THE
UNKNOWN
IACOCCA

Other books by Peter Wyden

Suburbia's Coddled Kids
The Overweight Society
How the Doctors Diet
The Hired Killers
Growing Up Straight (with Barbara Wyden)
Inside the Sex Clinic (with Barbara Wyden)
The Intimate Enemy (with Dr. George R. Bach)
Bay of Pigs: The Untold Story
The Passionate War
Day One: Before Hiroshima and After

THE UNKNOWN

IAC

OCCA

PETER WYDEN

WILLIAM MORROW & COMPANY, INC.   NEW YORK

This one is for Jeff.

Library of Congress Cataloging-in-Publication Data

Wyden, Peter.
  The unknown Iacocca.
  Bibliography: p.
  1. Iacocca, Lee A. 2. Businessmen—United States—
Biography. 3. Automobile industry and trade—United
States—History. I. Title.
HD9710.U52I28   1987   338.7'6292'0924 [B]
  87-15240
ISBN 0-688-06616-X

Printed in the United States of America

First Edition

1 2 3 4 5 6 7 8 9 10

BOOK DESIGN BY JAYE ZIMET

CONTENTS

THE
UNKNOWN
IACOCCA

1.

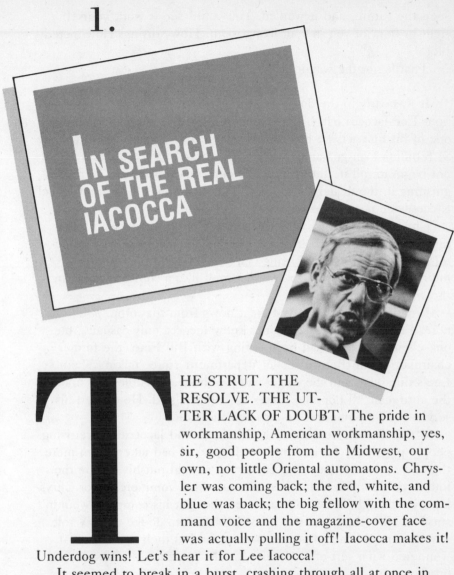

IN SEARCH OF THE REAL IACOCCA

THE STRUT. THE RESOLVE. THE UTTER LACK OF DOUBT. The pride in workmanship, American workmanship, yes, sir, good people from the Midwest, our own, not little Oriental automatons. Chrysler was coming back; the red, white, and blue was back; the big fellow with the command voice and the magazine-cover face was actually pulling it off! Iacocca makes it! Underdog wins! Let's hear it for Lee Iacocca!

It seemed to break in a burst, crashing through all at once in living color on the TV tube, the great American lifeline: the words that brooked no contradiction; the upbeat "Yankee Doodle" music; the pictures of bustling, beaming men and women in white coats closing ranks (yes, right up there on the TV screen) behind their leader, martially erect in the snugly tailored dark suit, jaw jutting out, booming confidence.

Confidence! Remember that old made-in-the-U.S.A. confidence? It's back! Like our other great TV star, Ronald Reagan, Iacocca had seen the future, and it worked. You could see it work yourself, right in front of you in your living room. How stirring! How incredible!

That is not the way it happened.

It was early in the do-or-die year of 1980 at Chrysler Corporation. Lee Iacocca had been Chairman for only a short time, and as one of his first acts he had cut his salary to $1 a year. Cash from the $1.5 billion loan guarantee he had pressured out of Congress would not begin to roll in until June. The current Chrysler cars were languishing in the dealer showrooms. The economical new front-wheel K-cars were not yet ready.

Chrysler was a high-wire act teetering over the abyss of bankruptcy. The press had already consigned the company past its demise. The papers were making Chrysler, the fourteenth largest industrial corporation in the world, smell like a corpse twisting in the wind.

Just then Iacocca received great news from that other *paisan* of note, Frank Sinatra. The crooner knew Iacocca only casually, but one evening Sinatra had been sitting with Bill Fine, the former chairman of the Bonwit Teller department store, talking about Lee's dilemma, and the singer had pronounced his blessing upon the auto man. "I hope he makes it," Sinatra said. He offered his services to help out and Fine passed the word.

It was like the coming of the Marines, and Iacocca's advertising people practically expired in their delight. It had taken them more than a year to convince Iacocca that he should put his ego on the line in public by agreeing to make television commercials for Chrysler even though The Chairman often thought his company wouldn't survive. Now there just was no way for him to dodge the TV role any longer, and the ad people, having landed their reluctant star, wondered what sort of production would bring out the best in him on the screen.

To their credit, they wanted nothing phony. Surely Iacocca would perform best if they simply let him play his favorite role, himself. But how?

For some time Iacocca had permitted cameramen with hand-held equipment to photograph him in action at Chrysler meetings. The advertising people liked what they saw, and they were ecstatic when they viewed films of The Chairman testifying calmly, colorfully, wittily, always in command, before the congressional committee weighing the federal loan guarantee legislation. That was it! He was a natural. Totally casual, natural commercials were the answer. Let Iacocca be Iacocca. And who could be a more natural partner for a commercial than Sinatra?

It would be the summit of selling power, a lovefeast.

Elated, Leo-Arthur Kelmenson of the Kenyon & Eckhardt ad agency, a loyal Iacocca crony, rushed to Palm Springs to confer with Sinatra about the details. Sinatra's public relations people were already unrolling press releases to herald the singer's rescue mission. His business manager, the normally implacable Mickey Rudin, waved the project ahead with unaccustomed informality. No papers were necessary.

"You don't want a contract?" asked Kelmenson, nonplussed.

"We'll set it up later," said Rudin.

"Lee, if you're working for a dollar, I will, too," Sinatra had said, according to the account in Iacocca's autobiography. In fact, the singer got some Chrysler stock options that eventually became very valuable. For the present, he received a free two-year "loaner"

of a station wagon and even this doubtful blessing worked out nicely. Chrysler had a terrible reputation for quality, yet Sinatra's car happened to serve him well (which was more than Gregory Peck could claim for the Imperial that Chrysler bestowed on him. Peck, who also helped the company, found that his car kept breaking down on the Los Angeles freeways).

And so Iacocca's new partnership with Sinatra was indeed a love-feast, but only until the filming of the commercial began in the Chrysler suite of Iacocca's favorite New York hotel, the Waldorf Towers.

The Chairman had been briefed that the ad people wanted to film a completely natural conversation between the two men. The encounter was to come off with no script, no preparation at all. According to this creative notion, the film crew would capture the spontaneous sparks of the two nimble minds accustomed to turning on vast audiences. Just let these two giants toss the verbal ball around and the commercial would all but drop into the can—so went the theory. For the paltry few seconds needed for the actual commercial, the ad experts would only have to cull out the choice highlights of the bons mots that were sure to fly through the air. It was a natural.

It didn't work.

"These two egos walked in and Lee was upset right away," says Bill Winn, an eyewitness and one of Iacocca's oldest buddies. Winn was merely uncomfortable during the filming; most of the other participants were "petrified" by the palpable tension, Winn recalls.

"Lee had no preparation and Sinatra worked with different ground rules. He had cue cards."

Like sturdy troopers, the two lions wrestled for half a day but brought forth no roars, even though some cue cards were finally scribbled for Iacocca in the course of the session.

"I'm a man in business myself," Sinatra intoned into the camera. Iacocca rambled, "We have what the car buyer wants." And then, not altogether convincingly, "We're in business to stay."

Both men looked overweight and grim.

"It was embarrassing," remembers John Morrissey, a Kenyon & Eckhardt account executive at the time and another Iacocca loyalist. "We put it on the air just once. They looked like two Italian grocers."

"Lee needs a script," says Leo-Arthur Kelmenson dryly. A script, yes, plus much reassurance to overcome Iacocca's reserve—inhibitions that he hides so well, that are seemingly so out of character, that even his friends sometimes forget them. Sometimes, but not often.

"What you see is not what you get," said Donald N. ("Don") Frey. I nodded agreement. We were talking about Iacocca, with whom Frey had worked closely for the better part of a decade.

I had by then been chatting with the Chrysler Chairman's colleagues, friends, relatives, schoolmates, and teachers for months, and as my search for the real Iacocca progressed, I found myself drawn into comparing their reminiscences with his own recollections and confessions as he shaped them for public viewing in *Iacocca: An Autobiography* (more than 2.6 million copies sold in hardback plus three million more in softcovers—an unprecedented record for the story of a businessman).

The discrepancies between the Iacocca version and the testimony of my eyewitnesses were puzzling and confirmed what Don Frey had just been telling me about the two Iacoccas: the qualities the public perceives in him as against his character as insiders know it.

Clearly more than one Iacocca had to exist, for what I had studied in The Book (as I came to think of the Iacocca megacreation) and what I had seen of the man on television, did not match up too well with what I was hearing from The Chairman's own crowd, many of them intimates who admire and even adore him.

Divergencies between perception and reality are an intriguing phenomenon to discover in anyone, but in the case of Lee Iacocca I find the differences spellbinding. After all, just about everybody in the United States "knows" this man. His "name recognition"—the pollsters' technical term for the percentage of people who can identify someone correctly—registers at an astounding 92.7 percent (70 percent is considered very high). Furthermore, most of the people (78 percent) who know Iacocca also say they *like* him; they buy him as he advertises himself in The Book and on TV.

As I pressed on in my search for the real person, it became clear that the differences between Iacocca as he appears from the distance and Iacocca as I was beginning to see him from up close are, well, spectacular, and the discrepancies unfold in specific contrasts that I found quite unexpected and unpredictable.

I had perceived the author of The Book—and the huckster strutting across my television screen—as a loud, brash, emotive trumpeter. According to the Iacoccalytes of my recent acquaintance, the man is in fact rather shy and inhibited—something of a wallflower, aloof with people he doesn't know too well and all but frozen stiff with strangers.

Though he comes across publicly as a smooth, hyperarticulate pitchman, he actually suffers from an acute case of social insecurity. His apparent love affair with television, for example, is imaginary, a myth. Although Iacocca's stature was created by TV, he detests the medium. It unsettles him, even in the company of Frank Sinatra.

While the polls certify him as a national hero figure, his image in his hometown, Detroit, has long been mixed at best. At least within the automobile industry his reputation is dirtied by nasty talk about his ruthlessness, his ego, his temper, and his ethics. Some of the stories are no doubt the ferment of sour grapes. Some are disturbing, for good reason.

Even physically Iacocca is not what he appears to be. To look at him on TV, to listen to the managerial voice that rings in confident cadence through the pages of The Book, he is a strapping superman, exuding fitness and strength. Yet according to the Iacoccalytes, he is a hypochondriac who feels forever cold and is riddled with symptoms that he feels certain are wracking his body.

I was stunned and confused by these conflicting impressions because like the people responding to the pollsters, I had been led to believe that Iacocca is pure, uncomplicated energy, all brains and guts. Perhaps unfairly I felt a little cheated when I became exposed to the more complex underside of the Iacocca personality, like a child learning there is no Santa Claus. I didn't seem to know the man everybody knows and likes.

I wanted explanations now. Don Frey was trying to help, and his struggle was itself a fascinating effort. Cool, amiable, an engineer by profession, formerly product manager at the Ford Motor Company under Iacocca, Frey is chairman and chief executive officer of Bell & Howell. Not the type who usually needs much time to explain a subject he knows well.

Iacocca happens to be one of his favorite subjects, and he had been wrestling with its complexities on my behalf for nearly two hours. It was time to leave, and Frey summed up: "I never worked for a man I learned more from, admired more—and who's a bigger prick."

Overdrawn? Not when it's one voice in a chorus, and I had been hearing lots of voices sound off in the same key, the blasts invariably coupled with admiring noises.

"Lee fancies himself a modern-day Don," said William ("Bill") Bourke, president of Reynolds Metals and once the number three man at Ford when Iacocca was number two. "But I learned a hell of a lot from him. I learned to act rather than react."

Such widely ranging sweet-to-sour superlatives carry extra resonance when you hear them on the hushed executive floors of such Fortune 500 enterprises as Bell & Howell or Reynolds Metals, where almost no sounds are permitted to intrude upon the thoughts of the ranking decision makers in their gym-sized offices with the costly artwork. Less highly placed men with close-up knowledge of Iacocca's ways—and, yes, they *are* all men—likewise speak of him in strong emotional terms. All have given the Iacocca personality intensive thought. The man seems to demand preoccupation with his psyche. It comes with his territory, the Horatio Alger storyboard enshrined in contemporary folklore.

Reviewed at one glance, the tale becomes pretty overwhelming:
Italian immigrant's boy claws his way up through the Ford Motor Company executive jungle . . . is anointed president . . . plots

to disown the WASPish proprietor but is decapitated. . . . Reborn at Chrysler, he snatches this ugly corporate duckling from death and turns it into the swan of proud new American workmanship. . . . He becomes a TV star . . . overwhelms the nation with the story of his turbulent life . . . adopts the Statue of Liberty as his leading lady. . . . Millions cheer and want him to be president of the United States. . . . Earns an astounding compensation of $23.6 million from Chrysler for 1986. . . . Listen again tomorrow for another thrilling chapter. . . .

If what you see is not what you get, then what *do* you see, in addition to energy and certitude? First, the face. It is a memorable trademark of a face. It reminds you of no one else, and it has stirred the viscera of authorities who handicap faces like racehorses, beginning with that ultimate prophet of magazine-cover horseflesh himself, Henry Luce.

"An expressive face," announced the founder of the *Time* magazine empire when he was introduced to Iacocca in the mob scene of a reception in Detroit. That was in 1962. Iacocca was a young man on the make; it was still two years before the debut of the Mustang, the car that made him a public figure. Luce, the kingmaker, had delivered another prescient judgment.

"Someday he'll put you on the cover," a henchman in the Luce entourage told Iacocca. "He likes expressive faces."

"Someday" arrived quickly, in 1964. The week the Mustang hit the dealer showrooms the Iacocca face appeared on the covers of both *Time* and *Newsweek*. It was an almost unheard-of stunt, a publicity H-bomb. The media crowd in Detroit is still arguing about how this hat trick was pulled off, still muttering about public relations treachery. Both magazines were transfixed by the Iacocca face. *Time* called it "hawklike"; *Newsweek* opted for "jut-jawed, Roman-nosed."

The curtain falls, rising again in 1984. Henry Luce is long dead. *Time* is discussing the post-Ford Iacocca as a possible presidential contender. He looked like a credible candidate to the *Time* flesh pickers. He had, they confided, "an expressive face."

In 1985 the magazine followed up with yet another Iacocca cover story. "A Spunky Tycoon Turned Superstar," the headline rhapsodized. And: "Straight-talking Lee Iacocca becomes America's hottest new folk hero." This time the story argued that his "tough guy face" lent credence to his "intense, you-gotta-believe-me manner."

By then other analysts had exhausted themselves over the Iacocca face and body. My favorite tone poem comes from a perceptive reporter, Gail Sheehy, author of *Passages* and other impressive best-sellers. She called on Iacocca for *Esquire* in 1978 and came away singing a chant that must have been a bit much even for the ego of The Chairman: "The brilliant, cunning, flat-eyed Florentine prince with the triangular face, wide forehead, aquiline nose, slash of mouth with jut of cruelty and contempt to it, the head carried on a stature of medium height and aesthetic build, with calves sheathed in high lustrous socks that might belong beneath a Renaissance doublet—how easy to picture him in a palace courtyard, toes arrogantly turned out, posing for a statue of a Medici prince."

I've not run across anybody else who spotted a Florentine prince in the charisma carrier from Chrysler, but Ms. Sheehy deserves to be cited because she is a pro, not easily carried away. She does not dwell on appearances unless they help to convey the substance and the dimension of a personality.

At six feet one inch, weight about 194 pounds, Iacocca would seem to be possessed of conventional dimensions. He does not, however, appear to add up to the sum of his parts. Mysteriously, there seems to be not only something other than what you see but something *more*, just more. Franklin D. Roosevelt projected this oversized personality. So did John F. Kennedy. So does Ronald Reagan. A lot of sharp kibitzers have noticed it in Iacocca.

"He looks like a goddamned colossus," says an advertising agency president who has worked elbow to elbow with him for a generation.

The bigger-than-life appearance impresses jaded politicians, too.

"He dominates every scene," says a senator's aide in Washington who watched Iacocca manipulate the United States Congress through more than a year of meetings and testifying.

He does dominate—seems actually to have something of a compulsion to dominate, the urge not merely to lead but to make his flock feel good about being led by him even if it's going to cost them plenty. It's no accident that Harold ("Hal") Sperlich, the president of Chrysler, a brilliant innovator, and several other Iacoccalytes, reached for the example of General George S. Patton when they attempted to explain the Iacocca personality to me.[*]

[*] General Douglas MacArthur also leaps to the minds of Iacoccalytes when they try to do justice to their hero. In Iacocca's office hangs a photo of MacArthur striding ashore dur-

Why pick "Blood-and-Guts" Patton, the arrogant World War II tank master with the swagger, the lacquered helmet, the pearl-handled revolvers—and the small regard for human life?

"He was the guy who gets the job done, sometimes not in the textbook way," said Sperlich. "He inspired the troops to follow."

A couple of times when my informants brought up the old general I ventured that Patton's manic visions of glory had eventually overcome him, that this hero had died in disgrace. The Iacoccalytes looked embarrassed, but only mildly so. Patton's sad end was not what they were talking about, they said. I think they considered me pedantic.

The Patton parallel does stand up perfectly when it comes to the weakness that the two giants share for low language. Patton and Iacocca are equally famous for it. When Don Frey described Iacocca as the "biggest prick" he has known, I think he was reverting to the time and ambiance of his service under this complicated boss, life with the "guys" and their "bullshit."

For Iacocca, the term "guys" describes car dealers, presidents of the United States, anybody. "Bullshit," probably his very favorite word of all, covers the scale from fakery to relatively gentle dissent from the views of others. But the unconventionalities go further. Iacocca's office language is routinely seasoned with every expletive in a sailor's lexicon, and sometimes this habit gets in the way.

Shortly after he went to Chrysler and gave his first major interview to the *Detroit Free Press*, the puckish managing editor, Neal Shine, decided to publish it as an unexpurgated transcript, gleaming with "shit" and the rest.

Furious, Iacocca summoned Wendell ("Lars") Larsen, his public relations chief.

"You want your wife to see this?" he demanded.

"Lee, you said it," responded Larsen.

He had hoped to teach the boss to be more cautious, but logic didn't work.

"Then he really got mad," Larsen remembers.

So what? Well, the episode sheds light on the ambivalence between the two basic Iacoccas, the public versus the private version. And it tells much about people's reactions to the man. The point is

ing an amphibious landing. An unknown wit has substituted Iacocca's head for MacArthur's, and the leader is surrounded by similarly faked images of the henchmen Iacocca brought in to help him save Chrysler.

that the four-letter interview hurt him not one bit. People were not upset. They laughed it off. Iacocca is human, they said. He cusses. Who doesn't?

I was startled by how freely some apparently negative observations were offered by the Iacoccalytes. But it would not be accurate to pass these comments on without noting that they were said with good cheer. People respect this strange, contradictory person. He does get things done, big things, good things, hard things, and if he thumbs his nose at textbook solutions that haven't worked, isn't it about time for some creativity?

People feel lifted by Iacocca, stretched, as his readers felt lifted and stretched by The Book with all its revealing misjudgments and omissions.

"It's like him," says Lars Larsen, laughing hard and with affection. "Some of it is even true."

Some of it?

It was a wisecrack and not helpful to my search. What parts of The Book were true? What parts were not? Are the public Iacocca and the private Iacocca really very different? If they are, do his less attractive private qualities leave the public persona invalidated, shattered? Or do the negatives help to flesh out the picture of the total persona? Are the respondents in the polls, heaven forbid, admiring a big man who isn't there? Or did the master salesman Iacocca sell us on a version of himself that has one dimension missing, not because he is a fraud but because he is human and therefore couldn't, as the poet Robert Burns has it, see himself as others see him?

The answers, as they do for all of us, lie scattered in the past and emerge most accurately not through autobiographical self-perception but through the lenses of eyewitnesses, supplemented by reasonably objective analysis of a person's actions, how he in fact met his challenges as he moved through his own developing history.

"Let's look at the record," said Governor Al Smith, and to judge by the polls, looking at Iacocca's record is a popular pastime. Even the limited self-perception of The Book has aroused much of the country sufficiently to see in him something great, at least something greater than outstanding leadership in business.

As this is written in the early summer of 1987, it seems highly unlikely that Iacocca, in his mid-sixties and suing his wife in an on-again off-again divorce action, will become ensnared in the game of politics, presidential or otherwise. He has said that he will stay at

Chrysler "for sure" until November 1990, perhaps longer "if it's fun." Yet the presidential boom, triggered by the rescue of Chrysler, a turnaround of epic scope, widely remembered and reinforced by the TV commercials that whooped up the Chrysler comeback, is surely a phenomenon as unconventional as Iacocca himself.

The boom lasted longer and touched more chords in the national psyche than most such unconsummated love affairs. The Iacocca-for-president sentiment actually gained momentum *after* he argued strenuously in The Book that Washington, politics, and politicians appeal to him about as much as leprosy. For five years he said no, no, no. Sometimes he delivered the message with a wisecrack, sometimes imploringly. Sometimes he cited the classic disavowal of General William T. Sherman. At still other times he weakened his no by delivering it in a teasing way, as if he wanted to leave the door ajar; he wouldn't run, he hinted, but he would tolerate being anointed.

Such coyness would normally evoke annoyance, but nobody was annoyed at Iacocca. He is exempt from such pettiness. Instead, a curious courtship dance was played out. Whenever Iacocca put the squelch on the boom, more or less, the politicians, the media, and the pollsters were freshly intrigued all over again, which caused them to renew their pursuit.

In Michigan the ranking Democrats, proud and powerful men, all but fell to their knees as they danced their courting maneuvers. In Washington a group of political pros set up shop as a Draft Iacocca Committee. Campaign strategy papers were composed and duly leaked. A business magazine published a cover photo of Iacocca, standing with hand raised and mouth ajar, in front of the presidential seal, ostensibly being inaugurated for the highest office.

Like kids snooping in the night for birthday presents to come, gifts to love or to hate, professionals began to comb through the noncandidate's voluminous public statements, hunting for tipoffs to President Iacocca's performance in a White House of the future. The carping and the adulation never did cease.

By early 1987 the boom seemed to be over, at least for the 1988 race.* Iacocca planned to confine himself to speaking and writing about presidential candidates. He would tell the country what he

---

* In the face of Iacocca's professed disinterest, his continued strong showing in presidential polls is extraordinary. In January 1987 a Gallup poll placed this noncandidate second among Democrats only to Gary Hart, then still the frontrunner. In October 1986 Gallup rated Iacocca as beating George Bush by 47% to 41% in a national vote.

thought of all the guys exhausting themselves in the campaign and perhaps go into the business of officiating as a power broker.

Politics did fascinate him, and 1992 presented an opportunity for direct intervention. Iacocca had given the eventualities his usual systematic analysis. For a businessman who claimed to be disgusted with politics, his look into the future was surprisingly canny and finally, very, very carefully, he left the door wide open for himself.

In 1992 he would be sixty-eight. That would make him a year younger than Ronald Reagan when he began his first term, hardly too aged to be called into service as a savior in a calamitous national emergency. Iacocca had given thought to such an emergency and had concluded that it just might cry out for another New Deal, another Roosevelt.

The Roosevelt scenario intrigued him. Whoever is elected in 1988, so Iacocca thought aloud to reporters at a press conference, is going to have an appalling time. He is "gonna feel just like Herbert Hoover" when Hoover followed the do-nothing Calvin Coolidge and let the country slide into the Great Depression. "He's gonna bear the rap," Iacocca predicted.

In 1992, following four years of economic travail, the nation would need a very strong leader to clean up the mess. Said Iacocca: "You're going to have a Roosevelt-type administration that's going to do something because the crisis by 1992 may be beyond belief."

Enter Franklin D. Iacocca.

The Roosevelt scenario fit neatly into my search for the real Iacocca. It revealed a great deal about him. For example, it was Iacocca, not the voters, not the politicians, not the pollsters, who remained in control throughout his curious presidential waltz of 1988. Control is crucial to Iacocca. If he couldn't be anointed, he wouldn't dance, not even into the White House.

Control. If he couldn't run the country personally, he at least wanted to exert maximum influence in helping to pick the fellow who would. Iacocca would run his own nominating convention. Why not? He knew what he wanted in a president, and he had earmarked the general characteristics of his contenders. They would be savvy, independent men, guys who stood their ground and knew how to dazzle on TV. Most of all, they would be "guys with balls." And Iacocca had a little list of names that he promised to talk and write about as the campaign progressed.* He'd be asking his candidates lots of questions. Eventually he'd make an announcement: "The guy who comes up with the best answers, I'm gonna say, 'You're my boy!' "

There was much ambivalence and poker playing in Iacocca, the noncandidate. For now, he wanted us to believe that he was the giant who wouldn't be president, a quaint twist of self-denial in the career of an executive so hyperambitious that he is sometimes accused of grandiosity. Does he sense that he must dodge the danger line of Parkinson's Law and quit pushing himself too far, beyond the ultimate level of his competence? Or was he still feeling his way onward?

As of mid-1987, Iacocca could still command some illustrious and die-hard backing. "I'd like to see Iacocca be president," I was told by the recently retired speaker of the House of Representatives, Thomas E. ("Tip") O'Neill. "We need something like him very badly."

Meanwhile, even if there is to be no Candidate Iacocca in 1988 and perhaps not in 1992, I still wound up my rounds in a wiser state. I learned about the contradictions of the public and the private Iacocca, and about the rest of us as well, about the qualities that make us worship a man, what it takes to become an American hero in these days when all our leader/gods seem to keep their feet ossified in clay and almost nobody is who he seems.

---

*In 1986 Iacocca told the writer Bob Spitz that Senator Bob Dole was his favorite Republican ("I'd pick a Dole over Baker or Bush"). Among the Democrats he didn't care for Gary Hart, who then was still the frontrunner for the nomination ("the guy's tentative!"). He felt that Senator Bill Bradley lacked pizzazz ("smart guy, Bill. Nice guy to be around. Too quiet"). Governor Mario Cuomo seemed to him the best bet at the time ("Probably the best debater. . . . He is pretty brilliant" . . . perhaps "a little too fancy," but Cuomo knew how to "handle the tube").

2.

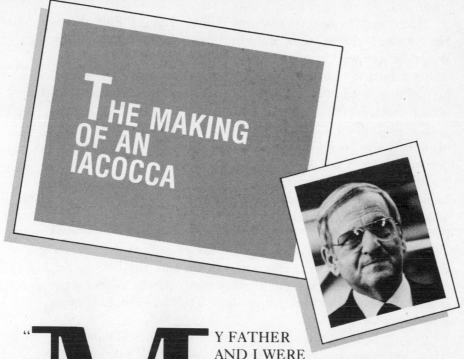

THE MAKING OF AN IACOCCA

"**M**Y FATHER AND I WERE VERY CLOSE," IACOCCA RE-CALLS IN HIS BOOK. "I loved pleasing him."

True. As Lee's friends and relatives remember it, however, the father-son relationship, while loving, was not nearly as placid and gentle as the son makes it appear in hindsight, perhaps even to himself. The eyewitnesses empathize with young Iacocca's need to toe his father's line. Or else. They remember vividly that father Nicola was not easily pleased and that life soured for everyone in Nick's orbit when this forbidding patriarch failed to get his way.

"Lee was always trying to ingratiate himself with his father," says Julius Iacocca, a cousin and Lee's look-alike.

"I think Lee was scared shitless of the old man," says another loyal Iacoccalyte.

"His father was very critical," explains Ed Charles, a chum who used to baby-sit for Lee when Iacocca was little. "Lee never got a beating. He didn't have to. His father's face made him run for cover."

"He feared his father," confirms William Denis ("Bill") Fugazy, Iacocca's very closest friend and best man at Lee's 1986 wedding. When Iacocca was about fourteen and got into a fight with his cousin Julius, so Lee told Fugazy, Nick got so angry that he tied his son to a post in the basement and left him there in the dark for several hours.*

So Lee learned in early youth that it was wise for him to hitch his behavior to Nick's expectations. The boy knew what it meant to measure up. And up. And up.

"He was the only son," reflects Ron DeLuca, another son of Italian immigrants and president of Kenyon & Eckhardt, Iacocca's advertising agency. "That's a very powerful thing in the Italian family. On him rode his father's hopes."

Attention must be paid to Nicola's hopes because they were the driving force behind the performance of the son, the 1988-model Iacocca, and the octane content of the fatherly propulsion ran high indeed. Nick's hopes were not modest. They were, in fact, boundless, insatiable.

Overtly Nick started out by living the stereotypical immigrant odyssey. He was twelve when he first glimpsed the Statue of Liberty, having quit San Marco, his scruffy native village in the foothills of the Apennines northeast of Naples. His initial exposure to the New World was in the home of a half brother who owned the company supply store in the dusty coal-mining community of Garrett, Pennsylvania, where life was hardly more promising than in San Marco. Never having acquired more than a fourth-grade education, Nick wound up in the mines, the fate of almost all the town's males.

But already the stereotype fades away. Nick quit mining on his first day, refusing to knuckle under like other immigrants. The work was filthy, but it was something more that drove him on. Nick hungered to strike out on his own. His one day in the mine, so he bragged in later years, was the only time in his life when he was not his own boss.

Like many of the boasts for which both Nick and Lee are

---

*The fight couldn't have been too serious. Cousin Julius cannot remember it. He does remember Papa Nick's punishments. Once Nick hung another nephew from a wall, suspended in a knapsack.

known among friends, this reminiscence contained exaggeration but not much. Nick did work at numerous jobs in Garrett and then in Allentown, where he went to live with another relative. Mostly he was an apprentice shoemaker, but the urge to function independently, to escape from the control of others, ran strong. He spent a lot of time running away from home—again and again. Making real money was on his mind, and only entrepreneurs made real money.

As soon as he had squirreled away enough savings by working in an uncle's hot dog restaurant, Nick opened his own place, the Orpheum Wiener House. It became the foundation of a miniconglomerate. His nephews still operate such places in Allentown. There are four of them now, called Yocco's Hot Dog King, that name being pretty much how the locals used to pronounce "Iacocca."* But Nick could not stop with hot dogs and never ceased acquiring.

Intensely curious, he sniffed out new opportunities, using his own style of market research. "Nick used to sit at a table in a restaurant listening to conversations around him," recalls Frank ("Buzz") Klotz, an Iacoccalyte for thirty years. "When he heard

---

*Nick pronounced his name "*Ya*cocca," and he never lost his strong Italian accent.

NICK IACOCCA:
"WHY WEREN'T
YOU FIRST?"

somebody talk about an interesting business, he'd say, 'Maybe we ought to try that.' "

Nick opened a movie house and soon owned two. He bought into one of the country's first car rental agencies, U-Drive-It, and expanded his fleet to thirty cars, mostly Fords. He plunged into real estate, pyramiding property on property, mortgage on mortgage. He relished his successes loudly. The old-timers remember Nick's jokes, his ebullient laughter ("a great toot"), his gusto, his publicity-grabbing promotions. At his theaters he offered free admissions to the ten kids with the dirtiest faces.

"Nothing worried Nick," says Buzz Klotz. "For him, yesterday was gone."

Short, bulky, and bald, Nick carried himself erectly, a little Caesar, relentlessly in a hurry, moving, moving, propelled by his energy and his hopes. He was seventy when Lee and a friend introduced father Nick to the game of golf at a Ford dealer meeting in Palm Springs. There may never have been a sight like it. Whenever Nick hit a ball, he started chasing after it on the run. "Pop, slow down," yelled the son. "Golf is a game of *walking*!" But overdrive was Nick's speed. Even at seventy he disdained walking when he could run.

Some years later he asked the wife of a Ford executive to dance with him at a company bash. She never forgot the effort. Nick dug both hands into her sides, his thumbs directly under her bosom, and bounced the much taller executive wife across the floor like a ball.

The Great Depression, triggered by the Wall Street crash of 1929 and grinding on for the better part of a decade, did slow down Nick temporarily. He lost all his properties—the building he had put up on Sixth Street, the three apartment houses—and he came close to having to abandon even the family's narrow little two-story brick row house at 440 North Seventh Street. His checks bounced, but his personal deposits of optimism and hope did not give out.

"Just wait," he told little Lee, "the sun's gonna come out. It always does."

The Iacoccas have a talent for bouncing back from adversity, but the Depression was a stubborn enemy; the sun was slow to reappear over the Allentown of the 1930s, and Nick did not manage his comeback without help. Old-timers credit Lee's mother, Antoinette, with holding together the family—and Nick himself. She knew how to settle him down, some of the time anyway.

"She had a thumb on Nick's forehead," Buzz Klotz remembers.

Nick had brought back his bride, a shoemaker's daughter, when he went to San Marco to take his mother to Allentown. Antoinette was seventeen, and he was in his thirties. Small and deathly scared, she came down with typhoid fever en route across the Atlantic, lost much of her hair, and should, by law, have been sent back to Italy when the couple reached Ellis Island. According to Lee, Nick managed to convince the immigration inspectors that she had merely been seasick. Apocryphal? The son says not.

". . . my father was an aggressive, fast-talking operator . . ." Lee explains proudly in passing along the treasured anecdote in The Book. Bill Fugazy, a confidant of both men, is convinced that Nick bribed the immigration inspectors, which wasn't uncommon then.

While the Iacocca women are careful not to steal any stray rays of limelight from their menfolk, they are anything but wallflowers behind the family scenes. And they all know how to work. As Nick struggled to recover from the collapse of his little empire, Antoinette sewed garments in an Allentown factory. When Nick opened the State Restaurant in the 1930s, he ensconced his wife in the show window and had her whip up spaghetti within view of passersby so they might be enticed to give the place a try. Nick knew that nobody in America made it without competing, competing hard, and that it was an entrepreneur's role to conjure up new tricks, to get an edge over the competition.

Just as his pre-Depression diversification had been made possible by capital generated in his hot dog enterprise, so Nick funneled his spaghetti income to finance new ventures. With building activity at a standstill he went to Washington and found out how he could hire carpenters and other workmen to fix up homes for less than standard pay. Eventually he moved back into real estate, buying, selling, moving into bigger deals. He became a contractor, too, rehabilitated a housing development that had sunk into default, and developed a 200-acre model residential section, Midway Manor.

Late in life he talked an Allentown bank into giving him a free option on farmland outside town, which he then unloaded on Western Electric. It was the start of an industrial park.

And he had fun. Nick always had fun. He made his own red wine at home, he coddled some grapes and a couple of fig trees into taking root in the backyard, and he always had the house teeming with family and friends on weekends. Antoinette cooked generous Italian meals. Never trusting a butcher's promise of freshness, she killed her own chickens. As in most Italian and Jewish families,

Lee and the other kids were allowed to sample the wine when food was served.

And games were played on Seventh Street, noisily, endlessly, sometimes all night on New Year's Eve. Mostly it was poker, always just for pennies, occasionally with the women joining in. The sounds and the theatrics made these sessions high entertainment; but winning was important, and Nick knew how to win.

"Nick was a great bluffer," recalls Buzz Klotz. "You never knew whether he was kidding."

In later years Lee tried to smoke out Nick's intentions. "Come on, Pop, play the game!" he shouted when the old man stalled. Nick, however, would not be jarred out of his center stage role as paterfamilias and principal attraction of the night. He liked to dominate his scene and knew that in the full-throated emotionality of the Iacocca home this was rarely possible by adhering to conventional rules.

Rules. Nick preferred to make his own. He liked "taking the shortcut," says Eddie Charles, the baby-sitter and Iacocca family friend, now a retired Ford dealer. Eddie thought of Nick as a second father. And Eddie was a shrewd observer. He analyzed how Nick dealt with the competition, engineering his deals so they would come out the right way, Nick's way. "His viewpoint was that [people] didn't understand [him] and they were behind the times and he'd go ahead and do it and fight [them] later."

Fight. Nick figured that one couldn't make it in business without fighting. He didn't mind. It suited his scrappy temper, and when an investigative journalist, Kirk Cheyfitz, went to Allentown in 1978 on behalf of *Monthly Detroit* magazine, he discovered the underside of Nick's ways, the fighting side, which his son, Lee, understandably fails to mention in The Book.

The name of the elder Iacocca turned up with surprising frequency in the local papers, Cheyfitz found, because Nick was fighting the law. Never anything terribly serious, but the stream of repeated minor infractions was obviously of a piece with the elder Iacocca's style. He was charged with violating state liquor laws. With operating as a realtor without a proper state license. With reckless driving. Even with assault. Conventional rules were not for Nick.

Sometimes his opponents fought back. Numerous businessmen with whom he had dealings took exception to his interpretation of the rules and sued him.

One confrontation in 1957, in particular, reveals Nick's unappealing side. Driving a late-model Ford that was registered in Lee's name, Nick passed through an intersection and almost hit a little girl. A school crossing guard tried to flag him down. Nick ignored the signal. The guard, a woman, shouted after him, making Nick furious. He pulled the car to the side, jumped out, and headed toward her on the run. His face was red with anger.

Cheyfitz located the school guard, Mrs. Marguerite Kase. She remembered the short, fat man vividly.

"Look, I got money," Nick told her. Mrs. Kase, startled, was not interested in money.

Nick tried another approach at intimidation. He hinted that his stature in town placed him above the law.

"You can have me arrested," he told Mrs. Kase, "but it ain't gonna be a damn bit of good."

Mrs. Kase stood her ground. "That little girl's life was at stake!" she shouted.

The confrontation was heating up. Witnesses later said that Nick shook Mrs. Kase and that he tried to put her in her place as he saw it. To him, this meant that she should have been at home, like a decent Italian wife, not out on the street like a prostitute.

"You whore," he yelled at her. "Why don't you go home and work in your kitchen?"

That outburst certainly did not help him with Mrs. Kase. Nick received a ticket and had to appear in court.

Cheyfitz talked to Bennie Rizzoto, the magistrate who heard the case and also clearly remembered Nick's fury twenty-one years later.

"I think the fact is he resented a woman telling him what to do," said the judge perceptively.

Rizzoto found him guilty of reckless driving and fined him a modest $30—hardly enough to change Nick's view of his seigneurial rights and the status of women.

It took a nosy journalist like Cheyfitz, by that time far more interested in Lee Iacocca's family background than in the father, to publicize the long-forgotten dirty side of Nick's two faces. When Nick died of leukemia in 1973 at the age of eighty-three, people remembered him as a marvelous character,* a bit rough at times,

---

*Jay Dugan, an early Iacoccalyte who was, among other creative talents, a magazine writer, once offered Nick to *Reader's Digest* as a subject for its "My Most Unforgettable Character" series.

perhaps, but a doer, a success, an optimist, a family man, generous to his own. Shortly before he died, he lavished $600 on fruit baskets for some friends. Sometime before, he gave his daughter-in-law, Lee's wife, a check for $5,000 and told her to get something special for her penthouse condominium in Boca Raton, Florida.

The headline of his obituary in the *Allentown Morning Call* said:

BUILDER NICOLA IACOCCA DEAD AT 83;
EXAMPLE FOR SON'S RISE . . .

"He built pleasant homes and other attractive structures that would be a credit to any builder," said an accompanying editorial of his public achievements. Mostly, though, the remembrance celebrated Nick's private legacy, his unflagging confidence, and the "fine family to which his devotion is almost legendary."

The *Call* had it straight. "His personal record is the most challenging of all," it said. Nick was a challenge, all right, and unquestionably an "example for [his] son's rise." On balance he made a beneficial model, though what you saw was hardly what you got.

3.

THE MAKING OF AN ANXIOUS MAN

"THE ANXIETY I FELT ABOUT THE FUTURE IS STILL VIVID IN MY MIND," IACOCCA REPORTS IN HIS BOOK. "No matter how I'm doing financially, the Depression has never disappeared from my consciousness. . . . It's not that I'm afraid of being poor, but somewhere in the back of my mind there's still the awareness that lightning can strike again, and my family won't have enough to eat."

The fear of physical hunger is not without foundation in fact. Eddie Charles, the baby-sitter, remembers days during the Depression that became memorable to him because Nick had made some money somehow and brought in several bags of groceries, enough for the Iacoccas and for Eddie's people. Even then, the meals were sparse. To this day Lee can't stand the very mention of polenta, the Italian cornmeal dish. "Don't talk to me about polenta," he has said to his friend Billy Fugazy. "That's all we used to eat."

But physical hardships were secondary. "Anxiety" is the principal operative word for this time of young Lido's life because the Iacocca of today—the cocky, pontifical folk hero—remains in his heart of hearts an anxious person. The anxiety is amply controlled; but it is undeniable, and its causes are not difficult to uncover. A long string of adversities account for Iacocca's feelings of insecurity; the Depression was merely the first blight to strike.

Lido* was only five years old when the collapse of the Wall Street boom market pulled the bottom out of the national economy in 1929, turning Papa Nick overnight from a wealthy man, by the modest Allentown standards, into a pauper (and causing him to switch his allegiance, at least during those lean years, from the Republican to the Democratic party). The Iacocca kids stopped getting new clothes in 1930. Mother Antoinette had to leave home to go to work. Little Lido was aware that they might really have to give up the cherished family home and discussed this barely averted catastrophe with his sister, Delma, who was two years older.

While such disasters—and worse—befell millions of families all over the country, the young Iacocca was then still too small to grasp events jarring the world outside his home. What was happening to him so very personally became all the more frightening because he was left to deal with his family's riches-to-rags metamorphosis quite on his own.

"I didn't really understand, and it wasn't the sort of thing my father could explain," he writes.

Couldn't, or perhaps just wouldn't, for Nick was not the sort to concede defeat at anything, not even to himself.

Bigotry, the second devastating force that pounded little Lido throughout childhood, also was never explained to him. It, too, remained mysterious and scary for years. Difficult as such a state of ignorance may be to remember in the light of Dr. Spock and today's openness and psychological sophistication, Iacocca's parents couldn't—or wouldn't—enlighten their son about discrimination or even about his own ethnic origin. "Being Italian was something you tried to hide," Iacocca writes.

That was probably it. Nick and Antoinette could have hoped

---

*Lido Anthony Iacocca was named for the famous Lido Beach outside Venice, where his father had been a visitor as a young man. This original name remains the Chrysler Chairman's legal one. It appears on formal documents bearing his signature, such as his two wedding certificates.

that if they tried to ignore the problem, it would not become known to their son and therefore wouldn't trouble him. Yet that was not possible in Allentown. The Allentown of the 1920s and 1930s needs to be understood as a two-faced world, one cozy, the other merciless. It was a pleasantly shady hillside place on the Lehigh River, somewhat isolated in rural eastern Pennsylvania and free of the grime and smoke belched out in the great steel center Bethlehem, almost next door, where many of Allentown's men labored in the mills.

Allentown was proud of its share in the making of America, its slice of history having been modest but picturesque. In 1777, when the British were about to seize the headquarters of the Continental Congress in Philadelphia, that city's patriotic colonists smuggled the Liberty Bell into Allentown and hid it in a church. Eventually the great bell was taken home to Philadelphia, but in Allentown a Liberty Bell Shrine was erected in its wake—a reminder of the city's part in making freedom ring.

The world of the Iacocca clan, the snug little island around North Seventh Street, seemed grown from the Liberty Bell tradition. The comfortable middle-class neighborhood where the Iaccoccas nested for thirty-five years was like a microcosm lifted from a Grandma Moses painting; at least that was how Lido's parents liked to remember it. Everyone left the front door unlocked; it felt safe, and it was. The atmosphere was congenial; the women gathered together in the backyards to preserve vegetables and fruit. To mother Antoinette it felt like home; the farmers' market on nearby Hamilton Street reminded her of her native village in Italy.

Lido retained considerably harsher memories. Kids being notoriously capable of cruelty toward other youngsters, the Iacocca children probably had reason to experience their being "different" (Iacocca's own word in The Book) more keenly than the adults. Little Lido, in any event, sensed the onus of differentness very powerfully. The feeling, like the threat of another depression, would never leave him.

"He had an early sense of social inadequacy," says Ron DeLuca, the Kenyon & Eckhardt president. "He's amazingly sensitive to his ethnic background."

Not really amazing, because the meaning of discrimination was left to fester unexplained in Lido's mind—one more terror among the insecurities of growing up—until he was eleven years old. It was only then that he managed to figure out, entirely without adult help, why most of the other kids in school spurned him as a second-class person and only then that he learned this didn't mean he was "bad" or guilty of a thing.

The bigotry around him was palpable, a constant physical danger, as he recalls. The other kids labeled him with ugly, diminishing names, "dago" and "wop," and they beat him up.

"I took a lot of abuse," he records bitterly.

Lido did not know the meaning of the epithets. Feeling that he was alone, that there was no one he could ask for help, the boy dreamed up a discreet (and heartrending) reach for impersonal aid. He searched for the bad words on a map of Europe, thinking that they might be the names of countries.

At eleven, he remembers, he learned "we were Italian." Not "Italian-Americans," not "of Italian extraction." Italian. Italy was a real country, he finally found out. And it was indeed a different, exotic land: It was the place where pizza came from. Lido loved pizza. His mother made the most delicious ones of all. Better yet, he discovered that the non-Italian kids in school never had pizza. They didn't even know what this delicacy was, not then in the mid-1930s, when pizza parlors did not exist. This information surfaced because the Iacoccas were having a great pizza party and Lido bragged about the event in school. At last the boy could seize an identification for himself, and a friendly and tasty one at that.

The enlightenment brought him some relief, though not a great deal. The adult atmosphere was less blatantly polluted by discrimination, but signs of it were never far under the surface. Some teachers referred to Lido as a "little wop" when they thought he wouldn't hear, or so he remembers. The majority of folks in Allentown called themselves Pennsylvania Dutch, and majority rule often turned mean in small towns during the bygone days of Lido's youth. The two Jewish kids in his grade-school class were treated worse than the Italian minority. They were "like outcasts" suffering from leprosy. There were no blacks. No matter. There were enough other targets for oppression, and young Lido felt he was one of them.

Such are Iacocca's memories, and his facts are not far off the mark. There *was* more stratification, more discrimination, more class consciousness in towns like Allentown during the 1920s and 1930s than today's youth would ever know. "The Italians were the peons; the

Pennsylvania Dutch were the aristocrats," remembers an Iacocca classmate of German extraction, and the Teutons were easily recognizable by names like Kuntzweiler and Schweinbinz.

Iacocca's emotional *response* to the status of "Italians" was abnormally sensitive, however. At least some dozen Allentown friends of his youth told me so. Unanimously they testified that Iacocca seemed to them, as Ron DeLuca, the friend of much later years, had said, "amazingly sensitive," and my Allentown eyewitnesses include several whose Italian background is obvious from their names.

Floyd Moschini, who became a ranking executive in the nuclear power division of Westinghouse, says he "never felt discrimination" in Allentown and was "surprised" to read about it in The Book. The mild-mannered Angelo ("Gene") Giancarlo, who became executive director of the American Newspaper Editors Association, went further. He was uncharacteristically rocked by Iacocca's recital of "abuse" and denigration.

"I couldn't quite fathom what he was talking about," Giancarlo says. "I never had that problem." Giancarlo likes and admires Iacocca, but he believes that Lido's ego led him into the extreme bitterness of his memories. Persecution? "I think he read a little more into the facts than really existed," Giancarlo says; it was understandable "if you wanted to be liked all the time."

The Iacocca ego, probably, is the key here, although the degree of his hypersensitivity to discrimination in Allentown is difficult to assess half a century later. Recollections soften. Memories screen out much unpleasantness. People don't like to disparage their hometowns. They hesitate to brand old neighbors as bigots, especially in these more enlightened times. Withal, the us-and-them dichotomy was real, and this was remembered in convincing ways when I talked to the two Jewish classmates Iacocca wrote about.

The cheerful, red-haired Ben Ami Sussman, an Allentown real estate man whose father was a junk dealer, used to live one block away from the Iacoccas on North Seventh Street. Kids used to call him "kike" all the time, and they followed him on the street singing, "Abie went to school one day on a Jewish holiday."

Sussman remembers Iacocca from grammar school. ("He always stood erect, proud, always proud.") Sussman also recalls the vibrations that seemed to radiate toward himself from the others, the "Dutch": "You could feel they were against us." He spoke wistfully, regretfully, but not with bitterness, not like a survivor, not like Iacocca.

Neither did Dorothy Warshaw, now Dorothy Saxner of Chicago, undisputedly the brightest of Iacocca's classmates. She said she was made to feel, as Iacocca says about himself, "different"; she knew she could never be crowned "Queen of the May," the school's highest social honor (although Lido was once anointed "King of the May"). How could she be sure she'd never be crowned queen? Well, kids just knew these things. Nevertheless, she, too, did not share Iacocca's bitterness, didn't feel that she had been dirtied by "abuse." He was more vulnerable to slurs than were his peers.

Luckily Lido had brains, lots of brains. In response to being classified "different" he turned introverted and sought his own world in books. And for books there was plenty of support at home. Like most immigrant fathers, Nick had recognized the central truth that education was the passkey to money and success in America. In his own indirect way he praised the boy lavishly for his school achievements by pressuring him to do better, always better. Enough was never enough for Nick.

The fatherly whip hit a receptive target. It's easy to detect the effect on the son and to visualize a well-remembered episode of his childhood, a scene that could have come straight out of Horatio Alger.

"Lido! Lido!" cried young Iacocca's chums under his window when he was absorbed in homework. "Come on out!"

He ignored the shouts, and when they continued, he'd yell back, "Go away! I've got to study!"

Most of his teachers appreciated such diligence. It set him apart from the others once again, but standards in class were different from those prevailing on the playground and in the street. In school it paid off to be different, and Lido loved the payoff. Achievement in school brought tangible rewards. Lido basked in being a favorite pupil, being singled out to clean the blackboard and ring the school bell. And he kept on doing well. In junior high school his overall grade average was 95.

It didn't come easily. Lido was not a natural intellect and charmer, nothing like Bob Beisel, for example, one of his rivals in high school—popular, easygoing Bob, a stylish WASP (his formal name was Wilford) who rose to rule as class president and valedictorian and ultimately achieved a vice presidency at Babcock & Wilcox, a national engineering firm. Achievement seemed to flow effortlessly out of Beisel. Nothing came to Lido without intensity, ferocious concentration, travail, sheer will.

"*Intense*" is the word I heard used most frequently to describe him through all his school days. Intense, serious, and reserved. "He absolutely listened a hundred percent," recalls a grade-school teacher; "his brow was always furrowed." Bob Romig, a classmate who became a police sergeant, remembers, "I never saw him smile."

The churning for achievement, the drive that was set off by the demanding father at home, was formalized into relentless organized competition at school as early as in the first grade. Here came the first stoking of what Paul J. Franz, Jr., an Iacocca schoolmate at Lehigh University who became vice president for development at that school and is a connoisseur of business success stories, calls Lido's "internal fires."

These flames never stopped burning brightly. When the Iacocca autobiography appeared, one of his closest associates at Chrysler wisecracked that a whip should have been displayed on the dust jacket, and this trademark would have been fitting as far back as Stevens School in Allentown. Iacocca was not the whipper then, he was the whipped, and the pressure on him even in those days was not simply to do well; the demand was to be the best, to be—in the leitmotiv phrase of Iacocca's entire life—*numero uno*.

No less. Sophisticated interpretations are not required to recognize how the psychological screws were brought to bear on this boy so he would strive for the scholastic pinnacle. Stevens School had designed a neat little system for the purpose. First, the school applied the whip by designating the various sections of each class grade sequentially, according to the collective achievements of the pupils. Thus Grade 1-1 contained the brightest little scholars of the first grade, and the maneuvering to squeeze into the first section remained stiff throughout the grades. Secondly, the top three scholars within each class were allowed to occupy places of special honor, the first three seats in the first row, and the ranking was subject to promotion and demotion each month, always in accord with the most recent scholastic efforts. The top student was known as "No. 1." *

---

*The *numero uno* theme, as we shall see, dominated Iacocca's career at Ford, and he even applied teasing parodies of shifting hierarchical rankings to his second marriage, his life with his wife Peggy, and their Yorkshire pup, Sassy, and to the couple's relationship with Peggy's kinfolk. *Metropolitan Detroit* magazine reported in July 1986: "The night before the wedding, over dinner at Nicola's, the toney New York Italian restaurant, Lee told Peggy's sister, 'Helen, I'm moving up to Number One. Sassy is Number Two. You're Number Three now.' "

As Iacocca remembers grade school, Dorothy Warshaw was always first in his class and he usually ran second. This is an intriguing switch of memories. Actually, it was later, at Ford, that Iacocca saw himself in danger of languishing forever as number two, outdistanced by Henry Ford II as a permanent number one. The facts at school in Allentown were more intricate and more revealing. For year after year the competition in Lido's class seesawed among *three* ambitious little scholars, two of whom were girls.

"It was musical chairs between us three," remembers Ruth Conrad, now the director of an Allentown church nursery school. "We were from lower-middle-class economic backgrounds, and we were concerned with survival in those days. Lee was aggressive. He wanted to be right. He sought perfection. He wanted to be number one." And the memories shared with me by Dorothy Warshaw are similar.

So this is how little Lido learned early about winning and losing. The lesson must have seemed all too real, for the downside entailed the ever-threatening drop-dead risk that he might at any time wind up in the cold—disgraced before his father, without any ranked place whatever in this not-so-innocent competition of musical chairs. Arguably, these years of being matched against two females also played some role in shaping Lido's feelings toward girls.

Did he dislike or disdain them? Or fear them as threats, competitors, perhaps somehow as unfair competitors? Did he experience them as brassy, the way some of his pals viewed his older sister, Delma? Memories are not sufficiently reliable to supply definitive answers. It is a fact, however, that Lido had little social contact with the opposite sex until after he left college; moreover, the courtship of his first wife extended across eight years.

Doubtless the musical chairs at Stevens School shaped Iacocca's almost overwhelming dread of losing, losing at anything.

"He's the absolutely worst loser in the world," reports Hal Sperlich, the president of Chrysler, and the vice chairman, Ben Bidwell, says, "The deeper the pit gets the harder he attacks. He just can't admit defeat." And to rate as number two is to be defeated.

This frustration is far from unique with Iacocca, of course. In the United States the overemphasis on competition and individual achievement has actually given rise to a condition called the "number one syndrome," which I found discussed in an insightful book by Dr. Philip G. Zimbardo, professor of social psychology at Stanford University.

Dr. Zimbardo recognizes that children who grow up under the flag of this syndrome are highly motivated but pay for their drive by undergoing some discomfort.

"To be loved, accepted, and valued, they must produce the desirable responses," he writes. "Recognition of individual worth is contingent on what people have produced, not on what they are. When our relationship to our fellows is purely utilitarian, it is natural to be *anxious about whether what they have to offer is good enough* or if we'll be cast off when we are no longer useful to them." (Emphasis added.)

Psychologists don't casually toss around such words as "anxious," so I recruited a psychologist expert of my own for clarification. My consultant wanted me to point out that he claimed no knowledge of Lee Iacocca. He was explaining concepts.

"The number one syndrome represents some very deep kind of insecurity," said the psychologist. "Nobody is your equal if you're number one." Since the basic definition of this syndrome comes from an authoritative book on shyness,* I was reminded that this problem had kept coming up in my research. And the memories of Iacocca's shyness are also traceable to the early Allentown days.

"Lido was a rare student," recalled Carroll Parks, his English and Latin teacher in the eighth grade. "He was all business . . . maybe a little shy."

Shy? Iacocca shy? Remarkably, yes, and more than a little. And he never quite defeated this handicap. Shyness—really withdrawal growing out of unease—is a trait that runs through his life like a red thread. All the Iacoccalytes brought it up and talked about their hero's many efforts to overcome this further adversity.

Undoubtedly thinking of the public Iacocca personality as suggested by his autobiography and his TV commercials, my psychologist expert launched into an explanation of a personality type known in his profession as "shy extroverts."

"These people function in a highly structured way," he said. "Their behavior may be scripted. Some of them can't deal with

Shyness by Philip G. Zimbardo (Reading, Mass.: Addison-Wesley, 1977).

spontaneity, ambiguity, novelty, whatever can't be put in a résumé. They're playing a role. There are limits on what they can and can't do. They may be full-time public persons—always 'on.' "

Marion Raber, Lido's ninth-grade teacher, was probably the first to come to his aid in this lifelong struggle. She knew something about developing the assets of shy children. She taught Lido the use of words, the excitement of communicating, the ability to make ideas march forth, and in the last stage of her campaign, she taught him the power to persuade—to assemble ideas and to make them attractive to others. In short, to sell.

"You know, Miss Raber," Iacocca told her at the twenty-fifth anniversary reunion of his class, "you got me out of my shell." The teacher was overjoyed, never having realized how deep-seated a problem she was battling—so severe, in fact, that she had merely cracked the shell and that Iacocca would still not quite have overcome the handicap in the 1980s.

Miss Raber started out by imposing a rigid requirement on her students to turn in a 500-word theme each and every Monday. It was her method for encouraging fluency in writing. To build richer vocabularies, she used the Word Power Game from *Reader's Digest*, a test that Iacocca still cannot resist taking every month. Finally she had her charges on their feet frequently to practice extemporaneous speaking, the scourge of shy people.

Having to deal with his stage fright was a particularly fearful test for the boy.

"At first I was scared to death," he writes in The Book. "I had butterflies in my stomach—and to this day I still get a little nervous before giving a speech." Profound self-discipline, however, is another Iacocca trait. He subdued his nervousness, practiced what Miss Raber preached, and went on to attack his phobia further by joining the Orotan Debating Society and becoming a relatively polished performer in that group. A fellow debater, Al Jenkins, who became a dentist, remembers how hard Iacocca worked on the team. It was apparent to him that Lido was absolutely determined to overcome his shyness handicap.

It worked. At least it enabled him to conquer the pitfalls of high-school-level debating. By the time Richard Snelling joined the Orotan in his sophomore year Iacocca was a senior who helped to recruit (and haze) the younger debaters. Snelling, an articulate boy who rose to head the debating squad and eventually became governor of Vermont, recalls that he had to muster all his determination not to be intimidated when Iacocca and another old boy, as part of the initiation rites, ordered him to make a speech analyzing the price of peanuts in India.

What Iacocca doesn't disclose in The Book is the key ingredient that first helped him to loosen up a bit: an audience. While most people enjoy showing off in front of an attentive crowd, Iacocca responded to the attention with unusual brio. For him, attention was the spinach that made the biceps of Popeye, the cartoon character, bulge. Iacocca would always adore working a crowd. He clearly craves its approval. Approval liberates him. It makes him whole.

Eddie Charles, his onetime baby-sitter, remembers an Iacocca performance at Eleanor's School of Dance in Allentown. Lido was eleven and detested dance classes. Nevertheless, he was given the lead role in the 1936 year-end revue. His solo number was the time step, but the dancing barely mattered. It was the sheer act of performing before obviously sympathetic spectators that fired the boy up as nothing else could.

Eddie Charles remembers the scene with amazement half a century later: "You could see he loved it—being in front of the audience and hearing the applause. He was a natural. He brought the house down." It was like watching a flower burst into bloom.

Others have witnessed similar dramatic transformations over the years. The blooming effect still keeps occurring, and my informants used powerful language to describe the flip-flop changes they have observed in the Iacocca personality.

"He starts out with self-doubt," says Ron DeLuca, the adman most responsible for turning Iacocca into a television star. "When he is put on a platform, the Jekyll and Hyde comes out in him. If he's engrossed, he turns into an entirely different person."

"This guy is really two people," confirms Bill Winn, an intimate for more than thirty-five years.

Here, then, in plain view, the private Iacocca—quiet, apprehensive, people-phobic—faces the public Iacocca—firm, boisterous, aggressive. The gap between the two is obviously nothing trivial.

When he was fifteen years old, Lido underwent still another transformation, and this one was most unhappy and intimidating. It happened in the watershed year of 1939; World War II broke out, and Lee contracted rheumatic fever. Gradually he had been turning less introverted and more active physically. He loved swimming, ice skating, and, above all, baseball. As a pretty good player he cherished the usual boy's dream of a career in the major leagues.

The illness upset all that and changed much more as well. It stopped young Iacocca and cast a cloud over the rest of his life.

In The Book he gives a graphic account of the physical impact that the illness produced on him.

In that time patients occasionally died of rheumatic fever, so when Lee first experienced heart palpitations, he was understandably petrified: "I almost passed out—from fear." The family physician, managing the treatment entirely in the home, prescribed that the boy place an ice pack on his chest. That truly "panicked" him. Ice on the chest? He says he thought, "I must be dying!"

More was involved than a threat to the heart. An infection settled in the joints, causing a high fever; severe pain immobilized wrists, elbows, ankles, and knees.

In those days before the invention of antibiotics the doctor prescribed birchbark pills against the infection. They proved effective but at a price: Young Iacocca had to take antacid pills every quarter hour to keep from vomiting. Worse, with modern painkillers not yet available, the doctor had to fight the inflammation of the joints by means of cotton wadding soaked in oil of wintergreen and set in place with crude wooden splints.

It was enough to scare the life out of anybody, especially a sensitive teenager at puberty.

The oil burned like crazy, the sense of immobilization was complete, and while the fever, the pain, the splints, and other manifestations of the illness in its acute phase eventually faded, the continuing danger of possible aftereffects to the heart did not. Consequently, in the opinion of the physician, six months of total bed rest were required.

Six months—something like a lifetime as a teenager's clock creeps.

For family and friends, a hearty bunch unaccustomed to serious illness, the boy became the center of loving attention. Visitors saw father Nick in tears for the first time. Antoinette cooked up large batches of chicken soup, the miracle drug favored by mothers. Cousins and cronies were permitted to call and listened more or less patiently to Lee complain loudly about his pain and, later, his eagerness to get out—just to get the hell out of that damned bed. Sister Delma brought the school assignments, faithfully each day, so Lee could keep up fully with his studies. And he read. And read. And read. And lost forty pounds.

In The Book Iacocca concedes that he had to give up athletics, which turned him toward chess, bridge, and particularly poker. He does not mention that he was considered so frail that even day hikes had become taboo for him. By the time he traded his former active role on the swimming team for the team manager's job he did so as a changed person.

The team photo shows him not as an expansive executive but thin to the point of gauntness, the jaw region of his face shrunk by the pinch of the illness, the narrow body wrapped up in suit and tie, sitting dolefully off to one side, looking like an isolate among his mates.

The Book fails to note that Lee had become a hypochondriac for life. According to conventional Freudian psychology, hypochondria is supposed to bespeak a lack of love and a search to find it. This interpretation is not relevant for Lee. His illness had simply shaken him up and scared him badly. No wonder. It had been a rough siege. His view of his invalidism had nothing to do with lack of love. It was a realistic assessment based on the physical facts. Not surprisingly, it left him permanently impressed with the fragility of the human body.

"He was always in a muffler with gloves and hat," remembers Bill Winn, "almost like a little old man."

And so Iacocca babied himself with the same diligence that he showered upon everything he did. Walking home with friends from high school, he would fall behind, trailing the others and reminding them that the doctor had told him to take it easy. On a camping trip to the Poconos after graduation the others slept in a tent; Lido curled up in his car.

The fearfulness over the delicate state of his health and the hypochondria of his later years were evidently no hyperreaction. I believe that his classmate Dr. George Rutt, who became a cardiologist, came up with the primary cause of Iacocca's delicacy that seems convincing. The doctor hit upon this interpretation inadvertently, decades later, which made it all the more persuasive to me.

Dr. Rutt had not been aware of Iacocca's bout with rheumatic fever at the time. However, when I asked whether he knew the doctor on the case, it turned out that Dr. Rutt had been well acquainted with the late Dr. Gerald P. Backenstoe, the Iacocca family physician who managed Lido's illness. Dr. Backenstoe was a competent general practitioner, no more. Yet Dr. Rutt recalled this colleague from medical society meetings as an extremely tall, forbidding-looking, commanding prima donna: "He was the authority, like a superduper specialist. He was God."

It requires no imagination to picture this medical deity putting the fear of the true God into a Lido Iacocca who was hypersensitive to begin with and accustomed to being browbeaten by his authoritarian father.

Nowadays, Lee's associates are familiar with an impressive range of Iacocca symptoms and do not take them too seriously. Like much of the older male population, he suffers from diverticulitis, a normally harmless if annoying intestinal condition that can cause occasional cramps and irregularity of the bowels. Iacocca brings Italian passion to his diverticulitis, as he does to all else. The disease caused him to become a student of the digestive process and an ardent advocate of a mild over-the-counter laxative, the natural fiber supplement named Metamucil. Many doctors suggest Metamucil with enthusiasm. To hear Iacocca delineate its bowel action—his cousin Julie, among others, was exposed to the full lecture on the subject, and he acted it out for me with gestures—is to gain respect for Lee's ability to invest the unlikeliest subjects with operatic drama.

He has also been known to tire easily. The condition is most likely to hit him when he is bored and disaffected and looking for an easy way of getting out of doing something that he doesn't wish to do. But warmth! Physical warmth is vital to his comfort. Iacocca views every cold as a potential pneumonia. "Lee gets the sniffles and he's going to die," says Lars Larsen, his onetime PR chief. An Iacocca limousine chauffeur's first job is to kick up the heater for The Chairman. When Iacocca viewed the great fireworks at the Statue of Liberty centennial, he huddled in the rows of coatless celebrities tucked up to his chin in a woolly blanket.

Iacocca fears his final illness, death, not as we all do, as a distant threat. He regards it as possibly imminent, a neighbor. Thoughts of death do not preoccupy him, but they can pop to the surface upon mild provocation.

David Smith, the editor-publisher of *Ward's Autoworld* magazine, an old acquaintance, was charmed when Iacocca decided to introduce him to his mother, the formidable Antoinette, at an auto industry gathering in the Greenbrier Hotel in October 1984. It was a frothy occasion, a dance.

"I'm happy to meet your mother," Smith told Lee. "She looks so young."

Iacocca did not focus on his mother's youthfulness.

"You and I will never make it to sixty-five," he told Smith glumly. "We live on a different track."

To Iacocca, the Lifeline is also the Deathline. He does not, however, bottle up his somber side in a depressive way. His candor about life's trials is refreshing, sometimes breathtaking, especially for people who cannot display their innermost thoughts with such openness.

Startled reporters were thus treated, at a routine news conference in Dallas on March 15, 1986, to The Chairman's casual disclosure that he had more than once contemplated suicide. (Suicide research concluded long ago that *thoughts* of killing oneself are universal; discussing such thoughts is unusual, even among intimates, unless the talker is contemplating suicide at the time, which Iacocca most certainly was not.)

Talk at the Texas news conference had been about the plight of farmers. Fresh government policies were needed, said the Chrysler Chairman, "to keep, as you read in the papers, farmers from committing suicide." This prompted him to volunteer, gratuitously, a thought about the depth of his despondency during Chrysler's difficulties in late 1980. He admitted: "I contemplated it myself, I'm not kidding you, a couple of times, when we didn't have any money in the bank."

And lived not only to tell the tale but to bask in popularity and prosperity that has become legendary.

Given the impact of his boyhood invalidism, Iacocca's comeback at the time was dazzling. A touch of hypochondria wasn't much residual damage when measured against all that went right for him. The time away from classes did not affect his grades. He was a member of the Student Council and one year became president of the whole school, though he lost the election the following year because of overconfidence. His name went on the honor roll in his sophomore year. The following year, 1942, he was graduated twelfth in a class of more than 900.

"Why weren't you first?" demanded father Nick, the insatiable, in one of his memorable kicks at his son's emotional shins, an authoritative reminder about the importance of being *numero uno*.

To young Lee the challenge did not feel devastating. It was another spur. He had overcome the blows of the Depression; the bigotry in his environment, perceived and real; his shyness; and a deadly physical affliction. The father's goading was no longer a threat. It had become a predictable tickle.

The son was well launched by then. Thanks to Miss Raber and his own diligence, he had mastered the written and spoken word; the word was power. His peers sensed that nothing was likely to hold back the thin, smooth-talking Italian kid with a jawbreaker name, the mop of black hair, and the penetrating eyes.

"Lee is a raconteur extraordinary," says their evaluation of him in *Comus*, the Allentown High School yearbook, "and not only can he quip with the best but he can pun with the worst. If knowledge really is power, he is omnipotent. This, together with the ability he has developed in managing and directing school affairs, will prove a great asset in his career of engineering."

Lee himself did not feel omnipotent, not yet. But he wasn't slowed by doubts about himself. Engineering had indeed been his perceived future ever since he fell in love with cars when he washed Fords in his father's car rental agency. Lehigh was his university, less than ten miles away from home. His vision was specific, and it reached well beyond college. The old advertising slogan "There's a Ford in your future" was something he was eager to adopt. And still more. His heart was set specifically on a vice presidency at the Ford Motor Company.

He had a plan. Planning, he was confident, was everything. "When you aim at anything you are sure to hit it." So said the motto that he gave to the editors of *Comus* to describe his assessment of things to come.

But the testing of young Iacocca was not yet done. The rheumatic fever had left no physical aftereffects, so when the physician who gave him his first life insurance physical found nothing wrong, he asked, in the brisk manner of doctors at the time, why he wasn't in military service. The answer was a source of deep shame to Lee.

In The Book he describes how Japan's attack on Pearl Harbor hit the nation in the middle of his senior year, and unlike the war in Vietnam, so much better remembered today, this was a conflict of good against evil: Democracy absolutely had to defend itself against dictatorship. Young men were eager to join up. Lee dreamed of flying bombers over Germany, but the army wanted no one with a record of rheumatic fever.

Young Iacocca, seeing so many of his classmates called up, so many eventually dead, felt understandably dejected when he was classified unfit, "4-F." It was an "enormous disappointment," a "disgrace." He was a second-class citizen all over again. It was some consolation, though only a small one, that all civilian students felt inferior during the war. An Iacocca college classmate recalls: "We felt the older people looked at us and asked, 'Why aren't you in service like my son?' "

In The Book Iacocca does not explain that by failing his army physical, he had flunked another test set up by his father, a test experience of Nick's life by which the father liked to measure his own manhood. As a patriotic young immigrant Nick had volunteered for military service as soon as the United States entered World War I. He was one of the relatively few people who then knew how to drive, and so he was assigned to train ambulance drivers at Camp Crane on the western outskirts of Allentown. He never served away from home; but his war record was a source of pride, and Lee heard it mentioned frequently around home.

"It must have killed him to sit back, inadequate in his father's eyes," says Ron DeLuca, the advertising man.

At Lehigh Iacocca was relegated to second-class citizenship for yet another reason. He was a "townie" who lived at home, not one of the regulars residing on campus. The Allentown students were assigned a special room for rest periods and lunches. They lived in somewhat segregated status, not part of the campus elite. Iacocca's perception of differentness was encouraged all over again, and so was his sense of distance from others.

He was never a loner in the conventional sense. He came across as sociable, talkative and was surrounded by a crowd of bright peers, communicative young fellows who became professional people: doctors; dentists; lawyers; executives. Until sometime after Lehigh, even after he received his graduate engineering degree from Princeton University, his typical contacts with women seem to have preserved considerable distance, however. He provided respectable Allentown girls as dates for college dances and for old friends returning to town on furloughs from the military. But he seemed hesitant to approach women on his own behalf.

Most of his male contacts in high school and college do not remember his dating at all, at least not with any regularity; much less was he involved with any *one* woman. I heard nothing of any sexual activity, at least not the intimacy that used to be known as "going all the way."

Iacocca's own memory offers a strange contrast. In a 1986 interview with Cindy Adams in *Ladies' Home Journal* he chose to identify himself as an overly liberated male, even though he wasn't even asked about his mores as a youth. Having merely inquired about the degree to which he supervised the dating of his daughters, Ms. Adams received this surprising response: "I'll be suspicious of anybody they go with. *When I was going out in high school and college, I was a bit of a rake.* [Emphasis added.] So now I look with a jaundiced eye on whomever my kids are seeing."

When I read this remark to one of Iacocca's closest friends from Allentown, Floyd Moschini, he laughed in disbelief and thought Lee was engaging in wishful thinking. "Maybe that was the Walter Mitty in him," Moschini quipped. I read the quotation to Moschini's wife, Florence, who had moved in the same high school social set, and she also thought it was funny. She related how their group had engaged in "ESP parties": The couples separated into two groups and thought they could send signals through the wall by means of concentrating on selected playing cards.

"That's as rakish as we'd get," Mrs. Moschini recalled.

Had Iacocca led a sleazy double life unknown to his pals? That's remotely conceivable, of course, but I doubt it very much, especially since I talked with Marjorie Flohr of Allentown, a "good friend" of Iacocca's since the eighth grade. She dated him occasionally on football weekends while he was at Lehigh and she attended nearby Moravian College.

Iacocca's self-description as a "rake" brought a burst of merriment from her.

"I can remember necking in the back of the car with him," she said. "He was always a gentleman. It wasn't a romantic thing."

Most likely Iacocca still remembers himself as rakish for having necked in the back of the car with Marjorie Flohr.

The absence of nonsexual intimacy was something else again. His reluctance to become emotionally involved with other people was unusual. Moreover, it was not confined to his cautious dealings with females. He is an *emotional* loner, anything but prone to intimacy. Even his smile is closed off. The thin lips hardly open, the teeth rarely show.

In The Book his campaign manager in high school politics, Jim

Leiby, is assigned the role of Iacocca's "best friend." Which absolutely floored Leiby, a political science professor once at Harvard, now at the University of California in Berkeley. A gregarious and cheerful connoisseur of human folly, Leiby, among his other books, authored a history of the United States welfare system.

He had a great liking for Iacocca, he recalls, and he still does, with some reservations about Iacocca's apparent lack of intellectuality. But the men have been out of contact for more than forty years, and in high school they must have been an unusual duo: Lido was as straight, materialistic, and establishmentarian as a kid could get, while Leiby was a bohemian who wore his hair very long (extraordinary in the 1930s) and played piano in saloons and Elks Clubs three to four nights weekly with a professional band. They did spend some time together, but as Leiby recalls the relationship, they were anything but intimates.

He was as much surprised when I told him that he had been singled out as Lido's "best friend" as I was to learn that Leiby had not taken time to read Iacocca's smash best-seller. On reflection the professor could offer no explanation for why he had been nominated to Lido's inner circle. He recalls having been a visitor to his friend's home just once, when Lido was ill with rheumatic fever. He never met Papa Nick, and there were no soul-to-soul conversations between the young men.

Of the friends and classmates to whom I talked—each of whom spent years with Iacocca at various stages from grade school through college at Lehigh University—not one claimed that his outstanding future success was predictable. In all the years, without exception, they saw him as a plugger, clever, appealing, striving, eager for acceptance, but far from brilliant or inspired.

"He wasn't the smartest guy in the class, but he worked the hardest" was a typical comment.

Several old-timers volunteered that their eyes had trouble dealing with the eerie contrast between the restrained, haggard Iacocca they remember and the fleshy, feisty, radiant leader who materialized like a totally unfamiliar personality on their television sets in recent years.

"The transformation is amazing," said one.

Strong strains of seriousness and anxiety about the future are nevertheless landmark themes for both the early and the current

Iacocca. In junior high school he wrote a poem published in the school paper. Its key verse:

> The battle rages on
> For the things we haven't won.

Such gravity was in character then, and it sounds much like Iacocca's recent foreboding rumblings about the trade deficit and other unmet challenges of the 1980s.

His well-honed sense of humor carried a somber, sarcastic undertone, then as now. Today he needles the new Fords, likening their shape to flying potatoes. Back in Allentown the darts he aimed at an eccentric physics teacher known as "Mouse" Frankenfield packed the same deadly zing. Dr. Rutt, the cardiologist, remembers thinking that Lido must have said "Gotcha!" to himself whenever he got off one of his wisecracks. The words are forgotten. Lido's joy over hitting his target is not.

"I can still hear his snicker," says Dr. Rutt.

While Iacocca would be a late starter in the climb to unusual achievement, certain leadership traits were in evidence early. Dedicated to diligence, he wanted to motivate others to follow the same austere road. As the eighth-grade class president he delivered little speeches at assemblies, exhortations that sound like forerunners of his later campaigns to whip his truck and car salesmen into shape. At the end of class sessions the teachers would reserve five minutes for students to use as their own. Time-conscious even then, young Iacocca urged his peers in his talks to use this precious period productively, to prepare for the next class, to brush up, not to waste these minutes! The idea to issue these reminders may have come from the teachers. The fervor of delivery was his.

"These five minutes belong to you!" he lectured, implying that frittering the time away with horseplay was tantamount to larcency.

His talent as a negotiator emerged at high school graduation time. The class of 1942, deciding to depart with a flash of glory, assigned Lido and another boy to hire the famous and hard-to-get Woody Herman band to play at the graduation dance in the former trolley car depot, which had been transformed into the "Empire Ball Room." Iacocca did the actual negotiating. The theatrical agent, true to his trade, tried to deflect him, insisting that the boy accept lesser talent. The arguments were protracted. Iacocca stood stubbornly firm. In the end he was able to sign the Claude Thornhill Band for $750. This was considered almost as good as getting Woody Herman, who would have cost $1,100. The negotiation turned Lido into something of a class hero.

At Lehigh there was no time for fun. World War II dominated the period. Iacocca pounded through the four-year course in three years. These were times bristling with Iacocca energy, ferocious energy, acute concentration, harsh self-organization, careful investment of every minute of his time. Nobody remembers Lido going out on a date or showing up, ever, for a beer at the campus pub. He was a grind, in class and out, repeating the pattern of Papa Nick, who had poured himself into so many businesses: Lido joined campus organizations wholesale. In the leadership groups photographed for his 1945 class yearbook, Iacocca appears, scrawny and grave, ten times, like the Scarlet Pimpernel, the fictional hero of the French Revolution who popped up everywhere all at once.*

He joined up, yet he would not veer from his private agenda. A college acquaintance recalls arriving at the campus newspaper to deliver a story he had written. The place was bedlam. The staff was whooping it up, everybody except Iacocca, the news editor. Occupying a desk near the center of the room, Lido sat immobile, immersed in a textbook, oblivious of the tumult. He accepted the story being delivered, edited it without a word, and redirected his attention to his book.†

He was cramming, preparing to face his next taskmaster, another father figure, a man as unyielding as Nick, who would whip him into condition for the demands of life in business, the do-or-drop of competition as practiced by adults.

---

*Among his causes: the Interfraternity Council; Arcadia (student governing body); Cyanide (junior honorary society); Omicron Delta Kappa (senior leadership honorary society); Pi Tau Sigma (engineering); Pi Delta Epsilon (journalism); *Epitome* (yearbook); American Society of Mechanical Engineers (student branch); Theta Chi (social fraternity).
†This is one of the very few vignettes that have survived of Iacocca in college. Even though he was such a hectic joiner (or possibly because he spread himself so thinly over so many activities), his presence at Lehigh is remembered only dimly. I wrote to forty-seven alumni who had posed with him for various group photos in the *Epitome* yearbook; to their embarrassment or amusement, the great majority retained no memory whatever of Iacocca.

4.

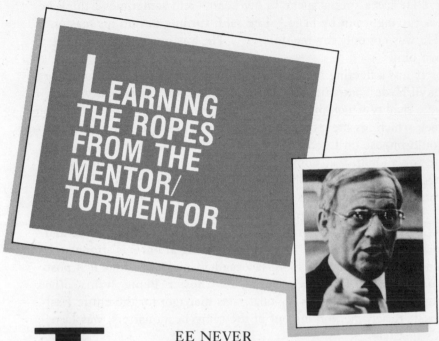

LEARNING
THE ROPES
FROM THE
MENTOR/
TORMENTOR

LEE NEVER
CALLED HIM "CHAR-
LIE." In more than a quarter of a century,
working in tandem, pushing millions and
millions of cars upon the public, Charles Ru-
fus Beacham always remained "Mr.
Beacham," even after Iacocca ultimately
became Beacham's boss at Ford in Detroit.

In his autobiography Iacocca reports that
only Papa Nick radiated more influence
upon his life than Beacham. Just as he does when he reports on his
feelings for his father, Lee fails to register the fact that fear, not
devotion alone, permeated his relationship with Beacham as well,
that both fathers worked their will upon the young man by applying
their whips as diligently as their smiles.

On one occasion Iacocca did let slip that pain was a routine feature of life with Beacham. Speaking at a Ford dinner in 1970 celebrating his great victory, his ascendancy to the presidency of the
company, Lee camouflaged the acknowledgment of Beacham's
darker side with a "gotcha" quip. Given even Iacocca's reputation

for virtuosity with words, his characterization of the older man, then five years in retirement, was striking.

"He has a special niche in my heart—and sometimes I think he was carving it out by hand," Lee said, turning toward his master. "He was not only my mentor. . . . He was my *tor*mentor, but I love him!"

It was a fleeting revelation, the merest glimpse of the love/fear Jekyll/Hyde contradiction in Charlie Beacham's personality, the same duality which marked old Nick Iacocca's life, the same double track which his life experience—the torment of his upbringing—would impose on Lee. While Nick and his iron discipline shaped the son's identity at home, Charlie Beacham and his distinctive methods for extracting obedience from his disciples would leave whiplash marks on Lee's professional persona.

In Iacocca's autobiography Beacham materializes posthumously as "Charlie," a warm, brilliant southerner with a radiant smile and an appealing manner, a "motivator" shining at once as strong and generous. They met in 1948. Iacocca had just landed his first post-training post in Ford fleet sales at the Chester, Pennsylvania, office outside Philadelphia. As regional sales manager for the entire East Coast, Beacham, working out of the same headquarters, was Iacocca's first boss.

Lido was still so shy that he mumbled every one of his sales spiels for practice, verbatim, time and again, before he dared place a call to a client. He remembers Beacham as a cheerleader who encouraged him, draping a protective arm around his shoulder when the twenty-four-year-old junior manager became discouraged by a month's poor sales result.

Lido applauded his boss's unequivocal values—"Make money, screw everything else" was the way Mr. Beacham encapsuled their world—and Iacocca worked so fiercely that he did not feel guilty when Beacham, wishing to shut off alibis at sales meetings, listed in one litany all the excuses his men had lately trotted out in fruitless efforts to deflect him.

When he entertained visitors from outside the automobile industry years later, Iacocca sometimes converted Beacham into a wise old character actor who tested a superbright apprentice by sending the little star on comical missions. Once Beacham dispatched Iacocca to Pottstown to resolve the fate of forty feeble used trucks that a dealer had found unsalable. Iacocca telegraphed Beacham that he had moved this "used iron" by slashing prices drastically.

CHARLIE BEACHAM (RIGHT): "SONNY, WHAT'RE YOU-ALL SUPPOSED TO BE DOIN'?"

Instead of the expected praise, Beacham responded with a terse wire instructing Lee to proceed to Tamaqua, Pennsylvania, to unload a similar pile of junk that had been unforgivably cluttering a truck lot for longer than thirty days.

In Iacocca's ex post facto reminiscing, Beacham became miraculously softened, much as a drill sergeant turns into a lovable curmudgeon once the war is over.

The Iacoccalytes who shared Lee's formative years in Chester under the reign of Beacham drew a more ambiguous portrait of the boss. It isn't altogether grim. With his imposing height and bulk, his severely brushed-back dark hair, his you-all drawl, and his off-color jokes for all occasions, Beacham could come across as an unlettered redneck. His cigars did not help. The doctor had told him not to smoke, so he chewed them and waved them at underlings to reinforce his commands, periodically cutting off the desiccated ends with a pocketknife and leaving them in a trail that reminded Iacocca of rabbit droppings.

Beacham was a college man, however. And while he never graduated from Georgia Tech, he could quote Shakespeare, and he excelled at ferreting out human failings. After he finally made it to a vice presidency in the Glass House headquarters in Dearborn at the age of sixty, he managed to captivate the dyspeptic Henry Ford II with his robust charms and could actually—miracles were still possible—make the prissy visage of Ford President Robert Strange McNamara break into a chuckle.

From the Chester days the Iacoccalytes fondly remember their chief's "Beachamisms," phrases that tended to delight in droll cruelties from the animal kingdom: Car buyers became weasels to be hooked while still asleep; some young automobile salesmen were so green that the cows ate them in the springtime. And the disciples admired how Charlie Beacham—like Nick Iacocca—lived by rules of his own design.

Beacham's dicta were firm. They covered a goodly range and disdained reverence for Ford's Detroit bureaucrats. Beacham preached often upon the value of clarifying mushy ideas in one's head by setting them down on paper. But he abhorred routine home office paperwork and, while still in Chester, instructed his disciples that the drumfire of paper from headquarters could be ignored. If an inquiry was urgent, let the boys in Detroit ask a second time. If his men wanted to hang up the phone on someone, they were to do this always when *they* were talking. A key management rule for making the most of an invariably endless Detroit meeting was to visit the toilet beforehand so no bureaucrat could slip something past while a good man from Chester was out of the room.

Most vividly, the Iacoccalytes remember Charlie Beacham's insistence upon—in fact, his absolute obsession with—*performance, performance, performance*, selling the goddamned cars! Whoever failed to *perform*—the word would become a neon-lighted imperative in Lee Iacocca's lexicon for life—was no better than cow droppings to Charlie Beacham, regardless of the offender's status.

The young men under his command were stunned to note the rank of some of Beacham's victims and the verve with which he mowed them down. One great day the Detroit manager of all fleet sales marched into Beacham's office in Chester, looking every bit as mighty as his title. Beacham welcomed the dignitary with cordiality and purred, "You're down here to help me, aren't you?"

The dignitary allowed that this was his mission.

"When did you ever do a good job anyplace?" demanded Beacham, and he recited, in perfect sequence, the wreckage of assignments that the visitor had muffed. Beacham was a dedicated student of failure. He knew the clinical details of a sinner's record and how to rub them in. The errant fleet manager remained in Chester only very briefly, and this was not unusual. Beacham once instructed his principal assistant that he needed to fulfill but one function during another official visitor's stay: to make sure that the fellow left town on time.

This, then, was the bright side of Beacham and his crusades. Unfortunately he usually didn't pick on sinners of his own size. Early Iacoccalytes like Jay Dugan remember smarting under his guilt-inducing "plantation attitudes." The best praise for Beacham that occurred to the diplomatic Buzz Klotz was a bloodstained allusion to boxing: "When he knocked a guy down, he took the time to pick him up." Larry Domagall remembers that Beacham used intimidation as an everyday tool of the management trade, as practiced by him, and he mused that old Charlie would have made one hell of a courtroom prosecutor.

Gar Laux, who eventually replaced Beacham and is an all-time great among the giants who ride herd on the car industry's unruly potentates, the dealers, was still traumatized more than a decade after Charlie Beacham had passed on to the great dealership up in the sky.

"I virtually had a fear of the man," Laux reflected. "He chewed you out in front of a roomful of people."

Laux also offered a two-faced compliment for "Mr. Beacham." "He sensed when to get on you and when to get off you," Laux said, but he recalled that the second part of this equation was sometimes not invoked until the ultimate stage of the intimidation game had been reached. On one occasion Beacham chewed out Laux so insultingly that Laux told his boss he'd resign on the spot, he wasn't about to take such abuse even from Mr. Beacham. Whereupon Beacham said he would never strike so hard at anyone who mattered less to him. Laux stayed on, but the call was close.

Brinkmanship was one of Beacham's bedfellows. He had been showing a film to a group of salespeople, and the room was still dark when he began to question one man about an item that he had found neglected in the past.

"Bob," he said, "what about that?"

Bob said that the matter had been attended to.

"Do you know that for a fact, Bob?"

"Yeah, absolutely!"

Whereupon Beacham placed the last bullet in his barrel and released the safety.

"Bob, do you want me to turn the lights on and ask you one more time?"

Like a badly jaded psychiatrist, Charlie Beacham was not certain that his methods were efficient. In moments of introspection he questioned whether adults were capable of changing their slovenly selves. Sometimes he said that attempts at behavior modification were probably useless to turn upon anyone past the age of twenty-one. Still, he refused to be guided by such a downbeat theory. Who really could tell? Maybe some of his sinners could be saved from themselves after all; maybe just one could be saved, maybe an Iacocca. Beacham was the quintessential salesman and therefore an optimist and a boomer at heart. He *never* gave up, just as Nick Iacocca had instructed young Lido *never* to give up.

And so Charlie Beacham goaded his troops and humbled them and rode them and drove them as close to the breaking point as he dared, and he made them squirm under his ridicule. Oh, how

Beacham could mobilize his phrasemaking talents to pile ridicule upon the head of a sinner, preferably in the presence of the culprit's peers! A man never forgot such occasions.

In particular, the Iacoccalytes remember their shame when Beacham taxed them with his "gonna barrel." This was Beacham's weapon against dithering, postponing, not closing the sale. More contemptible even than a salesman's sin of procrastination, Beacham believed, was the sinner's airy vow that he was "gonna" take care of such a lapse at some indefinite time in the future. Such an open-ended promise constituted treason to Beacham.

"You're gonna stick it in your 'gonna barrel,' eh?" So he would sneer, his voice dripping with sarcasm and disbelief.

"Performance" was the correct answer, the only answer, and to exact proper performance, Charlie Beacham, overriding his detestation of paperwork, wrote out weekly lists for himself, carefully sequencing each task according to its priority. He prepared his list every Sunday. On Monday morning he began working it off, item by item. He demanded that all his disciples, his sinners, make out their own lists, too, and then he applied his own system for tracking their progress by following up in his own idiosyncratic manner.

Encountering one of his charges in a corridor during the week, anyone at all, anytime at all, he'd stop him, and apropos of nothing at all, he'd inquire pleasantly, *"Sonny, what're you-all supposed to be doin'?"*

Charlie Beacham preferred to presume guilt rather than innocence. One could flush out more sins that way.

Thus he managed "by objective" and "by walking around," in his own stealthy style, long before more sophisticated manipulators invented the "one minute manager" and other Pavlovian psychological challenges. Beacham believed in the stick, not the carrot. Outright approval, much less praise, seemed never to pass his lips. His rare praise was always qualified. Once he managed to tell Iacocca, "You're the best guy I've got," yet right away he followed up with a "but." Iacocca still didn't delegate enough tasks, Charlie Beacham preached; he tried to do too much himself. He'd have to watch that weakness. . . .

Iacocca flourished under the treatment; he positively bloomed. It was just like home! He understood the system. It was simple: Approval was signaled silently by the absence of punishment, and Iacocca was deeply dedicated to his labor so that Charlie Beacham would not find him sinning. The Iacoccalytes recall no instance of Beacham's needing to apply his methods to compel Lee to perform. Just as one look from Nick usually sufficed to make him shape up as a boy, so Beacham's presence, the mere threat that he might appear, was discipline enough, and this included Iacocca's conduct on Saturday, presumably a day off.

Charlie Beacham was not a believer in the five-day week. A salesman needed to be ever wakeful to catch the weasel, the customer; one needed always to think, to scheme, how to go about catching the tricky little animal before it could slink away. Perhaps Beacham felt that his life was empty whenever he was not thus preoccupied. So he made it a habit to drop in of an occasional Saturday morning upon those of his assistants who performed most closely in accordance with his perfectionistic standards.

Decades later these lieutenants claimed that they did not resent their boss's unconventional intrusions upon their privacy. Actually it was a bit of a privilege to sit about in leisure clothing on Saturday morning, reviewing the week, making small talk with the commander. Saturday tended to find Beacham in a jolly mood, and the lieutenants did not suspect that he had come to check up on them, to make certain that they would not temporarily neglect their life's responsibilities just because the workweek was officially over for the less dedicated members of the flock.

Iacocca, though, took Beacham's Saturday inspections to heart, and so Saturday morning could be a time of loyalties divided: his need for respite, on one hand; demands of the omnipresent Beacham and his radar eyes, on the other. On one Saturday morning, Lee told Jay Dugan, he was sleeping late, reaping his warrior's reward of rest after a week of exhausting chase after the weasels. It was one Saturday when Charlie Beacham did not show up. Not physically, that is. He did materialize vividly in Iacocca's dreams during the half-wakeful hours of early morning. In the dream he peered down upon Lee, sacked out in his bed of sloth, terrified under the silent questioning of the master.

"Can you imagine waking up and having Mr. Beacham look down on me?" he asked Dugan, shaking his head, half-amused and half-horrified. The two men agreed that it was a funny scene, yet, well, maybe not all that terribly funny.

Tracked by Beacham's radar, Iacocca was spurred on to devise new ways for digging into the wallets of weasels and for herding salesman/sinners along the path of righteousness. Prior to the days of intensive huckstering via television, selling lingered as a messy art. All too often the lack of system made the getaway too easy for the weasels. Iacocca picked up on the need to elevate his calling, to systematize it, to organize the basics, to zero in on the ABCs (as he called them), forgetting the bullshit, and setting proven methods firmly onto paper or, during meetings, pinning them down in black and white on the blackboard. That was Mr. Beacham's style, and Mr. Beacham was law.

With Jay Dugan, Iacocca wrote a handbook, "Hiring and Training Truck Salesmen"—not a subject on which much printer's ink had been previously spilled. Later, as zone manager in Wilkes-Barre and in other depressing stops along his district, he drummed salesmen into formal training courses, another revolutionary notion at the time. His Sunday nights were kept reserved (then and forever after) as inviolate private time for list making, soul-searching, a pause for scheming in the unending weasel hunt. Starting Monday mornings, he'd appear before some startled district sales manager and inquire, "What's your job?" Few had thought about such fundamentals.

As promotions came and his territory expanded southward, Iacocca's Italian heritage, ever the source of both pride and anguish, began to get in the way of efficiency. The trouble started on the phone. He had to make many long-distance calls, and in those days each call required an operator who inevitably had difficulty comprehending the correct spelling of "Iacocca." When the operator wanted his first name and he said, "Lido," she'd giggle. Which is how Iacocca says he came to call himself Lee.*

Beacham next went to work on his last name. He viewed the foreign identity as a handicap for his protégé. To assure smooth relationships, corrective steps were indicated, and before Iacocca embarked on his first trip south, Beacham briefed him on how to get along on Charlie's native grounds. First, Lee talked too fast. Beacham ordered him to slow way down. To soften the negative effect of the undesirable foreignism—Iacocca—Lee was to tell the folks that this was his first name, that his family name was "Lee," the name most hallowed in post-Civil War memories down south.

*According to other accounts, Beacham simply told him to change his name. In any event, Iacocca clearly enjoyed being able to muster a dual identity ever after, as if one persona doesn't suffice to do him justice. He has never let go of his "Lido" incarnation. Sentimentally he signs his old name when he writes notes to close friends and to the cronies he left behind in Allentown. His second wife also took to calling him "Lido."

Iacocca accepted this bizarre stratagem but improved on it. At his first sales meeting in Atlanta he wrote LEE IACOCCA in large capital letters on the blackboard and then, as if seized by sudden inspiration, wiped out the last name. The letters LEE were left looming large, and Iacocca pointed to them proudly.

"That really means something down in this country," he said.

The guys from truck sales loved the chivalrous gesture, and if Iacocca ever felt any twinges of conscience because he trifled with his identity, downgrading his background in order to clear his career path, he never mentioned it.

By then he was courting his future wife, Mary McCleary, the very pretty daughter of a local plumber. She was a receptionist at the Ford assembly plant in Chester, and Lee was so shy that he almost missed out on meeting her. It happened at a reception that Charlie Beacham was throwing after the introduction of the 1949-model cars at the Bellevue Stratford Hotel in Philadelphia. Iacocca quickly spotted the bouncy redhead. Beacham's deputy, Matthew ("Matt") McLaughlin, was watching as Lee eyed Mary. Concluding that Iacocca was too tongue-tied to walk up to her and introduce himself, McLaughlin took him by the elbow and performed the icebreaking rites. They began dating even though Mary thought Lee too skinny ("He was like a stick").

On the wall of the study in McLaughlin's enormous home in the suburban San Diego hills there still hung, while McLaughlin told me of their first encounter, a photo of the young Iacoccas taken at a Halloween costume party a few years after they were married. Lee and Mary posed in front of a prize possession, their Model A Ford convertible touring car.

Mary was done up as a flapper from the twenties, her silver sequined dress shimmering brilliantly under the photographer's flashbulb as she struck the pose of a gangster's moll. Her grin was lighting up her entire face. The heel of one shapely leg was kicking high. Her body was pressed tightly against Lee, whose expression was mock-sinister, the black fedora pulled into his face, the mouth clenched around an enormous cigar, the tuxedo doing duty as the uniform of a Capone mobster.

Here was arresting evidence of two people in love, having a ball, telling the rest of the world to go to hell.

The idyll had been a long time in the making. During their

MARY (AS A 1920'S FLAPPER) AND LEE (AS A MOBSTER) POSE AT A HALLOWEEN COSTUME PARTY DURING THEIR EARLY YEARS IN DETROIT

eight-year courtship their friends sometimes could not be certain who was courting whom. Lee attributed the tortuous path of the romance to his long absences on business trips. Mary tended to blame Nick. The lovers argued frequently because Lee liked to spend weekends in Allentown, usually without Mary. She resented being left home alone, and until their marriage in 1956 she still worked at Ford, still as a receptionist.

While theirs was not a shotgun wedding in the conventional sense, it required a crisis to make it happen. It was spring, one of the few weekends that did not send Lee back to Nick and the familiar comforts of Allentown. Lee and Mary drove to the Poconos with several other young couples. All the others were married. Mary envied them. Why, after eight years, was Lee so enslaved to his work and his parents that he would not marry her? On the way back from the mountains they quarreled and decided they would break up.

As Mary remembered the events, she came down with a high fever the following morning and was taken to the hospital later in the day. It was a case of pneumonia. At his office, meanwhile, Lee was nursing second thoughts, and when he called Mary's home toward five o'clock and was told that she had been hospitalized, he hurried to her bedside and visited often as she convalesced. He loved her, she loved him, they were reconciled, yes, but marriage?

Neither partner ever revealed what ended the long deadlock. Mary's mother tried to help. Tired of her daughter's anguish, the mother wanted to allay whatever doubts might by now have arisen in Mary's mind. She loved and respected Lee, she told Mary, and Lee's love for his father was not only a sign of Nick's need to dominate but proof of a loving and therefore a good parental relationship. Wouldn't a loving son make a most loving husband? Hadn't Lee shown in Chester that he was strong when he was on his own, away from Nick and Allentown?

And so the reluctant couple became engaged on Mother's Day and was married in Chester on September 29, the sales resistance of Lee, the salesman, finally broken.

By then Lee was assistant sales manager for the Philadelphia district, basking in the departed glory of Charlie Beacham, lately promoted to be chief of car and truck sales for the Ford Division in Detroit. Lee was knitting together his friendships with the Chester junta that Beacham would import to infiltrate national headquarters—McLaughlin, Buzz Klotz, and other lieutenants—and he was building influential friendships with kingpin dealers like Victor Potamkin, a Ford dealer in Philadelphia before his subsequent historic defection to General Motors.

Victor and Lee were two of a kind, caught up—enraptured almost—by the thrill of marketing, watching in suspense, like kids, to see what would happen the next time they kidnapped some hotshot's Cadillac at the Green Valley Country Club, substituting a Lincoln with a note saying that the car was a loan they were leaving behind with best wishes for happy trial driving.

Together the two men concocted a crack into the one market that most strongly resisted buying Fords, the Jews. Still disgusted by memories of notorious anti-Semitism practiced by the original Henry Ford and his gun-toting sidekick Harry Bennett, most Jews looked upon Ford automobiles as insults to their religion. Even a Jewish merchant like Potamkin suffered under the unofficial boycott until his pal Lee had an idea.

"Do you know this guy Chaim Weizmann?" he asked Victor.

Potamkin said that he didn't but that he knew a brother-in-law of the president of Israel.

"See if Weizmann will accept a Lincoln as a gift," suggested Iacocca.

It worked. Photos appeared in the newspapers of a Lincoln Cosmopolitan limousine being presented to Israeli representatives. Some Jewish car buyers around the country were made to feel cozier toward Ford. Potamkin and Iacocca took delight in the success of their joint caper, and Lee would remember a lesson for life: Never underestimate the power of a gimmick. A gimmick might not move mountains, but it could move automobiles, lots of them.

And a gimmick of cosmic proportions was needed in 1956, the year Ford bet prematurely on new safety equipment as a way to attract buyers. Safety became the basis for an elaborate sales campaign. The effort bombed disastrously (see Chapter 14), and nowhere were the results more dismal than in Iacocca's district. Sales there were the very worst in the country. In desperation Iacocca cooked up an idea. He called the scheme "56 for '56," and it sounded strained, to say the least.

Under this plan Ford would sell a car for a down payment of 20 percent plus three years of payments at $56 a month. Philadelphia salesmen were unleashed upon supermarket parking lots with bags of potato chips and cards called "wujatak," a new word for "would-ya-take." The salesmen would tape the tickets on the windshields of parked cars, filling in their buying offers and leaving behind a bag of chips marked "The chips are down. We're selling cars for $56 a month."

Complicated, weird, silly, call it what one will, the weasels went for the bait. Within weeks the Philadelphia area led the country in Ford sales. In Detroit Charlie Beacham made sure that Ford's new leader, Robert McNamara, knew who had originated the happy avalanche. Minus the potato chip detour, the Iacocca scheme was adopted for the rest of the country, and since McNamara was the ultimate maven on numbers, he later announced that 75,000 extra cars were moved as a result.

The gimmick sufficed to secure Iacocca's future in Detroit. Its effects were instantly electrifying. He was about to get married, finally; he was getting promoted to a bigger job in Washington; he was inspecting the new carpeting in a new suburban Maryland house; everything was on the move up, up, and just then Charlie Beacham called him into his office in Detroit and said that McNamara wanted him to become national truck marketing manager in the Glass House headquarters. Iacocca never spent a night in the Maryland home.

The protégé was poised now on the final trajectory. Charlie Beacham had been the perfect front man and would continue to function in the same role through critical years. Iacocca found his counsel sound and lived by the Beacham rules, driving himself and his underlings hard, intimidating them when necessary, delegating whenever possible, but watching them, questioning them until the bullshit was purged, was oozing out of them, never letting up, not on Saturday morning, not on Sunday nights, when next week's lists were due, getting everything down on paper, crisply, the ABC style, no bullshit, never forgetting that the idea was to "hawk" the car, as he put it, to push it out of the goddamned showroom, and don't forget the options, lots of options—"class for the mass," as Iacocca called the high-profit extras.

There was, however, one Beacham advice that Iacocca was finally too impatient to heed. Beacham had warned him to stay as far away as possible from Henry Ford II. Mr. Ford, so Mr. Beacham preached, was a most dangerous man, especially when drunk but also when sober. Over the years Beacham had repeated the warning again and again. For a long time Iacocca plotted his Ford career accordingly. But not in the end. In the end Charlie Beacham, the judge of people, the mentor/tormentor, was gone, and Iacocca, left on his own, headed for the great fall.

Five days before he was fired from Ford he was still lecturing an interviewer about the greatness of Mr. Beacham, remembering how Beacham had cut him short when Lee used to barge into his office with a brainstorm. "Stop comin' in here and selling me with your hands," Charlie Beacham had drawled. "Write it down! If you can't put it down succinctly, you haven't thought it out."

Iacocca thought it all out, or so he believed, Beacham having taught him the rules so well that he could now teach them to others and become a mentor/tormentor himself. He was no longer a Willy Loman hustling up and down rural roads in Pennsylvania. He was what Willy Loman had dreamed about becoming and had never become.

5.

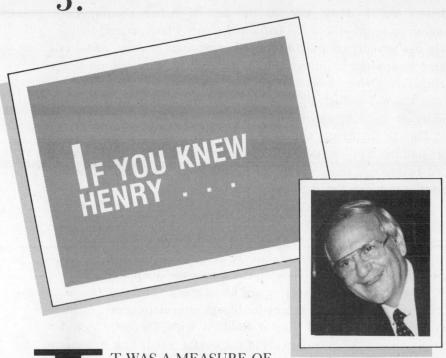

I F YOU KNEW
HENRY . . .

I T WAS A MEASURE OF
HENRY FORD'S OLYMPIAN
PERCH IN THE UNIVERSE THAT IACOCCA
NEVER EXCHANGED MORE THAN A FEW
FORMALITIES WITH HIS CHAIRMAN UNTIL
DECEMBER 1960, FOUR YEARS AFTER MCNA-
MARA AND BEACHAM HAD SUMMONED LEE
TO MOVE INTO THE GLASS HOUSE. And even
then the meeting was only for a bit of pleasant fakery.

McNamara and Beacham had convinced Ford to
make Iacocca general manager of the Ford Division, the company's
crown jewel. Ford had agreed. McNamara and Beacham had informed their protégé of the promotion, set up an appointment with
the chairman, and instructed Lee on his conduct. Under no circumstances was he to let on that he had been entrusted with advance
knowledge of what was happening.

Iacocca was so awed by the occasion that he had no trouble carrying off the formality of the charade with reverence. "It was like
being summoned to see God," he recalled years afterward.

If this was a case of mistaken identity, it was not far out of place. Henry Ford II (almost nobody used his nickname, Hank the Deuce) *was* a deity, one of the last of America's imperial owner/managers—those old-fashioned giants who operated industries *and* actually controlled them like one-man grocery stores. His name was on the building, as he sometimes liked to remind lesser beings, the *family* name, his very own grandfather's name, and Iacocca was old enough to know all about the impact of that first Henry on the daily existence of everyone alive.

Though frequently chronicled, the sweep of the Ford family history and the dynastic gyrations of Henry II must be freshly appreciated before the choreography of Lee Iacocca's rise and fall and rebirth can make the slightest sense.

The Fords and the Iacoccas. There could not be two American families less alike, more out of sync and sympathy, more polarized in values. The love of automobiles—and "love" is the correct word—pulled them together, but the differences of genes and environment were bound to blow up their marriage of convenience.

This was not some soap opera like *Dallas,* renamed *Detroit.* Even two extravagantly successful blockbuster fictioneers, Arthur Hailey with *Wheels* and Harold Robbins with *The Betsy,* could merely hint at the convolutions of the conflicts that tore this macho scene apart. The reality was too large, too intricately pressured, too primal for these contemporary storytellers to master. Here was classic Greek tragedy in overdrive. Nothing but the willfulness of Henry and Lee kept their unlikely bond functioning, more or less, for as long as it managed to survive: nearly twenty years of excruciating drama.

In the beginning there was only the creator, quite alone, Henry Ford I, a farm lad who had difficulty reading except at very slow speed. To recognize him as an engineering original, a genius, would be like dismissing Napoleon as a clever fellow with firearms. In love with machinery, the first Henry, in effect, invented mass production. The simplicity of his unique Model T was as breathtaking as its small price. Ford placed an entire nation onto wheels, squeezing down the cost of the Model T from $690 in 1910 to $360 before World War I, cheap enough to sell 730,041 automobiles, unbelievable for that time, and ultimately crowning Ford as the nation's first billionaire.

Unfortunately his biographers—and they were still juggling ad-

HENRY FORD II:
"MY NAME IS ON
THE BUILDING"

jectives for him and his clan in the 1980s—saw him flawed in the extreme. He was unpredictable, unembarrassable, and bigoted, his loudly proclaimed anti-Semitism extraordinarily virulent. He was also greedy, paranoid, dictatorial, and his interpretations of history were eccentric enough to have grown in the garbage dumps of mental hospitals. Hitler cited him as a source of inspiration. Ford spied on his workers, forcing them to communicate in quasi-ventriloquist grunts known as the "Ford Whisper," and his plants were so high-charged with tension that his people suffered from "Ford Stomach."

Nobody, however, claimed that Henry I didn't dote on his four grandchildren, the most coddled of the lot being, of course, the eldest, his namesake, Henry II. Little Henry was exposed to automobiles early and impressively. In the arms of his grandfather at the age of three the boy held the torch that ignited the new blast furnace of "the Rouge," the founder's great monument. It was the torch that set in motion an empire: the River Rouge automobile manufacturing plant, a near-autonomous territory of ninety-three buildings, ninety-plus miles of rail track, and, eventually, 75,000 workers. And before he was ten, the youngster raced about Fair Lane, his grandfather's ninety-acre estate, in his own miniature British sports car, bumping and denting it for the fun of it.

While Lido Iacocca and his piously Catholic family scratched for polenta in Allentown, Henry II grew up as a princeling of privilege, attended by relays of servants in his parents' sixty-room house at Grosse Pointe, where even affluent Catholics were unwelcome. The Ford boy's self-possession was remarked upon. When His Royal Highness the Prince of Wales came to visit and asked him, "How is everything?" Henry, then seven, pointed at his younger brother and announced, "He just threw up and Grandmother is hiding behind the screen."

While he could rarely be faulted for lack of candor, young Henry was not generally considered likable. He was tough, shrewd, mean, spoiled, cranky, and, well, unattractive. Known as "Lardass" at the Detroit University School, he was driven by chauffeurs, attended by bodyguards, held in awe by fellow students and, about equally, by the instructors.

Outsiders never forgot that they were dealing with a crown prince of industry, and Henry liked testing the limits. At Yale he reached them. He was found out at having had a senior thesis ghost-written by Rosie's, a tutoring service, and dropped out of the university without a diploma.

In all his days, the weaknesses of the second Henry induced a blindness in other people. It was a chronic miscalculation that toppled big men off their high horses, including, in the end, Iacocca. He and all the others simply underestimated Henry.

It was easy to do. In his private life Henry, presumably in pursuance of his perceived royal rights, often came across as an incredible buffoon. When he stated that he enjoyed "fooling around with the broads," this coltish admission covered such habits as his fondling, when drunk, freshly accosted female acquaintances very fully, persistently, front and rear, up and down, and very much in public. His copious drinking, usually red Château Lafite-Rothschild wine, bottle after $70 bottle, was commonly publicized. So were his divorces and marriages (three, including the one to Cristina, a gorgeous and wily Italian model); his extracurricular escapades (notably the California arrest for drunken driving with another model, followed by his historic celebration of the art of stonewalling: "Never complain, never explain"), not to forget the lawsuits in which he starred for weeks as the defendant on the witness stand.

The very grossness of young Ford's leisure pursuits encouraged people to undervalue his accomplishments at his work. It happened that his successes, especially in his early years, were nothing less than historic. And they centered, of all things, on his canny management of people. Somehow, somewhere, certainly not from his grandfather, not at Yale, not during a bored stretch in the navy, he had fathomed that people, not inanimate engineering devices, made good things happen.

Perhaps sheer necessity was the mother of his brilliance, for by the end of World War II the looniness of old Henry had turned the For Motor Company into a bleeding hulk. The chaos was fantastic: In one department, Henry II revealed years later, bookkeepers were estimating costs by actually weighing piles of invoices on a scale.

With a strong boost from his mother and the restless family's stockholdings, young Henry captured control of the company by pushing aside the feeble grandfather; he purged the gun-toting thug Harry Bennett, whom old Henry had selected as his successor; and while he shrewdly stepped back, mostly to observe, spending years to learn the industry, the grandson brought in not one group of sharp new managers but two teams to nurse the company back to health.

Sons of titans are often eaten alive by their overwhelming fa-

thers, and Edsel, the son of the first Henry, was no giant slayer.
The women of the family said, when Edsel died of stomach cancer
at forty-nine, that the first Henry had pressured his son to death.
But the second Henry had been sheltered from this struggle, and
he was strong.

From General Motors he lured away its financial wizard, Ernest
R. Breech, a specialist in cost analysis, along with several of his GM
assistants. Ford was able to recruit Breech because he impressed
him as a bright, earnest, altogether worthy young fellow and because the messes that bedeviled the company presented a proverbial challenge to a great problem solver. "I said a few prayers for
guidance," said Breech when asked why he signed on.

The second new broom came to Henry over the transom in the
form of an arrogant telegram that not every executive would have
taken seriously. It offered him the services of a complete management team whose members all but guaranteed up front that they
would save his company. Intrigued, Ford investigated and found he
was dealing with a group of junior air force officers who had revolu-
tionized decision making in the Pentagon by introducing sophisticated new types of statistical controls. He had stumbled upon a
package of talent that would become celebrated in histories of management as the Whiz Kids.

The team leader, Charlie Bates ("Tex") Thornton, would leave
Ford within two years to form Litton Industries. J. Edward ("Ed")
Lundy would stay on to become Henry's indispensable adviser: one
of the nation's least known but most influential financial men (see
Chapter 6). Bob McNamara would contribute the most to make the
company profitable and efficient after the war before leaving to become President Kennedy's secretary of defense. Like
McNamara, Arjay Miller would rise to the Ford presidency, though
he was shoved aside by Henry before long and wound up as dean of
the Stanford School of Business.

When young Ford first faced these potential stars, they were
freshly unfrocked soldiers who knew a good deal about numbers but
nothing about cars. Henry took to their brashness and shrewdly
guessed that by hiring this risky crew of unemployed youngsters, he
would enter the Ford Motor Company in the field of "human engineering," an activity lately popularized by the labor leader Walter
Reuther. Here was a new idea that appealed to young Ford for a
very profound reason.

"I think Henry always wanted to compete with his grandfather,"
Arjay Miller told the author Robert Lacey in 1986, "but he didn't

want to compete head on. He knew he could not invent something—and this 'human engineering' offered him the way. He was
going to do to people what his grandfather did to machines." The
Whiz Kids could get him started in that direction and young Henry
was smart enough to embrace these snotty saviors.

The sole aide he would trust in those days when he was new at
his job was John Bugas, who formerly ran the FBI office in Detroit,
and so Henry asked Bugas to grill Tex Thronton and his Young
Turks.

"What do you think of them?" Henry asked Bugas later in
private.

"They're all smart, almost too smart," said Bugas. "They want
about twelve thousand each, but I think we can get them for ten."

"Pay them the twelve thousand," Ford ruled.

Henry II was anything but a buffoon, at least not in the day-
time. His detractors tended to forget that after a dissolute night he
might arrive at the office hung over and grouchy, but he was invariably sober, in full control of his faculties; and history had proved
that these were very formidable indeed.

Iacocca, of course, knew his Detroit history, and he recognized that
one had better be serious about the whims of Mr. Ford (it was always Mr. Ford; as in Mr. Beacham, rank was rank). He realized
that these whimsicalities were made of the same stuff as when
Henry had bashed his sports cars at the age of ten and that Mr.
Ford's adult whims were exercised for precisely the same reason:
for the hell of it.

Mr. Ford's own cars always had to be black, never red, because
he detested red cars. The products of his factories could never be
equipped with Michelin tires because Mr. Ford couldn't abide "frog"
tires. His favorite dish, hamburgers, was never satisfactory outside
Detroit because only Mr. Ford's own cooks ground up filet mignon
to make them.

Iacocca felt that Mr. Ford was perfectly entitled to any eccen-
tricity, and in his first years in Detroit he humored the owner sub-
missively, he knew his place. People who listened while he talked
to the boss on the phone often heard him say only, "Yes, Mr. Ford.
Yes, Mr. Ford . . ." His loyalty to *numero uno* was total.

"Hell, Mr. Ford is No. 1 in my mind," Iacocca told a writer
from the *New York Times Magazine*. "Always has and always will be.
He hired me, he brought me along, he gave me my opportunities."

To make the most of them, Iacocca kept building up control over himself and over those others he needed to succeed at Ford. Always he had a plan, as Mr. Beacham had preached. On Iacocca's bedside table he kept a chart of dates showing when he was due to reach which rung of the corporate ladder, and when his vice presidency came eighteen days after his thirty-sixth birthday, not at thirty-five, the deadline he had prescribed for himself, he felt somewhat diminished.

He worked persistently on his shyness, feeling much liberated by a Dale Carnegie course in personality improvement and public speaking, to which the company sent him. In his autobiography he included a generous and detailed commercial for the Dale Carnegie Institute, and he spelled out the ways in which its coaches relaxed him. Unmentioned was another guide who, according to the Iacoccalytes, did even more to unlimber Lee.

The unsung teacher was Barry O'Daniels, an ex-vaudeville hoofer, a living caricature of Boffo the Clown, a comical figure with a bulbous nose and marvelously nimble feet that could perform a great tap dance while Barry was sitting down. Like Dale Carnegie, Barry was hired by the company to polish the public image of its executives. He was a likable character who loved telling dirty jokes, but he knew a lot about projection, enunciation, and he taught tricks that produced a more surefooted stage presence.

He again told Iacocca what Mr. Beacham had warned him about: that he was in too much of a hurry, it showed in his speech, he needed to slow down, way down, and he was still too tense, and that, too, showed. He should reduce pressure on himself while he was on the speaking stage by imagining that one man in the audience was sitting out there without any clothes. He was not to imagine a naked girl, however.

"She'd take your mind off your speech," Barry said, cackling.

To increase his mastery over what he called the people side of the business, Iacocca introduced what his autobiography describes as a system of quarterly reviews. He adapted the idea from Wall Street, he reports. If the stockholders were entitled to quarterly reports on the state of the company, why, the managers could surely check every quarter to see whether goals were being reached by its executives, whether *performance* was being delivered. Fair was fair. The book sets the procedures out sedately, a quiet formality like bookkeeping.

Iacoccalyte loyalists and Iacocca detractors, alike, remember the realities of Iacocca's reviews rather differently. They speak, still a bit cowed, of his "little black book" and how scared they were of it. It was his whip, and he used it as such. Actually it was not one book at all, and it was not so little. The performance records constituted a rather weighty library, some twenty loose-leaf binders, eight by ten inches, with black plastic covers, and Iacocca kept them close at hand on a credenza behind his desk.

Everyone saw the books lined up there, knew that Iacocca consulted them with regularity, knew that they contained indisputable evidence of everyone's conduct, of the record of weasels that were caught and those that got away, of the bonuses and demerits meted out by the keeper of the books, the holder of the whip.

At times Iacocca felt that the passive presence of the books was not good enough. To demonstrate his displeasure at a meeting, he'd pull one of them out, wave it at his guys, and remind them: "You're all in here, your destiny with the company is in here!" This was the Iacocca version of "human engineering" or, as he put it, "bringing a man face to face with his mortgage."

Like a field marshal surrounding himself with the most loyal officers for a chancy amphibious assault, Iacocca picked and quickly inspired a coterie of supporters, bright guys, not yes-men, car guys open to new ideas, and one of them was an engineer, a young product planner named Donald Frey, the future chairman of Bell & Howell. Frey was an iconoclast, a former university professor; but he appreciated flair and decisiveness, and he would never forget pitching an idea at Iacocca in a conference shortly after they met. The idea was about grease fittings. It would cost about $1 a car, require an immediate expenditure of $5 million.

"He picked it up in two seconds," Frey says. "It was immediately approved."

And how Iacocca could talk and how his mere words could sell!

It was not only that he could wrap his charm around the weasels, the car buyers trying to find true north in the jungle of the marketplace; that he could hook the dealers, the boomers, who could see through a selling technique as if it were another card trick; no, he could decimate a rock like McNamara, who had numbers coursing through his veins instead of corpuscles, who always searched for exits that he called "options," who X-rayed every proposition through his granny glasses and found something wanting . . . this McNamara could be sold by Iacocca.

Matt McLaughlin, Lee's deputy, watched it done. The two of

IACOCCA AND HIS FEARED "LITTLE BLACK BOOKS": "YOU'RE ALL IN HERE!"

them went from the fifth floor up to McNamara's office on the twelfth, lobbying to give a new car the name Galaxy and wanting an increased ad budget for it.

"If you're here to name the car Galaxy and increase the ad budget," so McNamara greeted them, "the meeting is over."

It wasn't. It lasted two hours, and McNamara surrendered in the end.

"Lee sold him," says McLaughlin. Rigorous preparation had much to do with it. Iacocca would not go against McNamara's numbers without numbers of his own. But he could make his numbers dance with his words.

Mr. Ford himself found that he became tempted to fall under Iacocca's spell, though never quite all the way, and sometimes he pulled Lee's leg about all that eloquence. Once Iacocca pushed one of his ideas so passionately that Henry stopped him: "All right, Lee; now let's get the facts or you'll sell us without our knowing them." That was selling, although Iacocca would probably have called it bullshit.

Not everyone was completely sold. One power center at Ford was the design shop, and its vice president for nineteen years, Gene Bordinat, tried to hold out a measure of independence for himself. He felt crowded by Lee's imperial style, worried that it would get Lee into trouble, that he was beginning in some respects to out-Ford Mr. Ford himself, which made Lee not healthy to be too closely allied with. Lee had to be handled with utmost care, especially because he never wanted to lose face, so Bordinat relied largely on oral communications and never included touchy matters in memos to Iacocca because these might be seen by others and boomerang.

Bordinat's diplomacy was especially helpful in connection with the company plane. Mr. Ford rarely rode in the 727 jet. But Iacocca sometimes requisitioned it to have his parents flown up from Allentown for parties and Lee seemed to consider it his personal transportation. Gene Bordinat had to have the plane's interior rebuilt to suit Lee's needs, and he delivered. The bed was queen-sized; the ceiling was dropped to become square. The faucets were gold-plated. The galley could turn out a choice of three hot entrées. Iacocca valued men like Bordinat who could accomplish such chores. But he kept a careful eye on Gene.

During one of their many trips on the 727 to Europe the two men sat facing each other. Bordinat was reading. Iacocca seemed to be sleeping. Suddenly Lee opened his eyes and made what Bordinat considered a most un-Iacocca-like remark.

"Gino," he said, "I might need you, but don't ever forget you need me." Whereupon he closed his eyes again, shutting off any discussion.

Many years later Bordinat was still taken by the revelations of that moment. "I was startled, shocked by the way he used the first person," he recalls. "It was a confession to me and also a threat."

Which, no doubt, was exactly what Iacocca had intended. This was the way politics was best played in a political company like Ford: cautious in risky relationships, aggressive everywhere else.

The Detroit environment helped to keep him charged up. It is quintessentially a town for guys, not for women, a company town, a lunch-bucket town (as some still say), a raw, ugly town made for work. Iacocca was out of the house at 7:15 A.M. or earlier, speeding toward Dearborn down the wide freeways that slice up the interminable urban and suburban sprawl, the way knives whack through pizza. Often he did not again hit the freeways to Bloomfield Hills until after eight in the evening. There was no time left for niceties.

Except for certain genteel enclaves dotted with mansions and clubs, Bloomfield among them, a permanent layer of grime seems to keep Detroit hostage. Even in the suburbs, miles of blocks of shops are boarded shut. Unemployment runs epidemic among the young blacks in this black town; violence rips through the schools; the murder rate is shameful, by far the highest in the nation.

Although Iacocca can hardly be faulted for the city's epidemic of crime, the automobile industry is no uninvolved bystander. The more it automates, the fewer semiskilled and unskilled workers it needs. The idled employees tend to be blacks with small chances for employment elsewhere. And Iacocca? Well, there is no evidence of outstanding civic leadership from him or Detroit's other big business problem solvers, even though the cancer of crime keeps growing and is as deeply imbedded in the industrial environment as the robots on the assembly line.

At the very least, the violence is a public relations liability for Chrysler and the other automakers because Detroit's reputation as "America's murder capital" makes sizzling copy for media around the world. Could a presidential candidate overcome the political handicap of such a lawless hometown?

More to the point is the stark tragedy of the scene.

"The more closely one looks at Detroit, the more violently it returns the look," began a seven-page spread in *Der Spiegel,* the prestigious West German news magazine, in 1987. Its headline was this remarkable quote from Mayor Coleman Young: IF YOU LIVE HERE, YOU HAVE TO BE ARMED, and the article started off by describing the 1986 murder of Jefferey Hilson, age eleven.

Jefferey's mother, Luvinia, had given him a special red shirt that cost $19.38, and the boy wore it proudly on his street in the West Detroit ghetto, when two local kids, Tim, fourteen, and David, fifteen, confronted him:

"Check in your shirt!"

"No," yelled Jefferey. "Never!"

So Tim and David—nobody was sure which one pulled the trigger—shot Jefferey in the stomach with the .38 pistol they had lately bought without the slightest difficulty in the neighborhood for $20. Jefferey was the thirty-second child under seventeen to be murdered in Detroit that year. By the end of 1986, 648 people had been murdered, including forty-six under the age of seventeen. Jefferey Hilson died at Henry Ford Hospital. When his mother got the word, she was working the night shift—at Chrysler.

Detroit isn't all murder, of course. Some spectacular buildings, ancient and contemporary, two excellent newspapers, and a fine symphony light up the clutter here and there, and a surprising degree of attention is paid to art by a few enthusiasts, but reminders are everywhere and emphatic: This is Chicago without the light side and no town for civilities.

Nowhere else in the world have I ordered a beer in a top-ranking hotel and been asked, "Want a glass with it?" You don't need a glass to make a car.

At strategic places along the freeways billboards keep flashing the continually updated state of Detroit's blood pressure: the numbers that tell instantly what this city is really about, the annual sales volume of American automobiles. The freeways that unfold beneath these statistics are named for Henry Ford, Walter Chrysler, and their fellow titans—what other titans are there? And when the automobile industry takes ill, all Detroit feels faint.

Fat books have been written lately about the decay in this most American of industries and about its nastiest ailment, arrogance*—

---

*Even the imperious Henry Ford II finally pleaded guilty to the charge. Addressing the Society of Automotive Engineers in Detroit in late 1986, he conceded that American automobile makers had brought their problems upon themselves during the 1960s and the dunderheadedness, what looks in retrospect like an almost suicidal stupidity that kept Henry Ford, Lee Iacocca, and all the guys making too many gas guzzlers that spent too much of their tinny lives in the repair shop while the Germans conquered America with feisty beetles and then the Japanese all but ran away with the ball game because their tight little vehicles kept running and running, the way the Japanese themselves keep running; and the cars were politely abstemious at the gas pump.

At the time, in the early sixties, the marketplace was not all that easy to assess. McNamara had been eons ahead of his time. He had plugged hard for safety, and the theme had bombed. He had made a small, very plain economical car, the Falcon, and it had won, won big, selling 417,174 pieces in its first year. But where was the encore?

Iacocca and his assault team did not believe, as McNamara did, that Americans looked upon their cars as mere transportation, that they would want their new cars to be clones of the Falcon—a granny car to fit the tastes of McNamara with his granny glasses, as the gag went. So what would they want, those weasels, the shifty consumers?

Iacocca, the sales guy who postulated that it was equally fatal to run more than two years behind or two years ahead of the market, hitched his career trajectory to a radically opposing trend; plainness made him ill. McNamara had left for the Pentagon. Iacocca was Ford's new powerhouse, and he was gambling that Americans wanted power, speed, and pizzazz in their automobiles, a rakish look, a little excitement. McNamara had taken Ford out of car racing. Iacocca put Ford back into it. "Race 'em on Sunday, sell 'em on Monday" became another of his famous phrase coinings.

Now he had to have a zippy new car, something fresh to dazzle "the lively ones," the restless youth market, the first postwar generation just coming along, the kids and the new-married suburbanites in the once-empty acres where Iacocca was pushing his reluctant Ford dealers to move and join the affluent settlers.

Out of this urge, this inner fire, he produced the Mustang. It was greeted as a revolutionary vehicle, it made Iacocca a national

---

1970s because they turned "careless and conceited." As he explained his industry's blindness, "We began to believe our own propaganda that we had all the answers, that our critics were at the very least misinformed and misguided and that all we had to do to win was show up for the game."

figure, and he wanted to be dead sure that he, only he, would be known to history as the Mustang's "father."

Was he? The paternity controversy was still afoot in the mid-eighties. Some Ford contemporaries and historians said the credit belonged to Don Frey, who first sketched the car on paper. Other guys said the semen came from Gene Bordinat's design shop, where the concept was turned into clay and then into metal. Both progenitors were still stirring up the competition to unscramble the Mustang's genes, the stakes in history were that high.

"That car," Bordinat pronounced in a retirement interview, "was developed seven months before he [Iacocca] saw it. That car would have made it to the marketplace without Lee."

"Most of the market research stuff was done after the fact," Frey told another interviewer. "They made it all up afterwards—somebody did—in order to sanctify the whole thing. . . . The market research that you read [of] is a bunch of bull."*

Such details were accurate, but they amounted to little more than footnotes. It was Iacocca, first of all, who issued the call for the car that would beget a new category of vehicles for which an entirely novel name would eventually be invented: "small-sporty." The call came in the privacy of a dining room at the Fairlane Hotel, about one mile from the Glass House. Iacocca and his assault group began to meet there weekly. Frey was there, naturally, and so was the production man Hal Sperlich, a scrappy character who figured later in other revolutions and bailed out Iacocca after Lee's head rolled at Ford.

They called themselves the Fairlane Committee, and at first the coalition talked over dinner. As pressure on the project mounted, it convened, true to the tradition of Charlie Beacham's work hours, for breakfast at 7:00 A.M. on Saturdays.

From these labors emerged the clay model of a little two-seater sports car that looked like a rocket, its air scoop openmouthed, and it was Iacocca who recognized that so much pizzazz was not practical for what he had in mind: capturing the mass market. Confirmation came, paradoxically, from experts who adored the model. They were racing car drivers and buffs whom Iacocca invited for an early look and who went crazy for it.

*To Iacocca market researchers were like bean counters: mostly excess baggage. He didn't think much of asking customers about their preferences. "They don't know what they want," he said some years after the Mustang had pretty much proved him right about such research. "Ya gotta have an idea and then ya gotta push it down their throats."

As he recalled the scene, "All the buffs said, 'What a car! It'll be the greatest car ever built!' But when I looked at the guys saying it—the offbeat crowd, the real buffs—I said, 'That's for sure not the car we want to build, because it can't be a volume car.'"

More influential was the reaction of Ford's financial guys. They were appalled. The minirocket would sell maybe 35,000 pieces, they said. After Iacocca's initial modifications they upped their estimate to 50,000. It was Iacocca again who made another difference. He came up with the idea that triggered a quantum jump. It was an obvious thought; but it was indisputably his, and it alone turned the Mustang into a revolution. He made it into a family car by adding two bucket seats in the rear. It was guessed that as a four-seater it would sell around 100,000 pieces.

Iacocca did not believe it. His nose for poker told him that the car would do far better. Bill Bourke, Ford's number three man, remembers being taken to the rotunda of the design center, where he was shown the clay model of the hot little novelty that the Fairlane boys had been puffing about.

" 'That's the Mustang,' " Bourke was told. " 'Iacocca thinks he can sell two hundred thousand, that it might create a new market!' " Bourke thought that was crazy. But when the car sold 418,812 pieces in its first year, 1,638 more than McNamara's Falcon, Bourke, a tough man who was no unqualified Iacoccalyte and would never become one, arrived at a judgment about the Iacocca mystique, and he shared it with me in 1986: "The guy's a genius! He gets a gut feeling from a piece of clay."

Stodginess that prevailed among his competitors helped, and so did a bit of industrial spying. Work on all new models in Detroit is supposedly secret. This old industrial practice helps to explain Iacocca's tendency to press his cards all the way to his vest even when the stakes are less than momentous, but there are always people who take interesting photos for which there is a profitable market.

And so one day Don Frey popped excitedly into Iacocca's office with a grainy picture. Obviously taken by a telephoto lens, it showed a competitor's 1964 model.

"You've got to see this, Lee!" Frey bubbled.

Iacocca looked at the photo, and a grin spread across his face.

"So that's what it's going to look like. It looks as if they are going to go sedanish instead of sporty. That's good news."

One obstetrician who never questioned Iacocca's paternity of the

Mustang was Henry Ford. For reasons nobody was able to fathom, Henry had right along been cool toward the car. It couldn't have been its cost because the Mustang was not really such a novelty, which is why it became so hugely profitable. It used the platform and engine of the Falcon and required only a relatively piddling $75 million investment for retooling the plant. Perhaps Ford kept resisting the new model only because he was feeling poorly, coming down with what turned out to be a debilitating case of mononucleosis.

"I don't even want to talk about it," he said when Iacocca finally persuaded him to come to the design center. He walked out and was driven straight to the hospital.

Iacocca never tried to sell Ford head-on. He worked on this prickly customer gradually, informally, outside of company channels that could activate sabotage from the financial guys, the hated bean counters. He encouraged an early look at a clay model, dropped hints of sales projections, tried to awaken proprietary instincts for the venture in Mr. Ford.

In the case of the now manifestly endangered Mustang, the customary bait had not worked. Iacocca was very upset but not discouraged. He had turned around other defeats at Ford, and Papa Nick had told him *never* to give up. He began to drop hints about the Mustang's promise to wider circles in the company, even to the gossipy automobile press, knowing that word would bounce back to Mr. Ford that the car was thought to be hot.

And yet, when the owner returned to the design center once more to see the car with Iacocca and Frey, he was still sour and petulant. In *The Reckoning* David Halberstam caught the memorable scene:

"I'm tired of hearing about this goddam car," the owner said.

Iacocca and Frey both thought that this might be the car's death sentence.

"Can you sell the goddam thing?" Ford demanded.

Iacocca assured him that they could.

"Well, you damn well better."

And so he did. In point of fact, the Barnum hoopla that Iacocca brewed up to huckster the Mustang—it made its debut on what became to him a sacred day, April 17, 1964—was so intense that Ford insiders fix the event as the genesis of Lee's decline in Henry's eyes. The same had happened to other operating executives struggling to survive under the thumbs of chiefs with monster egos: The only risk greater than failure was success. And Iacocca compounded his risk unnecessarily by grabbing credit for the Mustang so brazenly that the insiders were shaken from the start.

The jackpot of the sales campaign was Iacocca's simultaneous manipulation of his distinctive face onto the covers of *Time* and *Newsweek,* a feat of dexterity that he did not leave to the guile of his hard-pressed publicity people. Preparation was, as always, crucial. He dispatched Frey with pictures and sales spiel to *Time,* where Don knew a ranking editor. Iacocca personally lobbied the *Newsweek* editors and put on a masterful song-and-dance number. In each shop at least one principal executive was sufficiently impressed to order a Mustang sight unseen.

If Iacocca's two magazine faces launched a thousand clucks from the insiders, the texts of the articles sounded even pushier to them. *Time* described the Mustang as Iacocca's sole property, a car "he can call completely his own." Frey thought that Mr. Ford was left by the publicity salvo looking like a flunky in his own shop. At subsequent meetings the owner permitted himself bitingly to compliment Lee on taking time out from posing for pictures and sitting for interviews. To Mr. Ford, the Iacocca performance with the Mustang was of a piece with the man's checked and royal blue suits, his arm waving, his huge, pungent cigars, his torrents of language, his filthy words in front of women. Too loud. Too pushy. No class.

But this primitive made money, a great deal of money. The Mustang became a diamond mine, and then came years and showrooms full of further Iacocca successes: the little Maverick, the big new Thunderbird, the huge Mark III, Mark IV, Mark V, the mid-sized Fairmont, the European-made Fiesta, and the subcompact Pinto, which was another money machine until it became engulfed in the flames of its gas tank (see Chapter 14).

Nothing matters in an automobile company except new models that generate profits, always changing new models. Nothing, that is, except men to make them, and Henry Ford seemed to feel that he needed to turn over his managers much as he had to change the models of his cars, to change, churn, turn over, to keep the family enterprise in a state of constant renewal, revalidating the name on the building.

Ernest Breech, his teacher, went out the door in 1960 after an embarrassingly public show of no-confidence by Mr. Ford at a managers' meeting. Arjay Miller was neutralized in 1968. The same year

John Bugas was kicked out—Bugas, the old FBI hand who used to warn intimates that Ford fell in and out of love as easily and stormily with men as with women. Cristina Ford pleaded with Henry to post Bugas to Australia. "No," Henry said, "he's got to go." And 1968 was also the year Ford brought in a top executive from General Motors, the big, handsome Semon E. ("Bunkie") Knudsen, and made him president, the operating head of the company.

Bunkie was a vigorous fifty-five, a member of the Detroit establishment, a class act, and Ford thought Iacocca needed further seasoning. "You're still my boy," he told Lee. "But you're young. There are things you have to learn."

Iacocca disagreed. At the time he kept uncharacteristically quiet, but on another occasion he remarked, "I am the product man in this company. I am the one who moves the iron." Knudsen, he thought, was dumb and had to go.

"The day Bunkie was hired, Lee declared war," Frey remembered. Indeed, Iacocca announced that he would devote himself to "making life miserable" for Knudsen.

The war began on most days around 7:00 A.M. when Knudsen, an early riser, liked to appear in the design center for what came to be known as his "dawn patrol." He would order changes in designs Iacocca had approved. Later in the day Iacocca would appear, explode at the changes, and be informed that they had been made by Knudsen. "Tell Bunkie to bag his ass," said Iacocca.

The principal victim in this civil war was Frey, who had the misfortune of having known Knudsen earlier. Bunkie, no alley fighter like Iacocca, failed to bring along his own team of hatchet men when he came from GM, so at the first Ford reception that was given for Knudsen he greeted Frey warmly, put an arm around him, spent considerable time chatting with him. Later he went out of his way to praise Frey's judgment. Iacocca, smelling disloyalty, used Frey, in turn, as a carrier of rebellious messages to Bunkie.

Frey felt like the filling of a sandwich, and after a visit to the design center with Mr. Ford and Iacocca in the summer of 1968 he knew he had fallen off the bread slices and landed on the floor.

The three men were inspecting an abbreviated version of the Lincoln, approved by Iacocca. When Frey was asked for his judgment, he said he considered it still too heavy, realizing at once that he had committed a possible fatal blunder. Iacocca did nothing to disabuse him of this conclusion, and so Frey quit, and Lee made sure he didn't get his final bonus.

Bunkie was a tougher target to remove, but Iacocca was helped by Herb Siegel, an old Lehigh man who ran Chris-Craft. Siegel offered to hand him $3 million just as a bonus for joining up. Iacocca was tempted but said that automobiles were his life. Siegel warned him that Ford would never hand the presidency of the company to a loud Italian kid. Mary Iacocca supported Siegel. She had always felt high-hatted by the Detroit society women.

When Iacocca decided he should stay in automobiles, Siegel helpfully suggested that Lee use the Chris-Craft offer as a lever to push Knudsen out. Soon the rumor mills were grinding out word that Iacocca was thinking of quitting. Henry Ford became depressed, then alarmed. Even Ed Lundy, the financial man who frequently opposed Iacocca, thought that either Lee or Bunkie had to go, and he advised Mr. Ford that it be Bunkie. Lee was a winner. He had much support within Ford. He was backed by a solid constituency. Bunkie had none. He was the lonely outsider from GM.

The ax fell shortly after 6:00 A.M. on Labor Day 1969, when a Ford public relations man, deputized by Henry Ford, called on Bunkie at his home and said: "I've got a sad tale to tell you. You're not going to be with the Ford Motor Company after tomorrow."

"It just didn't work out," Henry Ford told Bunkie the following day, and when the firing was announced at a large press conference in the Ford auditorium, Iacocca sat at Mr. Ford's right, "smiling," as William Serrin recorded in the *New York Times Magazine*, "the faint, tight smile of a Mafia don who has just consolidated control over Chicago." Two reporters told Serrin that Iacocca had performed a triumphant obscene gesture in their direction from the stage.

Fifteen months later Lee A. Iacocca was named president of the Ford Motor Company and, ecstatic, immediately phoned the news to Mary and to Nick.

Henry Ford's hand had been forced, and he didn't enjoy the humbling experience. Increasingly he found Iacocca's swagger offensive, and as far back as in the early seventies the executives closest to the chairman began to pick up hints that the owner was actually feeling slightly threatened by his Italian sorcerer's apprentice. Traveling in a car to the Ford factory in Cologne, Germany, the chairman, a bit tipsy, suddenly turned to Bill Bourke and demanded: "Who do you think is the boss of Ford Motor Company?"

"You, Mr. Ford!"

"Well," grumped Henry Ford, "I hope so."

By Iacocca's fiftieth birthday, October 15, 1974, Henry Ford's unease had not diminished; nor had Lee's imperious strutting; nor had the one-for-all martial esprit of the Iacoccalytes. At his birthday party his followers gave their hero a T-shirt with the words "Numero Uno" printed up front. There! The word was out in the open: To his flock, Lee was the maximum leader, the number one.

When Ford heard about this display of affection—or more—he was furious.

6.

THE INVESTIGATION: HUNTING FOR SKELETONS IN IACOCCA'S CLOSET

LMOST THE MO-
MENT I ARRIVED IN DE-
TROIT TO RESEARCH IACOCCA'S
CAREER, VARIOUS MEDIA PEOPLE BE-
GAN TO TELL ME, ALWAYS "OFF THE
RECORD," THAT UNAPPETIZING SE-
CRETS WERE SAID TO LURK IN
THE CLOSETS OF HIS PAST.
"There's nobody in Detroit that
there've been so many rumors about,"
confided a mild-mannered, recently retired editor of a respected au-
tomobile trade magazine.

"But nobody ever found anything," I said, thinking of several
discussions I'd read on the subject, including one in Iacocca's autobiography.

The old editor did not look convinced.

Since Iacocca led a very public life for more than thirty-five
years without solid evidence of scandal coming to the surface, I
considered the remark outrageous and silly. Yet how thorough had

the scrutiny of my hero's life been up to 1986? What ugly bones might be dug up by investigative reporters if Iacocca were to move into public life, if not a presidential race, then perhaps Senate confirmation hearings for a cabinet post?

"He'd be fresh meat for five thousand Woodwards and Bernsteins," mused the publisher of another major automobile publication.

It was a daunting image, though not as intimidating as the thought of a single person, Henry Ford II, at the most damaging moment, planning seeds of embarrassing leaks aimed at his archantagonist. Such a scenario had been conjured up by still another knowledgeable old auto editor.

"Not that Henry would show up on 'Face the Nation' to blow the whistle," wrote Brock Yates in a *Car and Driver* article I found in the files for 1985. "He would be more subtle—and more devastating. Suddenly Dearborn would become a wellspring of hundreds of 'Deep Throats,' 'undisclosed sources,' 'former employees' and 'insiders' whose lurid tales about Iacocca's Ford adventures would serve as retribution for his portrayal of Henry II in the autobiography as a drunken, racist paranoid."

Lurid tales? What lurid tales?

Well, said Yates, rubbing in the libel further: "All the rumors of kickbacks and payoffs and shady business dealings." And in case he still hadn't made himself clear, this old editor camouflaged the canard as pious advice. He called his article "Don't Do It, Lee." That is, don't leave the relatively cozy haven of private citizenship.

I was becoming interested. What was this "lurid" smoke all about?

In The Book Iacocca relates how the tales were hatched after Henry Ford called him into his Glass House office in the summer of 1975.

"I know Fugazy's a good friend of yours," Ford began. "But I'm starting a full investigation of him."

"What's the problem?" asked Iacocca.

"I think he's mixed up with the Mafia."

This was a declaration of war on two levels. The ebullient, boyish-looking William Denis Fugazy (pronounced: Foo-gay-zee), operator of a New York travel and limousine company, masterminded the elaborate, very costly Ford dealer incentive promotions and had performed valuable legitimate favors for the company. And he was not a "good friend" to Iacocca. He was his *best* friend, and in 1986 Fugazy was the best man at Iacocca's wedding.*

Iacocca tried to reason with Ford. He reminded the boss that Fugazy maintained golden connections with the "right people." Bill had ingratiated himself with tycoons, cardinals, ballplayers, politicians, a who's who of VIPs. Iacocca had had dinner with Bill and Francis Cardinal Spellman. When Pope Paul VI visited New York, Fugazy arranged for the pope to travel around the city in a Lincoln, not the usual Cadillac.

Ford wasn't impressed. He said limousine companies are "always Mafia fronts." Iacocca countered that if Fugazy were a mob man, his business wouldn't lose so much money.† Henry refused to relent, and the ensuing investigation escalated into a remarkable witch-hunt. It went on for five months, cost the Ford Motor Company $1.5 million or more, and involved interrogations of some 500 witnesses, including 55 Ford executives. Fugazy obviously was only its secondary victim. The true target was Iacocca, and Henry's initial assault was directed against another Iacocca lieutenant, Paul Bergmoser.

Bergmoser was the logical beachhead. He was the chief of all Ford purchasing operations and the threads of Fugazy's dealings naturally had to run through his office.

"Aren't you afraid of Fugazy?" Ford asked him. "Aren't you scared of ending up in the East River with a pair of cement boots?"

Ford was obsessed with Italian gangsters. His grandfather's muscleman Harry Bennett, the revolver-wielding villain whom Henry II had to purge to gain control of Ford, had used such gunslingers. Henry's own son, Edsel II, had once liked a girlfriend whose family Henry suspected of being possibly linked to the Mafia, and Henry had been furious.

Fugazy, too, had come under Ford's suspicions earlier. In the late sixties Henry had received complaints from Bill's competitors in the dealer incentives business. Contracts in that industry were awarded according to competitive bids plus the bidders' ingenuity for developing novel travel schemes for wealthy, jaded dealers craving junkets that offer ever-lusher frills. Fugazy usually scooped his

*For an analysis of the Iacocca-Fugazy relationship, see Chapter 13, "The Company He Keeps and Keeps," page 221.
†While Fugazy is a spectacular promotion ballyhoo artist, his reputation as an indifferent businessman has remained a persuasive defense against allegations of supposed connections to organized crime. In 1984 his limo operation, Fugazy Express, lost $10 million.

competition. His rivals claimed that he could win because "someone" at Ford was feeding him inside information.

Then, in 1969, auditors found that Iacocca's friend had charged Ford $300,000 above his estimates, and Bill had to repay the money. Fugazy blamed faulty bookkeeping, but the incident did not increase his popularity with Henry Ford.

By the time Bergmoser faced his inquisitors his records on Fugazy's dealings with Ford had been sweated down to the last decimal. The figures were combed by a partner in the accounting firm of Coopers & Lybrand; the more distressing personal accusations came from the prestigious Detroit law firm that had long represented the Ford family: Bodman, Longley, Bogle & Armstrong.

When I talked to Bergmoser, by then retired but still looking and acting like a German field marshal, he vividly remembered the grilling he twice took from a team of the firm's lawyers.

Did Lee Iacocca ever tell him to favor Fugazy? Why did Bergmoser go to New York to have dinner with Fugazy on such and such a date? And then came the night when Judge Souris personally pelted Bergmoser with questions until past midnight.

Theodore Souris, senior partner in Ford's law firm, had been a justice of the Michigan Supreme Court, but Bergmoser was not enamored of the judge's professional manners on this occasion. "He made clear I was guilty until proven innocent," Bergmoser told me. Nothing incriminating was found, he said.

Fugazy told me much the same. At the time his business was affiliated with the J. Walter Thompson advertising agency, so Ford called its president and demanded cooperation. While Fugazy was away in Florida, the investigators were given keys to his office and carried off stacks of his files, including his income tax returns. Later they interrogated him for two afternoons.

"We know you and Iacocca are involved with the Mafia" was the premise preceding the questioning about how he ran incentive deals. Nothing came of this examination except that, as Fugazy says, he lost $7 million a year in business.

After getting nowhere with Bergmoser and Fugazy, the investigators fanned out systematically, starting with a meeting of Ford dealers in the easy-money atmosphere of Las Vegas. The California executive in charge of the expense accounts that were run up at the meeting was summoned to World Headquarters in Detroit and questioned about several dealer dinners.

Had Fugazy been present? Were any women with Iacocca? Were

any executives given cash for gambling? And then: Was Iacocca given any money for gambling?

Angry Iacoccalytes also claimed that the investigators listened to bugging devices in hotel rooms and bribed show girls to find out whom they were "dating."

The expense account supervisor from California was instructed not to talk to anyone about the proceedings, but as the investigation spread to Ford suppliers, their employees and their books, companies like U.S. Steel, Budd, Kenyon & Eckhardt, the secret of its existence and its obvious purpose leaked, much to Iacocca's embarrassment.

"Were they in to see you yet?" became a standard inquiry among potentially damaging witnesses against Iacocca.

Larry Domagall, Iacocca's executive assistant, told me that it began for him with a letter from Henry Ford announcing the special "audit." He was urged to hold back nothing. When the investigators appeared, it became clear at once that the Fugazy-Iacocca link was the focus of their curiosity.

How long had Domagall known Fugazy? How had the advertising agreements with Fugazy been worked out? And so on. The following Saturday night one of the questioners phoned and wanted to go over some of the same questions again on the spot. Domagall was going out to dinner with his wife and hung up. He could afford it. He was close to retirement.

So, fortunately for him, was Paul Bergmoser. The purchasing executive's fate was settled at a meeting between Henry Ford and Bill Bourke, the company's number three executive. Bourke had picked up scuttlebutt about the investigation earlier and had seen the rumors confirmed when Iacocca, whose office was two doors away on the twelfth floor, had been "unavailable" for an entire day because he was closeted with Judge Souris's lawyers.

Ford was incensed. If he couldn't catch Iacocca at any misdeeds, it would be a long-term problem to get rid of him; Iacocca had fans among the outside members of the board of directors. But the heads of lesser-ranking men like Bergmoser could be given less careful handling. Moreover, Bergmoser had been insubordinate. When his questioning yielded nothing interesting, he had actually had the nerve to call on Ford and demand an apology. Ford had coldly refused. He was convinced that Bergmoser was holding out on him, that he had been less than fully candid with the investigators.

"I'm going to fix that son of a bitch," said Ford to Bill Bourke. "He clammed right up. He's more loyal to Iacocca than to me."

That was the ultimate sin, now openly defined.

Bourke was instructed to tell Bergmoser that he would never get another salary increase, never another stock option. This was Ford language for top men when they were through, and Bergmoser, of course, knew it. He asked Bourke if Ford wanted him to quit at once. Instead, Bourke worked out a face-saving deal: Bergmoser could stay on until the following May, when he would be sixty-three, and then leave with his pension. At least there were no tears this time, as there had been when Hal Sperlich, a younger man, was purged outright only to move to Chrysler ahead of Iacocca.

The executives who were retained found themselves caught in the atmosphere of a banana republic. All generals suspected of loyalty to the maverick Iacocca were kept under observation by Mr. Ford's operatives as if they had been plotting conspirators. Iacocca's refusal to withdraw his friendship from Bill Fugazy was particularly galling to Henry.

"I am the king," Ford sometimes said into his shaving mirror half-kiddingly, "and the king can do no wrong."

Loyalty to Bill Fugazy was lèse-majesté. That man had to be handled like a leper around the Ford Motor Company, but in the process some of Ford's managers developed schizophrenic tendencies.

Ben Bidwell, in charge of all sales operations, was explicitly instructed by the chairman not to "associate" with Fugazy, not to "talk" to him. Bidwell had adhered to this order, but one Sunday evening Billy phoned from Iacocca's home, where he was staying, just a couple of hundred yards from Bidwell's house.

"I've got to talk to you," Fugazy said excitedly.

Bidwell pondered. Fugazy was always excited. But he was the president's close friend. The president was Bidwell's immediate boss. Also, Bidwell liked Iacocca. But he had unambiguous instructions from the chairman.

"I'm absolutely booked," he told Fugazy.

"I'm around the corner," Fugazy pleaded. "Can I ride into town with you in the morning?"

Bidwell, feeling trapped, lied that he'd have to leave the house at 5:15 in the morning. Fugazy said that was just fine with him. Finally they negotiated that Bidwell would pick up Fugazy at Iacocca's house at 7:00 A.M.

Driving south on Southfield Road at dawn, while Fugazy chattered with his usual urgency about an emergency that was no great emergency, Bidwell wished he were invisible. Traffic is slow on Southfield at that hour, bumper to bumper. Everybody drives a car to work in Detroit, and automobile people have learned to watch their chiefs the way Muscovites keep an eye on the men in the Kremlin. In times of crisis—and the Ford Motor Company had certainly been thrown into crisis by Henry Ford—it could be useful to know who was talking to whom.

Bidwell, over six feet tall, tried to crouch in his seat all the way down Southfield Road, wondering if hundreds of eyes kept staring at him. He felt jittery, guilty. At the executive garage for the Glass House headquarters he leaped out of his car, raced to the dispatcher's office, pointed at the startled Fugazy, and yelled, "Get this man to the airport immediately!"

Then Bidwell, relieved, went to a meeting of the product planning committee, where he was told to call Henry Ford. Bidwell phoned at once.

"Mr. Ford, this is Bidwell."

"What were you doing with Fugazy?"

When Bidwell related the story to me in 1986, it sounded like slapstick from a Marx Brothers flick. To Bidwell it wasn't very funny, not even in 1986.

These were all the "lurid" tales I could find. They seemed to leave Iacocca untouched, a conclusion that appeared safe since it took Henry Ford three more years to jettison Iacocca and nothing damaging had leaked from him or any other informed source before or since. And yet I felt restless.

I could not hope for access to the Coopers & Lybrand audits or the testimony accumulated by Judge Souris and his emissaries. Could any substantive Iacocca flaws still be hidden eight years after Iacocca's firing? I had a journalistic as well as a pointedly personal interest in this question. I'd look pretty foolish if I pooh-poohed Henry Ford's efforts and then had to sit still while he dropped a nuclear bomb or two on Iacocca's head once this book was in print.

A source in Detroit whispered that I should have a chat with Harold Soper, and I looked him up in his retirement home at scenic Holland, Michigan, on the banks of Lake Michigan. Soper, a CPA, had left Ford in 1977 as comptroller of the Parts and Service Division. He had been an "E-roll" (top-salaried) executive, supervising 440 auditors. I learned that Soper was a Republican conservative whose fastidious (some said nitpicky) ways of accounting for promotion and personal expenses had thrown him into frequent controversy with Iacocca (see Chapter 15, "The Iacocca Values," page 251). Might Soper know about true skulduggery, food for "lurid" scandal?

Like most auditing practitioners, Soper proved a circumspect conversationalist.

"Where'd you hear about me?" he wanted to know first of all.

He did not care much for Fugazy or the way Billy did business and wielded power. "You wouldn't want him for an enemy," Soper said.

Yes, he had gone through a great many of Iacocca's expense accounts and admired them, although he was somewhat grudging about it.

"Never could we tie Iacocca directly to anything illegitimate," he said, sounding slightly pained. "Everything was always well documented."

Soper's memory of the Coopers & Lybrand no-holds-barred audit was sketchy, he said. He had seen a preliminary report, but not the final version, and he could remember only this draft's overall tenor.

"I would be very embarrassed by that," Soper said; "whether Iacocca would be I don't know."

I left with the impression that Soper held strong objections against Iacocca's style and some reservations about his values but that, at bottom, he was full of admiration.

"The guy was profound," Soper said, "just profound. Such a fertile, innovative mind! And his questions: brilliant!"

Still curious, I contacted Franklin Murphy, whom I've known for nearly forty years. He had been dean of the Kansas University Medical School when I was a newspaper reporter in Wichita. I'd been much impressed with his incisive ways, and we'd kept in touch over the years while he became chairman of the Times-Mirror Company of Los Angeles and a director of Ford.

Murphy, who is a physician, had served on the Ford board's auditing committee in the mid-1970s, and Iacocca cites him in The Book as authority on the outcome of Henry's investigation. "You have nothing to worry about," he quotes Murphy as telling him. And Murphy had ridiculed Ford's efforts: ". . . he came in with a cannon and went out with a peashooter."

I thought I detected possible ambiguities even in these statements and asked Murphy if some report that could blow up Iacocca could possibly slumber somewhere.

"There is no such report," he told me.

Reassured but still not satisfied, I tackled the unequivocally ultimate authority, Ed Lundy. J. Edward Lundy, Ford's retired executive vice president for finance, is one of those colossi of power that almost nobody outside the industry had ever heard about, and he had remained near anonymous until 1986.*

He had moved into Ford in the 1940s along with Robert McNamara and the other Whiz Kids. Unlike the rest of that crew, he stayed on, had never married, and had become Henry Ford's most treasured confidant, the keeper in chief of company secrets. If there was dirt on Iacocca at Ford, Lundy absolutely *had* to know. There was one drawback to Lundy from my perspective. He had never, absolutely never, been interviewed by a writer, not by Halberstam, not, as far as I could discover, by anybody else.

I wrote to Lundy at his home in Dearborn, told him of my problem, and followed up with a phone call. Lundy reminded me about his policy toward writers and said he was not about to alter it. I said I thought Iacocca was entitled to reassurance that no alleged skeletons were kept hidden from him. Lundy said he was sorry but couldn't help. I said that I'd talked to Franklin Murphy but that I realized that even directors sometimes did not see some important papers.

"That's right," said Ed Lundy, the sphinx, and bade me farewell.

What was that again? Was Lundy confirming a routine operational fact known to everybody—namely, that outside directors lack time to look at many interesting documents? Or was he trying to imply that Murphy and his fellow directors had not been shown papers which, if they surfaced, could torpedo Iacocca's life story? My impression is that Lundy was merely being civil and literal, so that the former interpretation is most likely true.

Back in 1975, Billy Fugazy believed that Iacocca's headaches with Henry Ford were finally over and said so to his friend Lee. Iacocca knew Henry better than that and told Billy he couldn't be more mistaken. "Now our troubles start," he said.

---

*In that year David Halberstam managed to piece together a marvelous portrait of this éminence grise in *The Reckoning*, especially pages 248–260.

THE LOUDEST FIRING SINCE MACARTHUR

"THERE WAS NO DOUBT THERE WAS A HIT LIST," SAYS JAY DUGAN, WHOSE NAME WAS AMONG THE IACOCCALYTES MARKED FOR PURGING BY HENRY FORD.

Dugan, one of the old gang in Chester, coauthor with Lee of the pioneering handbook on truck sales, was too close to Iacocca to be tolerated. Jay had never moved from Pennsylvania. He liked living there, and he didn't have to be stationed in Detroit to do his work for the Ford Motor Company. For twenty-two years the company had been the sole client of his business. Each year he put together the catalog of colors and upholstery available for the various new models. The deal would run to around $2 million, and nobody had ever complained about Dugan's work.

In the spring of 1978, when Henry Ford's campaign to rid himself of Iacocca was approaching its climax and Dugan's contract was up to be renewed for another three years, the purchasing department sent word that another firm had made a more attractive proposal. About a month later came evidence that this was no routine dismissal of a contractor.

"I was told not to set foot on company grounds again," Dugan recalls.

Iacocca was not surprised. Some time earlier Leo-Arthur Kelmenson at Kenyon & Eckhardt had fielded an angry call from Henry Ford. Ford attacked at once:

"Leo, do you have a peddler working for you named Bill Winn?"

"Yes, why?"

"You get that peddler the fuck out of this company or you're through!"

Kelmenson was not mystified. Winn worked on promotion strategy for the new-model Fords and had been an Iacocca intimate even longer than Dugan. Lee and Jay went back to their roommate days during Iacocca's training in Dearborn in 1946. When Kelmenson told Iacocca about Winn's fate, Lee sighed and said that Henry Ford obviously thought that like Bill Fugazy, any friend of Lee's must somehow be taking advantage of the company.

Winn was naturally upset at his removal, and he was very worried about the air of conspiracy and persecution, the banana republic syndrome, that had taken hold at Ford. Winn was a punctilious type, spotlessly groomed, careful in speech, methodical in his work, obsessively scrupulous. To make certain that he could account for every step of his activities, he had long kept a detailed diary. Now he placed this record in his lawyer's safe. There seemed to be no telling what Henry Ford might question in order to get at Iacocca.

Ford's most exposed target turned out to be Hal Sperlich, the temperamental products man who had become part of Iacocca's inner circle at the time of the Mustang. Sperlich was very special. He was one of Ford's best and brightest, memorably outspoken, a driven soul, hyperenergetic, a supertoiler among workaholics, at his desk long before sunrise, sometimes at 4:30 A.M. His relationship with Iacocca was likewise out of the ordinary, even for a loyalist. Hal managed to get away with arguing long and loudly with Lee, right from the beginning. Sometimes he even presumed to poke fun at his mentor, even kidding him about his clothes, which then tended to be a bit too flashy. Lee was only a few years older but acted as something of a father to Sperlich during the mid-seventies when Henry Ford made the shrapnel fly throughout the Glass House.

Sperlich was the most free-spirited of all the Iacoccalytes, by far the most rambunctious of the species, and while he did not socialize much with Iacocca—whom he regarded as his boss, rather than Henry Ford—the bond between Lee and Hal was strong and public. This was particularly true during the two most furious battles of the 1970s, both ending in cataclysmic defeats. Together they were the Ford Motor Company's own Vietnam War: the years of abortive debates about downsizing and about the proposed brand-new small vans, first known as the "Mini/Max" at Ford and later as the "minivan" at Chrysler.

The downsizing controversy, which raged for two full years, from 1974 until 1976, stemmed from Sperlich's belief—in fact, his fanatical conviction—that Americans were finally going to demand smaller, more economical cars after all.

Iacocca bought this prediction and came up with an elegant solution to implement it. He personally struck a deal with Soichiro Honda in Japan: For the remarkably low price of $711 per car, Honda would furnish the engine and transmission for a U.S. version of Ford's little front-wheel Fiesta, which had cost $1 billion to make but had set off a huge sales bonanza in Europe. The new "American" model was going to be called the Tiger.

Henry Ford threw the deal out. "No Jap engine is going under the hood of a car with my name on it," he announced indignantly.* No doubt he meant it. But the sentiment did not tell most of the real story.

Ford did not believe that the American market would undergo much change, a notion probably grounded in wishful thinking. Henry did not like small cars and had a slogan to institutionalize his disdain. He called them "little shitboxes" and said: "Small cars mean small profits." This was a catchphrase at Ford Motor Company, a shibboleth to be ignored only at one's extreme peril.

But Sperlich had no respect for clichés. He fought Ford at meeting after meeting. He was relentless not merely with his facts but in his tone. Iacocca warned him that he was going too far, that he was "telling the chairman that he's full of shit," that Henry couldn't possibly be expected to stand for such treatment.

---

*Publicly no automaker has been more vociferous in his Japan bashing than Iacocca. With him, however, business is always business. After he took over Chrysler, the company purchased a 25 percent interest in Mitsubishi and markets that company's cars in the United States.

Sperlich would not desist. He bickered, he attacked, and he kept feeding fresh arguments to Iacocca, often during meetings of the product planning committee, where Hal sat at Iacocca's left while Ford was positioned at Lee's right. The very visibility of the alliance against him made Henry seethe. He told Iacocca that he didn't want to be ganged up upon, that he didn't like Sperlich's "pissing" in Iacocca's ear, he hated "that goddamn" Sperlich, he simply hated that man.

Iacocca told Sperlich to change his seat at the committee meetings, which accomplished nothing. Hal would not subside. He kept arguing for the Tiger even after the decision against it had been rendered. Ford had called Iacocca to tell him so, claiming that there weren't sufficient funds for the required investment. At the next meeting Iacocca had quit arguing. Sperlich didn't. He kept his cannonade going until Ford snapped: "I don't want to hear another damn word out of you. Just shut up, dammit."

Not that Henry vetoed the Tiger because of Sperlich. "He didn't want it because Lee did," recalls Matt McLaughlin, Iacocca's deputy.

The feud between the chairman and the president was turning into a deadly duel, and the inevitable consequence was a state of near paralysis throughout the company.

"They couldn't agree on anything," McLaughlin says.

And so they couldn't agree on the Mini/Max van, even though the debate about it became the longest-running drama in town. It wouldn't stop for a dozen years.

Back in the late 1960s one of the designers in Gene Bordinat's shop had come up with a brainstorm for this new kind of family vehicle, a novel substitute for the station wagon, something roomier than a wagon but still manageable for suburban housewives. It was a simple and ingenious thought, but it set in motion every crosscurrent, every vested interest, every insecurity in the company.

Iacocca did not become an enthusiast until market research revealed that consumers might pay as much as the then enormous price of $10,000 for a small van. Bordinat was hot for it all along, and Sperlich argued for it as aggressively as only Hal Sperlich could campaign. The research people projected that the Mini/Max could sell as many as 800,000 copies in its first year, an outlandish figure that almost nobody could believe.

Ed Lundy and his bean counters were dead set against this innovation. If the Mini/Max were to turn out sufficiently light and low so women would find it attractive, it would need front-wheel drive. It would have to be a brand-new vehicle costing hundreds of millions of dollars to develop.

Henry Ford was sour on the idea. Who was for it anyway? Bordinat and his elves, the designers? They wouldn't have to drum up the financing or sell the damned car; neither would the market researchers. Iacocca? His influence could stand further curtailment. And Sperlich, that goddamn Sperlich? It was time for that troublemaker to go.

The Mini/Max debate kept bubbling on until Iacocca and Sperlich got their revenge by making the van at Chrysler, where management had also been arguing about it, albeit only since 1974, and where the project had been stalled for an actual lack of investment funds. The exuberant Ford sales projections turned out to have been correct, and Henry Ford could easily have scooped Chrysler with the van. Instead, he walked off with Hal Sperlich's scalp.

It was done with no warning while Iacocca happened to be in New York and staying at the Waldorf.

"Lee, before the sun sets tonight, I want Hal Sperlich out," Chairman Ford instructed him on the phone.

Iacocca protested, but not long. Henry Ford was obviously in no mood to listen. Sperlich was too disruptive, too argumentative, and Mr. Ford didn't like him.

Iacocca dialed Bill Bourke in Detroit. Bill was next in line in the chain of command. He was stunned. Fire Sperlich, one of their best? Was Henry drunk again?"

"He's directed me, and I'm not there. You are, so I'm directing you," said Iacocca.

"Christ, what am I going to tell him?"

It was a rhetorical question. Bourke had fired executives before. He knew what to do. He also knew that the most searing aspect of getting axed in the automobile business was not what preoccupies a decapitated man at the time of execution. The toughest part of becoming unemployed was long-term. The number of important employers in the industry is limited to three, and one of these, General Motors, almost never hires from the outside. Unless a man works in finance, where skills are transferable to other industries, a firing from Ford could signify a disastrous dislocation for the victim and his family. But that thought usually did not hit a man until sometime after the fact.

What would most trouble an exceptionally competent and conscientious manager like Sperlich immediately upon receiving the news, as Bourke well knew, would be the surprise and the indignity of being discarded, the injustice of it. Bourke therefore delayed the confrontation until 4:00 P.M. This was his normal practice when he had to let somebody go. It allowed the victim to go home, "cry, get drunk and kick the dog." It was not unusual for a fired executive to cry.

When Sperlich showed up at four o'clock, Bourke said, "Hal, I'm not going to beat around the bush. . . ." Sperlich was to consider himself dismissed.

The surprise was total. "What the hell for?" Sperlich demanded. His performance record showed nineteen straight ratings of "outstanding"! But all that was irrelevant.

"What shall I do?" he asked Bourke.

Bill suggested that he cool off and then see Mr. Ford.

Sperlich moved himself to an obscure office so that his old associates would not have their style cramped by having to encounter him, and some days later he was given an appointment with Mr. Ford. He pleaded his case for his competence and his innocence of any wrongdoing. As Henry Ford later told Bourke, he cried.

When the chairman told him vaguely that things would work out "better this way," Sperlich was no longer surprised. He did feel considerably let down when he confronted Iacocca and Lee said there was nothing he could do.

"My father is supposed to save me," Sperlich still mourned many years later.

When Sperlich departed to take his talent and his drive to Chrysler in 1976, Iacocca was busy struggling to save his own head. Well-meaning people had been warning him for years that his coexistence with Henry was life on borrowed time. Lee had been installed in the Ford presidency for only a few months when a friend of both men told the *New York Times Magazine:* "Henry will come in with a hangover some morning and that will be the end of Lee." In 1972 Iacocca's Italian pal Alejandro de Tomaso left the sports car manufacturing business which he had sold to the Ford Motor Company and walked out disgusted. He had seen Henry drunk too many times, and he had advice for Iacocca.

"Lee, I am leaving now," he said. "You will be the next one. The guy is jealous. . . ."

In The Book Iacocca berates himself for not having quit Ford perhaps as early as the end of 1975. He attributes his inaction to "greed," which he calls his worst weakness; he just couldn't walk out on $970,000 a year. For that kind of money he could absorb considerable indignity: being introduced by Henry Ford as "my young Italian friend"; not being admitted into the chairman's social circle; indeed, being shut off from all intimacies with *numero uno*.

The Fords and the Iacoccas had dinner *en famille* on only one occasion, which was indicative of the distance between the two clans. In truth, Iacocca didn't altogether mind. He hated the conventional social drill of automobile executives, the country club affairs, the incestuous cocktail parties. He couldn't abide polite small talk and much preferred his boisterous poker cronies in "Lido's Lounge." Furthermore, by keeping out of Henry's way after office hours, he avoided some stiff and potentially embarrassing occasions.

"You don't get close to the king," Iacocca told his wife, Mary. And yet he hated to be shown, however indirectly, that he was supposed to know his place as an employee, not an equal.

At home in Bloomfield Hills, tension was rising, but Iacocca found unwavering support all the same. His command center was the most frequently used space in the house, the small family room off the kitchen, known as the "keeping room," in accordance with the custom of the Pennsylvania Dutch in Allentown. On top of the television, overseeing all, roosted a bronze bust of Nick Iacocca, his face a bit grim, a reminder never, never to give up. And this was also the motto of Mary Iacocca, the plumber's red-headed daughter.

And she wanted more than resistance. Mary detested Henry Ford with Irish fervor. She wanted to get even. Her husband was going through hell, wasn't sleeping properly; the pressure on him was affecting her own precarious health. Her diabetes was getting worse, and she went through her first heart attack. More and more often an ambulance would carry her through the night to the hospital, struggling through a diabetic coma.

Diabetes dominated much of the family's life. "We lived with it every day," remembered Kathi Iacocca, the older of Lee's two daughters, who runs the Iacocca Foundation, which devotes itself to diabetes research.

"People say, 'How do you get so involved? You have diabetes, you take a shot. Big deal!' Wrong. I lived with paramedics, and I lived with emergency rooms and IVs all my life. I mean, being a young girl and never knowing when your mother was coming home again . . ."

When Mary wasn't hospitalized, she carried on in the tradition-bound way of the Iacoccas. Spaghetti was Lee's favorite food of all, so Mary made her own noodles. Thus the spaghetti would be done "from scratch," as Mama Antoinette Iacocca always preached. "Father likes home, and he likes his food cooked at home," Mary said. "He's a fussy eater."

Lee, who called his wife Mother, was devotedly protective, raging wildly at her whenever he discovered evidence that she hadn't given up cigarettes as the doctor had ordered. Throughout the ordeal Mary remained her combative old self, smoking in front of trusted friends, begging them sheepishly not to betray her to Lee, stationing them as guards in front of the airplane toilet while she smoked inside. Resenting her handicap, trying to wish it away, she would forget to take along her candies, the emergency sugar supply that she was supposed to carry at all times.

Feeling snubbed by the executive wives corps of Detroit, Mary was not above lashing out with verbal kicks in return, and if she sniffed scents of disloyalty toward her husband, she could turn remarkably rude. Bill Bourke was, quite unjustly and not for too long, on Lee's list of Henry Ford's partisans, and this placed him on Mary's private blacklist.

Bourke recalls how Mary uncorked her spitfire tactics at a Ford cocktail party for the board of directors of Time, Inc. The gathering was held at the Renaissance Center, or RenCen, the cluster of dramatic black towers sponsored by Henry Ford at the Detroit River in his attempt to help shore up the disintegrating downtown area, and protocol called for everyone's politest smiles.

At this party Bourke encountered a lawyer acquaintance he had not seen since his own teens.

"Do you realize I used to mow his lawn?" Bourke exclaimed to Mary.

"As far as I'm concerned, you should still be doing it," said she.

It was as if she needed to show Lee's workaday colleagues that ailing or not, she was as strong as her husband, that she stood with him, not behind him, like some plastic Detroit society lady, and with Mary Iacocca this was no act. She was turned on by her husband's power, his brute strength, and didn't mind that he liked to flaunt these qualities.

In the Iacocca living room a *Wall Street Journal* reporter once spotted the surrealistic oil painting of a bull, given to Lee by Vic Damone. Then, on the coffee table, the visitor saw the crystal statuette of another bull. On the wall hung a large, gaudy painting of a bullfight. "Lee is bull crazy," Mary explained, delighted that her man had adopted such a powerful, stubborn creature as his trademark.

To survive in Ford's Glass House, Mary thought that Lee was, if anything, still not bull-like enough. She wished he would fight Henry more aggressively, going so far as to suggest, quite seriously, that she was willing to front for Lee, to assault Henry physically, to punch him to the floor if she could, she hated that tyrant so much, his drinking, his womanizing, his insulting treatment of her husband.

Barring mayhem, she urged Lee to keep notes of what was happening at Ford, to throw no papers away; he might someday want to write a book to get even with that bastard Henry. The suggestion appealed to Iacocca's bent for marshaling masses of data, for memorizing and systematizing, as well as for vengeance. He scribbled and squirreled away so much information that he could eventually show friends a remarkable hoard: boxes and boxes crammed with personal papers, the eyewitness record of his fall and comeback, enough drama for more than one book.

Henry Ford was most unhappy. Lee's imperial manner was doing far more than just annoy him; it suggested that his number two man, "that goddamn wop," wanted to take over the company. The thought was intolerable. Iacocca was personally objectionable. He was removable while Henry was not, and Mr. Ford made dead certain that all his people got this verity straight in their heads. He proclaimed it loudly before a large audience.

More than 300 Ford executives were all ears at a company convention in Boca Raton when Henry, after a few drinks, stepped up to the podium and said: "I want you Iacoccas and the rest of you bastards to know that you may not be here to stay but there'll always be a Ford at Ford Motor Company."

Henry's objections to Iacocca were also substantive. Lee's ascent to control of the Ford Motor Company would have violated one of Ford's principal operating strategies. Despite his own arbitrary ways, Henry admired collective leadership, the committee system as practiced at General Motors. This had been one reason why he had brought in Ernest Breech and Bunkie Knudsen from GM.

Iacocca was too willful. He was dangerous, too much of a loner. The future of the company should not be entrusted to such a one-man band, a man so vain that he was satisfied only with Table No. 1 when he lunched in the London Chop House, reputedly Michigan's best restaurant (there is the *numero uno* theme again). The trouble was that Iacocca wouldn't leave quietly like Breech and Knudsen and Bugas and Arjay Miller and all the others with whom Henry had grown disenchanted.

Yet, if one couldn't live with Lee, one could perhaps not live without him either. The man was a politician; he had created a state within a state for himself, an all but autonomous constituency. He wielded power. Ford could whittle at the Iacocca empire by purging such vassals as Bergmoser, Fugazy, Winn, and Dugan. But could he dispense with the one inconvenient manager who had kept the company hugely profitable ever since the Mustang bonanza of more than a decade ago?

Mr. Ford did not think so, at least not yet, not on May 26, 1974, when he was interviewed on the Lou Gordon television show in Detroit. Gordon, a rich man in his own right, was famous for asking tough questions in interviews. It was he who had killed a presidential boomlet for George Romney, chairman of American Motors, by squeezing him to admit that he had been "brainwashed" by the American military on a visit to Vietnam.

"Will Lee Iacocca be the man who will succeed you?" Gordon asked Ford.

Ford waffled. The board would decide. Iacocca is "a great fellow." He was doing an "excellent" job. And so on. But Ford would not respond about the succession issue until Gordon posed it for the fourth time: "And would you like to see him succeed you?"

"Yes," said Henry in a low tone of voice and looking less than delighted, a man trapped and hating it.

The following year, in November, a seismic tick of nature set in motion the chain of happenings that had to lead to the end of Iacocca's tenure at the Ford Motor Company. Strolling in his Grosse Pointe neighborhood, Henry Ford felt a sharp pain in the left side of his chest. Winded, faint, he had to sit down on the curb. Neighbors, running out to help, were shocked; he could barely talk.

It was not a heart attack. It was the onset of angina, a disease with which his mother had lived for many years. The disease was not life-threatening.* The attack was a signal, however, to which even kings respond sharply, the signal of mortality, an urgent hint

* In 1987, at age seventy, Henry Ford II, long retired from his company's day-to-day affairs, still held on to crucial power as chairman of the finance committee. All policy and personnel decisions of consequence still required his approval.

that the succession question had to be settled.

The angina warning was quickly followed by another kind of heart trouble. Ford's marriage with Cristina, the tempestuous Italian, had been falling apart for some time, and his difficulties with her hardly made Italians more popular with him. He had secretly been courting his future wife, Kathy DuRoss, on numerous "business trips." Some weeks after the angina attack Henry finally left Cristina. The divorce would be messy and would drag on for years.

And so would a spectacular lawsuit against Henry, filed by Roy M. Cohn, the notoriously ruthless onetime red-baiter who did dirty laundry for Senator Joseph McCarthy. Ostensibly Cohn's assault was mounted on behalf of small Ford stockholders, but these turned out to be relatives of a Cohn law partner. To this day no one knows who put Cohn up to his campaign or who furnished him with so much juicy and very, very detailed information that had almost certainly to have come out of either the Ford Motor Company or sources with uncanny access to its files.

Flying through the courtroom came all but the kitchen sink from the company's executive dining rooms. Ford was supposed to have made the company pay more than $1 million toward a duplex in New York's Carlyle Hotel, with "a tulip wood desk valued at $82,000," for Henry's exclusive use. He was supposed to have received a $750,000 kickback from a duck-shooting pal in exchange for a company catering contract. He was supposed to have told Ford advertising agencies to pay "unlawful" fees to a modeling agency in which his future wife had an interest. And much more in a similar vein.

The complaints carried the ring of plausibility and had much in common with Henry's charges against Iacocca and Fugazy, Billy being one of Cohn's oldest and closest friends. The allegations added up to favoritism, abuse of company office. But the charges were never substantiated. Eventually Cohn signed a statement admitting that "it now appears that there was no wrongdoing by Henry Ford II." The suit was dropped, yet the whispers at Ford never ceased that it could have been Iacocca, perhaps through Fugazy, who had something to do with the fanciful leaks of inside information to Cohn—speculation which also was never remotely substantiated.

In The Book Iacocca offers a different version of the Cohn vendetta. He identifies Cohn, who was eventually disbarred, only as the "prominent New York attorney," which is a little like describing Hitler as a prominent German politician. Iacocca says that he did not know whether the charges against Henry were true, but he takes the occasion to recall that he once used the company plane to carry a fireplace from London to Grosse Pointe for Mr. Ford. Cohn's suit was settled out of court, he writes, without mentioning Cohn's formal admission that the charges were groundless.

Iacocca's bottom line on the affair: "Henry got off easy once again."

Severely frightened by his health problem, preoccupied with fighting off Cristina and Roy Cohn, Ford was further beset by unaccustomed burdens in his business. Huge lawsuits set off by the Pinto were coming home to roost, and the American automobile industry was at last collecting its comeuppance: Business was awful. All the winds in Ford's life were blowing in one direction: If the Ford family was to have an honorable future, his Iacocca problem had to be resolved.

So in 1977 he hired the management consulting firm of McKinsey & Company, ostensibly to advise him on the company's image. Iacocca smelled trickery at once. "What is this shit?" he demanded of friends. "What the hell do we need outsiders coming in to tell us who we are?"

Shortly there came public evidence that the company's identity was not what Henry Ford was most interested in. He wanted to revise *Iacocca's* identity. Henceforth Lee would be number three on the company leadership ladder, no longer number two. The latest ranking was established by the appointment of Philip Caldwell as vice chairman, and the memo that announced the news spelled out its meaning beyond doubt. It stated: "The Vice Chairman is the Chief Executive Officer in the absence of the Chairman."

The demotion was especially galling for Iacocca because he felt vast contempt for Caldwell, who had been one of his subordinates as chief of Ford in Europe. Caldwell was a prissy product of the Harvard Business School, a collector of exquisite antiques, methodical, snobbish, slow, and supercareful about making any decision, definitely not a real automobile guy—a personality grossly incompatible with Iacocca.

Lee felt deeply humiliated, and Henry saw to it that the disgrace was all but posted in the public squares. At company dinners Ford was host at the table marked "No. 1," Caldwell headed Table No. 2, and Iacocca was at No. 3. Everyone in the Glass House could tell: Henry was trying to persuade Iacocca to quit, to embarrass him into turning tail, to run. He ignored Lee at meetings, and by 1978 the chairman and the president, still occupying adjoining offices, had not spoken for months. Top managers like Bourke and Bordinat had to carry messages back and forth between them.

It was a grotesque way to run a business, and then in June 1978 Henry tightened the screws still further. He announced that William Clay Ford, his brother Bill, the Ford who owned more stock than anyone, was joining the office of the president as the company's number three man. Which sent Iacocca tumbling into the number four slot.

Everyone at World Headquarters could see that the status quo was untenable. Something or someone would have to give.

Throughout the 1970s Iacocca's discomfort at life with Henry Ford kept escalating, first into anxiety, then into abiding hatred. Friends of both men were telling each other that even a squad of psychiatrists might find it difficult to untangle the emotional circuits that tripped up these two egocentric lordships.

Their dissimilar backgrounds notwithstanding, their personalities had much in common, and so did their management techniques, yet the similarities somehow drove them even farther apart. Not long after Iacocca became president of Ford, Henry instructed Lee that he must never let his managers get too comfortable.

"Keep your people anxious and off-balance," advised the chairman.

When Mr. Beacham had advocated the same course, Iacocca had approved and patterned his own style accordingly. When Mr. Ford advised the identical ruthless technique, Lee was disgusted. Mr. Ford could do no right.

When Henry began to turn his pressure tactics on Iacocca, Lee did flirt briefly with the idea of resigning as soon as he would become eligible for a pension in 1978. His friends found him depressed, reclusive, all but immobilized, and they wondered how long he could live in this uncharacteristic style. He was too quiet. When Phil Caldwell was about to be moved into the hierarchy over his head, Lee's stance remained defensive. He seemed principally interested in saving face.

Flying to Florida in the controversial company plane late one Saturday, Iacocca opened negotiations with Ford about his strange status, and when they reached Boca Raton, the men kept talking all night. As both related it to associates later, Iacocca proposed conditions under which he would withdraw from contention for the chairmanship of Ford but keep his reputation intact.

"If you don't want me to take over the company," he said, "make me vice chairman and make Bill Bourke president, and I'll resign if you pass on. I'll give you a contract that I'd step out."

Ford nevertheless insisted on going ahead with the Caldwell appointment, and in the summer of 1978, inevitably, the ensuing crisis became the business of the only jury with jurisdiction over Henry's duel with Lee: the company's outside directors. Iacocca did all he could to encourage the entry of the directors into the shootout. He had powerful friends among the board members, and he thought they would help him to put over the plan that had ripened in his mind.

As late as in 1984, writing in his autobiography, he denied any design to seize control of the company.

"I never had any illusions about becoming number one," he claims.

Friend and foe disagree. Without a dissenting voice they assured me they were certain that Lee was determined to risk a putsch, that he seriously believed he stood a chance to take over the holy Ford empire.

"Wine 'em, dine 'em, and screw 'em." Thus Henry Ford II reportedly expressed his sentiments about his directors. Certainly he wined and dined them sumptuously. On top of the Glass House he had provided a penthouse with a roof garden and the dining room for key company executives, and above that he had installed yet another floor, the summit, the fourteenth, with bedrooms exclusively for the directors when they convened, usually for an afternoon, plus the evening and the following day, once a month. It was a rarefied environment. Nobody had to scoot in and out of hotels and restaurants. No amenities were lacking.

As for screwing the outside directors (that is, the nine board members who were not Ford employees), Henry really had no need. They had never failed to go along with his wishes and their complaisance made good sense; the Ford family controlled 40 percent of the company shares. Yet these directors made some difference because they were by no means ciphers.

At least four of them felt considerable fondness and respect for Iacocca, and they were executives with minds of their own: Joseph Cullman III, chairman of Philip Morris; George F. Bennett, president of the State Street Investment Corporation in Boston; Marian Heiskell, née Sulzberger, of the *New York Times* publishing dynasty; and my old friend from Kansas days, Dr. Franklin D. Murphy, then chairman of the Los Angeles Times-Mirror Company.

Murphy felt close to Henry as well as to Lee. He held the confidence of both, suggesting diplomatic skills of a high order. It was natural that this negotiator would become the most active conciliating force in the Ford wars, and this did not surprise me when I first heard it. I remembered that Jim Hagerty, President's Eisenhower's press secretary, once told me that Eisenhower thought Murphy was astute enough to be president of the United States, and I had other memories suggesting that Ike was probably right.

When I first met Murphy, he had become, at age thirty-three, dean of the medical school at Kansas University and I watched him sell a hugely expensive system of mental hospital reform to the Kansas legislature, not then a hotbed of sophistication. It was an inspired bit of soft-soaping. Without his nose for politics Murphy also would not have survived later, when he was made chancellor of the university and became the target of an eccentric governor who was determined to purge Murphy by incinerating the school's budget.

Trained as an internist, Murphy decided he at least knew more psychiatry than the other directors, and he went to work.

Psychiatric counseling was the specialty that the Ford deadlock manifestly called for when the board gathered on June 7, 1978, for its monthly session. Henry was very worried about his heart. Business was still terrible. Cristina was picking up momentum in her divorce vendetta. Roy Cohn had just launched his court challenge. The Pinto was within three days of being recalled. And threatening to bring this witch's brew to a boil, Henry Ford disclosed to the directors that he was about to fire Iacocca, thereby pushing the board members closer to the edge.

"You had a situation tailor-made for the devil," Murphy recalls.

Without dissent, the directors counseled caution. Nobody wanted a public explosion that would affect the price of Ford stock. Everybody was cognizant of Iacocca's successes, his value to the company. Several directors were acutely concerned about Henry's drinking and his generally somewhat erratic performance of late. At a meeting which preceded dinner on the evening before the board's formal session, the directors eventually persuaded Ford to postpone a decision while they would launch efforts at conciliation.

As a first step Murphy shuttled to Iacocca's office to calm him. "Things are quieting down," he said. "You're not going to be fired."

But Lee was none too receptive to counseling. Murphy had been working at the task with little success for years, trying vainly to persuade Lee, for instance, to tone down the filthy language that made Henry wince, at least when the chairman heard the four-letter words at formal gatherings. And now Iacocca was acting more defiant than ever.

"Lee was terribly insecure, almost irrational," Murphy told me, "and Henry was less rational than normally. He worried about the Iacocca team, the people loyal to Lee. And the more Henry tried to reduce Lee's role, the more Lee pushed. It kept spiraling."

Iacocca was candid with Murphy. He told the doctor that he wanted to be named "head" of the company. Murphy told him to relax. This was not the time. His time would come. "You're going to have to wait your turn," Murphy counseled. Iacocca would not see his situation that way. He told Murphy he was convinced that now was the time for him to make his move.

Did Iacocca really think he could succeed? One Iacocca watcher did not believe that he thought so, although even a polygraph test might not have yielded the truth.

By chance, the writer Gail Sheehy called on him six days before the great firing. The smell of blood hung in the hallways. Neither the interviewer nor interviewee alluded overtly to any unusual tension within the Ford Motor Company, but Sheehy's questions were to the point.

"How did you learn to get along with Mr. Ford?" she asked brightly.

"First of all, you gotta perform," said Lee. "Meet commitments, follow through, produce results."

Then he voiced the sort of unreality that makes Pinocchio's nose grow extra inches—or suggests considerable self-deception.

"Nothing else really counts," claimed Iacocca.

Had he ever challenged Henry Ford as a man or as a leader?

"That's the first art of diplomacy," said Lee. "Never threaten your adversary."

What was Iacocca's worst fear at this point in his life?

"Fear?" Iacocca repeated the term as if he'd never heard it. "If I have a fear, it's what do you do when you've been embroiled in an activity like this and it suddenly stopped."

Sheehy's conclusion later: "Despite the brave front, I think Lee Iacocca knew that day the game was up."

Whether he knew or not, he did not act as if he knew.

While Henry Ford was away on a business trip to the Far East, Iacocca took the company plane to Boston and New York to build up support from Bennett and Cullman, the two directors most likely to help him actively in a showdown. In his autobiography Iacocca downgrades the conspiratorial overtones of this lobbying mission. He says the trip was the idea of the two directors, that it was no secret, that he submitted expense accounts for it to the company. The venture was, nevertheless, a desperate move, a reach beyond the borderline of accepted corporate behavior, a bid for power that Henry Ford was certain to interpret as a disloyal act.

Which was indeed Ford's reaction as soon as he returned to Detroit, so when the directors convened again on Wednesday, July 12, the stage was set for a scene worthy of *High Noon*.

Ford definitely wanted Iacocca out. Iacocca definitely wanted Ford neutralized. The directors were working up proposals toward a compromise. They could not understand how Lee could expect to win control over the owner of the company, and yet it was Iacocca who had forced the issue by plotting with the directors.

"It was an act of insanity," Franklin Murphy told the author Robert Lacey. "He just didn't have the cards."

I thought the gaming metaphor was relevant to the combat tactics of a poker player like Iacocca, but "insanity"? That sounded like a rather broad diagnosis, coming from an internist. I asked Murphy whether he had thought Iacocca was afflicted with megalomania. "Oh, no," said the doctor, "I think his ambition got the better of him." Which suggests miscalculation, not pathology.

Henry Ford was totally sure of himself. He showed no interest in the directors' various attempts at compromise. Finally he smiled and said, "It's him or me," and offered to leave the room so the directors could discuss this ultimatum without the presence of the two contenders.

"No, Henry," said Franklin Murphy, "you don't need to do that." He presumed to speak for the entire board because the upshot was beyond discussion. Iacocca was dismissed without a dissenting vote. He just didn't have the cards.

That happened on Wednesday night, the twelfth, without Iacocca's knowledge, although he realized, of course, that the board was meeting, that his neck was on the line. All of Detroit knew the same thing, which posed an annoying professional problem for Keith Crain, the publisher of the authoritative weekly trade paper *Automotive News*. His paper was poised to go to press. If Iacocca were going to get fired in the next twenty-four or forty-eight hours and Crain were to come out without the story, the publisher would look foolish.

On Thursday morning he called Iacocca at his office and challenged, "Say it isn't so!"

Iacocca said he didn't know exactly what was happening. "It really looks bad," he said. "I've got a meeting with Henry at three." Crain explained his deadline problem. Iacocca agreed to phone him after the meeting.

When he didn't, Crain reached him at home shortly after 5:00 P.M.

"What happened?"

"He fired me." Iacocca managed to sound calm.*

He wasn't, naturally, although the forty-five-minute meeting with Ford had started calmly enough. Bill Ford had been waiting for Lee along with Henry, which made Lee feel considerably better. According to Iacocca's recollection, Bill had "promised" that he would "fight" for Lee in the event of a showdown. But Henry gave his brother no chance to speak, even if he had wanted to.

After some hesitation Henry said that the association with Iacocca had been "nice" but that the company would be better off if it ended. "I think you should leave," said Ford. Iacocca claims that he looked at the chairman in disbelief. Then he asked for an explanation. Ford said it was personal, "just one of those things." Iacocca pressed for more justification. Ford shrugged and said, "Well, sometimes you just don't like somebody."

Iacocca demanded to know what Bill thought. Henry answered for his brother. The decision had been made, he said.

They talked about the financial settlement that Iacocca would

---

*Crain's persistence had paid off with a major coup because there was no other word until the Ford Motor Company held a press conference the following day. By that time *Automotive News* had released its story, and major newspapers and wire services around the country credited Crain's paper with his exclusive. It was treated as news of considerable weight. On the *CBS Evening News*, Walter Cronkite said, "It sounds like something from one of those enormous novels about the automobile industry." And the columnist Nicholas von Hoffman captured the bells of fear that must have been set off in the minds of many wage earners. He asked: "If a guy like Iacocca's job isn't safe, is yours?"

have coming to him, and it was then, when clearly nothing could be changed, that Iacocca took over the floor at length. He had to justify himself, his record, his performance. More, he wanted to make Henry Ford feel bad for reasons of business, make him worry, make him think he was making a business mistake that would cost him billions, yes, billions.

And still more. Other men who had just been handed their heads might have pleaded or argued for a reversal of the decision. Or bitten their lips and walked out. Or erupted into yelling fits. Or cried. Or taken refuge in self-pity. Or taken some other way to betray weakness, self-doubt. Iacocca chose a different course, a direction characteristic for him whenever he is pushed into extremity. He attacked. And he salvaged his self-respect. This man knows how to make lemonade out of the most resistant lemon.

He lectured Ford. He reminded the owner of his thirty-two years of service and pointed out that the company had just enjoyed two years of unprecedented profits, $1.8 billion each year. It would probably never happen again, he warned Ford, not because the industry was in trouble but because "you don't know how the fuck we made it in the first place!"

Iacocca was angry now. His voice was getting louder. Henry was not looking him in the eye, so as Lee recalled it, Iacocca issued an unusual command: "Look at me!"

It must have been an affecting performance because Bill Ford was stirred at last into attempting to reverse his brother's decision. Bill had enough stock to make his wishes felt. But he lacked the requisite aggressiveness and had never taken an active interest in the company management. He got nowhere with Henry. When the meeting broke up, Bill walked out with Lee and had tears in his eyes. He kept lamenting that the breakup should not have happened and told Lee how much he admired the way he'd taken on Henry.

Iacocca appreciated the friendly gestures but knew they changed nothing. He told Bill that he and Henry were living survivors. He was not. ". . . I'm dead," he said.

Several friends who saw him that week described his state as "stunned." They, in turn, were surprised, shocked at the firing once it came, even though it had been unmistakably in the cards for years.

"I don't know how the guy can make it," Bill Winn had said to his wife when he saw Lee go "into a kind of funk" after the Fugazy investigation and Mary showed signs of further deterioration. Lee seemed not to want to have fun anymore. The clamorous Friday poker sessions stopped.

Still, when Winn's wife heard the news on the radio and called Bill and said, "Did you hear about Lee, he was fired?" Bill was shaken. "You're kidding!" he said. He rushed to the Iacocca home and found Lee sitting alone in the family keeping room off the kitchen. "He was like a guy who just witnessed an accident—stunned," Winn recalls. He was also relieved. A couple of times he said, "Thank God, it's over!"

It wasn't. Driving to work the next morning, Iacocca located his new office in a warehouse on Telegraph Road, miles from the Glass House. He had difficulty finding the place and thought it was hardly more than a cubbyhole. His secretary pointed wordlessly to cracks in the linoleum floor and to the two plastic cups on the small desk. Tears filled her eyes.

In 1985 the indefatigable author Robert Lacey inspected the office and found it cheerful, modern, measuring twenty-one by fourteen feet. He also discovered that it had seen service, for twenty-eight years and until recently, as space rented by Ernest Breech after his reasonably friendly departure from the chairmanship of Ford. During nearly all of that time Breech had officiated from this headquarters as chairman of TWA.

Iacocca experienced the place as "Siberia," a "humiliation," and he used the scene of defeat, his arrival in this ignominious exile, in the Prologue of his autobiography. In his eyes the banishment to the warehouse was of a piece with Henry Ford's vendetta against him, a campaign to destroy him, to wipe out his influence forever.

Even after the firing there was fresh evidence that Henry did not consider the case against Iacocca closed. Walter Murphy, a principal public relations man at the Ford Motor Company, an Iacocca-lyte who had been part of the Fairlane Committee that produced the Mustang, became still another victim of the Iacocca purge. He had worked until 11:00 P.M. on the day of the firing and had just gone to sleep when Henry Ford phoned him at home. It was after 2:00 A.M.

"Do you love Iacocca?" Ford demanded.

"What?"

"Do you *love* Iacocca?"

"Hell, yes, I like him very much!"

There followed what Murphy years later recalls as an "inelegant" exchange, in the course of which Ford told him he was fired. In fact, Murphy "retired" about two months later, disgraced because he *"loved"* Iacocca.

Some days after the firing the Detroit press quoted a Ford family spokesman as saying that Iacocca had to be let go because he was "pushy," that he "lacked grace," and that—here came the meanest cut—"the son of an Italian immigrant born in Allentown, Pennsylvania, is a long way from Grosse Pointe."

Iacocca was naturally incensed when he read about this low blow. He never forgot it. "I'll never forgive the bastard," he told Tom Brokaw during a 1985 NBC special about the Iacocca career. I couldn't recall ever having seen a documentary preceded by a network warning that it contained language that some viewers might find offensive. This one did. Lee's feelings about Henry would ever remain unspeakable. But he was far from "dead."

8.

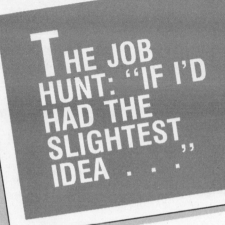

THE JOB HUNT: "IF I'D HAD THE SLIGHTEST IDEA . . ."

THE FIRST CALL CAME FROM CLAUDE KIRK, A FORMER GOVERNOR OF FLORIDA AND A LONGTIME IACOCCA CRONY. Kirk is a lawyer and deal maker who gets much done by introducing his friends to each other. Would Lee have lunch in New York with two members of the Chrysler board, J. Richardson Dilworth, the manager of the Rockefeller financial holdings, and Louis Warren, a Wall Street lawyer with a thirty-five-year-long connection to Chrysler?

Lee would. He had already listened to something like a dozen serious bids for his services. Charles Tandy of the Radio Shack chain wanted him to come and write his own ticket. International Paper and Lockheed made offers. Two business schools tried to make him dean. His reputation had remained gratifyingly intact. Chief executives around the country knew enough about Henry Ford's eccentricities not to hold the famous firing against the latest victim.

Iacocca had waved away the job offers. They were flattering but of no interest. "Cars were in my blood," he writes. More, Henry Ford was in his craw. Iacocca was obsessed with getting even. That could only be made to happen on Henry's turf. That didn't include Renault, for example, the French car manufacturer, where he would have felt sidetracked, out of the American mainstream, and where he was offered only a consultancy. He was an operator, and he wanted to be master of his own shop ("I had been number two for too long"). All of which made Chrysler an obvious and seductive possibility.

And so in that steamy August 1978 the luncheon with Dilworth and Warren became the overture to the minuet that usually orchestrates job hunting at the highest levels. In this case, the ritual reveals a great deal about Iacocca's skill at maneuvering when he selects a new challenge for himself.

At the opening luncheon Dilworth and Warren merely mentioned their measured concern about the state of Chrysler. Iacocca voiced his sympathy and ate two dozen excellent raw clams on the half shell. All three men, of course, knew the appropriate dance steps: who would unbend and how far and at what stage. At the moment the parties were only gathering preliminary information.

Like everybody else in Detroit, Iacocca knew that Chrysler was having "a hell of a tough time."

During the fiscal quarter when the company began to woo him it was losing a record $158.5 million. Internally it was a caricature of corporate competence. Its chairman, John Riccardo, was barely speaking with its president, Gene Cafiero. Its products were not moving—and for excellent reason. Word had long gotten around among consumers: Chrysler was making lousy cars.

Iacocca thought he wouldn't have much trouble turning the company around in a couple of years. It seemed to have a solid base to build on. Its engineering people were tops in the industry; Iacocca knew he could bank on that asset because he used to raid Chrysler for some of this technical talent. They made the best transmissions and engines in the business and came up with the very first hydraulic brakes. They just were not given enough money to turn out their best.

To an auto buff like Iacocca, much else seemed attractive about Chrysler. The history of the company's founder, Lee remembered, was the perfect script for his own post-Ford career. Walter P. Chrysler had quit almighty General Motors in 1920 because he wasn't given enough authority over his Buick Division. How he'd gotten even with GM! He reorganized two moribund companies, Chalmers and Maxwell, bought out Dodge and Plymouth, and even showed his face in the advertising of his new Chrysler Corporation. ". . . my kind of maverick," says Iacocca.

Conveniently crowded out of his normally superb memory was the depressing record of Chrysler after 1957. That year the company introduced rear fender fins, the "flight-sweep" design that looks silly in retrospect but was much beloved then and sent sales up. In management's haste to cash in, it created disaster. The doors and windows of the cars leaked, transmissions collapsed, ungalvanized steel led to early body rustout. Many of these stylish models had to be towed in by dealers and rewired for furious customers.

It was a telltale omen. In the next twenty years Chrysler chiefs toppled like Politburo apparatchiks under Stalin (one president fell under payola charges after a tenure of sixty-four days. He owned an interest in Chrysler supplier companies). Enough years were profitable to keep the place afloat, but the tailspins triggered massive purges: 7,000 workers one season; 11,000 another time. Morale was near zero. Factory recalls cost as much as $200 million a year. A string of European car companies was acquired, proved to be losers, and had to be jettisoned to raise cash. Corporate debt was up to $791 million by 1970.

All this time, amazingly, Chrysler was churning out more poor cars. "It was the lowest-quality product on the street," I was told by one of the engineering executives of that time, and the company's agony was very public. Just when it began its conversations with Iacocca, Michigan Governor William Milliken had been persuaded to drive the first of the New Yorker models off the assembly line. As cameras rolled and a big crowd applauded, the governor turned on the ignition. Nothing. He tried once more. Nothing. He never could make the car move, just as nobody could make the company move.

The stunning Chrysler mismanagement could fill books—and did. At least two entire works have been devoted to X-raying this corporate cripple in recent years.* Thumping sections of other

*_Going for Broke: The Chrysler Story_ by Michael Moritz and Barrett Seaman (New York: Doubleday, 1981) and _New Deals: The Chrysler Revival and the American System_ by Robert Reich and John Donahue (New York: Times Books, 1985).

books joined in the lament. In *The Reckoning*, his 1986 history of the American automobile industry's decline, David Halberstam holds up Chrysler as "the embodiment of what had gone wrong with American heavy industry in the last twenty years. As more was required, less was put in. . . . It was rotting."

Iacocca acknowledges that he did not realize the starkness of the trouble when Chairman John Riccardo phoned him at home to follow up on the ground-breaking luncheon with the two first Chrysler scouts, Dilworth and Warren. No doubt Iacocca's ignorance about the true state of Chrysler was real. But in The Book he further asserts that no amount of money could have lured him to Chrysler if he had had the "slightest idea" of what he could face there—a speculative and mighty iffy claim.

He would certainly investigate Chrysler's situation, but first he had to smoke out precisely what Riccardo had in mind for him. Even this could be sticky business. He hardly knew the Chrysler chairman. They had only met casually at civic luncheons and Motor Vehicle Manufacturers Association meetings. But Riccardo—slight, gaunt, and pasty-faced from overwork—had a pungent reputation. A bean counter who came out of the Touche Ross accounting firm, he had driven trucks across the Burma Road in World War II and was known in Detroit for volcanic outbursts that earned him the nickname the Flamethrower.

Iacocca also knew good things about Riccardo. He was not one of the ultracautious financial jugglers who acted as if Detroit were in the business of selling figures, not cars. Though starved for cash, the Chrysler chairman had listened to the lobbying of the persistent Hal Sperlich and come to a terrifying decision: Chrysler should spend the necessary $700 million to bring out Sperlich's gas-economical front-wheel K-cars in 1980. He also hoped to go ahead with Sperlich's minivan. Some Riccardo fans still maintain that these two plans—not the coming of Iacocca—saved Chrysler.

"He had all the ducks in a row," says one of these admirers. Which overlooks that Riccardo, presiding over Chrysler's rot for a decade, had built no system for turning out quality vehicles that could compete with the Japanese imports. It also ignores the tragedy that Riccardo lacked the funds to finance his excellent intentions; that he had no prospects for getting the money; that he had worked himself to near death trying to raise it. For, as Iacocca didn't know when he began negotiating with Riccardo, the chairman was suffering from heart disease and needed to lighten his crushing work load.

He was determined to capture Iacocca. Effectively he had little choice. He had tried to contact other prospects, but they hadn't even returned his calls. Besides, Iacocca was the logical candidate. Three Chrysler directors had independently come up with the same proposal. But the talks were begun at Riccardo's initiative. He could (and would) always claim that it was he who brought in Iacocca.

"I picked Lee for the company," he said later correctly and with pride.

Something about one-industry towns encourages intensive media coverage and, thereby, the leaking of secrets. Washington is a notorious example. So is Detroit. The recruiting minuet had to be kept quiet, especially since Gene Cafiero, the Chrysler president, was not to hear of it."* Security precautions were agreed upon beginning with the first encounter between Riccardo and Iacocca in a suite of the Hotel Pontchartrain overlooking the Detroit River downtown. Iacocca drove there in his own car and ducked in through a side door. Dilworth was present on behalf of the directors but said little.

Riccardo, to begin with, didn't say much either. He was the one who still had a job (despite Chrysler's extremity, it had paid him a remarkable $770,000 the preceding year). Iacocca was the one looking for work. The corporate negotiating ritual called for casual reconnaissance. Riccardo confined himself to remarking that Chrysler was giving thought to making a change.

Iacocca, enacting one of his favorite roles, the poker player as negotiator, challenged, "What are we really here to talk about?"

Riccardo folded quickly. He said he wanted Iacocca to come to Chrysler as chief operating officer.

Iacocca responded that under his severance agreement with Ford he was immobilized until after October 15.

---

*He never did. On the last Friday of October Riccardo and several other Chrysler executives informed Cafiero at the old Detroit Club that he was through. When reporters asked for details on the courting of Iacocca at the job announcement press conference the following Thursday, the new Chrysler president stonewalled and said with a grin, "Johnny called me and said, 'Why don't you come over and give me a hand?' " Cafiero called on Iacocca and argued for his retention by hinting none too gently that the Chrysler crisis was Riccardo's fault, but Iacocca knew by then: The malaise was rooted mostly in operations, Cafiero's territory.

Riccardo thereupon felt forced to drop all caution and laid open the central truth of the hiring dance: He was under pressure while Iacocca was not.

He told Iacocca he was disappointed. He had wanted to present a deal to his board at its next meeting around October 1.

Iacocca repeated that this would be impossible and stretched his timetable further. He was really tied to Ford until he would leave the payroll November 1.

Undiscussed but no secret was Iacocca's trump card: He could retire at his present age of fifty-four and never reenter the corporate pressure cooker because he was rich, very rich. In the preceding six years Ford had paid him $4.2 million in salary and bonuses. He owned Ford stock worth $3 million. His severance package included $400,000 cash on departure, $270,000 the following year, retirement pay of $178,000 a year until age sixty-five and thereafter a pension of $175,000 a year for life.

Capitalizing on these formidable assets, Iacocca proceeded to stab at Chrysler's Achilles' heel. "I need to know how bad things are," he said. He wanted figures, operating plans for the coming year, the works.

At their next meeting—this time in a room of the Northfield Hilton on Interstate 75, way north of town—Iacocca pulled out still another weapon: his skill at dropping informed, searching questions. Fortuitously he was in an ideal position to conduct this interrogation. Or so he thought. He had been briefed.

That summer he had been entertaining a visionary project of his own design. He called it Global Motors. The notion was to put together a consortium of American, European, and Japanese carmakers, possibly Chrysler, Volkswagen, and Mitsubishi. He saw himself as the successor to the automobile magnate he admired most of all, Alfred Sloan of GM.

Activating his personal old boy network, he got another crony, Billy Salomon of the Salomon Brothers investment banking house, to research the feasibility of such a grandiose merger. Salomon reported that the government climate of that time would sink the deal under the weight of the American antitrust laws. As part of the research Salomon Brothers had put together the basic data on Chrysler, and as his negotiations with Riccardo progressed, Iacocca went back to the firm for more ammunition. He cross-examined Lee Higdon of the banking firm's staff and drew up a list of ten pointed interrogatories. The answers were supposed to place him truly on the inside of Chrysler's travail.

Riccardo was shaken by this inquisition. "He knows more about us than we do," he told an intimate at Chrysler headquarters in Highland Park. "He's had Salomon Brothers do some work on us."

The wary Chrysler chairman was not exaggerating: Iacocca was indeed digging out more about the company than its own executives knew. Only some time after Iacocca had moved into Highland Park would he learn that he *still* hadn't probed deeply enough. Not nearly enough. Riccardo wasn't faking. The trouble was that his managers did not realize the severity of their own afflictions, and neither did he.

At the Northfield Hilton Iacocca properly zeroed in on the crucial item: Where would Chrysler get the money to finance the K-cars? To start up the manufacturing of the engines would cost $300 million. Another $200 million would have to be invested in the transmissions. The overall estimate of around $700 million probably would not cover all costs. The total might come to nearly $1 billion.

"An expensive mother," as Iacocca remarked to Riccardo.

Figures were Riccardo's home ground, and his projections added up to optimism that did not seem unreasonable. "It wasn't John concealing anything from me," said Iacocca subsequently, "but in looking at it, I thought, 'Oh, boy, not much cushion here!' "

By this time Iacocca was more than intrigued by the Chrysler job. He *wanted* it to work, and it was natural that he would rely heavily on counsel from a trusted inside source, his old sidekick from Ford, Hal Sperlich. When they had gotten together casually that summer to talk about Global Motors, Iacocca had learned that internal information was not as easy to come by within Chrysler as it had been at Ford. Sperlich said that he sometimes had to go researching on his own. But at bottom Sperlich had sounded optimistic about the outlook.

Now he drove to Iacocca's fifteen-room five-level home in Bloomfield Hills. He wanted to show the K-car designs and the sketches for the minivan. He hoped they would help to recruit the one man he considered capable of getting his babies born. "I didn't lie to him," he says. "But I was selling him. I didn't go out of my way to portray all kinds of problems."

The designs and sketches looked excellent to Iacocca. They touched the product man in him, the marketing man. These were automobiles he could sell! Getting them made would be a headache, but all that would take was money. Banks had lots of money.

Product was the hard part. Not everybody had a great product. Chrysler did. He had seen the plans now, and he knew Sperlich. Sperlich was the right man. He would make the product come out right.

Additional support came from that feisty Irish lady Mary, his wife. Although her diabetes was steadily worsening, the firing from Ford had brought her closer than ever to Lee, emotionally and literally. Iacocca rarely went to his office in Ford's Siberia that summer and fall. He worked at home. Mary officiated as his secretary and assistant. Her grudge against Ford was as unyielding as her husband's, and she knew Lee was far too restless to retire.

The Chrysler deal looked appealing to her. "Let's give that bastard Henry a shot he'll always remember," she told her husband. That was massaging Lee's heart of hearts.

Further meetings with Riccardo had cleared all but one possible obstacle toward the deal. Iacocca had anticipated trouble when he told Riccardo bluntly that he required an absolutely free hand. Remarkably that had posed no problem. Riccardo said that Chrysler should have only one boss and that he would leave within a year. So all that was still needed was agreement on Iacocca's compensation.

The compensation committee met in the Chrysler suite on the thirty-sixth floor of the Waldorf Towers. Iacocca, still keeping the talks under wraps, took the elevator to the thirty-fourth floor and walked the rest of the way. He needed to fear no real difficulties. The compensation group had already been duly impressed by his qualities. Iacocca had seen to that.

The committee was chaired by William Hewlett, the billionaire cofounder of Hewlett-Packard. The old boy network moved again. One of Hewlett's board members had been an Iacocca partisan on the Ford board, and Iacocca made sure that this friend would give Hewlett a useful version of his wars with Henry.

The compensation meeting went smoothly. On going to work with Chrysler, Iacocca would forfeit $1.5 million of severance pay with Ford. Chrysler would pay him that amount to come aboard, thereby, in effect, buying out his contract. His base pay at Ford had been $360,000 a year. Chrysler agreed to match it. The important element of compensation, as Iacocca has never been embarrassed to concede, is recognition—acknowledgment that he has made it to the top. As he had done now. Again.

* * *

It had been a virtuoso performance in self-management. Though he had been fearfully wounded in the automobile business, he retained the insight to realize that this was not the time to run away from the familiar battleground; much was left for him to achieve in the ballpark he knew best. He felt convinced he could handle the challenge if only he were allowed to function without interference, if his personal feelings, his plans, his hunches, his decisions, were to prevail. His confidence in himself had not been shaken by Henry Ford. Old Nick Iacocca was still at Lido's side, reminding him that the sun never failed, it always came up again.

He knew that the demands made upon a top manager—"*numero uno*" he again called the spot—would be more intense than anything he had experienced previously. It would require growth to master these demands, and so he was shifting gears to make space for the expansion of his horizon. Old Nick and Charlie Beacham had been outgrown as his principal models. They still had value as silent cheerleaders, but now Iacocca was lifting his sights, connecting himself to Walter Chrysler, the engineer turned empire builder, and Alfred Sloan, the master manager who put General Motors on its seemingly permanent giant pedestal. Old Nick had not been satisfied when Lido graduated in twelfth place out of 900 students. Why hadn't he been first? Lido was acting on that message now.

His negotiations with Chrysler were finessed masterfully. He waited for the company to take the initiative and to come to him, not to volunteer his availability. Almost from the moment the hiring dance began, Iacocca seized control of both its process and its substance, the pace and the contents. He refused to be rushed and set his own comfortable deadline. He fortified himself with inside information from Salomon Brothers and Hal Sperlich and used the new data to dig out more. Like a dive bomber, he burrowed in on the softest target: the lack of cash to finance new products.

If he still didn't tunnel down deep enough to uncover the full extent of Chrysler's decay, he compensated for this serious failure by placing his emphasis on assets that were undeveloped and barely visible but unquestionably real. The K-cars and the minivans had the right smell, the right feel for the developing market. Their time was at hand, and he wouldn't even have to look for the man who could bring them in. Sperlich was in place. Enough advance work had been done so it wouldn't take forever to cash in. This was a formula for salvation, and events would prove the analysis was dead right.

Would Iacocca really have stayed away from Chrysler if he had gleaned the "slightest idea" of what was in store for him there? I don't believe it for a minute. This after-the-fact assessment is hyperbole, an outburst of pride and relief, maybe a little wonderment and self-applause, a bow to the audience with a smile that says, "Hey, you didn't think it could be done, did you, but I did it!"

I think Iacocca was turned on by Chrysler the way a cancer surgeon is intrigued by an appalling assignment in surgery. And he was protected by a color blindness common to entrepreneurs. If they didn't wear rose-colored glasses and mobilize their basic optimism (remember Nick Iacocca's comebacks from financial destruction?), they could never break away from the scheming, digging, negotiating phases of a future enterprise and go with their instincts, take the plunge.

Conceivably Iacocca might have made his move just to nettle Henry Ford. It almost sounds that way in The Book. Iacocca writes that he heard it was "a real jolt" to Henry that his axed Italian underling wasn't fading away as decapitated victims were supposed to do; that when Henry got the Chrysler news, he drowned his frustration in two bottles of Château Lafite-Rothschild every night (supposedly now at $120 per bottle). I could hear Lee snickering the way his old Allentown school chum George Rutt remembers him snickering with the gleeful air of "Gotcha!"

In the end Iacocca took on Chrysler in order to silence his nastiest critic of all, the doubter who gets under his skin more irritatingly than Henry Ford: himself.

Not long after he made the move to Highland Park he had a call from a close friend from Ford, Hank Carlini, who would soon join the Iacoccalytes at Chrysler. Hank had told him that the Lamborghini sports car people in Italy might want Lee to take over their business. Iacocca had asked Carlini to look into the proposition. Now the deal was dead,* and Iacocca felt he had to explain himself to Carlini.

"I had to do it," he said. "I had to prove to myself that I've still got it."

---

*In May 1987 Iacocca made up for the lost opportunity and spent $25 million to acquire Lamborghini for Chrysler. He wanted to become the world's largest producer of such "ultraluxury" cars as Lamborghini's best seller, the 150 mph Countach, selling for $128,000.

9.

THE MAKING OF THE BORN-AGAIN CHRYSLER CORPORATION

"**W**HAT'S TODAY'S SURPRISE?" ASKED IACOCCA, STARTING THE MEETING. A litany of unexpected disasters had been blowing up in his face since he came to Chrysler. He was beginning to get accustomed to his fate, liking it less and less.

"You know how many used cars we own?" countered Gar (for Elgar) Laux (pronounced "Low"), the genial Iacoccalyte from Ford whom Iacocca had persuaded to take over Chrysler marketing.

"We're not in the used-car business," snapped the new president.

"Well, we're owners of fifty-five thousand used cars."

Iacocca greeted this revelation with the disbelief that marked his early months at Chrysler. His first day in Highland Park headquarters had gone well enough once he found the place. At Ford Chrysler had been considered a backwater, and he had trouble locating the proper ramp off the Davison Expressway. But when John Riccardo ushered him from the cavernous fifth-floor hallway of the K. T. Keller Building* into his introductory meeting with the thirty-one-member Officers Council, he was met by a standing ovation, and when Iacocca lighted up his Monte Cristo, Riccardo, in some embarrassment, announced he was then and there rescinding the rule against smoking.

The new order was by no means in place, however. Other long-entrenched Chrysler ways did not change readily, and Iacocca was shattered as he peeled layer after layer of decay from the company's deformed skeleton. His dream of a speedy turnaround had been wishful thinking. "You son of a bitch, why didn't you tell me it was this bad?" he demanded of Hal Sperlich, and Sperlich allowed that he feared the full story would have scared his mentor away.

Iacocca was, he said later, "starting from scratch." And like so many of his sweeping claims, this one, too, was essentially on target.

Even in the retrospective light of the years that have passed since then, the Chrysler malaise was so fundamental, so downright primitive that its scope is difficult to exaggerate. The same can be said of the hardships Iacocca endured to bring about ultimate rehabilitation. The Chrysler transformation stands as an awesome achievement and offers a rich case study in the facets of leadership. While nothing about the works of an old establishment shines under the new broom of a reform regime, the before-to-after sequence of the metamorphosis in Highland Park has been subjected to sufficient expert study for a reliable perspective to emerge.

The performance lends credence to another hyperbolic-sounding assertion that Iacocca has repeatedly flung out in recent years: Given twenty-five loyalists of his choice, he says, he could engineer a similar about-face in the workings of the federal government.

Grandiose? Not necessarily. It is easy to underestimate Iacocca. Skeptics often fell victim to this temptation, especially in the boardrooms of businesses where a civil service committee mind-set is considered safe and tends to be confused with competence. Executives given to openness, facile expression, unconventionality, ex-

---

*The incongruous dimensions were relics designed to accommodate a long-gone past: Maxwell cars were once manufactured in the building.

tremes of any kind are not shunned as automatically as in generations past, but they get eyed with suspicion still.

In the automobile industry the Iacocca face and decibel level loomed like the Matterhorn against the range of nameless, silent corporate figures in charge at the other big-name brands—workaholics like Iacocca but with a passion for anonymity. To make a comparison between the two styles seems unfair. The Iacocca presence stands out in any company short of a De Gaulle or Churchill.

"Everything about Iacocca is monumental," says Ron DeLuca of Kenyon & Eckhardt, his image keeper. The outsized effect has a flip side. It can be overwhelming. It is also resented by competitors and other critics with a stake in dismissing the Iacocca ways as surface bombast, a pitchman's smoke screen, a con.

And so Iacocca's takeover at Chrysler was met by doubtful clucking. Executives who knew him by reputation dismissed him as a huckster, a bully, and, in view of his final vaulting ambition at Ford, a bit of a megalomaniac. He was supposed to lack skill at analysis and a feel for finance. He was seen as a spender while Chrysler desperately needed cost controls. The perception was that he could create and sell product by intuition and dazzle but only if others footed the bill. And the toughest rap of all: He had never handled the job of ultimate boss. Some people grow into the *numero uno* state. The glitz of marketing stars often covers up lack of substance.

People who had worked closely with Iacocca at Ford knew a more authentic picture of him. They recalled how his lushest box-office hits, the Mustang and the Continental, were largely patched together from available components and required little development money. These witnesses saw him juggle numbers at Ford—including a $1 billion budget cut in 1974–1975—to match the most miserly of bean counters. And during the time when he had indeed been boss of Ford (in fact and in responsibility), he had displayed agility at a prime leadership skill—moving through his workday while switching between two sets of lenses: one to give him a hands-on close-up of such details as really mattered; the other set for the corporate overview.

He could listen for an hour or more without moving a muscle, but when he detected a note that troubled him, he leaped like a leopard. People froze when he interrupted to yell, "Hold it! Hold it! Hold it!" Or when he purred, "Why do you say that?" Excessive detail quickly made him restless. All he needed, as he kept saying again and again throughout his working life, were the "ABCs."

His mastery of the auto industry's gestalt enabled him to X-ray Chrysler rapidly once he moved inside. The parallel with government in Washington comes to mind again because a car company, too, is divided into three roughly coequal branches that must mesh: manufacturing (including engineering); marketing; and finance. At Chrysler these functions operated almost as if each were located in another town. They were barely in touch with each other. They didn't know what impact their work had on the fellow down the hall. Nobody reported to anybody. The system was that there was no overall system.

Iacocca was reminded of the chaotic way Italy was governed before 1860. "Everybody had his own little empire," he said. And the troublesome quirk that Sperlich had causally mentioned during the preceding summer—that he had to do his own digging for answers that should have been at hand—was symptomatic of a chronic paralysis. There was no way of extracting meaningful data out of the near-autonomous duchies.

Iacocca was stunned. At Ford an easy flow of operating information had been taken for granted. Since Chrysler had always been run by bean counters, he assumed that its financial controls were in good repair. On closer inspection it developed that while accounting and auditing controls were in place, there was no system for flushing up the numbers needed for operating decisions.

It was like running a household without knowing whether the grocery bills were out of line, except that it took the new Chrysler regime a lot of time to install a responsive reporting system. Many months after Iacocca had persuaded his old Ford friend Paul Bergmoser to leave California retirement and take over purchasing, Bergmoser winced at the mounting deficits and said, "I have a terrific accountant's report that tells me we lost a billion dollars this year. What I don't have is an analysis to tell me how we lost it."

The most grotesque sleight of hand at Chrysler was the manipulation of the car inventory. This self-deception was known as the "sales bank," which sounded like an asset. It wasn't. It was a backlog of deteriorating cars jamming acres and acres of mud and weeds during the closing phase of each model season. Iacocca had heard about it, and it made him furious each morning because he had to drive past an old Ford plant in Highland Park which Chrysler had to rent from Ford to help tuck away the embarrassing overflow.

But he did not know the fantastic extent of this practice, didn't realize it was a way of life seriously affecting the company's total performance. The awakening came when R. K. Brown, the old marketing vice president, approached him at a Las Vegas dealer convention for money to underwrite a season-end promotion. The books were closing in a month. The sales bank contained nearly 100,000 automobiles.

Grimly Iacocca demanded how the hell Brown expected to move so many cars so quickly.

"That's a spring ritual around here," lectured Brown. "Everybody goes into the Tank."

Iacocca had not heard of the Tank. Brown explained that the corporate sales force would be assembled with each man assigned to sell a quota of hundreds of cars at chillingly low prices. Like hucksters of dubious penny stocks, they would dial into the night. The 4,800 Chrysler dealers, confidently waiting out the accustomed windfall, would snap up the bargains plus the attendant personal giveaway goodies. A hot tub was the prize for taking five cars that stood rotting in the sales bank. For taking twenty-five, the award was a junket around the globe.

R. K. Brown was soon replaced by Gar Laux, and the old dealers, grown jaded by having to unload so many boringly styled lemons for so many years, were joined by lustier types. One of the converts was Victor Potamkin, wiry and exuberant, the old Iacocca pal from their days together in Chester, Pennsylvania, now the world's biggest GM dealer, famous for the ease with which he seemed to sell Cadillacs the way other pushed motorcycles.

A $2 MILLION VOTE OF CONFIDENCE IN CHRYSLER AND IN LEE A. IACOCCA, trumpeted the fat black letters of the headline announcing a new Potamkin Dodge dealership in a full-page ad in *Automotive News*. The industry took the hoped-for notice. Confidence was building. True, Potamkin was very rich and could afford to take chances. "What's a friend for?" he asked. Potamkin was also very shrewd. He didn't care what GM or Henry Ford thought. He had faith in Iacocca. Iacocca would make it.

"He's the smartest automobile man in the world," Potamkin yelled at me, vindicated, when I called at his block-sized New York headquarters in 1986. "Not in the U.S., in the world! The smartest!" Potamkin wanted me to get further confirmation from another Iacocca fan, a competitor, the former head of the Ford Dealer Alliance, and got him on the speakerphone. In no time they were chatting about Iacocca's qualifications for the presidency of the United States, a subject I had not brought up.

"I'd give him five million bucks," Potamkin shouted into his speaker, "and I could raise five million more!"

Like a newly elected president arriving at the White House with a mandate to switch policy and management, Iacocca had to put together a new team to head his Chrysler divisions. Unlike cabinet offers in Washington, unfortunately, the Detroit jobholders didn't conveniently resign. Almost all had to be fired.* Eventually thirty-three of the thirty-five most important desks were filled by new executives. Remarkably, considering the Iacocca reputation for crudity and ruthlessness, not one protested publicly or leaked nasty stories to the media.

Iacocca was astounded by so much feeble acquiescence. "You know something," he said to his intimate, Wes Small, "not one of those guys came in here and said, 'Lee, you're making a mistake. Here's what I've done, and here's why I shouldn't get fired.' " Iacocca shook his head. Losers! It was depressing as hell. "If a guy can't stand up for himself, he wouldn't be able to sell anybody else."

Wes Small thought his boss was telling him that the purged executives must have been screwing up too dreadfully to permit the making of any sort of reasonable case for themselves. But other factors kept down the noise level of the bloodletting, and it was not merely resignation to Detroit's inglorious history of headchoppings. Iacocca's skills with personnel contributed much to keeping the peace.

A number of the departing officers were not formally dismissed but allowed to retire gracefully, and the full firing/hiring wave was phased across three years. Financial settlements were reasonable. Iacocca, no doubt remembering his own firing and that of Hal Sperlich from Ford, performed the wrenching act personally each time. He displayed consideration that those who stayed behind found touching and remained on friendly terms with several of the men he let go. He is proud of that and likes to talk about it.

---

*Among lower-level employees, firings and forced retirements also grew into a Detroit-style epidemic. From white-collar ranks alone, 8,500 people vanished in the first months of Iacocca's tenure. The very day the K-cars finally went into production Chrysler was forced to lay off nearly half of its 6,500 engineers.

I spoke to one survivor who watched a decapitated leader emerge from Iacocca's office with tears in his eyes. "He talked to me for an hour," the victim said. "It wasn't so bad."

To fill his vacant cabinet posts, Iacocca looked for loyalists he could trust, safe, deeply experienced men whose performance record he knew at first hand. He had no margin for error. Each man absolutely had to be a top-quality manager. Such men do not search the want ads for jobs. They must be carefully wooed and motivated to undertake a drastic change in their lives. And on the surface of his situation Iacocca could offer only a spot on a listing (if not sinking) whaling boat.

Gar Laux, the new marketing boss, had been division sales manager at Ford when the Mustang was launched. He was a "dealer man," friendly, folksy, but sharp underneath, and a consummate organizer. When his advancement at Ford seemed blocked by the coming of Bunkie Knudsen, he moved on to head the Dallas Chamber of Commerce. Then he ran a highly profitable Cadillac dealership with golf champion Arnold Palmer in Charlotte, North Carolina. Iacocca sweet-talked Laux into becoming a consultant and shortly chained him to a full-time line position.

Paul Bergmoser had been Ford's purchasing guru for thirty years. He did "materials control," bringing in the best parts and raw materials as cheaply as his no-baloney methods could knock them out of the suppliers. It was Iacocca who once flattered this dictator by calling him "a goddamn Prussian general." He was sixty-three when Iacocca phoned him in California and sang, "Bergie, I'm all alone at Chrysler." Bergmoser signed on "temporarily"—and stayed to succeed Iacocca as president when Lee became Chairman.

Iacocca cherry-picked his players all over the industry. Dick Dauch and Baron Bates left the security of Volkswagen, and others left safe berths elsewhere. "He got people to throw away their pensions," marveled Hal Sperlich. "He really is a great salesman."

Mostly the rescuers came from Ford to side with Lee and join the excitement at Chrysler. Jerry Pyle came to run sales, Robert S. ("Steve") Miller to be assistant treasurer and eventually vice chairman, followed by many more colleagues, so many that Detroit wags gave Chrysler the nickname Little Ford.

As a pied piper Iacocca moved with deliberation. He almost never approached a potential recruit personally. As his middleman he deputized his old Chester associate Jay Dugan, known to a generation of Ford men as a supplier of promotion materials and an Ia-cocca pal. Dugan would call at the home of a targeted executive and announce, "Lee wants to see you." It usually worked.

The piper was able to put his finger upon the choice talent be-cause he possessed the key divining rod, his detailed diagnostic rec-ords on all Ford managers—his notorious little black books with the periodic performance ratings. Bill Ford had given him permission to take the books along, a priceless parting gift.*

To install the crucial financial controls, Iacocca needed someone permanent and special. Again, the little black books helped. So did a bit of luck. It happened that a few months before he was fired Iacocca had consulted Ed Lundy, the old Whiz Kid who had be-come the ruler over Ford finance, about Lundy's own staff. Who were the potential top managers who should be pushed ahead?

From his black book he pulled out five or more names and showed them to Lundy who identified one "sleeper": Gerald Greenwald, forty-three, president of the Ford subsidiary in, of all places, Venezuela. The son of a St. Louis chicken farmer, Green-wald was a Princeton economics graduate and—most unusual among high-level auto managers—Jewish. Known as a maverick, he had long tried to move beyond finance into operations. Given his chance in Venezuela, he performed spectacularly, increasing profits by ten times in less than three years.

"Don't call back," advised his wife, Glenda, when Iacocca phoned in December 1978 at the enormous mountainside hacienda where the Greenwalds were ensconced in Caracas. She guessed at once that their grand life-style was in danger, and it was.

Critics say Iacocca is impatient. Greenwald saw no sign of it. In four months of negotiations, through meetings in Las Vegas and Miami, Iacocca pursued Greenwald's tracks to convince him that he should return to the rigid discipline of finance after enjoying free-dom in operations. (Nobody at Ford understood why Greenwald was leaving, except Henry Ford. Greenwald suggested to Ford that he turn back thirty-five years and remember how *he* had put to-gether a new crew and turned around his grandfather's faltering en-terprise. Ford appreciated the message.)

The Iacocca whaling ship got under way with a prime crew aboard. The recruitment had been a phenomenal tour de force. "None was a cast-off," wrote two tough *Time* reporters, Michael

*The notebooks are no longer a physical presence, but their system of goal setting and performance rating are institutionalized in Chrysler's regular quarterly reporting system.

Moritz and Barrett Seaman, in their book *Going for Broke: The Chrysler Story.* "They did it for the thrill and for Lee Iacocca." David Halberstam, though scathingly critical of the Iacocca style in *The Reckoning,* allows: "Probably no one but Iacocca" could have resuscitated the "dying company." And Halberstam pinpoints the rescue leader's foremost asset at the start of the trip: "What legitimized the rescue operation first in the business community and then in the Congress was Iacocca's name and reputation."

The cabinet worked out well for the long pull, too. Greenwald rose to be chairman of Chrysler Motors. Sperlich became president. In 1983 the high command was joined by Ben Bidwell as vice chairman of Chrysler Corporation, the parent firm. Bidwell had worked with Iacocca at Ford and then become head of Hertz Rent-a-Car. In 1986 Iacocca collared an alter ego, Bob Lutz, born in Switzerland, educated in Berkeley, and another maverick. He came from Ford, even though he had to give up his ambition to become president there.

While they are publicly overshadowed by their flashy Chairman, all of these four men had earned reputations within their industry as exceptionally strong characters. Aside from Bidwell, at sixty perhaps a shade too old to succeed Iacocca, all are driven, hyperenergetic individualists, charging about with the proverbial marshal's batons in their knapsacks. Lutz liked to speed to work on a motorcycle. Sperlich enjoyed kidding Iacocca as being too old to understand the youth market. Bidwell would stick his head through the Chairman's door and inquire, "Is Mr. Modesty in?"

Although reverence is alien to these lieutenants, they survived. Their very strength is their survival secret. Iacocca holds yes-men in vast contempt and knows that he and the stockholders benefit from the frankness of his cabinet. Nobody has been as aggressively noisy about it as Sperlich, by nature a tomcat, but all the advisers make their points forcefully. Iacocca has no trouble hearing them out. According to all testimony, he is an attentive, analytical listener, even when advice is unflattering.

Ben Bidwell read portions of The Book in manuscript and told Iacocca outright that this oeuvre was impolitic. "Don't print it," he said. Iacocca thought it over and decided to go ahead. The Book's reception made publishing history, just as television history was made when Iacocca overruled the advice of his respected PR chief,

Lars Larsen, who didn't want Lee to make the case for Chrysler in TV commercials. The point here is that principal advisers felt they could dispense counsel freely.

By no means everybody on the Iacocca payroll will do so. Among some in the lower ranks, men less strong, less sure of themselves, less proved by fire, Iacocca is a threatening, fearsome figure. "He's an intimidating guy," says an adviser who does speak up, Ron DeLuca, the adman. "He exudes power. You don't want to be wrong with him. I think some of his people have a fear of that. That's why they don't venture opinions."

"When he sets his jaw and gets that look in his eye, they get round heels," says Gar Laux, chuckling because his heels never buckled.

"He likes vigorous dialogue," says Sperlich, who has survived years of shouting matches with his mentor. "You have to be strong to stand up to him."

Don Frey remembers an executive who gave a market research presentation and then wilted under Iacocca's questioning: "Lee cut this man up and left him goddamn near bleeding on the floor." But Frey also saw the weakness of the victim: "I went up to him after the meeting and said, 'You know, George, you get treated the way you let yourself be treated.' "

Iacocca realizes that his forbidding tactics sometimes squash opinions he needs to hear. This troubles him and can lead him to bark commands not everyone can handle. Another executive genius, the moviemaker Darryl F. Zanuck, once commanded an underling, "Don't say 'yes' until I've finished talking!" Iacocca once instructed Leo-Arthur Kelmenson of the Kenyon & Eckhardt agency, "Don't say yes to me when I'm wrong!"

Some associates might have fled from such a risky injunction. Iacocca no doubt sensed that Kelmenson would draw encouragement from it. Iacocca knew that Kelmenson's ego is about as mountainous as his own, having been nurtured by what the adman proudly calls "my ten years on the couch."

Iacocca's ego never needed years on the couch or, so far as anybody has been able to uncover, so much as a single day with a psychiatrist. His frustrations also require no outside attention. Unlike executives who bottle up their emotions and let them fester into ulcers or worse, Iacocca knows it's healthier to blow off steam. He is not, however, a "rageolic," which is how one authority on human aggression describes someone given to untrammeled rage. Iacocca knows how to limit his steam emissions.

Lars Larsen, who drafted speeches for him during Iacocca's early days at Chrysler, observed how the famous temper operates.

"Larsen, get your ass in here," the boss would shout into the phone when he received a text he didn't like.

"This isn't worth a shit," he yelled when Larsen hurried into his presence. Whereupon Iacocca dumped the manuscript into a wastepaper basket.

Larsen noticed, however, that the act was controlled. The manuscript went flying in a graceful wide arc. It was carefully aimed.

Nobody I could find had ever seen (or heard of) the Iacocca temper careening out of control. Paradoxically its outbreaks are regarded as overblown self-assertion. "It's a mechanism *of* control," says a Chrysler manager, which means that it works much like the sound effects Iacocca gives off when he wants to dominate a poker game.

Larsen found that the explosions blew over swiftly and the fallout was never radioactive.

"Talk to somebody who knows how to do this thing right," Iacocca would grumble by way of ending the eruption.

Five or ten minutes later the phone would ring in Larsen's office. Calmly, pleasantly, Iacocca would address himself to new business. "It's his way of saying, 'Don't worry about what happened,' " Larsen explains. Other associates, not necessarily Iacoccalytes, confirm: Iacocca is invariably considerate, even deferential, about personal concerns. They offer accounts similar to Larsen's experience when his wife underwent hernia surgery. Each day Iacocca phoned to inquire how she was getting along.

"Lee likes to thing he has the hide of an elephant," Kelmenson analyzes, "but inside he's a mushcake." And nothing softens him as much as a man's worry about his spouse because this was Iacocca's own most vulnerable territory for nearly a decade before his first wife died in 1983. She suffered from juvenile diabetes, a volatile, unpredictable condition. Often away on business, her husband could never know when Mary might be rushed to the hospital, ambulance sirens screaming, in the middle of the night.

The stress of the crises during the final years at Ford and the initial phase at Chrysler hardly helped to manage the disease. Mary was given an artificial pancreas; it was an experimental procedure and didn't work. A 1983 insulin reaction produced the heart attack that brought her to the hospital in critical condition. Nobody could tell Iacocca anything about the heartache of years with a dying wife.

If the days at home were life on borrowed time, so was life at Chrysler. The company was often actually in bankruptcy, kept alive by supplier/creditors who were lenient about collecting on their bills. Sperlich pushed every limit to get out the K-cars, but there was never enough cash. The pressure could have caved in any man. It was life with the bailiff. "Every Friday at 4 o'clock," Iacocca remembered later, "I looked for $260 million to meet my payments."

This was the time when he flirted briefly with thoughts of suicide. "I got scared," he recalled. "It was just overwhelming, almost like events outrunning your ability to cope with them, and you suddenly say, 'Oh, my God, I'm going to drown.' " The texture of events was different from the cliff-hanger-phases that all chief executives must live through at some time. The watery abyss under Iacocca's cliff was too close. It could have been paralyzing.

And still he manipulated and motivated himself and the players without whose help his crusade would have collapsed. In a historic realignment he converted to his cause the most powerful adversary of the automobile industry's management, its labor union, the United Automobile Workers (UAW). It was like the Hatfields and the McCoys abandoning their ancient rivalry and marching arm in arm to meet an outside foe.

No union played the negotiations game with greater virtuosity than the UAW. At contract renewal time it would target the most vulnerable of the Big Three automakers and bludgeon its victim with money demands, political pressure, headline-making strikes, anything legal to gain maximum pay increases and other concessions, which could then apply to all three companies. Signs of management weakness worked as a red blanket for the union's bull tactics.

To engineer the turnabout in Chrysler's chronically poisonous labor relations, Iacocca reached out to make a friend and ally of the union president, Douglas Fraser. They seemed an unlikely pair. Like Iacocca, Fraser dominates groups by his brains, his height (six feet three inches), his leonine head, and the convincing manner and speech of a scrappy immigrant (he was born in Scotland).

Both men had come up from poverty, Fraser starting as a metal finisher for Chrysler, working for only one month during his first year and laid off the rest of the time. For most of their lives, however, the two men had represented polarized vested interests that could not have kept them farther apart. They were Mr. Capital and Mr. Labor, and in United States labor relations the twain did not meet.

Until 1979. Drowning, Iacocca appealed to Fraser. "We can't follow the pattern," he said. Chrysler could not survive a labor settlement identical with Ford and GM, he argued. It absolutely had to work with lower costs. Fraser did not want Chrysler to drown. Nearly 150,000 jobs were at stake. So were the pensions for retirees. But in the climate of the 1970s unions still flew the banner of Samuel Gompers, a founder of the labor movement. When he was asked for labor's goals, Gompers answered with one word, "More!" Iacocca was asking Fraser to change the slogan to "Less!" That became a survival cry in the 1980s. In 1979 it was revolutionary.

Fraser said he could not sell the idea to his people on his own. Iacocca would have to go before the committee of the UAW leadership and tell the members why they should agree to concessions. This invitation also sounds unremarkable in retrospect, yet in 1979 no ranking auto manufacturer had ever appeared before the committee and tried to make his case.

Iacocca came twice and was a hit. Jocularly he addressed the labor representatives by filthy epithets. They loved it. He brought out detailed charts documenting Chrysler's pitiful economics, and they appreciated his candor. "It was a breath of fresh air," said Doug Fraser. It convinced him to join the Iacocca bandwagon ("I bought a Chrysler because of Lee Iacocca," he told me), and it sold the union on wage cuts and other concessions adding up to $1.07 billion.

It was another Iacocca solo performance, and its clincher brooked no counterargument: "We've got lots of jobs at $17 per hour. We've got absolutely none at $20." It was his way of cutting the hourly wage by $3, and at the same time he volunteered to cut his own pay to $1 a year.

As his improbable romance with Fraser warmed, Iacocca asked the UAW chief to join the Chrysler board of directors so the union could share management's secrets on a continuing basis. In Sweden, Germany, and elsewhere such sharing was traditional. In the American automobile industry it was a first, an absolute heresy, and was received with equal incredulity by management and labor across the country.

Fraser had some doubts about accepting such a position of trust; he feared it might appear self-serving. Iacocca sent word: "It's you or nobody." So Fraser took his seat on the board, though not the director's fees.

Iacocca was not sleeping much. Helpers like Leo-Arthur Kelmenson, the adman, would be awakened by his calls with new ideas in the middle of the night. In the office Lee would sometimes brood and act distant. To intimates like Hal Sperlich he expressed doubts about the company's survival chances. The constant public burials in the press bothered him. Still, for the outside world he maintained an ebullient facade.

"It was one of his biggest bluffs," says his old pal Hank Carlini with admiration.

Yes and no. Iacocca's good cheer was not all front. Throughout, he kept his eye on the main chance, the ripening Chrysler product, especially the minivan. "Product in the end decides," he insists, and here was a fresh concept, a new configuration that could cash in on the rich suburban mother-taxi market in love with the station wagon, a high-profit category dominated by Ford. Wouldn't it be poetic justice to hit Henry where he felt unassailable?

The moment the running prototypes were completed Iacocca walked into the high-domed styling studio for a first look at the stylish little vans. Smiling from ear to ear, he circled the models, looking as if he could not quite believe his good fortune. Still grinning and circling, he exclaimed, "I've got 'em, I've got 'em!"

10.

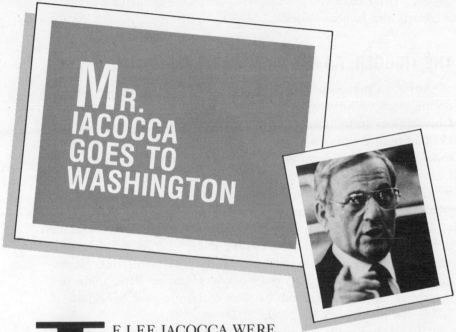

MR. IACOCCA GOES TO WASHINGTON

IF LEE IACOCCA WERE EVER TO BECOME PRESIDENT, HE WOULD BRING TO THE WHITE HOUSE THE PERFECT EXPERIENCE FOR A MOST USEFUL PRESIDENTIAL REQUIREMENT: SQUEEZING WHAT HE WANTS OUT OF CONGRESS. In the last four months of 1978 he charmed, cajoled, bargained, and bludgeoned the legislators into handing him $1.5 billion to put Chrysler on its feet. The deal was the nation's most elaborate financial transaction ever, involving not only 535 senators and representatives but the cooperation of the president, 452 banks, the governments of four states and three foreign countries, 1,500 suppliers and dealers, the UAW, and five other unions.

Supporters called it a "loan guarantee." Opponents dismissed it as a "bailout" and a "con." The controversy is vaguely remembered from the TV news, but it's instructive to break out just those elements that illuminate Iacocca's role.

His performance adds up to a textbook exercise in the engineering of consent, the more notable because the battleground was not his familiar industry scene in Detroit but pure politics, politics at highest levels in Washington, played out to the tune of a national debate. The fate of Chrysler now became an Issue with a capital *I*. Herewith the Iacocca episodes.

THE TRIGGER: A FAST-BREAKING EMERGENCY

Although preoccupied with firing, hiring, sweeping out corporate debris, Iacocca knew that his efforts might become academic. Chrysler was scraping bottom. The company's share of the car market had plunged from a onetime record of 26 percent to a sickening 8 percent. V-eight gas guzzlers were still selling, but thousands of Chrysler's small Horizons and Omnis—a three-month supply— weren't moving, and even $1,000 rebates failed to diminish the stockpile of the little Japanese-built Colts.

Then, as so often happens in Detroit and Washington, a sudden new crisis, triggered by uncontrollable events far away, made a bad situation immeasurably worse. On January 16, 1979, less than ninety days after Iacocca started work in Highland Park, mobs in the streets of Tehran caused the shah of Iran to pilot his Boeing 727 out of his country for good.

"The Day the Shah Left Town," Iacocca would call it, but the impact was no joke. For American car owners it was an enormous pain; for Chrysler it extinguished the light at the end of the tunnel.

Gas prices doubled wherever gas could be found at all. Chrysler's van sales slumped 42 percent. The overall market share for small vehicles rose 15 percent (any 2 percent swing was normally considered serious). The revolution had spread from the streets of Tehran to dealer showrooms and gas stations all over America. Never had the automobiles business been shaken so violently so quickly. If a road to survival existed, Chrysler could not go on without drastic action. Nor could it even field the kind of crew that stood a chance of marshaling a rescue operation.

BUILDING THE RESCUE CREW

John Riccardo, still the titular chairman even though Iacocca was running the company, started shuttling to Washington in Chrysler's white-and-blue Gulfstream II jet. First he tried to lobby for a freeze on government pollution regulations that were costing the company a lot of money. The congressmen were not interested. Indeed, they resented Riccardo. He was saying insulting things about environmental controls they had worked hard to make into law.

In July Riccardo tried for a refundable $1 billion tax credit. The Treasury Department turned him down.

Riccardo, loyal and tireless, had become a liability. He was still the "Flamethrower." He kept losing his temper, which didn't work in Washington. Treasury Secretary W. Michael Blumenthal thought Riccardo hadn't done his homework; the old Chrysler man failed to realize the devastating seriousness of the company's cash problem and seemed oblivious of the research effort required to document what was, in effect, a financial underwriting.

Worst, Riccardo was too visible a reminder of the pre-Iacocca Chrysler. He was a symbol of the rotten management responsible for its cancer. Iacocca decided he had to go. Lars Larsen, his vice president for public affairs and an old Riccardo confidant, engineered the exit.

"We did something that was very dramatic and very cynical," Larsen disclosed to Harvard economist Robert Reich in 1984. "We helped John Riccardo see that the company would be better served if he resigned." Larsen arranged for Michigan Senator Don Riegle to meet with Riccardo in Detroit, where the senator told him straight out that no relief could get through Congress as long as he was in charge. Riccardo was ready to call it quits. His doctors were telling him that he would almost certainly die if he continued to expose himself to still more stress.

The following Sunday Larsen went to Riccardo's home to settle details. "I'd written my master's thesis in English literature on scapegoat symbolism in Faulkner," he recalled. "That came in handy. I told John that Congress and the country weren't going to act until we staged a morality play, and I told him how he'd been cast: John Riccardo takes on himself all the sins of commission and omission, we drive him into the woods, and the company is pure again. At the end of the day we drafted his resignation statement. The script was for Riccardo to fall on his sword. . . ."

Ill and weary, Riccardo agreed and the tactic worked. The way had been cleared for Iacocca to take charge of Chrysler's future and to map his own campaign for getting there.

In early August the Carter administration gave its first sign of relenting. When he had been chairman of the Federal Reserve Board, G. William Miller had belonged to the large contingent in Washington that wanted Chrysler to slide into bankruptcy. Now, having succeeded Blumenthal as secretary of the treasury, he announced that the government would consider a loan guarantee.

Iacocca had all along hated going to Washington as a supplicant. As a free enterpriser by practice and conviction he opposed the idea of government in business. In the past he had argued in Washington against it. Running there now to cry for a handout would make him look inconsistent and helpless.

Most of his associates also opposed trying for a loan guarantee. Gathered in the rarely used ornate directors room on the fifth floor of the K. T. Keller Building—the place was so large that the rectangular table with its fifty chairs looked almost lost—they argued one by one against government aid. Hal Sperlich, as usual, temperament flaring, was the most vociferous. He opposed the loan on ideological grounds and because in Europe the public had tended to lose confidence in companies when government moved in.

In the end Iacocca said, "You guys tell me what the alternative is."

Nobody found one, so he deputized Larsen to orchestrate a campaign in Washington.

FACING A WALL OF OPPOSITION

The opposition was so overwhelming that Larsen remembers feeling at first like a leper. And the uproar seemed to pour in from everywhere.

Republican resistance on Capitol Hill was to be expected, but even one of Michigan's own congressmen, David Stockman, later to become Ronald Reagan's budget director, heaped contempt on the Chrysler cause. He wrote an article for the *Wall Street Journal* entitled "Chrysler Bailout: Rewarding Failure?" and another piece for the *Washington Post* demanding, "Let Chrysler Go Broke."

In a Democratic administration the strident opposition from the chairman of the crucial Senate Banking Committee, William Proxmire of Wisconsin, was more serious. In much the same language the senator warned again and again: "If we provide loan guarantees to Chrysler, we will be saying, in effect, to every business in the country that it doesn't matter if you no longer make products that enough people want to buy . . . so long as you are big enough and can muster enough interest groups to fight your cause in Washington."

Bankers lined up against Iacocca with almost no exceptions.

Walter Wriston, chairman of Citicorp, called the Chrysler plea an attempt "to move economic resources to places where they would otherwise not go. Such distortions inevitably lead to less, not more productivity. . . ."

Conservative economists such as Milton Friedman and Alan Greenspan were still holding out against the Chrysler guarantees years after the loans had been repaid with interest, with Greenspan lecturing: "Policies focused on protecting jobs in moribund industries must eventually fail and, in the end, destroy more jobs than they save."

The assault from the left of the political scale was more vitriolic yet. Ralph Nader weighed in with twenty-five pages of consumer complaints about Chrysler, which he submitted to the Senate Banking Committee. In his follow-up testimony the consumer activist, drawing on his reputation as author of the auto industry exposé *Unsafe at Any Speed*, demanded: "Don't guarantee a mismanaged company so that the executives can proceed with the public's guarantee and further their own tired managerial practices and policies."

Most hurtful to Iacocca was the one enemy with direct access to the public, the press. Here he faced near-unanimous opposition, especially from that bible of business the *Wall Street Journal*. Relations between him and the *Journal* had been touchy for a long time. The paper called him "Motor Mouth" and seemed to delight in pricking his ego in its commentaries and deflating his exaggerations in the headlines and text of its news columns. The blood feud—it was precisely that—was still running in 1986, even though Iacocca had tried to end it by a *cri de coeur* delivered in a speech after Chrysler had been rehabilitated.

"Screw the *Wall Street Journal*!" he could shout by then, having risen from the grave that the newspaper had dug for him.*

While the decision on the loan guarantee still hung in doubt, he

---

*The *Wall Street Journal*'s power playing with the auto industry dates back to 1954, when a reporter named John Williams did the unforgivable. He rejected the then-prevailing trained-seal habits of the Detroit press. He shunned the Off-the-Record Club, where the carmakers took journalists into their confidence in return for relying on formal press releases in writing important stories. Well in advance of the prescribed date, Williams wrote a carefully researched front-page story on the most treasured secret of the year: the radical changes being incorporated in the 1955 models. Williams even printed (it was the ultimate lèse-majesté) drawings of the new cars. General Motors, the newspaper's most important advertiser, canceled all its advertising. Locally the unruly writer was shunned as an outcast. But everywhere else GM was branded as a bully. It canceled the boycott with an apologetic statement within two months. The *Journal* had established its independence from the carmakers.

had had to be content with writing self-serving letters to the editor which did nothing to deflect the *Journal*. Its editor, Robert L. Bartley, won a Pulitzer Prize in part for an editorial entitled "Laetrile for Chrysler." Another piece, "Let Them Die with Dignity," suggested that the company be "put out of its misery," causing Iacocca to write to the editor that the patient was still alive and that he was "grateful you're not my family physician."

And the ridicule! Chrysler was hitting a new low in its identity crisis. It was still far from becoming the scrappy underdog the audience loved to cheer on, much less the victor over adversity, the role that eventually landed Iacocca back again on the cover of *Time* magazine,* on this occasion as "Detroit's Comeback Kid." The company was still the flabby has-been everybody liked to kick, especially the cartoonists.

Herblock of the *Washington Post* showed a dejected Chrysler executive in line at the welfare office. Paul Conrad in the *Los Angeles Times* cast Chrysler as a sinister stickup man in a bank. Johnny Carson seemed unable to get along without Chrysler; the company was, as one of Iacocca's friends moaned, Carson's longest-running joke. Perhaps his most biting gag was the new definition of the meanest man in America. According to Johnny, this was the fellow who called Chrysler and asked, "How's business?"

THE TEST WAS PERSONAL

To Iacocca the meek are not blessed, and he detested his role of supplicant. Testifying repeatedly before House and Senate committees, TV lights glaring in his eyes, the lawmakers peering down on him accusingly from their daises, he fielded the hostile questions, explained the dire necessity for a handout that went against his own entrepreneurial grain but was simply unavoidable—and felt terrible.

"I was the defendant," he writes. "It was murder." And: "It was personal."

To Iacocca, any unadmiring sentiment about him can seem personal even when it's not. This time there was no mistake, however. The digs at him were explicit.

"You are now asking the Government to risk $1.5 billion," lectured Senator Proxmire in the high-ceilinged hearing room. "If it

---

*All told, he appeared on the cover four times.

fails, the taxpayer takes a painful bath. If it succeeds, you will be a famous success and be made very, very wealthy."*

Proxmire's principal aide, Elinor Bachrach, feeding her boss written ammunition from her seat directly behind him, asserted that Chrysler was not even the issue. "The federal government was not asked to save Chrysler," she remarked, "but to build a monument for Lee Iacocca."

Throughout, Iacocca's infamous temper never surfaced. He might be a flamethrower at heart, like his predecessor Riccardo, but outwardly he kept cool control. "He couldn't afford to lose his temper," the UAW's Doug Fraser told me years afterward. This is true, but it is not the central truth. The point is that Iacocca can subdue his internal flames when it counts. And he can accept advice from his staff.

The most provocative test came in his encounter with Congressman Richard Kelly of Florida, a gangling, stooped former circuit judge known to fellow legislators as the "hanging judge from Disney World." A passionate free-enterpriser, Kelly was gunning for Iacocca, eager to milk the most out of a rare opportunity for an obscure congressman to shine on national TV.

"This guy is going to nail you," Lars Larsen warned his boss. "If you confront him, he'll go nuts. Just smile and be nice."

Kelly lived up to his nickname. "I think that you are trying to put a con on us," he accused Iacocca. Chrysler, he said, had been rejected by the marketplace. "You couldn't make it," Kelly taunted; Iacocca was trying to fool Congress with "baloney." Kelly marshaled all the inflammatory buzzwords that would make the evening news jump: "The Chrysler bailout will be the beginning of a new era of irresponsibility in government. The Chrysler bailout is a ripoff of the American worker, American industry, and the taxpayer and consumer. The Chrysler charity is the most blatant con job in our time."

Con job, bailout, rip-off, charity—Iacocca absorbed every insult with outward equanimity. Inside, he was boiling. "He had to grovel," says his old friend Bill Winn; "it was humiliating. He was disgusted."

---

*The debate over the justification of federal loan guarantees—and Proxmire's opposition to them—never ended. In September 1986 the senator told the *New York Times:* "The principle is so bad. Last year there were something like 57,000 failures. Now how can you justify bailing out Chrysler and not bailing out every little business in the country? The heartbreak, the loss of jobs, was probably greater for the small businesses. . . ."

"It really killed him," says Bill Fugazy, the leader of the Iacoccalytes. Physically he came close to buckling. Walking up a Capitol Hill corridor, feeling stressed, he began to see double and felt dizzy. He thought he might faint. Doctors in the House infirmary diagnosed an attack of vertigo, a transitory and innocuous problem of the inner ear. It didn't stop him from continuing his rounds.

Away from the public eye he remained true to his shy self when his internal limits felt threatened. At least up to a point. During one of the negotiations Treasury Secretary Miller explained why he thought Chrysler should make only small cars and stay out of the luxury market. Though he was seething, Iacocca listened quietly. Profit margins on small models were modest. Chrysler could never survive without the markups on luxury cars. Finally he ripped off his glasses, banged them on the table, and said with some emotion that the running of his company was his business, not that of the secretary. Miller accepted the rebuke.

While roaming from one office to another, pleading his case—he made five lengthy pilgrimages to Washington that fall—Iacocca would invoke his sense of privacy whenever he couldn't go on gladhanding. His strategist, Lars Larsen, recognized the limits of the public Iacocca the day he asked his boss to contact Senator Bob Dole, the minority leader.

"You're going to have to call him," said Larsen.

"I've never met the son of a bitch," snapped Iacocca. "I'm not going to call him." And he didn't.

MOUNTING THE COUNTERATTACK

Striking back, Iacocca performed brilliantly, as he invariably did when he faced a large audience. Testifying under the TV lights before the House Banking Committee's Subcommittee on Economic Stabilization, he made clear at once that he was no John Riccardo. Nobody could accuse him of doing too little homework or being insensitive to the psychology of his listeners.

"Quite frankly, I would rather not be here at all," he began. "I am a strong advocate of the free enterprise system. I grew up in it and slugged my way through it for 33 years."

His punch line was frightening and came quickly. Not only were 140,000 Chrysler jobs at stake, but the "awesome total" of 2 million Americans would be "severely impacted" by the company's demise. (Analysts later noted that this was the highest of many wildly varying expert estimates.) According to a study made for the Congressional Budget Office by Data Resources, Inc., Iacocca pointed out, the cost of Chrysler's death to taxpayers would run $10 billion during the first year alone.

Going into bankruptcy, he testified, could never prevent Chrysler's death. It would hasten it. "We're dying out there with just the talk of it." Its domino effect "could completely paralyze us in a few short weeks. . . ."

In the ensuing days additional calamitous facts and figures emerged from independent studies, and Iacocca made certain that this ammunition was spread in influential places. Chrysler's bankruptcy would be the largest in the nation's history and cause a drop of some 0.5 percent in the gross national product. Unemployment would rise nationally between 0.5 and 1.9 percent. Welfare payments could go up $1.5 billion.

And why, so Iacocca kept punching, were his critics acting as if a congressional loan guarantee to Chrysler would set a ruinous precedent? They talked as if they were being asked to finance a whiskey subsidy for alcoholics. Yet over the years they had approved guarantees to Lockheed, Penn Central, and many other corporations for a breathtaking total of $409 billion.

"Don't stop now, men," Iacocca urged his congressional audience. "Go to $410 billion for Chrysler. . . ."

What irked him most was the largess Congress had shown toward American Motors of Wisconsin. Five times between 1967 and 1979 this ailing Chrysler competitor had received financial favors from the federal government without dissent from Wisconsin's Bill Proxmire, now Iacocca's most influential opponent.

Iacocca dared to attack the senator in front of his own committee. "I remember you were the prime mover for loan guarantees for American Motors and they're owned by the French," he challenged. "So you were aiding and abetting the French government."

Proxmire struck back by matching his inconsistency against Iacocca's. "More than any other executive in Detroit, you have led the anti-Washington campaign," the senator said. Yet here was Iacocca pleading for government aid. "Doesn't this fly in the face of what you have been preaching so eloquently for so long?"

"It sure does," Iacocca answered. "I come here with great reluctance. I am between a rock and a hard place."

The confrontation ended with unexpected praise for the witness.

"I am opposed to your request," said Chairman Proxmire. "But I have rarely heard a more eloquent, intelligent, well-informed witness than you have been today. You did a brilliant job. . . ."

Before every other Washington audience as well, Iacocca mastered his complex sales pitch much as a symphony conductor extracts the most from his last bassoon. Even some critics applauded. Felix Rohatyn, the investment banker who had engineered the rescue of New York City from bankruptcy in 1975 (with expensive congressional help), had come up with a plan to save Chrysler. The company had turned it down. Nevertheless, once Iacocca's salvage operation was over, Rohatyn praised him effusively: "Lee is a man who can install leadership in a crisis. He knows his business from front bumpers to back ends. He is the right man at the right time."

Iacocca knew that putting over his message in Washington was not enough. It had to be magnified, trumpeted to the taxpayers over the heads of their elected representatives and the skeptical snipers in the press. So while an internal debate about his personal appearances in television commercials seesawed unresolved (see Chapter 11), he asked Ron DeLuca of Kenyon & Eckhardt to write a series of full-page newspaper ads which appeared throughout the country over his signature.

Together the two men sweated over the texts. The wording was combative. No, the loan guarantee was not a giveaway and was not a precedent. No, Chrysler hadn't waited too long to build small cars. Yes, Chrysler management had become strong enough to turn the company around.

The grand-slam manifesto, baldly headlined "Would America Be Better Off Without Chrysler?," marshaled Iacocca's case with crisp persuasion, and the feedback on the unconventional series of ads was gratifying. Iacocca and his people heard that copies were being shown from office to office in Washington. Chrysler dealers around the country saw smiles for the first time in a long while.

Iacocca also learned how to organize Washington's toughest hired guns to strong-arm Congress directly. He obviously couldn't exert $1.5 billion worth of pressure in person. Professional muscle was needed, and Larsen recruited the best lobbyists to graze each side of the political aisle. Thomas Hale ("Tommy") Boggs's law firm fielded a dozen attorneys full-time. Boggs's ties to the Democrats were superb: His father had been House majority leader, and his mother inherited the seat. The other Chrysler lobbying arm, Bill Timmons's company, worked the Republicans; Timmons had been an aide to Presidents Nixon and Ford. More, two former Michigan representatives and one retired senator were put on the payroll to buttonhole their ex-colleagues and the influential UAW lobbying staff went to work on congressional liberals.

MAKING THE STEAMROLLER MOVE

Chrysler's home ground, Detroit, was not hard to mobilize. The company was the city's largest employer. Some 25,000 blacks worked there and would have great difficulty finding other jobs. A Chrysler bankruptcy would increase the city's unemployment rate, already chronically steep, by another 10 percent. Coleman Young, the black mayor, a onetime UAW organizer and one of President Jimmy Carter's first supporters, put his political clout behind Iacocca. He pulled key strings in the administration and spread word that 1 percent of *all* income of America's blacks derived from Chrysler.

Larsen knew that the company's urban grass roots carried weight. A leader in the Lutheran Church, he found time to preach a Sunday sermon at the city's biggest black church. "We had prayer meetings, bake sales, everything," he remembered. "Save Chrysler" petitions were circulated by many churches, and when a group of ministers delivered the signatures to Senator Riegle's office in Washington, they decided to remain in town and deployed for additional personal lobbying.

Chrysler and Dodge dealers all over the country were drummed into a massive lobbying army that fell upon Capitol Hill like paratroopers. These were hard people to ignore. Articulate, wealthy, active in community work, they were often heavy political campaign contributors. They tended to be Republicans and were therefore particularly effective with conservative legislators who were ideologically opposed to saving Chrysler.

Larsen, a onetime army intelligence officer, targeted the Iacocca shock troops for all-out assaults. Each morning the dealers descended from their 1,800 hotel rooms to be briefed in a ballroom on the latest tactical situation and to receive the day's assignments. Equipped with lists of "talking points" and tips on the dos and don'ts of congressional etiquette, the dealers knew precisely where to hit and how to slant their pitch.

Accustomed to the aggressiveness of pressure groups, the congressmen were nevertheless impressed. Some received twenty visits from as many dealers. "They're hunting us in packs," wailed one victim. And at night Larsen reassembled his men to receive target-by-target results and to collect congressional requests for information which he normally had ready by morning.

Each congressman was confronted not only by a generalized appeal for assistance but with hard data documenting his own district's economic benefits from its ties to Chrysler. Once again Iacocca's zeal for homework, preparation, precision salesmanship paid off. Computers broke down data on every dealership, supplier, and plant, district by congressional district; only 2 out of 535 lacked a Chrysler involvement. All others received printouts spelling out what jobs and sales would be wiped out locally by a Chrysler failure.

One congressman in Indiana learned that 436 companies in his district stood to lose $29.2 million in annual sales. These were economics lessons that congressmen understood.

Iacocca even converted his Italian heritage into an advantage. The House of Representatives had thirty-one members whose ancestry bound them together in an Italian-American Caucus. Iacocca walked into their meeting with the senior man, Congressman Peter Rodino, chairman of the House Judiciary Committee, who invited the Chrysler Chairman to give a sales talk. He did, and all but one member eventually voted for him.

"Screw the Republican or Democratic party lines," Iacocca told economist Robert Reich later. "They voted the Italian party. It was because I'm Italian, I guess. You used everything in the book. You pulled out all the stops. . . ."

TURNING THE PRESIDENT AROUND

Among the few outright volunteers in Iacocca's oddly assorted assault force was the hyperactive young Democratic congressman from Chrysler's home district, whom no ranking executive at the company had previously even known, the boyishly fluffy-haired, round-faced James ("Jim") Blanchard.* Having won in a primary without UAW support, he had clinched the general election with billboards announcing his phone number and the slogan "If I can help you let me know."

---

* Largely on the strength of his role in the Chrysler fight, Blanchard was elected governor of Michigan.

As the only Michigan member of the House Banking Committee, Blanchard now repeated the same offer to Chrysler management. Having at last been noticed by its strategists, he put his formidable supply of adrenaline behind the cause at key pressure points, especially the White House. Angered by the Carter administration bureaucracy's slow pace in committing itself to a loan guarantee—particularly Treasury Secretary Miller's lassitude—Blanchard decided on a dramatic maneuver to put the president on the spot.

The occasion was a Democratic gala dinner to solidify Carter's nomination for a second term. Detroit Mayor Young was seated on the dais next to the president.

"I charged through the doors of the Hyatt Regency like a bull at Pamplona and told every person I knew that the administration was flushing Detroit down the toilet and Carter didn't even know what was going on," Blanchard wrote later in the *Detroit Free Press*. "I told everyone what a bastard Miller was and pointed so he could see me."

Blanchard was causing the desired stir in the hall, but Mayor Young was beginning to wonder whether the young congressman was ruffling too many VIP feathers.

Blanchard remembered: "Coleman Young shot a glance at me that said, 'Cool your jets, squirt.' "

"These guys are going to kill us," Blanchard hissed at him. "They've stabbed us in the back!"

"He told me to keep my shirt on," Blanchard remembered, "and he'd see what he could do."

What the mayor did was turn to the president then and there and remind him of the city's immediate need in explicit street language. That did it. Immediately after the dinner the president called his domestic policy adviser and told him to meet at once with Secretary Miller. Within days Carter had approved the loan guarantee, and the House passed it by a vote of 271 to 136.

It happened just before Christmas 1978, on December 18, and only after the speaker of the House, rising to address his colleagues as "Tip O'Neill, the congressman," delivered a final extraordinary plea. Aware that many of the representatives were too young to remember the Depression, O'Neill evoked the picture of the unemployed of Boston standing in the morning chill, begging for jobs shoveling snow. Now almost 1 million Chrysler people were about to lose their jobs.

"That is how depressions start," the speaker warned.

For Iacocca it was an effective reminiscence coming at one of several climactic stages of his campaign. Other, narrower escapes from failure were facing him in the Senate.

TAMING THE SENATE

The Senate version of the loan guarantee bill called for a freeze on wages. Iacocca told his men in Washington he couldn't live with such a provision. It would keep him from attracting badly needed experienced executives and craftsmen. The key man was Indiana's Republican Senator Richard Lugar. Without his support five or six Republican votes would be lost. This was an emergency concerning a subject that the UAW lobbyists were best qualified to deal with.

The union had been lining up votes right along. It was difficult for liberal congressmen to turn the UAW down, in effect telling workers, "I won't vote to save your job." Dealing with Republicans like Lugar was more delicate for the labor people, yet by the day prior to the Senate vote Doug Fraser had sweet-talked Lugar around, and on the day itself the UAW chief was working two telephones in the office of his old friend Vice President Walter Mondale, directly off the Senate floor. While his chief lobbyist lined up senators on one phone, Fraser—he had earlier testified "brilliantly" in public, Iacocca said—cajoled other senators on the second line.

Vice President Mondale, ailing with the flu, was pressed to come to the Hill to preside over the Senate. Iacocca, at home in Bloomfield Hills, called Senator Charles ("Chuck") Percy of Illinois and, finally overcoming his shyness, Senator Dole. The president phoned a number of undecided senators. Gloria Steinem, the feminist activist and a UAW friend, called Oregon's Senator Bob Packwood. Union muscle was so totally mobilized that the Senate reception room seemed to overflow with labor lobbyists.

"It was like an American Labor Hall of Fame," marveled a Senate aide. "I would have believed it if [the late] Walter Reuther had been there."

The vote was 53 to 44, but the Senate version was harder on Chrysler than the bill passed by the House. The two measures would have to be reconciled in conference. Congress was rushing toward Christmas adjournment. Chrysler's latest projections showed it would run out of cash by mid-January.

Alerted to the danger of a delay in funding by Congress, the

Treasury panicked. Assistant Secretary Roger C. Altman phoned Larsen in alarm. News that Chrysler could collapse in January would send down its stock price. Altman would have to disclose this to the public. That could close down Iacocca's game.

"I called Lee and told him that the world would soon know that Chrysler was going to die in a few weeks because Roger Altman got scared by some lawyer," Larsen told Robert Reich in 1984. "Lee said, 'It can't happen or we're dead. Go stop him!' "

Larsen hurried to Altman's office, pushed past his secretary, and pleaded the case. His entreaties got nowhere. Whereupon he says he told Altman he would not leave, and he promised to "gun down" anyone trying to move out of the office with a press release.

No release was issued that day, and by the time word reached the public some days later Iacocca had squeezed sweet lemonade out of this lemony news by putting on one of his most agile press conference performances. He neatly turned the Treasury's alarm into further pressure upon Congress.

"The current softness in the economy and in the car market are eating a cash drain at Chrysler and interim funding will be necessary in January," he told reporters. "Only prompt action in the legislature will provide enough time to put in place a program of interim financing."

Meeting on December 20, the critical session of the Senate-House conference committee provided the Iacocca crew with a final *Perils of Pauline* cliff-hanger. Senator Proxmire, Chrysler's most determined opponent, arrived with a series of unexpected last-moment proposals and pushed his papers across the committee table at startled colleagues. The changes were technical restrictions, but Michigan's Senator Riegle recognized at once that they could have sabotaged Iacocca's efforts. Congressional courtesy evaporated.

"This is bullshit," Riegle yelled, red-faced with fury.

"It's not bullshit," yelled Proxmire.

Despite the inflamed atmosphere, cool Republican heads, prompted from the sidelines by Iacocca's Republican lobbyists, wheedled agreements out of the conference committee while noisy Christmas parties cranked up on Capitol Hill. Outside the committee room Larsen, holding a tattered piece of paper in his trembling hands, read Chrysler's message of thanks to reporters. The words had just been dictated to him by Iacocca, who was in New York attempting to quiet down the company's bankers. They were in an uproar.

TAMING THE BANKS

Chrysler's debts to banks and insurance companies totaled a staggering $4.75 billion, and these creditors cared little about Iacocca's talk of saving jobs. They didn't want to be sucked into the financial equivalent of Vietnam, a parallel that Peter Peterson of Lehman Brothers had suggested in his testimony before Congress. The moneymen wanted their dollars back.

Again Iacocca was careful not to overmanage. He had delegated most of the haggling with the politicians to Lars Larsen, who knew how to massage clamorous Washingtonians. It had worked. Now Iacocca would leave the bankers in the hands of his financial strategists Jerry Greenwald and Steve Miller.

Greenwald set up twenty-two task forces, and it took them nearly six months to forge a settlement. Three times they faced "D-D Days" ("Drop-Dead Days"), when all cash ran out. The first time they delayed paying suppliers. The second time they suspended payments to their Japanese creditors. The third time they persuaded the banks to waive their rights to Chrysler's Peugeot stock; Iacocca had pledged the shares to the French carmaker in exchange for a $100 million loan.

It was a bizarre period. One night the Chrysler men ordered sandwiches and found that the delicatessen would not make a delivery to the company without cash in advance. Another time Miller pulled out a toy pistol and threatened to blow his brains out in the middle of a difficult conference.

So many pieces had to fit into the puzzle that Iacocca wondered how the company could possibly emerge from the chaos as one enterprise. More than fifty law firms participated in the final negotiations. Chrysler's legal and finance bills came to $20 million. The financial advisers, Salomon Brothers, took a fee of $13,250,000.

By June 1, 1979, the most resistant remaining holdout was David W. Knapp, president of the American National Bank and Trust Company of Rockford, Illinois. Other banks were ready to settle for thirty cents on the dollar. Knapp wanted his entire debt of $65,000 repaid. One holdout might have encouraged more resisters. Steve Miller met with Knapp in the Rockford mayor's office, briefed reporters on the City Hall steps, and stayed on to watch citizens—many of them employees of a nearby Chrysler factory—withdraw deposits and picket the bank. Knapp surrendered.

The finale began at dusk on June 23 and unfolded like a Hollywood script. Greenwald was walking toward the principal lawyers' offices in the Westvāco Building on Park Avenue in New York City, where the final papers were being put together. He encountered Steve Miller, and together they watched fire trucks screech to a halt in front of a skyscraper some distance down the street. Black smoke puffed out of a high window.

"Can you imagine if that was our building?" asked Greenwald.

It *was* their building. The fire was a bad one, and the stakes were incalculable. Chrysler could absolutely not tolerate any delay in getting the deal signed. Greenwald and Miller were certain that a pact involving such a large number of diverse interests would not hold together. So at 2:00 A.M. Miller and some twenty fellow executives got permission to enter the thirty-second floor to evacuate the precious documents stored there.

The firemen were still at work. The smoke was so thick that the rescue party could not see all the way down the hall. Many of the documents were covered with brown soot. Without regard to their order, the executives stuffed the papers into mail carts, and around 2:30 in the morning they wheeled a dozen of the carts containing Chrysler's destiny down the middle of Park Avenue and into another law office at Citicorp Center.

There, ten hours later, about 100 people gathered in a conference room. Speakerphones linked them to offices from Washington to Paris. A lawyer called the roll: "U.S. Revolver Bank Group, are you ready?"

"Ready."

"European banks, are you ready?"

The calls went on and on.

"Japanese banks, are you ready?"

"Ready."

Any negative responses could have blown up Iacocca's house of cards.

The Canadian banks, the Peugeot people in France, and the Loan Guarantee Board representatives in Washington were heard to speak in hollow tones through speakerphones.

Steve Miller was the last to be called. He thought they'd never get to him, but after an eternity he heard the call: "Is Chrysler ready?"

Miller hesitated. Should he utter something grand for history? Then he said, "Aw, shucks, I guess so," thereby pronouncing a happy end to the year-long rescue drama starring Lido Anthony Iacocca, formerly of Allentown, Pennsylvania.

PERSONAL LOSSES, PERSONAL TRIUMPHS

The victory was an obviously personal one, and it aroused resentment that focused upon the single perquisite dearest to The Chairman's heart: his fleet of private Gulfstream jets hangared at the executive air terminal in Pontiac, not far from his home. Sometimes he used one of the planes to stop at a ball game—or his wife's hospital bed—in Florida. Or he'd schedule a quick visit with his mother in Allentown. His staff insisted that his air force conserved his time and nerves and made his presence quickly available wherever it was needed. No doubt it kept The Chairman functioning at peak speed and efficiency. But mostly, as with Henry Ford and the 727, the planes were an issue of rank, status, ego.

The government Loan Guarantee Board supervising the disbursement of federal money wanted to humble its haughty protégé. The government people flew commercial; Lee could fly commercial. "It was unseemly for the government to be subsidizing these traditional perks," Robert Reich was told by one of the bureaucrats. When Iacocca refused to sell the planes, the board leaked a nasty newspaper story about this unnecessary frill. The Chairman, furious, kept up his resistance.

"Iacocca thought this was really doing him in," Reich was told by Michael Driggs, who moved in as the Loan Guarantee Board's staff director when Ronald Reagan became president. "He came at us directly; he called congressmen; he even called the White House." Iacocca got nowhere, and his intense dislike of Donald Regan, then secretary of the treasury, is rooted in the airplane episode. It was Regan who insisted that the planes be sold, and they were.*

As soon as Chrysler recovered, Iacocca got his wings back by

---

*"That fucking Don Regan" (in Iacocca's phrase) was also the muscleman when the Reagan administration fired Iacocca from the Statute of Liberty Commission in 1985. Iacocca hates Regan almost as passionately as Henry Ford. "Don Regan shouldn't be president of the United States—and he is!" he told an interviewer in 1986. "Make no mistake of it. He is the president of the United States today! But people say, 'Nah, you're going too far.' Well, all right, go talk to them. See who runs things right now. See who gets the guys together on Nicaragua or Libya. Don Regan!" There is no record of Iacocca's language when he learned that Regan quit under fire because of his conduct in the Iran/contra affair.

---

simply buying the Gulfstream company for $242 million. In the Chrysler executive lunchroom The Chairman's imperial action brought cheers and some cattiness. "Lee wants to be sure nobody'll ever take his plane away from him again," said one of the Iacocca-lytes.

By then Chrysler and Iacocca were rich. Better, they were free. For in the summer of 1983, seven years ahead of time, Chrysler with one check paid its government loans back. The country was impressed. Iacocca basked. He announced the payback in an elaborate ceremony at the National Press Club, playing what he enjoyed best, the role of statesman, and sounding almost like Churchill fighting off the Nazis at the beaches.

"I think it shows that the system can work if everybody pulls together," he said. "We just got everyone working together. We cooperated; we fought for each other; we sacrificed equally. In a way it was social democracy at its best."

It was also Iacocca having a ball. By extraordinary coincidence, the date was July 13, precisely five years to the day of his firing by Henry Ford. Understandably he was gloating.

"The people in Washington have a lot of experience in handing out money," he lectured, "but not much in getting it back. So maybe the surgeon general should be standing by in case anyone faints when we hand over the check."

The early liquidation of the loan was indeed such a novel sensation that it took the federal authorities a month to figure out a way legally to accept Chrysler's last payment. Iacocca finally managed to present it to his bankers with another public relations stunt, a ceremony at which he posed, beaming and glass in hand, before a mammoth blowup of a check for $813,487,500.

His heady mood represented yet another comeback from a very personal disaster, for less than two months previously Mary had died, following a stroke, at the age of fifty-seven. Somehow she had maintained her spirit until near the end. Though she needed a wheelchair to move about, she went bowling and even square-dancing in it. "Mary was a real fighter," said her friend Ila Small. "She would have lived to a hundred and forty if her body had been as strong as her spirit."

Among the honorary pallbearers at her funeral was Maurice Duncan, the shoeshine man in the executive barbershop back at

Ford. Duncan did weekend yardwork for the Iacoccas, and he and Lee and Mary were friends.

Lee was devastated by Mary's death but also relieved that her many years of suffering had ended and that he no longer had to watch her decline.* At least she had lived to see their enemies get their comeuppance: Henry Ford, that bastard Henry, Senator Proxmire, and the rest of the princes, naysayers, and nitpickers. Most satisfying, perhaps, had been the fate of Lee's prime tormentor on Capitol Hill, Congressman Kelly, the hanging judge from Disney World. Kelly had been caught in the bribery schemes of the Abscam scandal and sent to prison.

And in Iacocca's latest comeback, the titanic triumph at Chrysler, the most dramatic element had, of course, been television.

---

*He often takes flowers to her grave in the cemetery near the family home. In 1985 he and his younger daughter, Lia, visited the site on July 16 at precisely 9:07 A.M., the moment of Lia's birth.

11.

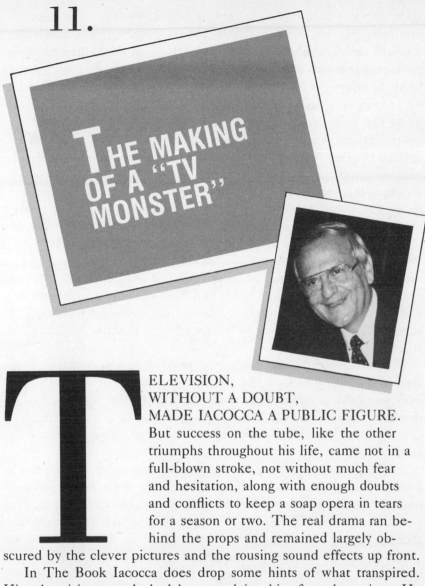

THE MAKING OF A "TV MONSTER"

TELEVISION, WITHOUT A DOUBT, MADE IACOCCA A PUBLIC FIGURE. But success on the tube, like the other triumphs throughout his life, came not in a full-blown stroke, not without much fear and hesitation, along with enough doubts and conflicts to keep a soap opera in tears for a season or two. The real drama ran behind the props and remained largely obscured by the clever pictures and the rousing sound effects up front.

In The Book Iacocca does drop some hints of what transpired. His advertising people had been nudging him for a long time: He should personally plant the Chrysler flag onto TV. Before he signed up Kenyon & Eckhardt, the people at Young & Rubicam, the old Chrysler agency, had begged him to step forward and do it. And when the seesaw loan guarantee fight inevitably became a spectacle on the nightly news, K & E turned on the pressure hard.

The media mavens put up persuasive arguments. The country was getting the idea, all too graphically, that Chrysler was about to go under. You had to be crazy to buy a car for which no parts or service might exist next year. Who but the chief surgeon, the boss himself, the personification of the struggle, might convince national audiences that he could breathe life into the seemingly terminal patient, to assure car buyers that he and his outfit would stick around?

Iacocca concedes that he fought fiercely against the idea of being cast in the would-be savior's role. The fact is that he kept up his resistance for more than a year, and in The Book he ticks off a barrage of reasons for his coyness. He goes on and on about it. Making commercials is slow, tedious labor, he complains ("like watching the grass grow"); he couldn't possibly spare the necessary time. The public might overreact to his personal appearance, interpret it as Chrysler's last stand, an act of ultimate desperation (which is exactly what it was), and be finally, irretrievably turned off.

Besides, very few chief executive officers were then appearing successfully on TV. Some who had tried had not done well, such as Frank Borman of Eastern Airlines and Frank Sellinger of Schlitz. Frank Perdue, the chicken king, was an outstanding exception, sure, but chickens couldn't be compared with a sacred American institution like automobiles.

And still more, Iacocca wondered whether he was being suckered into allowing himself to be set up as a scapegoat. The Chairman was a vulnerable asset after all. "If the ad fails, it's *his* ass on the line," Iacocca writes. That's if *the ad* fails. He does not speculate about the fate of his posterior (or his employability) if *the company* fails.

More pertinently, he offers a passing reference to deeper grounds for his recalcitrance: his shyness. "I'm really a very private person," he finally allows, well into the twenty-third chapter of The Book. He hated the idea of "some guy" barging in on him without warning "every five minutes" while he was trying to enjoy dinner in a restaurant. He *is* a very private person. Lee's teachers recognized it way back in Allentown, and all my Iacoccalytes insist that their hero has never fully overcome this handicap.

Unmentioned remains this further bit of historical background: Iacocca used to be a poor performer on television. His instructors at the Dale Carnegie course had helped him to live with his stage fright, but not enough to cope with the demands of TV.

"He was terrible," remembers Gene Bordinat, chief designer and a ranking vice president at Ford for more than twenty years. That memory reaches back to the 1960s, when Iacocca's flop could do little damage. He was introducing the Falcon and was seen only by dealers and employees on a closed circuit.

"He's just basically shy," says Lars Larsen, the former Chrysler public relations chief. "He hates to talk to people he's never met before. He has a hard time making small talk. At parties he'd stand in the corner. I'd bring people to him and he'd almost bow."

"He doesn't meet new people easily," remembers Don Frey of Bell & Howell. "He likes his own boys around him."

"Lee just isn't comfortable socially," says a long-retired Ford executive who worships Iacocca but demanded anonymity. He still fears his old boss and can't abide having his name attached to even a mildly negative observation.

Iacocca has developed private strategies for coping with his reserve. "We'd go into a meeting at the design center," recalls Bill Bourke, the former Ford number three man, "and he wouldn't say, 'Good morning, guys.' He'd single out an individual he knew, walk over to him, and say, 'Hello, George.' " The others in the room presumably would not mind being ignored by their supreme leader.

"The shyness is most noticeable at large gatherings," says Wes Small. "We'd be off on a ten-city series of dealer meetings, the 'America tour.' There'd be cocktails from six to eight P.M. in every city, and the invitations would go out in his name. After the first couple of cities he'd say, 'Do I really have to do this?' Well, he'd make a circle around the room, but then he'd take a fifteen- or twenty-minute rest. He needs a push. He's just like an actor. He has to psych himself up even though he has a common interest with the people in the room."

The Iacoccalytes recognize, of course, that shyness in a noisy, overtly open, and evidently gregarious public figure is something of a paradox. It begs for explanation, and they have talked and thought about this quite a lot. Some told me that they suspect Iacocca holds back with strangers because they represent the unknown. The unknown cannot be controlled as long as it remains unknown. And Iacocca, these thinkers suggest, absolutely needs control to perform at full capacity.

Gar Laux, the Iacocca sidekick who has served with The Chairman since they were both harangued by Charlie Beacham in the 1940s, offers more benign reasoning: "He's shy, yes. He feels like he has to *earn* his status. So he starts quietly. After a meeting he'd feel free. He'd let people know what he stood for." The audience had done its work.

Ah, the audience, he had to feel the audience. The audience is more than a sounding board. It is the ultimate control. At the least, interaction with it is vital to Iacocca. It functions as an enabling mechanism and opens him up. It always worked that way. Eddie Charles noticed the process in operation long ago in Allentown when little Lee blossomed under the applause in dancing class.

But what about the situation in television when the audience is enormous and is perhaps sensed but normally remains unseen, silent, unavailable to lend encouragement, perhaps adulation? How does a "very private" person become a TV star?

The answer is: slowly. Slowly, with enormous determination and self-discipline.

Unmentioned in The Book is the fact that Iacocca's first commercials for Chrysler were like the appearances for the Falcon in the 1960s, terrible.

The venture was launched while Iacocca was flying to New York with a media adviser of long standing, the gangling John J. Morrissey, head of the Kenyon & Eckhardt office. They were arguing back and forth about Iacocca's becoming Chrysler's pitchman on TV.

It all had been said before. Leo-Arthur Kelmenson, an Iacocca intimate and his oldest friend at K & E, had warned that Chrysler had very little credibility left with the consumer. Could Iacocca on his own hope to produce more? The Chrysler product was still nothing to rave about; the peppy K-cars were a year away. Lars Larsen, the PR chief, argued vehemently against using Iacocca on the tube; like many PR people, he feared the drawbacks of openness and favored a low-key strategy. Theatrics from the top man were likely to be counterproductive. Theatrics were undignified. They could backfire. Let the company get rebuilt first. Let there be credibility.

Larsen was also being protective of the boss. "We didn't want to get him hung out to dry," he says. And he brought to the deliberations the professional PR man's respect for and apprehension of the press. "Until they say you're well, you ain't well," he told Iacocca.

While the arguments had grown stale, Chrysler's situation was heating up. Cash, the lifeblood, had all but drained from the company. The federal loan was set, but the money had not yet been paid. The point of do or die was at hand. The assembly lines were churning out cars like crazy. They weren't moving. They absolutely *had* to be made to move.

In this context the argument between Iacocca and Morrissey on the New York plane took on the tone of crisis. Morrissey is a droll Irishman, but he was not being one bit funny that morning. He was pushing The Chairman as hard as he could, but Iacocca was preoccupied with the fragility of Chrysler.

The place might really go belly-up at any moment. The publicity would then descend in a howl of I-told-you-sos. Among the bodies in the wreckage would have to be that of The Chairman. No matter how hard a fight he would have put up, no matter how impossible the odds, it all would become academic. His reputation would be shot. Henry Ford would snicker. So would all the people he had fired and his many enemies in the industry. The hated *Wall Street Journal* would pat itself on its vast ego. It would be an ignominious defeat and very, very public.

Worst, worst by far, Iacocca would be cast in the one role which—as all his friends have learned—he can tolerate not at all. He would stand in the debris as a loser.

His ass, as he would put it himself, truly was on the line. If the game were to fold, his grandstanding on television would not have helped the company and would have blackened his personal future all the more. As a poker player he had to ask himself: What could be riskier? Was this the time to bluff and to act out that bluff on national television?

Iacocca was still not convinced he was going to make it. Sometimes, in fact, he was pretty sure that he would not, his public protestations notwithstanding. He could not let his doubts leak out, and they didn't. But he could play his cards close to the vest, and he did.

All the network talk shows were constantly pleading with him to appear. He was the classic embattled titan, a great story. The *Sixty Minutes* program offered him an entire hour to make his case. Again and again he rejected the opportunity.

As late as in January 1980 he turned down Phil Donahue. "Are you kidding?" he confided to a media friend. "I think we're going bankrupt, and I'm not going on."

Yet television did offer a possible way out of his predicament, a seductive lifeline, a proven, unexcelled sales tool. Ever since Iacocca had learned, a generation earlier, that American TV sets stayed turned on for an astounding average of 42.7 hours per week, he had been "awed" by the power of the medium and had committed millions and millions for commercials. At Ford he once purchased 100 percent of all time available for one season of NFL games. TV might be the escape hatch for his present extremity.

But the cards he was holding were not promising.

"I don't want to do it," he told Morrissey on the plane.

"That's not the question," Morrissey shot back. "You've *got* to do it."

And so the Iacocca television career began—with a whimper. By agreeing to go on the tube, he had not consented to star in a blitz of hype. The reality of his situation would have made any crowing sound ridiculous. He was still a prisoner of his situation. His release would come very slowly.

Seven years later I saw a film of all his commercials unroll in sequence at the K & E offices in New York. It showed a remarkable progression.

The first Iacocca spots cast him in the hated role of supplicant, an immobile talking head against a fragment of boring office background. The head was saying very little, and what it did say could hardly have been more defensive.

"Compare, that's all we're asking," intoned the head gravely. Beyond that plea he merely promised that Chrysler would fight on "against whatever odds."

Iacocca came on only fleetingly in this debut, making the curtain speech at the close of a routine pitch for car sales. And "curtain" was the best word to describe his appearance.

"He looked tired," says Leo-Arthur Kelmenson. "He was taking this terrible beating from the press, and all he could say is 'Trust me.' "

The ad people needed a specialist to make the most of Iacocca, and accident brought them a maven in the most relevant specialty, politics.

The expert was no less than Harry Treleaven, a pal of John Morrissey, who ran into him one morning in the lobby of the Pan Am Building when the morale of the ad makers had dropped to its lowest. Although his name was still not precisely a household word, Harry was a force in the media world. He had the touch for bringing out the television best in problematic public personalities, and there was a whole book to prove it: *The Selling of the President* by Joe McGinniss, a smash best-seller in which Harry was, well, the hero/villain. It was Treleaven with his trenchant memos who coached Richard M. Nixon as close to media swanhood as that grim performer would ever rise.

At the time liberals were scandalized by the revelations of McGinniss's hatchet job. But the book established Harry as a ranking political cosmetic surgeon. In 1966 he took George Bush into the streets and factories of Houston, had him take off his preppy coat, and made the future vice president the first Republican congressman ever elected in that Democratic stronghold.

Treleavan remembers his encounter with Morrissey in the Pan Am Building and how urgently the agency needed a second opinion on the Iacocca problem.

"They were unhappy with the commercials," he says. "They wanted me to take a look, so I went to K and E and looked at all the films for two or three days and gave them a report."

The ill-fated Sinatra commercial, in particular, saddened Harry. "They had their jackets buttoned, and both were a little overweight and looked uncomfortable." Harry winced as he recalled the filmed wreckage of that summit meeting.

The other commercials made him no happier.

"There was a lot of stiffness," he remembers, "and the environment was wrong. He was behind a desk, but you can put a man in the environment where he's most comfortable. I said, 'Get 'im the hell outta the office!"

The K & E people had been thinking along similar lines, and Morrissey was happy to see the politically seasoned Treleaven confirm his own diagnosis that the Iacocca problem was much like the manicuring of a candidate for public office. It had occurred to Morrissey that each sale of a Chrysler car was really a ballot cast for the picturesque Chairman.

"In a way, we were trying to get him elected," he remembers. "We wanted people to vote for him."

In 1980, with the government loan assured, K & E brought aboard an in-house creative executive with a record of bipartisan political media experience. Ken Duskin had polished commercials for the Republican Nelson Rockefeller as well as for the Democrat Hubert Humphrey, and the ideological undertones of the Iacocca account stirred his sense of civic duty.

"The one thing we tried to do is not make him sound like a car salesman," says the lugubrious Duskin, his double-breasted black suit fronting as assurance of corporate solidity while a huge bush of untamed dark hair promises artistic verve. "He wasn't just selling automobiles! He was keeping all those Chrysler people working and off the welfare rolls!"

When I talked to him six years later, Duskin still exuded ecstasy. He warmed again visibly to the excitement of the corporate turnaround that he had helped to engineer and the challenge posed by the personality whose leadership qualities he did his share to place in public view. "It's not every day you get to be part of history," he says with pride, ever careful to claim no undue credit for himself and the other technicians supporting the star from the wings.

"You don't manufacture something like this," says Duskin. "He had it in him. You *had* to believe the company would survive. He just doesn't look like a person who's going to be blown away. The worst you can do is make him look like an actor."

Right. Fortunately, Iacocca was able to *focus* like an actor. The K & E people had witnessed all along that their man possessed not merely the capacious memory common to many giants in politics and business; he could draw on truly extraordinary powers of *concentration*. They had watched him sitting silently through meetings lasting an hour or an hour and a half and then, without apparent effort, rapidly recapturing all essential points and shaping them into an action plan. He did it all without taking a note, and months later he could quote back long excerpts from statements made by others. Watching the Iacocca memory in operation was a marvelous show— like witnessing an intellectual marathon with nobody else in the running.

Duskin marveled at the same powers when he saw them in action during a twelve-hour marathon filming session at Chrysler's Jefferson assembly plant in Detroit. K & E had at last taken Iacocca out of his office and planted him into his home environment ("his candy story," said John Morrissey), and there Duskin marched his man, step by step, with hardly a hitch, through seven commercial scenes in a single tour de force.

Iacocca hated it. When he autographed a copy of his autobiography for Duskin, he expressed his gratitude "even though you created a TV monster."

A monster! The term comes up often with Iacocca. Sometimes television itself ("that cursed tube") is the monster. Sometimes he is himself the monster. He worries about it. He doesn't want people to think of him as an actor—like Reagan, of all the many people he holds in contempt. He doesn't want his commercials to be mistaken for the substance of his achievements. And he fears that when he dies—remember, death might strike anytime—people will remember him for his commercials more than anything else. That would be monstrous indeed.

And it *was* onerous labor, hateful, tedious beyond reckoning, the kind of footslogging that is a trial to the souls of professional actors and quickly becomes sheer hell for a notoriously impatient, authoritarian boss accustomed to command, not to being commanded. It is precision work regimented by scripts, prompters, stopwatches, floor diagrams, monitors, absolute conformity. The penalty for deviation is endless repetition. It feels like a life sentence. A wrong syllable, an awkward emphasis, three seconds too long or too short—everything requires retakes, more retakes.

Ronnie DeLuca of K & E was the ringmaster. He is a deceptively gnomish figure: short, gray, so fragile that you think he might break. He is a little stooped and so quiet. But he was the right fellow. He held Iacocca's respect. He had the smarts. They had worked in tandem on the signed Chrysler print ads, and DeLuca had made them work. He wasn't full of bullshit like other ad people everybody knows. He was Italian; he knew exactly how Italians speak with their hands, when a pointed finger looks right and when it looks phony. And he knew how to handle Lee when Lee was difficult, and Lee was always difficult, requiring infinite handling in the early days of making the commercials.

Not just difficult. Explosive. The stage directions blew his mind.

"Jesus Christ," he bellowed at DeLuca, "do I *have* to do this?"

DeLuca lowered his voice to a near whisper: "Lee, I think it'll help the company."

That would quiet the star down, but the next eruption was never far off.

"He's yelling and screaming at me," DeLuca recalls with the smallest of smiles. "He hated the script, he hated doing it, he *couldn't* do it!"

And so they did it and did it, and he kept up his complaining. His kids said he looked too fat on TV. The camera people were commanded to make certain that his nose wouldn't look too big. Then came the day in Los Angeles in 1980, when they had to make a mammoth commercial introducing the K-cars and Iacocca had to work on a Hollywood set for the first time. DeLuca was seriously worried. A Hollywood set is no place for an amateur, let alone a sensitive, essentially shy prima donna suddenly required to perform at something new, to *walk* for the first time, to march according to an intricate, confining, tightly prescribed pattern with his—as it turned out—slightly bowlegged gait.

It was like Iacocca's dance class back in Allentown all over again. The stage was full of *people*, human support, everybody was sure the K-cars were going to sell, Chrysler *was* coming back, and on the set they were tootling the "Yankee Doodle" music for the first time. Lee was feeling good, up; those legendary powers of concentration were set for "On!"

"Jesus, it was incredible," says DeLuca, still awed. "He was able to concentrate on the monitor and didn't flub a line."

What came through on the screen was authority personified, total control. DeLuca has seen it in Iacocca many times since then: "All he needs is a swagger stick, and he's Garibaldi, a general. When you put him onstage, he performs. All of a sudden he's a tiger waiting to strike. The television tube has a tendency to diminish most people. Others become overenlarged. They dominate it. It's what we call 'busting through the tube.'"

This is what I was seeing when I watched the entire inventory of commercials being played back on film at Kenyon & Eckhardt not long ago. Gradually Iacocca's painful defensiveness ("we're in business to stay") faded away. By 1981 the change of tone made you sit up. Here came the first scenes shot with factory backgrounds, manufacturing noise, moving parts, industrial power.

"No one can say our cars don't stack up," The Chairman was booming, and here was proof: He introduced the then-revolutionary guarantee for five years or 50,000 miles. How about that, Henry Ford and GM and *Wall Street Journal* and you other bad-mouthers, eh? Would they think he was crazy? To hell with them! The Chairman gave them their answer right on the air: "We're not foolish, we're confident!"

I was beginning to experience the commercials like an escalating suspense film. What were they going to try next? And indeed, there was a climax. It came orchestrated with pictures of men in white laboratory coats scurrying in the background, assembly lines cranking out cars, wheels whirring, lights flashing, sparks popping like firecrackers, and then, as the high point of this industrial Fourth of

July, The Chairman threw out the line that would become famous and widely parodied: "If you can find a better car—buy it!"

"That one was my own . . ." claims Iacocca in The Book.

Well, yes and no and not quite and maybe I'm quibbling.

Ron DeLuca remembers the meeting well. They were working on strategies to introduce the high-priced new Chrysler LeBaron. It looked like a difficult sell. Fresh ideas were needed. The Chairman felt frustrated.

"Hell," he exploded, "I don't know what the hell else I can put in those cars!" Pause. "Goddammit, if people don't want 'em, fuck 'em!"

DeLuca pounced: "Holy shit, it's right there! If they can find a better car, fuck 'em!"

Fantastic! This was true confidence. It only needed the tiniest bit of cleaning up.

It also marked the liftoff of an image-making campaign that hasn't ended yet. DeLuca was at the heart of it. "The process was carefully designed, brick by brick," he says. "Nobody, including our client, has ever had it explained to him. It was built on a series of plateaus related to real events."

The process didn't have to be explained to Iacocca, as DeLuca knows. Iacocca *was* the process.

"He recognizes what's important," the adman says. "We held a postmortem, and he said, 'What do you guys think is the most important thing that happened in the TV commercials?' He answered himself: 'That it made "Made in America" mean something again.' "

DeLuca says: "That posture set the stage for a lot of things that happened since."

The first thing to happen was a new identity for Chrysler that prompted the audience to associate the name with quality. "At Ford quality is Job One," the Ford commercials would echo, but that was much later. Iacocca had taken the popular pulse correctly once again. He had felt the patriotic beat and scooped the competition by making the trend his own.

"We were desperate to separate ourselves from GM and Ford," DeLuca explains. "We were saying, 'We're different from those bad guys. We are going to treat you better.' "

It was the Mustang revolution as it would be reborn again with the minivan:* Iacocca had brain-picked the ideas from others, thereby performing the job of an inspired executive; he packaged

*Which is manufactured in Canada.

them brilliantly, and pushed them hard. Now he had latched on to another bandwagon, the vehicle pioneered for the early eighties by Ronald Reagan.

"The two men epitomize the rebirth of patriotism and pride," says DeLuca. "But with a difference. With Reagan it was almost a naive belief. It was simple: His country *must* be right. Iacocca feels it necessary to *force* his belief." And if he makes a lot of deals with Japanese manufacturers, even markets their cars in the United States, so what? Reagan makes deals with the Japanese; they can't simply be told to get out of town.

The process of moving from plateau to plateau clicked almost too well. The cars were selling like crazy. Success was at hand. Watch out! Iacocca had banked heavily on audience sympathy for himself as a struggling boxer. "When you've been kicked in the head like we have . . ." was the way the theme was hammered by the commercials. Success made this appealing posture obsolete.

"We were working the underdog theme," remembers DeLuca. "Now that we're here we have to be very careful. He can puncture his own balloon."

Chrysler had become the fastest-growing car company. New routes had to be found to the next higher plateau. The suddenly looming Jolly Green Giant had to keep on looking jolly. Which is why billboards were calling new Chrysler cars "An American Adventure."

The strut. The Iacocca stride through the commercial scenes. What was all that movement *for*?

Russell Baker, the resident humorist/philosopher of the *New York Times*, was struck by the question and it worried him a little.

"Where is he headed in these incessant televised walks?" Baker wanted to know in one of his columns.

Maybe Iacocca was responding to an urgent call: "Lee, they need you up in radiators right away." But was the tube perhaps telling less than met the eye? Baker wondered: "Suppose he is just walking dynamically through the factory because a television genius said it would make a nice picture?"

That impression was what Iacocca absolutely had to squelch. If he had the admen make him into a television monster, well, it had to be. He would make up for it by becoming a man of letters as well.

12.

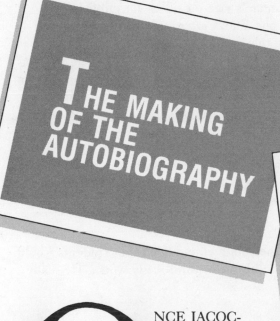

THE MAKING OF THE AUTOBIOGRAPHY

ONCE IACOCCA'S AUTOBIOGRAPHICAL EXTRAVAGANZA HAD SECURED A PLACE IN THE PUBLISHING HALL OF FAME, STUART APPLEBAUM WAS NATURALLY EAGER TO MAKE CERTAIN THAT HIS PERSONAL CONTRIBUTION AS RAINMAKER AND CHIEF STRATEGIST WOULD NOT SOMEHOW SUFFER NEGLECT. Besides, the invention of The Book made a great story, and Applebaum, a promotion man by profession—if not almost by religion—was congenitally crazy about a great story. Up to a point where corporate discretion took over.

It was the summer of 1981, he remembers, and Bantam Books, the world's leading producer of paperbacks, had just made a decision that rocked the parochial little universe where books are born and raised. Hardcover and softcover publishing—or, in trade parlance, "hard" and "soft"—had largely coexisted as separate jurisdictions. Now Bantam was knocking down this wall between church and state. It would publish both categories. The company needed only some blockbuster projects to get the fledgling hardcover line launched.

Enter Applebaum, Bantam's vice president for publicity.

"I was sitting around one Friday afternoon with our president, Alberto Vitale, discussing this hardcover venture we had just embarked upon," he reminisces. "It was a summer afternoon; nothing was going on. I observed that business books seemed to sell well in hardcover—this was even before *In Search of Excellence*—and Alberto said he had always admired the business philosophy of Lee Iacocca. So I said we should get him to write his autobiography. So we got an appointment to see him and flew to Detroit, joined by Jack Romanos [Bantam's sales chief], and as we walk in the door, Lee looks at us warily and announces that he doesn't want to write a book, he has no time to write a book, and what did we want to see him about anyway?"

Applebaum to the rescue.

"I said that I thought he could write a book that students would read to understand how the business world really works. He really responded to that. . . ."

By the time I came upon this version of history, I knew that it skipped over a number of essentials.* Iacocca's phenomenal name recognition, his overwhelming exposure on TV, accomplished at Chrysler's expense, not Bantam's, beckoned more seductively to the publisher than Iacocca's "business philosophy." Iacocca was an established national brand. Marketing his book would be like pushing McDonald's hamburgers without McDonald's advertising expenses. And to Iacocca, in turn, the chance to get even with Henry Ford publicly, magnified by Mary Iacocca's same yearning for vengeance, loomed larger than the wish to enlighten America's youth about the joys of business.

Hal Sperlich, Iacocca's rambunctious protégé and fellow refugee from Ford, had analyzed Lee's motivation shrewdly for an interviewer from the *Washington Post*. He said: "I think for a man as driven as he is to win [his firing] was unconscionable, which I'm sure caused the book to be written. . . ."

* For the original Applebaum scenario, see "The House of Hits" by Terri Minsky, *New York* magazine (May 5, 1986).

I could understand why Applebaum might consider it indelicate to talk about such truths, but I wondered why his version of history omitted the key creative ingredient that he had himself supplied to the book venture: the maneuver that first brought Bantam, the irresistible force, into the presence of Iacocca, the immovable object.

It hadn't been easy to forge that connection because Applebaum and his colleagues had been unable to make contact with the Chrysler Chairman by conventional means. Iacocca truly wasn't interested in publishers. His every day was still a titanic struggle. He had not quite yet turned Chrysler around. The ups and downs of his wife's health were agonizing. He was still grinding out his TV commercials. Publishers had been pursuing him since the Ford firing, but for the moment he was preoccupied with plenty of higher priorities.

And so Applebaum hit upon a slender but ingenious link to his target in Detroit. He remembered that Gio Hernandez, the barber who cut his hair at the Bergdorf Goodman department store on Fifth Avenue, was also Iacocca's barber. This was clever rainmaking because Gio, then fifty-five, was no ordinary cutter of ordinary hair. He cut the hair of power brokers, and through the only-in-America alchemy that makes fame contagious, Gio had become something of a power broker himself.

IACOCCA DOING HIS THING AS A TV PRO, HIS EARLY INHIBITIONS FORGOTTEN

He didn't seem the type. Once a radio journalist in Cuba, Gio fled to the United States in 1962, the year after the Bay of Pigs invasion. He learned the barber trade and gained a reputation for craftsmanship and congeniality. He clipped Vic Damone, who recommended him to Billy Fugazy, who handed him on to Iacocca back in the late 1960s.

Lee and Gio became friends, sharing occasional dinners and confidences and making a very odd couple. Gio's English was broken and heavily accented. He was smallish, downright wispy in appearance, and a bit shy. Holding his head slightly cocked, he had the face, the huge, dark eyes, and the ingratiating manner of a choirboy. But he had proved himself canny and discreet, he knew everybody and introduced everybody to everybody else—George Steinbrenner of the Yankees; Roone Arledge of ABC; the idol Robert Redford; Roy Cohn, the lawyer who had tormented Henry Ford; absolutely everybody—and he drew them together when their hair was down so they could pull each other's wires and make deals.

"Gio is secretly running New York," Arledge claimed with tongue in cheek. Not quite. No one could doubt, however, that Gio was highly regarded by the power elite and that he was fiercely loyal, loyal, loyal to his friends, his own little club, his adored clients.

So he was naturally sympathetic when his client Stuart Applebaum confessed, while in Gio's chair, that his client Iacocca was giving Bantam the runaround. "If you can get us an appointment, we'll pay you a good commission," so Gio recalls being told by the rainmaker from Bantam. Gio further remembers that Applebaum promised him he'd "make a lot of money." Applebaum has a different memory. He remembers no conversation about money until much later, when the book was the number one nonfiction bestseller. He also says that Gio, not Applebaum, brought up the irksome subject of compensation.

By then this variance of memories was financially weighty enough to wind up for resolution before the New York State Supreme Court. And while Gio was happy to talk about it, Applebaum definitely was not.

Back in the fall of 1981 and through the summer of 1982 it didn't look as if there were going to be any book to fight about. Gio remembers talking to Iacocca about Applebaum's request for an appointment on two or three occasions over a couple of months. He kept assuring Iacocca that Bantam was a worthy outfit. Iacocca wasn't interested. But eventually, when Gio pressed again and urged, "Lee, why don't you talk to these people? You've got nothing to lose!" Iacocca said, "All right, tell 'em to call me."

Whereupon, in early October 1981, the Bantam delegation consisting of Messrs. Vitale (who was born in Italy), Applebaum, and Romanos, calling themselves the "Gang of Three," were ushered into Iacocca's office at Chrysler and were indeed pelted with a barrage of reasons why Iacocca wanted nothing to do with writing a book. Indirectly, however, he offered the delegation an opening for further exploration when he said that Chrysler wasn't safe as yet, that the "story" wasn't finished.

The Bantam people argued that the story they wanted Iacocca to tell *was* complete. They explained that they didn't want a book about Chrysler in particular; they wanted the personal story of a business success, the saga of the Italian immigrant's boy who slugged his way to the top in the cutthroat automobile industry. And if he preferred not to include a lot of gossipy details about the Ford firing, they wouldn't "necessarily" be upset.

Iacocca became interested and began to ask questions. How much work would it really take to turn out an autobiography? How could he carve out time for it? Would he be expected to do the writing himself?

The Bantam people were smoothly reassuring. He would need to do no writing at all. They would find a compatible collaborator and bring him around for Iacocca's approval. This professional writer would do the real work. Iacocca would simply have to submit to perhaps thirty hours of taped interviews. The sessions would be set up to suit his convenience. "We'll work around your schedule," promised one of the Bantam delegates.

Iacocca asked to see a proposal in writing, which Bantam promptly furnished, and then a marathon of agonizing began. Iacocca couldn't be moved to make a decision. Meeting followed meeting. He might go for it. He might not. Finally, in August 1982, after a session in the Chrysler suite at the Waldorf Towers, Jack Romanos, the marketing man, remained behind after his colleagues left and moved in to close the sale.

"Look, Lee," he said, "you're a marketing guy. You know when the time is right to do something."

"You're right," said Iacocca. "Let's do it." And they shook hands.

A contract was drawn up, reportedly calling for an advance of

$150,000 against author royalties—an unspectacular but reasonable amount. Bantam would also pay the cost of the writer, and the publisher's candidate had been waiting in the wings for about a month. He was William Novak of Newton Center, Massachusetts, a total unknown. It turned out to be a masterstroke of casting.

Except for marriage, a literary collaboration calls for more adjustments by the partners than probably any other formal relationship. The relative trust between the parties, any inhibitions against a free give-and-take, the disparity between what each stands to gain from the project's success, the way their biorhythms affect their best working hours, even the partners' respective coffee drinking habits, anything and everything can have a bearing on the outcome.

Considerable intimacy tends to develop between literary partners. Their dealings usually must be unreservedly open if their book is to ring authentic. It's not easy to maintain distance between collaborators if they're working well. But the Iacocca/Novak team was a gross exception. Its intimacy rating was nil. In fact, if surface signs had counted, the coupling of these men should have produced a catastrophe.

Why the opposite result occurred isn't easily explained because some of the participants still treat the making of The Book like a National Security Council mission. The secrecy symptom in Iacocca enterprises had become familiar to me, and here it was again, the fear, the fear of Lee, fear that he might dislike some unknown nuance of something someone might say, that such a slip might be leaked to the public and make him spitting mad.

"With Lee we tend to keep our conversations rather private," says Stuart Applebaum, curbing his promoter's instinct to gab.

"I'm not suing, my *lawyer* is suing," Gio Hernandez, the barber, told me. Panic-stricken, he was trying to put distance between his peaceful self and combative lawyers who are in business to foment trouble. Gio didn't want to be seen rocking Iacocca's boat.

"My job is behind the scenes, I can't talk about my writers," says Nessa Rapoport, the Bantam editor who recruited Bill Novak after numerous ruminative conferences between the ranking generals of the publishing house had reconnoitered the scene for promising recruits.

Their thinking was big, their budget modest. The CEO as cult hero had not yet arrived. Iacocca's reputation was still building. Nobody knew how much personal or other inside information this untried author might commit to paper. The longed-for blockbuster was a possibility, certainly, but it was not yet in sight. With a $150,000 investment on the line, Bantam declined to splurge on Hemingway-sized writing fees.

For a while authors with box-office names were nevertheless bandied about. One could dream. Among the five writers who were discussed was Gay Talese, son of Italian immigrants, friend of Iacocca, a brilliant and best-selling writer. But no, his ego was too vast and his price would be much too high. The Bantam high command also wanted no one from the fraternity of Detroit auto writers. Too parochial. They did want someone whose style would capture the distinctively colorful voice and manner of the Chrysler Chairman.

But the budget, the infernal budget; it dimmed the yearnings of the Bantam strategists. They thought they could afford a fee of $40,000 plus expenses but with no sharing of royalties. This was very small potatoes. In the lush 1980s, experienced writers were loaded up with projects of their own. If he'd consent to a collaboration of any kind at all, what respectable writer still wanted to immerse himself in a demanding project without participating in future earnings, especially when the start-up fee wasn't munificent?

And so Bantam's roving corporate eye fell upon Bill Novak.

Bill who?

"Why the hell did they call Bill Novak?" I was asked by Novak years afterward. He shrugged an appealing little shrug. He still could not fully explain why destiny had smiled upon him, Novak, of all the writers in the Western world.

Mostly it was because of Nessa Rapoport, who at the age of twenty-eight was a very precocious senior editor. She was a published novelist, a recent émigré from Canada. Having been signed on by Bantam after she had languished in a series of basement-level editorial jobs, she had proved herself a tactful and resourceful asset as the editor of former President Jimmy Carter's memoirs, another start-up project of the new hardcover line.

Rapoport not only knew Novak, she practically grew up with him in Forest Hill, the predominantly Jewish suburb of Toronto. They had been acquainted in high school, and when Bill became editor of *Réponse*, a Jewish quarterly, Nessa had contributed some reviews and poetry. They moved in the same circle of young Jewish intellectuals and kept in touch after both moved to the United States.

The notion of setting Novak adrift in Iacocca's lion's den was a riverboat gamble. Would the great carnivore eat young Bill alive? Novak was thirty-four and looked even younger with his tousled dark brown hair, positively boyish. He was mild of manner, almost meek, an egghead with not a smattering of interest in any business, let alone the automobile free-for-all in Detroit. He was writing books, but not biographies, and had never been tested in the crucible of a collaboration relationship.

His literary interests might have set Iacocca's eyes rolling in boredom. Bill had written about marijuana as a life-style. He had coedited a marvelous anthology, *The Big Book of Jewish Humor*. And he had written a well-researched romp of popular sociology, *The Great American Man Shortage*, which had earned respectful reviews, had had almost no hardcover sales, but had been bought by Bantam for paperback publication at the modest price of $35,000.

Still, Rapoport recognized relevant assets in her childhood chum from Forest Hill. He was diplomatic, extremely bright, sensitive, well organized, hardworking, a fast man in his head and on the typewriter. Two of his books had required extensive interviewing— the work on marijuana and the one on the shortage of males—and Nessa could detect in these efforts that Bill knew how to capture voices. He had an ear for the tone and essence of his interviewees and knew how to convey them on paper.

Another thing: He was available, although Rapoport did not then know how extremely available Novak was at the time.

Bill was reassessing his career during the summer of 1982. He was not a failure; but he had become a husband with a son, and while his wife, Linda, was running a dating service for Jewish singles, the couple still wasn't earning quite enough to maintain a family. Bill was thinking of transferring his writing talent to a public relations job with some safe corporation when Nessa Rapoport phoned him in his Newton Centre suburb outside Boston.

"Bill, would you be interested in a collaboration?"

Novak was floored and thrilled. No editor had ever called him before with any sort of offer. Yes, yes, yes, he was interested.

"I can't tell you who it is," said the discreet Ms. Rapoport. "We haven't signed him up yet. He's a prominent businessman."

Novak thought that it absolutely *had* to be Armand Hammer, the oil supertycoon, but Bill is also terribly discreet and refrained from sharing this speculation.

Some weeks later Rapoport phoned again.

"You can't tell a soul," she cautioned, "but it's Lee Iacocca."

Novak felt somewhat let down. "I knew he was some guy on TV," he recalled much later, but Iacocca surely wasn't as fascinating as Armand Hammer with his global political friendships, his billionaire life-style, and his mammoth art collections. Still Novak needed work, and when he said yes, he thought, "You can always say no later." Whereupon Ms. Rapoport asked him to compose a detailed letter so she could show her bosses what Bill thought the book would be about.

Novak took himself to the Newton Public Library, where, he wisecracks, he "found out how to spell Iacocca." He also dug out some magazine articles about his man and worked up a five-page letter/outline concentrating on the drama of the Ford firing and the making of the Mustang. "I spent a week on the letter," he recalled. "It was an employment document."

The Bantam commanders were impressed. So was Iacocca. The project kept being wrapped in secrecy, so Novak was never informed that he had become the only candidate to be presented to the big by-line from Detroit.

The first encounter took place in the Chrysler suite of the Waldorf Towers, with Rapoport and Romanos also present, in August 1982. Bill was nervous. "I thought I might not know what the hell he was talking about," he remembers. Going up in the elevator, he wondered whether to address The Chairman by his last or his first name. He figured he'd certainly call him "Lee" eventually, and since a switch might sound awkward, he'd use the first name from the start.

The conference had not yet lasted five minutes when Iacocca demanded, "So, Bill, how would you organize the book?"

Novak had no idea how the book should best be organized, so he responded with an intricate Jewish folktale about a traveler through the woods. He comes across an archer who has been shooting arrows into targets on trees. The marksman is evidently a terrific shot because there are lots of holes in and near the various bull's-eyes. Well, as Novak's story spun on, it turned out that the marksman has actually been shooting arrows at blank trees and has only then drawn targets around his hits.

"That's the way I work," Novak told Iacocca. "First you have to shoot the arrows in."

If Iacocca was nonplussed by this schmoozing detour, he hid it well, although the story clearly did not enchant him. "He didn't break into applause," says Novak. Nevertheless, The Chairman indicated his approval of the writer by pushing on to a discussion of how they'd work together. He'd obviously grown to trust the publishing judgment of the Bantam people. Moreover, once Novak began his many short visits in Detroit, it quickly became apparent that Iacocca had firm views about the way his opus should be organized.

It was his own superb idea, for example, to start The Book right out, bang, bang, with his getting fired from Ford. And while Novak feels it would be indiscreet for him to discuss it, other sources made it clear that the opportunity to spit at Ford's eye (and elsewhere) was indeed the most appealing motivation that made Iacocca put up with the tedium of producing the memoirs. I was informed that the villainies of Henry Ford came up at every one of the meetings that Iacocca held with Novak over a stretch of nearly two years. And always vehemently so.

Perhaps Iacocca's thirst for revenge was the *only* force that kept him going, for he made it painfully public that he regarded the book project as a dreadful pain in the posterior, an unwelcome diversion from his task of nursing Chrysler to health.

"I need a book like I need a hole in the head," he told some newsmen, making Novak feel even worse than Iacocca was making him feel anyway. Worse and smaller.

"Lee was not a barrel of fun," Novak recalls, and the difficulty of gaining physical access to his coauthor turned into a frustrating tug-of-war. "I had fantasies of living in his house for weekends," Novak says. "Would I have to go duck hunting and go through other things I didn't want to do?"

Such familiarities from Iacocca would have suggested concessions of intimacy, and intimacy turned out to be no cause for Novak's concern. The interviews never lasted for more than a couple of hours at most. All took place between 9:00 A.M. and 5:00 P.M., always between Mondays and Fridays. All broke up at prescheduled times; none was open-ended. Iacocca invariably wore coat and tie, and so, in response, did Novak. Bill was never asked to Iacocca's home. He never met, much less interviewed, his coauthor's wife or mother or sister, although Iacocca did make friends and associates available.

Novak had eagerly anticipated interviews with family members to flesh out his narrative. The possibility of such meetings was often discussed. Iacocca said he would arrange them. Yet somehow they never happened.

A great many meetings did take place between the collaborators, some of them aboard the Chrysler corporate jet, but all added up to no more than forty-eight hours of cool togetherness, perhaps only forty. The secretive Bantams never told Novak that they had enticed Iacocca into the project by promising him that thirty hours spent with a writer would be ample.

"I felt like I wasn't being taken seriously," Novak recalls. "I was very distressed. I was bitter. I felt the book was being sabotaged."

And yet he lived with his ignominy without losing his patience or temper, surprised and gratified that Iacocca never once raised his voice either. On only one occasion did The Chairman return some manuscript pages to his writer with the comment "Bill, this stinks." On reflection, Bill agreed.

Both men demonstrated commendable self-discipline and a nice sense of the role each was playing for the house of Bantam. Iacocca was hired to play Iacocca. Novak was hired to capture this character doing his act. Both did their stuff, no more, no less. But it was unquestionably an act.

"This wasn't journalism," Novak explained. "It was helping a man tell his story the way he saw it. I was the chauffeur. I was taking him where he wanted to go."

Where Iacocca wanted to wind up was as the author of a *business* book, nothing too searching, too personal. Novak's instructions were explicit on this point, and so he learned to cope with unspoken restraints. "It was clear he was drawing some line for how personal this was going to be," the writer said about his partner. That is why Bill steered away whenever the taped talk threatened to veer too far into the preserve of Iacocca's private life. Only once did Lee feel compelled to spell out limits and say, "I don't want to go into that."

Thus fenced off, Novak refused to become distraught over his lack of access to Iacocca's private papers. Bill did not know—as I told him I'd heard from Bill Fugazy and others—that his coauthor was hoarding "boxes and boxes" of mostly handwritten notes scribbled to himself, records wherein he kept track of important conversations, controversies, crucial encounters. The sharp-eared Novak did pick up that some papers existed in the off-limits Iacocca home in Bloomfield Hills; but he did not guess at the scope of the hoard and he was treated to but one delicious sample.

For one of their taping sessions Iacocca brought along a hand-scrawled memo he had composed following a one-on-one encounter at which Cristina Ford unpacked private morsels about her husband, Henry, whom she was then divorcing. So much for Iacocca's secret pumpkin papers in the making of The Book.

Withal Novak felt he should be grateful. Certainly Iacocca didn't waste time. Small talk between the coauthors typically lasted less than thirty seconds at the opening of a session. Then Lee would ask, "What are we doing today, Bill?" Whereupon Novak would pull out a list of queries he had prepared—never realizing that lists were what Iacocca also lived by.

At which point Iacocca was off, pithily unloading story after story, dialogue, atmosphere, drama, almost never repeating himself, month after month, his memory clicking away, unreeling "The Portable Iacocca," the saga of the survival of the fittest and the loudest, elemental experiences that no inhibitions could dilute by much.

Bitter or not, frustrated or not, Novak knew he should be pleased by this outpouring, and he was. "Every time I left I had good stuff on that tape," he recalled, still grinning years later at the richness of his haul.

His respect for Iacocca grew as their work progressed. Here was this fantastically busy man managing to get his autobiography written during snatches of his business hours, with never a phone interruption except for an occasional call from his family on his private line. This was a truly organized man, a man of action, putting out right in front of Bill's eyes. Sure, it was a performance, but a damned persuasive one. One could benefit from watching it, and Novak did.

"I wasn't nearly as aggressive as I am now," he says. "I was definitely influenced by Iacocca." Here was someone else for whom Iacocca became a learning experience.

Perhaps it was Novak's respect for his subject that made him prettify his man, thereby, paradoxically, causing a near shipwreck in the summer of 1983.

Bill submitted ten of his chapters to his employer, Bantam. Without Iacocca's ever having seen the pages, Bantam turned them down flatly as being too sanitized. "Unacceptable," judged the gentle Nessa Rapoport. The Bantam high command voted that the chapters were "too well written." They "didn't sound like Iacocca."

Rapoport instructed Bill: "Go back to the transcripts, make it sound more like conversation."

Devastated, Novak undertook months of rewriting. Painstakingly he roughed up his polished prose. Having removed "shit" and "fuck" and other Detroit pleasantries from the transcripts dozens of times, he now put them back into the manuscript. Let Iacocca sound like Iacocca.

In the spring of 1984, almost a year after Novak was supposed to have been allowed to turn to other work, the sensitive manuscript—Bantam kept it in a safe—entered the obstacle course of editing. Iacocca took the pages to a Long Island hideout for four days and worked hard over them, adding numerous punch lines and making hundreds of small changes which Novak admired almost without exception. Iacocca was handy with words, no question.

Some policy matters remained to be negotiated, and these were less easily settled. Meetings with Iacocca were convened by Bantam. The quota of recently inserted four-letter words was reconsidered at the highest executive level. The Bantam people thought there now were too many of them, so most were removed again. Novak had begun to feel possessive about these informalities and fought to retain at least one "fuck." He won. The expletive stayed in place within the account of the accusations Iacocca hurled at Henry Ford during the session of his decapitation.

Iacocca was less than delighted with Novak's chapter on automobile safety. He just didn't feel comfortable with it, tame as it was. At one of the meetings with the Bantams it was all but decided to junk the chapter altogether. Novak, his liberal consumerist passions aroused, objected. Again he won, this time for a good cause. Bill felt that he had at least made a strong case for seat belts—basic but not without importance. The chapter stayed in the book.

"Iacocca could have overridden me, but he didn't," the writer reminisced. "I'm proud of that."

Iacocca was himself overridden about a number of passages involving his favorite subject, Henry Ford. Novak won't talk about it, but I learned that the Bantam editorial and sales people objected to a number of Henry stories on grounds of good taste. Also, the lawyers contributed some clucks of caution even though the authenticity of the anecdotes was not in question and Henry, being a very public figure, could be libeled only if he could prove that Iacocca had treated the truth with "reckless disregard."

By this time Ben Bidwell, the Chrysler vice chairman, had read portions of the manuscript and advised Iacocca that he found their publication impolitic. Billy Fugazy had implored his pal to tone down his treatment of Ford, Fugazy's own fiercest enemy. Billy told Lee: "Hey, you made it! He's nothing today. Why dignify him with this? Just ignore him!"

And so Iacocca did not bristle when it was decided to blue-pencil two explicit sexual vignettes starring Henry Ford.

Having massaged the manuscript into the desired contours, the Bantam command felt rather certain that it had produced a winner after all. The text sounded like vintage Iacocca, and in the three years since its genesis the status of its hero had gratifyingly ripened to assume giant proportions. "He turned the faceless CEO into a cult figure," said Thomas J. Peters, the management consultant who coauthored *In Search of Excellence.*

The Bantam strategists projected a sale of 500,000 copies, a handsome figure, and while they did not pay Novak what Bill's agent had asked, which had been $65,000 plus 20 percent of Iacocca's income from The Book, they had upped their projected writer's fee from $40,000 to $45,000 ("Take it or leave it," Novak was told. And: "It's only a one-year project.") Bantam further offered a $10,000 bonus payable after a hardcover sale of 100,000 copies.

When *Iacocca: An Autobiography* finally landed in the stores in September 1984, Novak's travail paid off not only very big but with totally unexpected suddenness. It sold like toasted bagels, a truly hot book. Bill's bonus became payable instantly. The day after Bantam gave a sumptuous publication party at New York's Parker Meridien Hotel in October, Louis Wolfe, the company's chairman, presented Novak with a voluntary additional bonus of $10,000. And when the millionth copy was sold around Christmas, the ecstatic publishers handed him a further gift of $15,000.

This was also the juncture when Iacocca, his marketing nostrils aquiver, told his Bantam guys that he saw a "herd effect" in motion. Hundreds of thousands of copies of his book had to be lying unopened under the nation's Christmas trees. After the holidays further word-of-mouth publicity was sure to be placed in circulation by these new readers. Was Bantam prepared to unleash a second-phase push in the new year? The publishers said they were ready, and they did keep up their sales push and churned out ever new printings.

None of which helped Novak's finances. While his total take of $80,000 represented more than food stamp money, he understandably measured his earnings against the might-have-been. Some collaborators pocket 50 percent of a principal author's proceeds. As *Iacocca: An Autobiography* kept riding in the saddle of best-seller lists throughout the world, Novak kept calculating and calculating, finally computing that Iacocca might be wallowing in more than $12 million, eventually perhaps as much as $15 million from The Book.

The fact that Lee had decided to give all this income to diabetes research, in honor of his late wife, softened Bill's disgust only a little. His soul was nagged by the knowledge that he was missing out on millions of dollars that he could have earned, should have earned, had in fact earned! Even worse than this injury was the insult that everyone Bill met was convinced he had struck it as rich as the world's luckiest lottery winner when actually he had labored for two years at $40,000 a year.

"It's not easy to be a flat-fee author," he allowed. "It was the hardest thing I ever had to deal with."

And then came the distasteful fade-out: In the end his hero Iacocca disappointed him painfully. Again, Novak himself is mum on the subject, but a trustworthy source told me that Bill wrote Lee a pleading letter after the sale of the millionth *Iacocca* was punched up at the cash register.

Bill made no demands. Indeed, he wrote that he knew he had no formal right to make even a gentle request; he recognized that his deal was with Bantam, not with Iacocca. Still, the performance of The Book so extravagantly exceeded everyone's most outlandish dreams that Bill felt, in net effect, unfairly treated. He requested that at least a percentage of the upcoming paperback royalties be allocated to him, and sent off his appeal by Express Mail.

Iacocca never replied. He had no further need for his literary chauffeur.

Unfairly treated! The identical sentiment was plaguing Gio Hernandez, the barber. For three years he had been anticipating that "lot of money" he was going to make for brokering the book deal to begin with. Instead, he was reaping pleasant publicity for himself and for his own posh shop, which he had meanwhile opened in the

Pierre Hotel. And he was having fun. He basked as an honored guest at The Book's coming-out party in the Parker Meridien. His friendship with Iacocca made good copy for the gossip columnists—a king-and-commoner story.

"He was a way to get publicity for the book," says Jack Romanos, the Bantam marketing man. "We started to promote that. It was a nice item. The guy stayed with us as part of the story."

That was fine with Gio except that he was still waiting for his money. As the Parker Meridien party drew to its end, he took aside Louis Wolfe, the Bantam chairman, and said that now, with the approach of Hanukkah, might be an appropriate time for the publisher to let go of the money that Gio said he had been promised by Stuart Applebaum, the promoter, so long ago.

Wolfe said he'd see what he could do. The next day he summoned a meeting of his executives to deliberate the issue, whereupon Applebaum was dispatched to Gio's shop with a check for $5,000. "We decided that this amount was a nice token," Wolfe told me. "It was a finder's fee."

Gio did not think it was nice at all. He showed the check to his client Roy Cohn, the legal tiger, and the tiger growled. They agreed that the check was an insult and returned it. Cohn said it was no better than a tip for a haircut. He thought that $300,000 or perhaps $400,000 would constitute more appropriate compensation and wrote Bantam a nasty letter demanding that it do right by everybody's barber. When this produced nothing, Cohn upped the ante and, on June 19, 1985, filed suit for 10 percent of Iacocca's take, the normal commission of an agent.

The suit charged that Applebaum had in effect entered into a contract with Gio and that a breach of that contract had occurred. Moreover, Cohn, who died in 1986, charged Bantam with fraud. "In truth and fact," said the court papers, "the defendant [Bantam] did not intend to pay the plaintiff [Gio] the aforesaid consideration as Applebaum had promised, and made said false statements for the sole purpose of inducing the plaintiff to use his good will and friendship with Iacocca to assist the defendant to obtain the rights to publish Iacocca's autobiography."

In its formal response, dated July 24, 1985, Bantam admitted nothing about any promised compensation. It merely confirmed that Applebaum had asked Gio "to tell Iacocca that Bantam would like to meet with him to discuss his autobiography."

Which is where the controversy still remained frozen in early 1987, Gio having lost the $5,000 volunteered by Bantam, plus, presumably, legal expenses. The barber wouldn't tell me whether he'd discussed his hard luck with his friend and client Lee. And Applebaum, the rainmaker, would barely acknowledge ever having had his hair cut by anyone named Gio.

While fame was thus a fleeting thing for the barber, Bill Novak did much better. For him the Iacocca caper turned into a rewarding investment. On the strength of his virtuoso strumming at the typewriter he was hired as the Boswell for the whorehouse memoirs of Sydney Biddle Barrows, the "Mayflower Madam," which also became a best-seller. From this libidinous chore he advanced next to perform an autobiographical dance number of Capitol Hill, the rollicking memoirs of another great character, House Speaker Tip O'Neill. Most recently Novak worked on Natan Sharansky's own story for Random House.

Six years after Nessa Rapoport had intervened in his career, Bill still looked like a graduate student and still made his living as a hired gun, but he no longer toiled for a flat fee. Without a boost from Iacocca he might have vanished into the ranks of anonymous writers about business who grind out dull press releases for dull corporations. Iacocca saved him.

The immensity of The Book's success made it the subject of innumerable analyses by academics and experts in publishing, in automobiles, and in management. Iacocca's standing as a fixture in the national psyche; the public's readiness to admire a businessman for a change and hold him up as a role model to the young; the intrinsic drama of the Iacocca life; Novak's fine-tuned ear for his man's personality—all these elements helped to fertilize The Book's runaway sales chart.

Something more was at work. Pronouncing benediction on his own greatest story, Stuart Applebaum told me that The Book is the next best thing to knowing the admired author in person, to having him visit the reader's home. Which begs the question of why readers would be eager for such a visit. What do they feel links them with Lido Anthony Iacocca, the tycoon?

Iacocca himself divined the answer.

"They identify with a piece of the book they want to identify with," he has said, "such as life is full of adversity, but don't let it knock your socks off, okay? Keep your feet on the ground, grit your teeth, move along and in this great country you'll have a second life.

"It's adversity. They want to talk to someone who suffered a little. . . . They want to hear that you had a tough time and how you weathered the storm. . . ."

In his mind Iacocca hears people saying: " 'Look, he was on top of the world and he got fired, too. He came back, so you can come back.' I betcha that has been repeated 80,000 times at breakfast tables."

The breakfast tables where talk of The Book was least admiring were in the homes of some executives, the very business audience Iacocca had been hoping to influence. Some businessmen used the autobiography as a cookbook with recipes for success, but some reviewers for the business media disliked its inadequate attention to Iacocca's ruthlessness; his failure to issue a personal apology for the Pinto and other mishaps; his myopic inability to see himself in any but the most loving light; his touching belief in his uniqueness.

"Lee is good, but Lee is not the only guy that's good," Malcolm S. Salter, a professor at the Harvard School of Business, told the *New York Times*.

"Iacocca is on a roll," said David E. Cole, the automotive expert at the University of Michigan. "And when a guy is on a roll, sometimes he can believe things that may or may not be true. He may be thinking of himself in the same breath as God."

This would not be too bizarre a case of mistaken identity because publishing people kept pointing out that the sales of *Iacocca* were rivaling those of the Bible. Iacocca could shrug off elitists like George Will, the conservative columnist, who considered The Book primitive and dismissed it as "breathtakingly awful." But Lee was taken aback by the criticism from his own constituency, and he turned defensive.

"Maybe I shouldn't have written some of those things," he told *Time* magazine.

His contrition was brief. What the hell, he had his rights. "I took a lot of shots from critics in the business press who saw [The Book] in its narrowest view, that I was fired and had to get that off my chest. I wrote my life as I saw it. It was my catharsis."

Bill Novak had not seen this statement when I read it to him. "Catharsis?" he asked. "I'm surprised he put it that way."

That was another thing about Lee. He could always surprise you. There always seemed to be more insight—and greater emotional depth—to him than was apparent.

LIDO ANTHONY IACOCCA: MAN OF MANY FACES

YESTERDAY: CLAWING HIS WAY UP THE CORPORATE LADDER AT FORD MOTOR COMPANY

THE MANY
MOODS
OF . . .

TODAY:
PERSUASIVE,
PUSHY, PENSIVE,
BENIGN, AND
USUALLY TALKING

THE
EARLY
YEARS

COMBATIVE EVEN
AT THE AGE OF
FIVE

THE PARENTS:
NICOLA ("NICK")
AND ANTOINETTE
IACOCCA JUST
AFTER THEIR
MARRIAGE IN 1923

A STAR IS BORN: LIDO IACOCCA AS "KING OF THE MAY" (SITTING ALONE AT LEFT CENTER) IN GRAMMAR SCHOOL, ALLENTOWN, PENNSYLVANIA. THAT'S THE "QUEEN OF THE MAY" IN THE CENTER, OF COURSE

LIDO AT AGE TEN:
PAPA NICK HAS A
FIRM GRIP AROUND
HIS BOY'S WAIST

AFTER LONG SIEGE OF RHEUMATIC FEVER, LIDO IACOCCA, LOOKING FRAGILE (EXTREME RIGHT), WAS BARRED FROM ACTIVE ATHLETICS AND BECAME BUSINESS MANAGER OF SWIMMING TEAM

SOME OF HIS HIGH SCHOOL'S BEST AND BRIGHTEST JOINED THE OROTAN DEBATING SOCIETY: IACOCCA IS IN FRONT ROW, THIRD FROM RIGHT; HIS FRIEND JIM LEIBY SITS SECOND FROM LEFT. RICHARD SNELLING, WHO BECAME GOVERNOR OF VERMONT, IS STANDING THIRD FROM RIGHT

·comus·

HUNTER, JOHN   "Johnnie"

General

"Better than gold is a thinking mind"

John's record and personality need no apology. While attaining satisfactory records, he has also been a member of the band and the German club. He hunts, bowls, plays baseball, football, basketball, and is a sea scout. His ambition is to work for the Navy after a training at the United States Naval Academy.

Band 2, 3; German Club 4; Track 4

HUNTER, THELMA MARIE   "Toot"

General

"Stop, look, and listen! You might miss something"

Thelma's sunny smile and disposition will be a tonic to her patients next year. Her pet delight is to have people confide in her, and she returns their confidence with sincere understanding. She likes modern music, is an ardent collector of "in-the-groove" records, and likes nothing better than to "jive" out a hot jitterbug number. She has a way of saying things backwards that would confuse even the experts. Her latest interest is learning to drive her Dad's car, and when she gets out on the road, look out, brother! She knows what she wants and goes after it.

Basketball 1, 2; Gym Club 2

HUYETT, JOYCE ARLENE   "Yoikey"

Commercial

" 'Tick, talk, tick, talk,' says the clock the whole day"

Joyce is about five feet tall, small featured, and very pretty. Small as she is, there is a lot of pep in her, and she always wears that cute little smile. She gets along with her teachers and friends because of that happy way of taking things as they are. If she thinks she is right on any subject, she argues and pleads her point ill you agree with her. And almost everyone does.

IACOCCA, LIDO ANTHONY   "Lee"

Enginnering and Science

' When you aim at anything you are sure to hit it"

Lee is a raconteaur extraordinary, and not only can he quip with the best, but he can pun with the worst. If knowledge really is power, he is omnipotent. This, together with the ability he has developed in managing and directing school affairs, will prove a great asset in his career of engineering.

National Honor Society 3, President 4; Orotan Debating Society 2, 3, 4; Varsity A Club 4; Red Cross Council 4; Latin Club 2, 3, 4; Swimming Team, Manager 3, 4; Junior, Senior and Interclass Play Committee

Page Ninety-nine

THE FAMILY

PROUD PAPA NICK
IACOCCA STILL HAD
HIS HAND ON HIS
BOY

LEE HAD A
PROTECTIVE HAND
ON MOTHER
ANTOINETTE'S
SHOULDER, BUT
HIS EYES WERE
FOR PAPA NICK.
LEE'S OLDER
SISTER DELMA
WAS MARRIED TO
AN ALLENTOWN
FORD DEALER

THE MEN IN LEE'S LIFE

LEE AND BILLY: TWO MEN ABOUT NEW YORK AND DETROIT. IACOCCA AND WILLIAM DENIS ("BILLY") FUGAZY ARE THE CLOSEST OF FRIENDS

THREE MEN
SHAPED IACOCCA'S
LIFE: PAPA NICK
(TOP) AND
CHARLES
("CHARLIE")
BEACHAM, HIS
"MENTOR/
TORMENTOR" AT
FORD MOTOR
COMPANY
(CENTER) AND
HENRY FORD II,
WHO FIRED HIM

THE WOMEN
IN LEE'S LIFE

MOTHER
ANTOINETTTE
REMAINED HAPPY
AS A HOMEBODY

FIRST WIFE MARY (TOP) DIED OF DIABETES AFTER 27 YEARS OF MARRIAGE. THE RELATIONSHIP WITH SECOND WIFE PEGGY WAS STORMY

THE YEARS AT FORD

RELATIONS WITH HENRY FORD II (RIGHT) WORKED WELL ENOUGH FOR YEARS BUT WERE NEVER COMFORTABLE

THE MUSTANG WAS IACOCCA'S OVERWHELMING TRIUMPH AT FORD. HERE HE IS WITH THE 1964 (REAR) AND 1974 MODELS

THE YEARS AT CHRYSLER

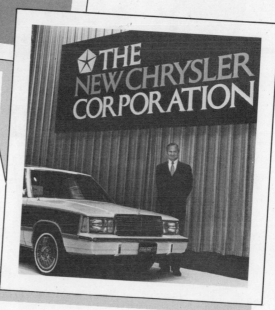

"NEW" WAS THE WORD FOR CHRYSLER UNDER IACOCCA. HERE HE IS WITH ONE OF THE K-CARS THAT STARTED THE COMPANY'S COMEBACK

PATRIOTISM AND SHOWMANSHIP HELPED BRING CHRYSLER BACK FROM NEAR-BANKRUPTCY

WITH AN UNCHARACTERIS- TICALLY BENIGN SMILE, HAROLD K. ("HAL") SPERLICH POSES FOR FORMAL CORPORATION PORTRAIT. IN ACTUALITY, THIS AUTOMOTIVE GENIUS AND LONG- TIME IACOCCA COLLABORATOR IS A DRIVEN MAN WITH A FIERCE TEMPER

EVERYONE IN IACOCCA'S CABINET AT CHRYSLER (FROM LEFT TO RIGHT), GERALD ("GERRY") GREENWALD, BENNETT E. ("BEN") BIDWELL, ROBERT S. ("STEVE") MILLER, AND ROBERT A. ("BOB") LUTZ CAME FROM JOBS AT FORD

THE
BOOK

"Gentlemen, let us open to page 82 of our Iacoccas."

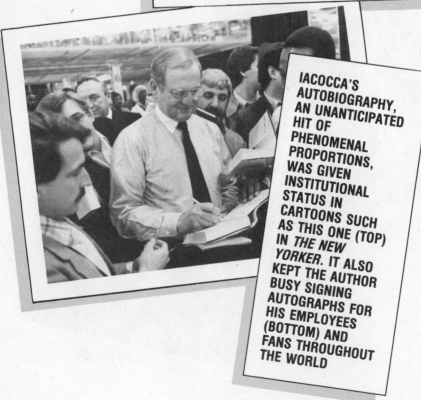

IACOCCA'S AUTOBIOGRAPHY, AN UNANTICIPATED HIT OF PHENOMENAL PROPORTIONS, WAS GIVEN INSTITUTIONAL STATUS IN CARTOONS SUCH AS THIS ONE (TOP) IN *THE NEW YORKER.* IT ALSO KEPT THE AUTHOR BUSY SIGNING AUTOGRAPHS FOR HIS EMPLOYEES (BOTTOM) AND FANS THROUGHOUT THE WORLD

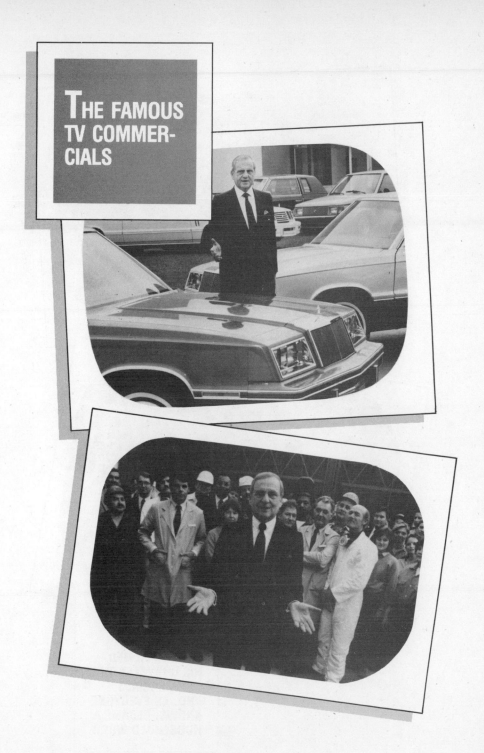

THE FAMOUS TV COMMER-CIALS

THOUGH RESISTANT AND SHY, IACOCCA FINALLY FILMED HIS CHRYSLER TV COMMERCIALS AND, AS EVERYONE KNOWS, BECAME A HOUSEHOLD WORD

13.

THE COMPANY HE KEEPS AND KEEPS

AT FIRST I COULDN'T FIGURE OUT WHAT THEY WERE TELLING ME. "I can't see you that week," I kept hearing from people I needed to interview about Iacocca. "I'm going to the wedding."

Wedding? This was June 1986, and the man had just gotten remarried in April.

When I was given the same story for the third or fourth time, always delivered with the same slight impatience, as if anyone familiar with Iacocca's life would surely know about *the* wedding, I finally inquired what very important personage was getting married this time. It turned out to be Iacocca's older daughter, Kathryn Lisa, aka Kathi. She was marrying Ned Hentz, a twenty-eight-year-old New York advertising copywriter, at St. Hugo of the Hills Church in Bloomfield Hills, and *everybody* was going because Lee absolutely, positively had to have *everybody* around him on this day of days.

Nearly every male member of Lee's gang came out of the automobile industry. They were "good car men"—there was no higher accolade—men who looked at cars with excitement and touched the vehicles sensually as if they were alive, beautiful women even, and all these members of the wedding and their wives went back a way with Lee, many of them a very long, long way indeed.

Here was Eddie Charles, Lee's baby-sitter during childhood in Allentown. Eddie had been a Ford dealer who loved Fords with such abandon that he traveled to see the old River Rouge plant on his honeymoon. Eddie had come to Bloomfield Hills to sit with Lee once more and stayed with him for days when Lee got fired by Henry Ford and was "so mad he couldn't look at you."

Here was "Zimmy," Frank Zimmerman, the madcap promotion genius whom Lee met on his first day in 1946 as a trainee with Ford in Dearborn. Zimmy had started Lee dating and relaxing a bit back then, and in the mid-sixties Iacocca had difficulty restraining Zimmy from letting a bear drive a Mercury Cougar coast to coast to demonstrate how safe the car was.

And Buzz Klotz was there from the training days in the forties in Chester, Pennsylvania, Buzz, who scoured the Amish markets with Papa Nick. Buzz was part of the Friday night poker gang that met in "Lido's Lounge." He was long retired as director of Ford's Used Car Division and spent most Thanksgivings with the Iacoccas in Florida.

And Bill Winn came, Bill, who had sauntered down Michigan Avenue in Chicago with Lee, both of them swinging hatboxes. They were in their twenties, and they'd just raided a millinery shop for headgear to present to their girlfriends. Lee and Bill were sharing an apartment in Dearborn at the time and they had been sharing ever since, Bill getting fired by Ford just before Lee got fired; both surviving the purgatory of the loan fight in Washington together; Bill accompanying Lee to the first nerve-shattering shoots of the TV commercials, even the disaster with Frank Sinatra.

And Murray Kester from Wilkes-Barre, Pennsylvania, Murray, the master salesman, who used to call customers and ask them how *their friends* liked their new car, its being Murray's theory, usually accurate, that car buyers loved to brag to friends about their new cars and wouldn't mind surrendering the names and phone numbers of these friends so Murray could call *them* and pitch them a new buggy.

And Jay Dugan was there, naturally, Jay who had largely abandoned his advertising agencies and had become a serious, widely exhibited sculptor. Jay had hammered out *Knowledge Ascending*, the enormous new memorial to Nick Iacocca on Iacocca Plaza at Lehigh University. He, too, had been with Lee since the Chester days. It had been Jay to whom Lee had confided his dreaded nightmares of their mutual boss, Mr. Beacham, the mentor/ogre.

And Hank Carlini, whom he had chosen as his companion at the vineyards Lee had purchased in Tuscany. Hank had been with Iacocca since the fifties, when Lee entrusted him with a then-revolutionary mission. Hank was to take a whole line of new Fords, in secret, to the countryside so the cars could be photographed for advertising against *natural* backgrounds. Natural backgrounds! Who'd ever produced such a spectacular before?

And here was Leo-Arthur Kelmenson of Kenyon & Eckhardt, who had put his advertising agency at Lee's disposal during the first Chrysler days, when everybody told Leo that this meant he was committing hara-kiri. Lee and Leo could sit and talk together about their personal values, their friendships, Lee's trust funds for his daughters, just about anything.

Ben Bidwell was there, like so many others from Chrysler, Ben, who'd endangered his career at Ford by driving to Lee's house right after Iacocca was fired to tell him he wasn't turning his back on him. . . . Ben, Chrysler's own Will Rogers, Ben, the ghostwriter of the immortal Iacocca line "Screw the *Wall Street Journal*!"

Joe Califano came from Washington, Joe, the senior politico who had phoned Lee to commiserate when Joe was secretary of health, education and welfare and Lee got fired from Ford, and then Lee had called later to commiserate when Joe was in turn fired by Jimmy Carter. Two geniuses with identical temporary setbacks! Joe had saved Chrysler tens of millions of dollars annually, at the same time providing its workers with better medical care by organizing a much more rational health system.

Alejandro de Tomaso, the onetime racing driver, had flown in from Modena, the ancient headaches with the controversial Mangusta and Pantera* forgotten, but with memories still fresh of the flair with which Alejandro told Henry Ford to go to hell and now his Maserati sports models were coming to Chrysler, ah, Alejandro, there was a loyal friend!

---

*Both cars were works of sleek beauty but unpleasant frailties. The Mangusta's braking and general handling were poor, and it offered almost no rear vision. The Pantera's flaws caused the National Highway Traffic Safety Administration concerns over numerous engineering problems, including the possibility of cracks developing in the fuel tank and a possible loss of steering capability.

And Carroll Shelby came, that other racing man who'd first introduced Lee to de Tomaso, of whom Carroll liked to say, "Alejandro is the most opinionated sumbitch who ever shit between two boots!" Shelby had forgiven Lee for making Carroll turn down a Toyota dealership that would have made him jillions ("We're going to kick their asses back into the Pacific Ocean," Lee had claimed in 1971). But Carroll remembered Lee's sadness when Mary died and Carroll came to the house, where Lee cooked him the favorite Iacocca Italian dinner of all, chicken wings with butter-and-garlic sauce.

Vic Damone arrived at the wedding with Diahann Carroll, and Vic sang Schubert's "Ave Maria" for Kathi and Lee's 400 guests at the church. Vic, another skinny Italian kid, had met Lee more than twenty years ago, when the singer crooned on *The Lively Ones*, a musical TV show for NBC, sponsored by Ford. They'd become great friends, visiting at each other's homes, nibbling prosciutto, and scheming bigger and bigger promotions to bedazzle the car dealers.

How they remembered 1966! That was when Lee had told Bill Fugazy and Bill Winn to outdo themselves for the introduction of the new Mercury Cougar, and they did. They hired the SS *Independence* at $44,000 a day and steamed all their favorite dealers—the ones who'd met their sales quotas, that is—to St. Thomas in the Virgin Islands. Everybody was enjoying a cookout on the beach when suddenly an LST disgorged a white Cougar and out stepped Vic Damone with a song on his lips. Iacocca remembered how all the guys went nuts then, and here was old Vic blessing Kathi's marriage, singing Schubert!

And the Smalls were present, Wes and Ila, Wes, who'd been a helper at Lee's side since 1948, Wes, the man who had to say yes when Lee faced a distasteful public chore and asked plaintively, "Do I have to do this?," and Isla, whom Kathi called "Gram" and who had arranged the whole wedding, including the separate table with the pizza and the salami and the tortellini. Together Wes and Isla had been working until 5:00 A.M., pinning down final seating arrangements, and Wes was managing the comings and goings of the out-of-town guests, juggling a fleet of thirty rental cars.

A sharp-eyed reporter from the *Detroit News* spotted housekeepers, guards, and secretaries, past and present, among the guests, as is customary at the populist Iacocca family doings, but even she failed to note that the crowd included Lee's favorite barber and sometime literary agent Gio Hernadez, who flew in from New York.

Some of the important people in Iacocca's life were not invited, however. Some were purely business contacts, nothing personal, people like Bill Novak, the autobiographer. Others had been divorced by Lee, yes, divorced, discarded like lovers in emotional breaks, charged with the highest of high crimes, disloyalty.

Bill Benton was among the missing ex-partners, debonair Bill, movie star handsome, beautifully attired, a recent defector to the advertising business from a Ford vice presidency. Bill had been another passionate partisan of Ford automobiles since his father drove the family from North Carolina to New York in a Model T when Bill was a boy.

Bill had been Lee's most intimate henchman and shadow at Ford. They did everything together, traveled everywhere, talked about the most delicate secrets. Bill was dispatched on the most sensitive errands, and people who knew both men were still speculating almost a decade later about their divorce. Neither man talked about the break; but it came sometime after Lee had been fired by Ford, and the charge was said to be disloyalty.

Well, what exactly? How? Why? The insiders reminded each other that Benton had bought a house on the street where Lee's most hated rival, Phil Caldwell, lived. They figured that this transgression alone might have sufficed to whisk Bill into a state of permanent banishment, along with other nonpersons who had once been intimates, especially certain fair-weather pals who were guilty of failing to return Lee's phone calls after Henry Ford had dropped the guillotine on his neck.

Defections! Defections from the ranks are punishable under Lee's private code of law—punishable and as unwelcome as having to cope with surprises. Or the prying glances of strangers. Or twinges of the diverticula. Defections are the rotten side of the coin called loyalty, and as Tom Clark, the Iacoccalyte who is president of the BBDO agency that does the Dodge advertising, says: "*Loyalty* is the one overriding word with Lee."

And the most ardently loyal of the Knights Errant at King Lee's Court, the first among equals, the noisiest, the closest to the king, the sidekick hovering most watchfully and possessively in the ruler's divine presence (and of course, a busily cheek-bussing guest at Kathi's nuptials), was that one-man circus Billy Fugazy, the fellow who first got Lee in trouble with Henry Ford.

"An unguided missile" is what the infamously outspoken Iacoccalyte (and wedding guest) George Steinbrenner of the New York Yankees calls Fugazy. "Iacocca and I always tell him he could screw up a two-car funeral," says Steinbrenner, "but there isn't anybody we have more fun with."

Fun? It is a precious quality of life for the famous. Many VIPs do not manage to get much fun because of internal and external pressures on their crowded days. To be looking for fun, reveling in it, yukking a few belly laughs, letting the hair down in prankish posturing is all to the good.

But I had never equated Fugazy with fun. I had heard whispers about him around New York for years, rarely anything as sinister as the suspicion of Mafia connections that sent Henry Ford into the furious inquisition of the Iacocca/Fugazy connection. But eyebrows were raised at Fugazy's boyhood friendship with a man-eater like the lawyer Roy Cohn, Billy's involvement in numerous lawsuits, his rapid maneuvering in the limo and travel business.

I had pictured William Denis Fugazy as a ferocious prima donna who (it was said) once threw a telephone through a window and snaps his clubs at golf (he plays in the seventies) as readily as other men break matches. I'd also thought of him as a tycoon rooting around in gold. Now I learned that he was both more and less than that.

The business press did not take Billy's enterprises too seriously. "He has a million friends and no money," a friend told *Manhattan, Inc.* magazine. "He has never been a good money man. He just doesn't care about it. What's more important is to have a picture with the cardinal on one side and Iacocca on the other."

Billy's million friends, what a club it is—almost every member a *numero uno*! It was Billy who introduced Iacocca to George Steinbrenner and Donald Trump in the first place—introductions are a big thing with Billy—and it's Billy who carries the message from Iacocca to another Fugazy buddy, Governor Mario Cuomo of New York, with Lee's complaint that Mario is too soft on liberals and should come out in favor of the death penalty.

Bob Hope, another Fugazy crony, is on the phone often, kidding around with Billy, and so was the late Terence Cardinal Cooke. "My best friends" is what Billy calls all these and many more first citizens and intimates.

He's not kidding, and the golden circle is still widening. In recent years the seventyish John Kluge became Fugazy's brother/father figure, Kluge being chairman of the billion-dollar

BILL FUGAZY (CENTER) GETS IACOCCA TOGETHER WITH THE FAMOUS. HERE THEY ARE WITH RETIRED HOUSE SPEAKER TIP O'NEILL

Metromedia television empire, and the image of this mogul as Bill's brother/father is no exaggeration. The two spend a lot of time playing backgammon, and when Kluge converted to Catholicism, Fugazy, who maintains close relations with the Vatican, became his godfather even though he is, at sixty-one, Kluge's junior by more than a decade.*

Although I knew in advance of his elite connections, I was bowled over when I spent several hours with Fugazy in his modest, crowded Fifth Avenue office. The effect is of a museum struggling to pay the rent. Photos of Billy's best friends papered all walls and spilled across all furniture: presidents of the United States at play and work, CEOs of industrial empires chuckling with cardinals and bishops, sports figures like Howard Cosell, and entertainment stars collected wholesale, like at Grauman's Chinese.

All but lost on one wall roosts an arresting picture of Lee Iacocca with Papa Nick, both men in sports clothes, Nick seated,

---

*The idyll dissolved in acrimony in April 1987, when Metromedia sued Fugazy for $35 million in actual and $250 million in punitive damages. The charge was fraud in connection with limousine operations which friend Kluge had purchased from friend Fugazy. Billy denied the allegations and said that Kluge and his people just didn't know how to run the business.

looking martial with a trace of grudging smile, Lee bent over the old man, grinning boyishly, one cheek squeezed so tightly into the father's that both faces are puckering.

Talk about close! The emotional meaning of the photo is rivaled only by a photo of Lee Iacocca on a ledge near Billy's desk. It shows Lee in front of a Mark V and is inscribed in Italian: *"Al mio carissimo amico Bill con i migliori auguri. Lido."* ("To my dearest friend Bill with the most sincere wishes.")

I found this dearest friend endearing: eerily juvenile in looks and manner, fidgety in the extreme, frantic in the conduct of his business on the phone—spending more than thirty seconds without a phone receiver at his ear is manifestly an act of sacrifice for him—and so entertaining and uninhibited that I had difficulty keeping my face straight.

Talking with Billy Fugazy is like watching a Charlie Chaplin movie. He slides so low in his armchair that he is practically prone. He unbuttons his shirt to scratch his chest vigorously and at length. He picks up the phone, barks at some best friend, "How ya doin', big man?" Fugazy talks to few little men. Within moments he signs off, exclaiming either "Love ya!" or "You're the best!" And when he was worried that he was perhaps committing a very slight indiscretion or wondered about my reaction to his performance, Fugazy lapsed into the most explicit body language I've ever witnessed. He covered his face with both hands and peered at me sideways through a small opening between two fingers.

One needs no road map to track what ego-inflating thrills and economic advantages a rainmaker like Billy—a practicing compulsive who collects VIPs like butterflies—gets out of his intimacy with Iacocca. Billy loves to be a nice guy, and he performs beautifully (and often unselfishly) in the role. He simply loves the gig. Perhaps this is why it seems impossible not to like Fugazy. But what explains the enormous intensity of Iacocca's feelings for this unlikely twin?

One must think Italian, think of the sharing not merely of roots but of the seminal Ellis Island experience, a joining of two clans in a remarkably fortuitous way. When Fugazy Travel happened to bid on travel services for Ford executives in 1959, Billy didn't get the business but struck up an acquaintance with Lee. They went to the World Series together (Billy can get tickets anytime to anything, absolutely anything at all), and they got to chatting about their families. Imagine! Nick Iacocca had known Billy's grandfather, Cavaliere Luigi V. Fugazzi, and he had known him very well. Conceivably old Mr. Fugazzi had been at hand when Nick bribed his sick young bride past the immigration men, had perhaps even had a hand in the transaction.

This was not farfetched because Fugazzi went to Ellis Island twice a week to help Italian arrivals with the immigration bureaucracy, to interpret for the refugees and to change their money. It was business, too, not philanthropy alone. Fugazzi had started a private bank and steamship ticket agency in Greenwich Village about 1870. This community enterprise had made him a patriarchal figure among the Italian-Americans. Nick used to visit often at the office in the Village.

Once Lee and Billy had unraveled the entwined threads of their past, Billy, in his smilingly relentless way, plunged into a friendship with Nick as well. "I was like his other son," Billy told me. Another mutual admiration society was in business.

Nick and Billy did a lot of traveling together. They joined in tweaking Lido's ego and tightfistedness. "Nick could do anything," Billy says, and Billy noticed, as had the folks in Allentown, that Nick didn't take pesty rules too seriously. For example, Nick taught Billy's fourteen-year-old son how to drive a car even though he was too young to get a license.

Business dealings got Lee and Billy closer together after the first failure to connect in 1959. It was Lee who got Billy started in the limousine business. Loyally Billy accepted the free use of some Lincoln Continentals when Ford wanted to break the hold that GM's Cadillacs had upon the lucrative Manhattan market. Billy somehow lost $3 million on this invasion, but Iacocca's Lincolns were visible in Fugazy's posh territory, ferrying Ford executives to the World's Fair.

Given Billy's loyalty, Iacocca made sure that his friend got a chance to bid on the rich contract for the introductory promotion of his beloved Mustang that year, and after that nothing could keep the pair apart. Billy harvested a vast volume of promotion and transportation business from Ford and Chrysler. He can drop Lee's name with his other best friends often and to good advantage. And although Iacocca is often moody and sometimes spends hours with Fugazy without either partner saying much, if anything, Billy does revel in the camaraderie with the Big Man from Detroit.

And Billy does get much done for Lee—a private audience with the pope, the real estate investment partnership with Donald Trump. Billy *is* a doer. He promoted the second and third championship fights between Floyd Patterson and Ingemar Johansson, the final voyage of the *Queen Mary,* and he is chief hustler for so many charity and fund-raising drives that the innocent act of finding themselves in his proximity can cost bystanders money.*

"Billy makes things happen," says another doer, Tom Clark of BBDO. "He's an organizer. The son of a bitch is always after me for something, and suddenly I'm standing in front of two thousand people because he asked me to. . . ." Clark laughed and shrugged helplessly, forgivingly, the way kings used to excuse the lapses of court jesters. Or the way Iacocca eventually forgave Billy for packing Lee's own wedding with guests neither the groom nor the bride had wanted.

"Why'd you invite all these people?" Lee had asked his bride, Peggy Johnson, as he looked around their reception in annoyance. Peggy hadn't. Billy confessed that at midnight he hadn't been able to help his Good Samaritan self and had invited a small flood of best friends at the very last moment. What was a best man for but to be good to his friends?

Ah, but everybody forgives Fugazy. Partly it's the schlemiel factor at work: Billy tries so hard and seems so selfless, so vulnerable, chronically losing money, so rarely out of the clutches of the limo drivers, the lawyers, flailing at obscure but messy emergencies, shaking his collection can for anonymous multitudes, ever enmeshed in the personal soap opera of his existence, teetering on some appalling brink in his Fifth Avenue picture gallery, his own worst enemy.

"He's a *loyal* fellow," Bob Hope said when he made some free TV commercials for Billy. "He's good to his friends." Loyalty again.

When one of Fugazy's benign conspiracies clicks, the emotional fallout is a veritable Chernobyl of goodwill. Which happened when Iacocca came to New York on business and looked forward to eating

*I was waiting for my first appointment with Fugazy. The receptionist smiled warmly at me and asked, "Do you like children?" She was swept away, she said, by her success with her fund-raising calls to important friends of Mr. Fugazy, who absolutely had to send money for some mammoth charity event by the upcoming Friday. I felt a direct pitch coming on just as, thank heaven, Billy dashed distractedly out of his office on one of his incessant emergencies and waved me into his sanctum while he continued his run in the opposite direction.

at one of his favorite Italian restaurants, Romeo Salta. Instead, Fugazy steered Lee and two additional associates to the Christopher Columbus Club. There they found themselves captured by the tedious proceedings of the annual banquet of New York's most distinguished Italian-Americans, but when Iacocca was introduced and became the evening's stellar attraction, he was greatly touched by the recognition and loved the respect shown by the diners who stood in line to shake his hand, courtesy of Billy.

And as they reap applause, so Lee and Billy are partners in sorrow. "When my daughter died, he didn't leave me for three days," Fugazy remembers.

Most men are too emotionally closed off to manage so intense a friendship with another male, and the flattery and fun and the links with the famous, all the goodies that Fugazy heaps on Iacocca, still cannot fully account for Lee's feelings for Billy. So what more does the Big Man get from the Little Fellow—one so rich, the other so struggling; the celebrity in lockstep with the celebrity collector; both chock-full of beans, guile, and guilelessness?

"Release," diagnoses from Tom Clark, the Iacoccalyte from BBDO. "With Billy, Lee shuts off all business." For a pressure-ridden workaholic, a brooder, a worrier with a perfectionistic streak like Iacocca, release from responsibilities is a blessing, a rare gift for a personality coping with severely loaded circuits.

"A claque," judges Don Frey, the former Iacoccalyte who moved on to Bell & Howell. "He *has* to have a claque; it's a protective cocoon against adversaries." Everyone faces adversaries; not many people manage to weave a cocoon strong enough to ward them off.

"Confidence," says the Supreme Iacoccalyte, Fugazy, "I guess he gets a lot of confidence around me."

Confidence? Does the Big Man still need infusions of confidence at this age and stage of his life? Yes, and his continuing shyness in front of strangers documents the inhibitions of this seemingly uninhibited giant. Fugazy doesn't see his buddy as merely "shy." Billy is one of those who go further and say, "He's bashful."

Iacocca's oversensitivity to the requirements of playing golf is a case in point. Fugazy, who attributes much of his social-cum-professional record to his superior golf game, declares that Lee should be proud of his golf swing. Golf is serious business with Billy, not anything he would fudge about, so this judgment deserves respect. Alas, golf cannot be played in private or just in front of friends. The prying eyes of strangers invariably play along, which is why Iacocca plays golf only a few times a year.

"He doesn't want to get up early and go to the club in Bloomfield Hills and *ask* anybody to play with him," Fugazy reports. "And he doesn't want to be seen and embarrassed because he isn't playing well enough."

So Iacocca lifts his inhibitions to play only with Fugazy and close friends because Fugazy does give him confidence. Billy, his vulnerable little pal, endows him with the freedom to drop the anxieties that make Iacocca bashful. I wouldn't be surprised if—as some of the more thoughtful Iacoccalytes believe—Iacocca is sometimes a bit jealous of Billy and wishes he could be as uninhibited as his court jester.

The Iacocca cheering section, the company he keeps and keeps, tolerates no females, no critics, no competition, no one better educated or smarter than the object of affection, no one unpredictable. These are shrewd men, for the most part—"country-smart" or "street-smart" might be better labels—and they're promoters of some sort, businessmen all, men who meet payrolls but are also rainmakers with imagination, not dollar shufflers who only buy cheap and sell dear.

Iacocca has long outgrown most of these awed flatterers, intellectually and by any other yardstick, but loyalties forged through adventures past and the comfort of familiarity keep him from abandoning the old-shoe bunch from the Friday Night Poker Society while his circle has grown to encompass East Coast city slickers like George Steinbrenner and Donald Trump.

Preserved, too, like the loyalties running back to the Ford days, are the ties going back farther and binding him still to North Seventh Street in Allentown and the school days, enshrined in memories stored for instant retrieval in Iacocca's formidable brain. So when a telegram signed by Henry Soltys arrived for him at Chrysler as the K-cars came out in 1981, he was not puzzled.

He had not seen Soltys, his music appreciation teacher at Central High School, in nearly half a century, and music appreciation had hardly been Lido's forte. But remembering that Soltys had been a blithe spirit, he set about at once to decipher the wire. It was in a strange private code of Soltys's invention and, like the old teacher himself, not uncomplicated.

Iacocca, master of crossword puzzles, deciphered that Soltys was buying a 1981 Plymouth Reliant but wanted Iacocca to issue certain instructions to his dealer. Soltys wanted, for instance, a car with a Chrysler (not a Mitsubishi) engine. Iacocca issued the necessary orders and replied to Soltys, using the teacher's own code: "Krellpuff yes, Chevpuff no, Gimmyjunk no. . . ."

Why shouldn't he fall in with Henry Soltys's weird little joke? Soltys had remained one of Lido's gang, and his membership would never lapse.

But how did Lido feel about the rest of us, people at large? How much did he care about humanity?

14.

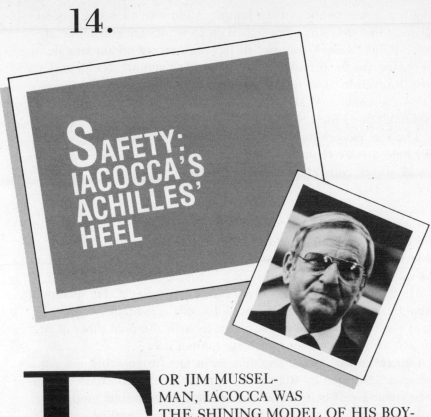

SAFETY: IACOCCA'S ACHILLES' HEEL

FOR JIM MUSSEL-MAN, IACOCCA WAS THE SHINING MODEL OF HIS BOY-HOOD. Jim could hardly have helped it. Iacocca wasn't even president of Ford yet when the principal of Musselman's Allentown school scrutinized the sixth-grade assembly and pronounced an exalted, if conditional, blessing. The principal moved his eyes across the scrubbed young faces and said gravely, "We can only hope there is another Iacocca out there."

Another Iacocca, another poor boy making it to the top, making it on brains and character; every youngster in Allentown had to ingest the Iacocca story at home and in school over and over through childhood and adolescence. How many small towns delivered such a folk hero to the nation? Here was the Allentown version of honest little George Washington who confessed that he chopped down the cherry tree and became president because he grew up as such a great kid.

For Jim Musselman, still moon-faced, apple-cheeked, and gangling but now a public-interest lawyer, Allentown's favorite legend collapsed in 1984, when Jim signed on to work with consumer advocate Ralph Nader* and studied Iacocca's record on automobile safety. Iacocca for president talk was getting around. Nader and Musselman didn't like to hear it.

"We're concerned about the momentum," said Musselman. "Nobody knows the real Iacocca."

The real Iacocca record on auto safety hardly deserves the angelic halo that he claims for himself. Nor is the performance as callous as Nader, Musselman, and their fellow crusaders cast it.

"I was a safety nut," writes Iacocca in an often-ridiculed passage of The Book. "I still am." And in his numerous pages on this dicey subject he presents himself as the lone principled choirboy of safety who out-Nadered the great Nader.

Musselman considered this self-image hypocritical. He was more taken by another widely circulated Iacocca quotation—"Safety doesn't sell"—which sounds suspiciously as if the pied piper of Allentown valued cash a lot more than human life.

Iacocca's initial record on safety is, in fact, impeccable and not in dispute. Inspired by Robert McNamara, a certified safety nut, Iacocca favored seat belts three decades before the public grudgingly began to accept them. He worked to have them installed in the 1956-model Fords, along with such other then-novel lifesavers as crash-padded dashboards and deep-dish steering wheels (to minimize the danger of impalement).

Loudly promoted and advertised, the "safety package" bombed at the box office. Nader was still in law school then, and people didn't want to think about accidents. Often they wanted the seat belts removed before they'd buy the cars. Iacocca had hoped that safety might be useful as a novel merchandising gimmick. When it didn't work, he complained that he was quoted out of context. He says he didn't snarl, "Safety doesn't sell." He remembers saying, more or less, "Look, fellas, I guess safety didn't sell, even though we did our damndest to sell it!"

*Nader, another poor boy, rose to national hero status on the critic's side of America's car wars. His 1965 best-seller *Unsafe at Any Speed* focused on the appalling accident record of Chevrolet's Corvair and was largely responsible for congressional passage, in 1966, of the nation's first reasonably stringent auto safety law. Since then Nader spawned a hutch of prolific consumer centers and has become, in his fifties, the grand old man of a new and respected consumerist establishment.

The semantics hardly matter. The point is that Iacocca continued to plug seat belts, and when drivers insisted on ignoring them, he became a pioneer for another unpopular but lifesaving cause—more than a decade before its time finally arrived: He demanded mandatory use of the belts. A year after becoming president of Ford he wrote to all fifty governors, advised them that the company favored such a stringent step, and urged them to get the necessary legislation passed.

Since such laws weren't adopted until the 1980s, Iacocca risked further public scorn by pushing a gadget called Interlock, devised by Ford engineers. It kept a car's ignition dead until the front-seat passengers fastened their belts. The National Highway Traffic Safety Administration made Interlock mandatory on new cars in 1973, but again drivers rebelled. Car owners having much in common with gun owners, they cherish their American right to kill themselves and others; they kept the belts buckled but without wearing them. Congress responded to this streak of cussedness by declaring the device illegal.

The laudable chapters from Iacocca's record on safety were not on Jim Musselman's mind on July 16, 1986, when he made his way to the front row at a Washington press conference summoned by the committee that had assigned itself the task of drafting the Chrysler Chairman to run for president (see Chapter 16). Jim had gained admission by smiling and saying he was from Allentown and wanted to watch a fellow townsman get a boost for the presidency. But he was furious. He had discussed his plans with Nader, who had agreed: A verbal stink bomb could benefit these proceedings by enlivening them. Iacocca boosters and potential boosters needed to be reminded of two odious stories, their hero's specific record on the Ford Pinto and on air bags.

And Musselman had decided to go further, for he had become convinced that his childhood idol did not exist, like Santa Claus. As soon as the meeting was opened to questions he rose, identified himself and began to read a statement:

Lee Iacocca has for years appeared to be a friend of the American public and the American consumer. Through his speeches and his television advertisements he has led citizens to believe that he has a deep care for the American people. Before citizens perpetuate this myth and push Iacocca for the presidency they should consider the following points.

First, under his leadership at Ford Motor Company and the Chrysler Corporation, Mr. Iacocca has allowed many unsafe vehicles to be sold to the unknowing American public. Many of these defects, including [those of] the Ford Pinto, were problems that Ford executives were aware of before the cars were placed on the market. Almost 900 people lost their lives because of the callous economic decision that was made about the Ford Pinto while Iacocca was president of Ford. . . .

How culpable *was* Iacocca in these deaths? Data are voluminous regarding the Pinto and the Ford Motor Company, the record having been dissected by swarms of analysts. Few were objective; most of them held some stake in the 117 lawsuits filed by owners of the Pinto and the nearly identical Mercury Bobcat, alleging a dangerous fuel-system design. Judges and juries had their unmistakably damning say about the culpability of Ford as a company. Information about Iacocca's personal involvement is considerably sketchier—he testified at none of the trials—but it reveals the way he operates when under great pressure.*

Among Ford people the Pinto was known as "Lee's car," and from the beginning it cast the spell of another breakthrough hit like the Mustang. Its concept was superb, actually overdue. It was a totally new subcompact, not just new "skin" (outside sheet metal) as were so many new models, and it would adapt European engineering practices for low-cost, low-weight, and low-fuel use to American car manufacturing.

To establish the project's internal top priority, Iacocca had come up with a trademark, a mantra all his own, a sloganized objective typical of his style. Everybody know that his "56 in 56" campaign had started his rise at Ford. Now, in 1968, Iacocca was shooting for the presidency of Ford, and the mantra was "2,000 and 2,000," meaning that the Pinto could weigh no more than 2,000 pounds and cost no more than $2,000. Nobody would question that this car, unlike the Mustang, was fully Lee's own.

The "2,000 and 2,000" formula was law. "Iacocca enforced

---

*The basic investigative research was done by reporter Mark Dowie and published in the September/October 1977 issue of *Mother Jones* magazine. I have relied for many details on the more carefully balanced account by Robert Lacey in *Ford: The Men and the Machine* (Boston: Little, Brown, 1985, especially pages 575–86) and on my own interviewing.

these limits with an iron hand," a Ford engineer who worked on the Pinto told *Mother Jones* magazine. Every expenditure had to be "re-justified" every month. The deadline pressures were killing. A wholly new car normally required forty-three months or longer to roll out; Iacocca rushed the Pinto through in thirty-seven months.*

Economy of weight was achieved mostly by truncating the rear end, and this proved fatal: It left the gas tank with its filler neck too vulnerable to impact on collision.

Before the launch of the car—but not until after the costly tooling was frozen—Ford engineers ran rear-impact crash tests on some European Capri models that had been modified to simulate the configuration of the Pinto's gas tank. They learned that even at low speeds the risks of rupture and fire were serious. It is not clear, however, how high through the many layers of the Ford bureaucracy this information penetrated upward.

Mark Dowie of *Mother Jones* asked the anonymous engineer who spoke of Iacocca's "iron hand" whether anyone had told Lee about the unsafe gas tanks.

"Hell, no," said the engineer. "That person would have been fired. Safety wasn't a popular subject around Ford in those days.† With Lee it seemed taboo. Whenever a problem was raised that meant a delay on the Pinto, Lee would chomp on his cigar, look out the window and say, 'Read the product objectives and get back to work.' "

I acquired my own inside source on the Pinto who was anything but anonymous. He is the twinkly, neatly tailored Harley Copp, and his survival at Ford for thirty years is a tribute to his unfailing good cheer and the precision of his work. He rose to be director of Engineering Technical Services before management slashed his epaulets away and demoted him for, well, insubordination shortly prior to his retirement in 1976.

Like all automobile authorities—even oppositionists like Jim Musselman—Copp operates on a stark premise: Human flesh being weak and metal being strong, there can be no such machine as an

---

*Iacocca's draconian rule got results. Unveiled in late 1970, the Pinto weighed in at 2,030 pounds and, inflation notwithstanding, cost just under $2,000. Managing by objectives—it could be done as the textbooks prescribed.
†No doubt the memory of the money that the company lost in the failure of the 1956 Ford "safety package" was still vivid.

absolutely safe car. Still, Copp had a thing about safety. He was in favor of it and hated to see human life placed needlessly at risk. This began to cause him difficulties with Lee Iacocca in the early sixties, when Copp, having gotten wind of defects in Chevrolet's Corvair, wrote a letter about the trouble to government regulators.

Although this unconventional leak was directed against General Motors, a competitor, Copp found that he became a nonperson to Iacocca. He dropped from Lee's field of vision like a victim of a Stalin purge. As Copp relates it, if he said something at a meeting, Iacocca acted as if the words had not been uttered. If he walked past Iacocca in the hall and said, "Hi, Lee," Iacocca would walk on as if Copp had not been there.

"I'd left his team," Copp explains, and he was exiled to one of Ford's European branches, out of Iacocca's sight, returning five years later, just as plans for the Pinto were being polished in the drafting room.

"How're you going to put a fuel tank in there?" he asked the engineer who was trying to squeeze essential nuts and bolts into the pretty drawings.

"The car is styled," the engineer said. "We have to find a place to put it."

I asked Copp whether it was possible that Iacocca knew the fuel tank was dangerous.

"I have no proof that he knew," said Copp, "but if he didn't know, he was a goddamned poor manager because he set up a climate of fear."

Fear. Fear of Iacocca, his power, his wrath, his toughness, the wand of his cigar, his capacity for punishing you by turning you into a nonperson, in effect locking you away for being "bad," just as his father, Nick, used to lock Lido away, lock him out of the family for violating Iacocca *standards*, standards of behavior that in the eyes of the father figure brooked no deviation.

They were law like "2,000 and 2,000."

Fear in the ranks was no doubt one reason why Iacocca would not have known about the findings of the crash tests. Other rationales for such astonishing ignorance have been advanced by students of Iacocca's behavior. First, American technicians in those days had little experience with taking weight out of cars. And Iacocca compounded this ignorance by a blank spot in his own past. In *Ford: The Men and the Machine,* Robert Lacey concludes: "The fundamental problem with the Pinto was that Lee Iacocca, who was its moving spirit, had only once before worked on a new car that was really new."*

But Lacey also offers a speaking platform to Gene Bordinat, Ford's vice president for styling, who attributes the Pinto gas tank episode to Iacocca's don't-bother-me-with-trifles haughtiness toward technicians.

"He sort of disdained engineers," Bordinat told Lacey. "When it came to confrontations, he liked to say, 'Hey, look, I've got a degree in engineering.' But I don't think he really knew didley-damn. He just let the engineers get on with it."

Lacey asked whether an engineer might have been "scared to confront Iacocca with the news that protecting the Pinto fuel tank would add weight to the car—and worse, might delay the launch of the vehicle by weeks, months, or even a year."

"Well," Bordinat said, "Lee had a tendency to intimidate people, and I'm afraid they may well have thought, 'He'll kill the messenger, he'll say, "Hey, don't bug me with bad news" '—particularly if it was going to have any effect on shifting introduction dates."

My own consultant, Harley Copp, placed the blame on Iacocca's role in the power struggle then raging for the body and soul of the Ford Motor Company. Iacocca was reaching for the top. Bunkie Knudsen was blocking him. Iacocca absolutely *had* to turn the Pinto into a triumph. It was the key to his kingdom. And speed was indispensable. Six years had passed since the Mustang. Iacocca absolutely had to pull off another success *right now*.†

"His ambition exceeded his morality," concluded Copp, and he pronounced this harsh verdict not only to me but in 1979 as part of his court testimony in Winamac, Indiana, during one of his lawsuits by Pinto owners against Ford.**

By that time the horrible fate of the 900 dead and mutilated Pinto drivers and passengers—the victims about whom Jim Mussel-man wanted to remind his audience at the draft-Iacocca press con-

---

*Iacocca's 1965 LTD/Galaxie was built from scratch. The Mustang, Maverick, and Continental Mark III all had very visible antecedents.
†If it hadn't been for the costly lawsuits, the Pinto would indeed have scored a huge commercial hit. People loved the smart, economical little car. It sold 400,000 pieces during its first year, 1971. But the controversy and its enormously damaging publicity dragged on until June 1978, when Ford finally recalled nearly one and a half million Pintos. Iacocca was fired the following month.
**As if in retribution, the durable Harley Copp carved out a busy and profitable postretirement career as a respected professional witness in cases requiring engineering expertise. He testified repeatedly against Ford's handling of the Pinto affair.

ference in 1986—had become routine fodder for courts and local TV news. Hardly anyone took notice of the Winamac case. What lingered in more memories was an earlier trial, one of the first and at the time possibly the most appalling, the Grimshaw case, which began on the highway near Santa Ana, California, in May 1972.

Eric Grimshaw, a schoolboy of thirteen, was a passenger in a brand-new Pinto driven by a housewife, Lily Gray. The engine stalled as she entered the merge lane. The car behind her couldn't stop in time; it rear-ended her Pinto, rupturing the fuel tank behind the axle, and starting a fire that incinerated Mrs. Gray's entire body. Some hours later she died in agony in a hospital emergency room.

Hers was a relatively blessed fate compared with that of Eric Grimshaw. His facial features were burned away as if he had been an A-bomb victim in Hiroshima, and he spent year after year in operating rooms while doctors labored unsuccessfully to fashion an ear and a nose from skin of the few unburned areas of his body.

Revolted by the testimony it heard about Ford's way of "thrifting" the Pinto into production, the jury awarded the Grimshaw family $3.5 million in compensatory and another $125 million in punitive damages. The judge accepted the first figure, reduced the second award to $3 million, and Ford paid $6.5 million plus interest after losing an appeal.

Understandably Iacocca doesn't mention the Grimshaw case in The Book. He is squeamish about gory details of the slaughter on American highways (42,500 killed per year, the third-ranking cause of death) and once became so nauseated while watching a safety movie that he hurriedly left the room. Nor does he mention the crash tests on the Pinto gas tank in any way, leaving open the question of whether he knew of the results or, if he did, knew enough about the engineering details to appreciate their significance. He employs the defense technique of denying what nobody except a professional crusader like Jim Musselman ever accused him of: knowingly making a dangerous car.

"The guys who built the Pinto had kids in college who were driving that car," Iacocca writes. "Believe me, nobody sits down and thinks: 'I'm deliberately going to make this car unsafe.' " Anyway, it was no longer "Lee's car." The car's cadaver belonged to the "guys who built the Pinto."

His other comments are carefully hedged. Iacocca does assume some share of the responsibility ("Whose fault was it? One obvious answer is that it was the fault of Ford's management—including me"). But even this tiptoe concession, which diffuses guilt to include Henry Ford, the engineers, and any number of other managers, seems not to cover the flaws in the Pinto's design and production but appears to apply only to Ford's shameful legal and public relations squirming once the lawsuits struck.

Iacocca says the company became guilty of "stonewalling" at this late stage of the industrial disaster. "Plenty of people" would condone this tactic under such immense pressure, he argues. He says he doesn't.

If the Pinto was ancient, if tragic, history, Jim Musselman's second cause was very much alive. In the statement he read to the draft-Iacocca press conference he charged further:

> Mr. Iacocca was totally responsible for stopping the introduction of the air bag as standard equipment on all vehicles. This technological vaccine, which saves over 9,000 lives a year and prevents thousands of injuries, was squashed by Mr. Iacocca in the early 1970's. Iacocca himself pressured the Nixon administration to drop the passive restraint requirement that would have made the air bag standard equipment on all vehicles. Since then 140,000 people have needlessly died on the highways.

Once again Iacocca did not disclose delicate portions of his past, this time a record built through many years of a tortuous controversy in which he played a starring role. He did declare himself in passionate opposition against the air bag, the folded-up plastic balloon that inflates and becomes a cushion when sensors activate it in case of accident. His list of caveats was so forbidding that you begin to think he's discussing leprosy.

He said the bags can be dangerous because they work only in certain circumstances and sometimes inadvertently or not at all, that they can lead "to injury and even death," that they would encourage owner lawsuits, that he wouldn't want to ride around with the particular chemical that inflates the bag, that the bags are far too expensive, and on and on. He called the device a false hope, "a red herring."

As a driver I was greatly relieved to read the convincing counter-arguments offered on these and other counts in the pamphlet *About*

Air Bags, published by the Insurance Institute for Highway Safety,* especially because self-interest lends great credibility to the insurance companies. They save money by saving lives. Iacocca can save money and sell cars by eliminating the costs and complexities of equipment that doesn't dazzle customers, indeed may turn them off. The controversy boils down to the state of the technology and (most particularly) to money, to costs versus benefits, real and perceived.

Money. Not lives but money. Money. The word kept buzzing through my mind as I read and reread a thirty-page document, a transcript from, of all things, the notorious White House tapes of former President Nixon.† I had read fleeting wisps of this transcript before, fragments quoted in various articles, mostly in small-circulation magazines such as the *Nation*, after the document came to light in 1982, eleven years following the fact. But only the full text, strewn with archival phonetics ("laughs," "uh," "unintelligible"), opens up what is helpful here: an opportunity to watch Iacocca at work under great pressure and in secret.

The secrecy is important and very real. The time was 1971, four months after Iacocca became president of Ford. The place was the Oval Office of the White House. Present were President Nixon, Henry Ford II, Iacocca, and the president's adviser on domestic affairs, John D. Ehrlichman. Air bags were about to become mandatory by federal regulation on every new car. Ford wanted the ruling rescinded. Iacocca did most of the talking.

So secret was this thirty-seven-minute meeting that even Nixon's secretary of transportation, John A. Volpe, heard only rumors about it afterward and never managed to get the White House to confirm that it took place. The fact that a crucial conference had occurred eventually became common knowledge, but what had happened? Years later congressional investigating committees tried twice to obtain a transcript but did not succeed. It surfaced in the November 18, 1982, issue of a lawyers' newsletter, and only through circumstances close to inadvertence.**

*This is not the place to do full justice to the controversy. Readers can request the pamphlet (third edition, 1985) from the institute at Watergate 600, Washington, D.C. 20037.
† "Part of a conversation among President Nixon, Lide [*sic*] Anthony Iacocca, Henry Ford II and John D. Ehrlichman in the Oval Office on April 27, 1971, between 11:08 and 11:45 A.M.," from the National Archives and Records Administration, Nixon Presidential Materials Project.
**People tend to think that all of Nixon's White House tapes are public property. They're not. Except for matters directly related to the Watergate scandals, the tapes remain under Nixon's control. The former president was subpoenaed to testify as a witness

Unintimidated by the aura of the presidency or its oval surroundings, Iacocca, early in the meeting, laid out its true stake, the strategic issue behind the air bag question, and its urgency.

"We will have our first major confrontation for real this time," he informed the president. "Uh, we've had threats before, but, uh, this brings up this whole issue of, uh, how important is safety."

The prime measurement, Iacocca made clear, is money: "We have on our cars today a hundred and fifty dollars of, I don't say all gadgetry 'cause the steering columns, I think, are saving lives, the collapsible column and the like, but the shoulder harnesses,* and the headrests are complete wastes of money."

Now salesman Iacocca, selling Nixon the way he sold Charlie Beacham, Bob McNamara, Henry Ford, his car dealers and their customers, pulled out the stops, hyperbole included: "When we have inflation on top of pollution [controls] . . . you can see that safety has really killed all of our business."

Safety hadn't killed some automobile business; no, safety killed *all* of it!

A moment later Iacocca pronounced himself helpless, and threw himself with emotion at the mercy of Nixon, the supreme arbiter: "We're not only frustrated, but, uh, we've reached the despair point. We don't know what to do anymore."

Next he conjured up the villain, the yellow menace, the small and none-too-popular "Japs" (that was Iacocca's word), who work for next to nothing. It was all their fault: "They are going to put whatever is demanded by law in this country on at a buck fifty an hour, and we're, we just cracked seven dollars an hour. . . . The Japs are in the wings ready to eat us up alive."

And the ultimate bosses, the voters? Did they truly want safety? Iacocca pleaded: "I'm in a position to be saying to . . . [Secretary] Volpe: 'Would you guys cool it a little bit? You're gonna break us.' And they say, 'Hold it. People want safety.' I say, 'Well, they, what do you mean they want safety?' We get letters (unintelligible). We get about thousands on customer service. You can't get your car fixed. We don't get anything on safety."

---

in the case of a suit for wrongful death filed against Ford in Pennsylvania by the parents of a teenage girl killed in the crash of a Ford car. Nixon agreed to release the 1971 tape as part of a deal to quash his subpoena.

*This reference to shoulder harnesses seems to represent a decided pullback from Iacocca's early enthusiastic endorsement of seat belts. The harnesses, now long mandatory, form part of the seat belt system and often keep heads from crashing into windshields in accidents.

President Nixon, who had been encouraging Iacocca's arguments right along with supportive comments, here responded with one word—"Right"—and accepted the Iacocca postulate, possibly accurate, that American drivers don't much care about safety until their own blood flows on the highway. From this Iacocca and Nixon concluded, jointly and inaccurately, that safety, specifically air bags, was unneeded, and the air bag ruling was shortly rescinded in the face of Secretary Volpe's disagreement.*

About four years before the text of the White House summit became public, Iacocca went out of his way to deny that the meeting had resembled its transcript. He took this position when he was negotiating safety matters with Brock Adams, then President Jimmy Carter's secretary of transportation, and Joan Claybrook, Carter's chief of highway safety.

"He's an enthralling performer," Claybrook told me in late 1986; "we were always just goo-goo-eyed when he came." At the close of one such performance Iacocca turned to Claybrook and offered an inventive version of the famous meeting with Nixon. "I bet you think we tried to get Nixon to kill the air bag," Claybrook remembers Iacocca saying. "That's not what it was about. We were talking about price controls."

The air bags issue has been stalking him like Banquo's ghost, and so insistently that he has said he is steeled for St. Peter to question him about air bags the moment he arrives to seek admission at the pearly gates.

When confronted unexpectedly, Iacocca overreacts strongly. The issue popped up to haunt him at a 1985 reception in Washington celebrating the introduction of the new Chrysler line of cars. Clar-

*By 1986 air bags still cost about $800. Safety advocates attribute the high price to small production caused by lack of demand. They say that the price can be whittled to $200 or even $100. Mercedes-Benz was supplying driver-side air bags in all new cars as standard equipment. Ford offered the bags as options on four-door Tempo and Topaz models. The technology of the systems had much improved. The Supreme Court found the air bag "an effective and cost-beneficial lifesaving technology" and instructed the Department of Transportation in 1983 to require automatic restraints, air bags or *automatic* seat belts, in all new cars or supply justification for not doing so. The department subsequently ruled that 10 percent of all 1987 models, and all models by 1990, must have "automatic restraints" unless laws mandating seat belts are passed in a "substantial" number of states. The bottom line, then, is that air bags have been authoritatively accepted as desirable. The question of how soon they will be widely used remains open, but in December 1986 Iacocca seemed to be throwing in the towel at long last. A tentative decision was announced to equip at least half of all Chrysler cars with air bags before long.

ence Ditlow, the director of the Center for Auto Safety, had been invited and took along a young blond Virginia housewife, Rosemary Dunlap, president of a lobbying group that calls itself Motor Voters.

Mrs. Dunlap, an ardent air bag advocate, had written to Iacocca, had asked him to meet with her and other air bag proponents, and had received no reply. When Iacocca finally made an appearance just as most guests were leaving the reception, Mrs. Dunlap approached him, smiled, and wished him *tante auguri* ("best wishes"). Iacocca was just newly remarried, and Mrs. Dunlap had lived in Italy long enough to have picked up some of the language.

Shy as ever with strangers, Iacocca kept smiling but was confused by hearing Italian spoken in Washington and kept repeating *"auguri, auguri"* until he understood and smiled some more.

Whereupon Mrs. Dunlap, who is small and weighs 115 pounds, pulled a copy of her letter out of her little handbag and tried to hand it to Iacocca.

Instantly she felt like a holdup man. "He stepped back, hands up, looking startled, very uneasy," she recalls. "His total demeanor changed. Maybe he was fearing service of process or foul play. He was looking at his guards, big guys, seven or eight of them."

Mrs. Dunlap happened to know about bodyguards and wasn't frightened. Her brother-in-law is a Secret Service agent and had served on the presidential detail. So she was not surprised when one of the guards seized her letter and assured her it would get attention. It did, in the form of a note from Iacocca: "I appreciated your bringing your views to my attention. It was thoughtful of you to take the time to address this issue, and I will be sure to keep your comments in mind."

This formality, too, did not surprise Mrs. Dunlap. "What surprised me," she said, "was that this was something he *feared*."

On June 10, 1986, viewers of NBC television received food for negative thought about Iacocca from a frightening and impressively researched documentary called *Safety Lost*. Its spotlight was on light trucks, and here was pretty Connie Chung saying in her demure manner that 5,600 Americans had died needlessly in 1985 in these enormously popular vehicles mostly because the trucks lacked passenger headrests, or because they were made without steel-reinforcement beams in the side doors, or because the strength of their roofs proved inadequate when the trucks rolled over.

Consumers didn't know, Chung said, that such lifesaving devices were required by federal law in passenger cars but not in the vehicles advertised as "fun trucks."

Iacocca was cast as the sole defender of his industry. He appeared twice, his mood and bearing so dramatically different each time that I was reminded of his friends who had told me that they knew him with two faces, the benevolent, public Dr. Jekyll and the hidden, mean, private Mr. Hyde. It was eerie to watch the change right on my VCR.

The first Iacocca was the happy warrior everybody knows from his commercials. Beaming, he drove a little light blue Dodge truck into a Chrysler Corporation plant filled with cheering employees. Head high, chest popping with pride, he addressed them, basking in his latest success story: Instead of one truck getting sold for every five cars, which had been the ratio only five years earlier, a truck was now marketed for every two passenger vehicles—a triumph for Lee Iacocca, the onetime truck salesman.

Then, flip-flopping to the negative side of the story, the film quickly zeroed in on victims.

A young daughter told how her father lingered five years before dying of brain damage he received when the rear of his unprotected head crashed against the rear window of his truck cab.

A young credit manager told how her leg was amputated because of a sideswiping collision.

A safety expert appeared on the screen and said the accident would have been a "walkaway" had the door of the victim's truck been reinforced by a steel beam.

The testimony of these and other witnesses was punctuated with film showing mangled remains of trucks, bodies lying on highways receiving blood transfusions and oxygen, bodies being whisked away on stretchers, bodies lying lifeless under white sheets in truck wrecks. They were sights for strong stomachs only.

Now the cameras let the audience meet Iacocca's other persona, head down, face grim and jowly, arms folded defensively in front of the chest, voice low, at least at first. Maximum safety was attainable by one simple rule, he said: "You must wear a shoulder harness and belt at all times, and you must get drunk drivers off the road and the rest is so minimal really."

Connie Chung inquired how he viewed the truck safety devices she had discussed earlier in the program.

"There are so many gimmicks you can put on that might save some injury or fatality," said Iacocca, his voice rising slightly; the ratios of cost versus benefits had been analyzed and had to prevail.

Chung asked what he meant by "gimmicks," her voice still quiet and barely quizzical.

"I don't think headrests in our array of facts are a factor in protecting a person that are meaningful," said Iacocca. And then: "Why talk about a lousy little beam?"

"While I was doing the interview, I could feel the heat," Chung told me. "He was very angry. I could sense more and more tension."

Once off the air, Iacocca seemed "very upset" and voiced his displeasure at Chung and at the Chrysler public relations man who had brought him to the filming. Iacocca felt his answers had been poor because he had not briefed himself thoroughly enough. He had been harpooned by his most feared bugaboo. He had been *surprised*. Surprises were almost always bad or very bad.

"She ambushed him," said Baron Bates, the Chrysler public relations man who had made the arrangements with Chung and was present at the interview. The possibility that the reporter simply had a more meritorious case than Iacocca did not come up in Bates's subsequent postmortems with The Chairman. The debacle was Chung's fault, no question.*

Shortly afterward Iacocca asked NBC for an opportunity to be interviewed again about truck safety. He'd find the time, but only if the first film would not be shown. The NBC programmers said they were ready to go anywhere to shoot more film, but they turned down his deal; they would not junk the first film. This standoff became the last word except for the words from relatives of the victims. They had spoken at the conclusion of the program *Safety Lost*. They could not forgive—"Safety? Ha!" one victim's daughter muttered bitterly—just as Jim Musselman, Nader's man, could not forgive.

For Musselman, Iacocca was a wonderfully visible fall guy whose record served him as a lever for getting more air bags into more cars and saving more lives. Musselman knew how to mobilize emotions and keep tears flowing. To the draft-Iacocca press conference he brought along a Washington attorney, Robert Tiernan, who founded the Airbag Information Center after his thirteen-year-old son had

*The defeat rankled. When Bates told Iacocca months later that a reporter was coming to see him," The Chairman growled, "It better not be Connie Chung!" Another time when Iacocca was given details about an upcoming press briefing on a new line of cars, he demanded: "Is Connie Chung coming?"

died from injuries of a 1981 crash in a Chrysler K-car. The boy had lingered in a coma for a year and a half. Tiernan joined Mussel-man's filibuster at the press conference and blamed Iacocca directly for his son's death because the K-car had not been equipped with an air bag.

Musselman, quiet, pink, boyish, said he planned to hound Iacocca with many, many parents of thirteen-year-olds like Eric Grimshaw and the Tiernan boy and with the relatives of older crash victims. There were so many of them with more tears still unshed. They were terribly angry, and their emotions could be easily channeled to worship the air bag and damn Iacocca and his "disinformation."

"If he makes such a decision on the air bag, what would he do as president about the [space] shuttle?" Musselman demanded. "It's like sitting on a vaccine for cancer."

He would personally appear whenever the Iacocca boosters held gatherings.

"I told 'em to save me a seat," he said.

Would voters care? Maybe not very much. Musselman's initial press conference caper captured little attention. The *Detroit News* was one of the few papers to perk up a bit (PROTESTERS ASSAIL IACOCCA ON AUTO SAFETY ran the headline on page 11). Most of the coverage barely alluded to the impassioned interruption on behalf of safety. The air bag issue bored the press and seemed largely dormant. In 1987, laws making seat belts mandatory were still fighting their way slowly toward acceptance by state legislatures a quarter century after Iacocca had first advocated them. Drivers still seemed none too interested in being saved from themselves.

To exercise leadership is to lead the parade but not to strut so far ahead of it that the leader can't hear the sound of the band. The Iacocca record on safety shows ambivalence with a touch of callousness—much like the record compiled by the rest of us, the public.

He shrugged off the safety issue. The loss of life appeared to leave him pretty much unmoved. Or was he going to great lengths to hide guilt feelings? That was possible, but it would be unusual for Iacocca. Emotions normally well up easily in this man. They seem to ooze out of his every pore, especially his feelings about the bedrock of his life, his roots, and his values.

15.

THE IACOCCA VALUES

H E CALLS IT VILLA NICOLA, AFTER HIS REVERED AND FEARED FATHER. It is an isolated stone farmhouse on twelve acres of wooded hills and vineyards in rural Tuscany, about an hour by car from Siena, on the Old World soil of his father's native Italy. Iacocca acquired this retreat in 1985 and revels in it with unashamed sentimentality. Thoughts of father Nick preoccupy him in Tuscany even more than normally. The farm is perhaps the ultimate symbol of success. It is as if the son were showing Nick that he was graduated as *numero uno* from high school after all.

Iacocca's roots are visible here, and he experiences them like tonic. The baking ovens in back of the house are hundreds of years old, hundreds! And there are fig trees, lots of the fig trees that Nick loved so much, not just a couple like the ones the old man coaxed out of the grudging soil back in Allentown. Lee shakes his head and says to his friend Bill Fugazy, "Can you imagine if Nick was here?"

Surely Nick's unquenchable enthusiasm would brim over if he could glimpse his son's vineyards. Nick would have remembered, as Lee remembers now, how the house on North Seventh Street in Allentown filled up with a pungent odor every fall when Nick made four or five barrels of red wine. And Nick would have chuckled, as Lee does now, at seeing the Villa Nicola vineyard workers stomping on the Sangiovese grapes.

That was real winemaking, winemaking from scratch, as mother Antoinette, too, appreciated when Lee flew her to the Villa Nicola for a long vacation. From scratch—that's the way Antoinette, now in her eighties, still produces her meatball soup and other dishes. (Reporters calling for her recipes always get firmly lectured first: "My cooking is always from scratch! Fresh! I don't care for that canned stuff! Our people cooked from scratch, and I cook from scratch!")

At the Villa Nicola son Lee also likes to cook himself, linguine and such, from scratch, of course, and when the place first came into the family, the friends whom Iacocca brought there to share the almost primal experience, men with Italian roots of their own like Fugazy (Fugazzi) and Hank Carlini, thought it would be an oasis of repose.

While the name of the nearest village was kept secret to assure the privacy of the *padrone*, its obscurity also helped. Chrysler Vice Chairman Ben Bidwell, the company's resident wit and assistant phrasemaker, was unable to find the place on his map and kidded Iacocca: "I know about unlisted phone numbers, but whoever had anything as exclusive as an unlisted town!"

The surroundings were as relaxing to Iacocca as the villa. His cronies drove with him to Siena, watched him glance through the *International Herald Tribune* while leaning against a building like a native, or soak up espresso, sunshine, and a cigar in the café on the square.

The bucolic lassitude was brief. Carlini was sitting with his chief, overlooking the vineyards, and the peacefulness was too much for them.

"You know," said Carlini, "that wine might be fantastic. Maybe Giorgio could do something with this."

Iacocca laughed off the idea at first but quickly reconsidered. The place was costing him a bundle. Its sentimental value was beyond price, but his Depression-born inclination to be tight with money, combined with his entrepreneurial itch, proved too strong. He told Carlini to talk to Anthony ("Tony") Giorgio in Detroit, another old pal of Italian ancestry. Giorgio, who manufactures industrial fasteners and controls other businesses, including a wine-importing firm, was enthusiastic about the five sample cases from Italy. A personalized miniempire was launched.

The wine, named Villa Nicola, in memory of Papa Nick, was dismissed as "unpretentious" by the *Wall Street Journal* and criticized as overpriced by some distributors, but the publicity about the brand's sponsor helped. The labels announce that it is *"imbottigliata per* [bottled for] Lee Iacocca" and carry the master's signature, as do all the corks.

In keeping with entrepreneurial religion, the growth of the business soon seemed assured. Some 10,000 bottles of the Iacocca product were sold right away in midwestern and eastern cities; another 60,000 bottles of wine from "neighboring places" moved about as rapidly. "Extra virgin" olive oil *"confezionato per* [manufactured by] Lee Iacocca" was the next import item, followed by eight-year-old balsamic vinegar which carried a similar personal sendoff.

"I invite you to enjoy its superb quality as I have in my own home," says the olive oil label over the illustrious signature. In short, if you can find better olive oil, buy it!

Then automobiles joined Iacocca's Old World idyll. It was inevitable. He had long maintained a love affair with the exquisitely designed and engineered Italian sports vehicles for connoisseurs, like the long-ago Mangusta and Pantera, those boutique cars as temperamental as their maker, that other Iacocca buddy Alejandro de Tomaso, the owner of Maserati in Modena. Some 75 percent of de Tomaso's workers were Communist party members, but Alejandro liked to say it was almost impossible to put together a bad car in Modena because the workers were too proud of their craft and refused to short-circuit quality.

In 1986 Iacocca bet that his old friend's happy theory made business sense. Communists or not, Chrysler took control of de Tomaso and Maserati, and in the fall Iacocca flew his board members to Modena. They looked around their exotic acquisition, test-drove the prototypes of the hot new models Alejandro was developing for them, and were bundled off en bloc to the Villa Nicola. At a board meeting convened in a small nearby spa, Iacocca's bunch celebrated the retirement of two members, but the high point of the junket, everyone agreed, was the outdoor cocktail party toward sundown at the master's villa.

Nobody had seen him so happy, so loose, so underdressed. Striding about in slacks and rugby shirt, he supervised the distribution of such local delicacies as wild boar sausage and the vino named for his father.

"The Godfather has returned to his home," one of the directors observed later, laughing, but there was nothing sinister about these proceedings. It was all fun. Vice Chairman Bidwell asked Lee how the wine was selling locally. All of it was exported, said Lee. What about penetration, Lee, don't we worry about market penetration? How can you penetrate the market abroad if you aren't penetrating locally?

The irrelevance of the joke was what made it so relevant. Iacocca just kept circulating, drinking a glass or two more than usual, and exclaiming, "Isn't this great?" Said one of the directors: "He was welling over with pride like a kid on Christmas morning showing off his new toys to the neighbors."

Showing off and gaining more and more acceptance.

Acceptance. Iacocca was reaping rich helpings of the precious stuff on his father's soil in Italy as well as in the finally booming world of Chrysler in Detroit, yet still not everywhere in Detroit, not in the class-conscious precincts of Henry II. It irked Lee that he was still put down as an Italian arriviste by Henry's crowd, and he determined to change this second-class status once and for all by jamming down roots in the precise spot where the Fords had traditionally tended theirs. The upshot was the sort of I-can-be-as-grand-as-you-are competition that nourishes the souls of society editors and real estate salesmen.

During all of his Detroit career Iacocca had lived in Bloomfield Hills north of town—a comfortable, even posh enclave of executives. The old elite nested east of town in Grosse Pointe, especially in Grosse Pointe Farms at the Lake Michigan shoreline. In 1943 Henry Ford and his first wife moved into their "honeymoon cottage" there, at 300 Provencal Road. The pillared brick colonial was relatively modest for that neighborhood: seven bedrooms, three acres. But Provencal Road was the ultimate. It was itself an example of the *numero uno* category.

Provencal is a perfectly private world of estates, a cul-de-sac one block long, flanked on one side by *the* golf club of the area, the Country Club of Detroit, and on the other by the Grosse Pointe Hunt Club. Provencal can be entered only through a gate watched by a uniformed guard. When they're not at their castle in Britain, Henry Ford and his third wife still reside there. They had little trouble acquiring a more elaborate home down the street from No. 300, but the universe of this neighborhood, a mere handful of homes, is difficult for ordinary mortals to penetrate.

A place on Lakeshore Drive, a block away from Provencal, became available in 1985, and Iacocca was seen inspecting it repeatedly. So, separately, was his then-fiancée, Peggy Johnson. Mysteriously the house was taken off the market and shortly sold to Edsel Bryant Ford II. Gossips whispered that the house had been commandeered by Henry Ford or one of his disciples. The defeat turned into triumph for Lee and Peggy a year later. The Ford honeymoon cottage at 300 Provencal came on the market! The Iacoccas snapped it up, and a *Detroit News* cartoon showed Henry Ford looking out the window and saying, "There goes the neighborhood."

In Grosse Pointe, the Iacocca beachhead was no joke. Some snickered at the eagerness of the newcomers to carpetbag on Henry's turf in an effort to become his equal. Lee's friends wondered about the new neighbors' readiness to *accept* him. One old pal, Bill Curran, was making worried calls, trying to soften up the officers of the Country Club of Detroit. Would these keepers of tradition accept such a brash squatter? Much as Curran loved him, he almost wished Lee had stayed out of Provencal. "I don't know what the hell he wants to leave Bloomfield for," Curran grumbled, mystified.

It was no mystery. For Iacocca, the planting and replanting of roots are a confirmation of his values, fundamental to the furious force of his striving to become *numero uno* beyond challenge, the drive propelling his bluffing, his diligence, his tenacity, his calculated rages and occasional ruthlessness, the eye always focusing hard, concentrating on the immediate goal and on the next goal and on the plan, the plan for getting there, for making it, making it as Nick had demanded it of him. Demanded!

Irresistibly the son whose favorite animal is the bull overrides adversity, though not always on the first try. Lee Iacocca has turned adversity into a value of itself: faith in renewal; the hurdle hurdled. He has overcome so many hurdles: the fear of the father and the fatherly goading; the resentment of the "abuse" in grade school because of his Italian origin; the disabilities of the rheumatic fever in high school; the 4-F rejection by his country at college time; the shyness always; the insult upon his integrity during the inquisition at Ford; shame of the social rejection and the firing by Henry; the resistances Iacocca had to hurdle during the revival of the Chrysler corpse; the replacement of the long-ailing spouse with a young new wife, the uncertainties of the separation from her . . . the hard realities of a hard lifetime.

If the hardness of experience has turned *him* hard, even callous, in his demands on himself and on the people who must face the bull side of his personality in business, life has not brutalized his innermost feelings or what he holds dear. The Iacocca who bubbles over in Italy when he can fill his friends with companionship and wine and wild boar sausage is real. He can indeed be a "mushcake," as the Iacoccalytes claim, and the evidence is ample and openly expressed.

Openly but not necessarily in public, at least not entirely in public. The Iacocca involvement with the Statue of Liberty—Peggy Iacocca thinks of the monument as his "other lady"—is a case in point.

The public side of the story received considerable attention. Miss Liberty and her base, Ellis Island, the admission gate where 16 million immigrants had to pass the U.S. government's stringent muster between 1892 and 1924 before being allowed into the country, were in need of urgent, expensive repairs. The government appointed Iacocca to raise the money and Detroit's great mover and shaker plunged into the mission with the gusto that had made him famous.

He announced that anyone could have a picture taken with him in exchange for a donation of $100,000. After one fellow came to his office to give him $1 million on the condition that his name would never be revealed, Iacocca teased his audiences by promising that anonymity would also be available to any other $1 million donor, if desired. In any event, he insisted, he would no longer grace any Statue of Liberty luncheons as a speaker unless the organizers *guaranteed* $1 million up front.

Lest anyone think he was turning elitist, he pleaded with equal fervor for nickels from schoolchildren and came away with equally spectacular success.

"Five million dollars of nickels I got!" he crowed.

The Iacocca publicity machine started grinding out words of supplication overtime, much of this inspirational material appearing under his by-line. "In Pursuit of Liberty" was the title of his article in *Parade* magazine, and it opened with a hazily remembered vignette of his being taken to the statue by Papa Nick in the 1920s, when little Lido was five, not many years after Nick had bribed the immigration inspectors to let his sick young wife into the promised land.

"The only thing I remember is climbing the stairs," wrote the son. "I remember my father hauling me by the hand up a long stairway that seemed to go on forever. I didn't know where we were going, or why. I couldn't understand what could be so important that my father made me climb all those stairs. And I don't think I understood for more than fifty years [that] . . . my father went back, maybe in his own way just to say thanks."

That sounded heartfelt, all right, but in all the verbiage, ghostwritten and not, in all the scurrying and cigar waving, who could separate authentic feeling for liberty and patriotism from hard sell delivered by automatic pilot? Were these sentiments perhaps interchangeable with Iacocca's car commercials on TV, trumpeting "The Pride Is Back—Born in America" or the billboards for the Chrysler LeBaron introducing its new model as "An American Hero"?

It certainly looked as if commerce and patriotism were one and the same thing when, at 7:45 A.M. on July 4, 1986, the *Queen Elizabeth 2* steamed into Upper New York Bay totally occupied by Iacocca's most elite troops. They were 800 Chrysler and Dodge dealers with some 800 escorts and guests, chosen salesmen who had done battle against their quotas and won. Their boss had ferried them to a choice spot amid thousands of assembled vessels and now, never mind the hour, they were toasting the refurbished Statue of Liberty in champagne and wearing jackets proclaiming "The Pride Is Back."

The scene, said the normally unflappable *New York Times*, was "of almost biblical proportions," and for Iacocca and his soldiers it was only the final act of a two-week spectacular, the "trip of a lifetime," as a dealer from Santa Monica, California, described it. Iacocca had flown the group to Paris for dinner at the Palace of Versailles, then on to London and, by ship, to Bermuda and New York. Buck Sloan, a dealer from Waxahachie, Texas, reported that the group had drunk several of the ship's bars completely dry.

The action in New York harbor fit the dealers' jubilation. The trip of a lifetime, Chrysler Corporation saved and prosperous, the Statue of Liberty saved, the champagne flowing for breakfast, the *Queen Elizabeth* releasing 2,500 red, white, and blue balloons, a ten-piece band playing "Yankee Doodle Dandy," the fireboats spraying red, white, and blue geysers, it was almost too much good fortune, and the dealers and the country owed it all to Lee Iacocca.

"Lee Iacocca is today's ultimate American hero," said Maddy Miller, wife of Wendell Miller, owner of three dealerships. And after a special mass attended by Iacocca at St. Patrick's Cathedral, John Cardinal O'Connor explained the Iacocca appeal to reporters: "I just think people see and hear what they perceive to be authenticity."

This worried the Republicans in Washington and, as every TV watcher knows, the Reagan administration decided that Iacocca's yeast was rising too high, and it fired him from one of the two Statue of Liberty committees. The dispute between Iacocca and the piously indignant Interior Secretary Donald P. Hodel (who huffed: "The statue is more than Lee Iacocca") was basically about what to create on Ellis Island. Hodel & Company wanted a hotel and conference center. Iacocca considered this too commercial, a desecration. He preferred a Williamsburg-style restoration so visitors could "see exactly what your mother or father or grandparents saw." He wanted to re-create what he called "an island of tears." His opponents lampooned this concept as an ethnic Iacoccaland.

How to use the $250 million raised by Iacocca remains an unresolved question at this writing, but the teapot controversy presented him with a fantastic chance to shove his famous face onto the network news, to denounce President Reagan's man Hodel as a pipsqueak and ingrate ("*I* got the nickels!" thundered Lido), and to enact the role of David slaying the Goliath named Washington, D.C. That wasn't exactly what was happening, but whatever was transpiring was making Iacocca look terrific.

"It was," said *Newsweek*, "yet another proof that in a time of dim gray men and prepackaged politicians, Lido Anthony Iacocca knows how to shine."

The private side of Iacocca's affair with Miss Liberty is quieter and more revealing of the man. It began early in 1982 in the office of the then Interior Secretary James Watt. The secretary faced the problem of getting the dilapidated statue and its island shaped up without using public funds. He had seen Iacocca performing his commercials on television and thought he'd discovered the perfect fund-raiser.

No way, said the peppery Charles ("Chick") Cudlip, Chrysler's Washington lobbyist, when the Interior people brought the proposition to him. Iacocca was far too immersed in Chrysler's comeback problems to subject himself to yet another uphill struggle, this one without budget or staff. But Chick promised to put the matter to his chief and to pass along reading material about the statue and the island that the government delegation had left with him.

Iacocca went through the material, reading excerpts from it aloud to his dying wife, and reported later that they both got goose bumps as they learned how refugees used to be herded into the Great Hall where Papa Nick twice started life in America, once when he arrived as a lad, the second time when he brought over his bride.

The discussion between Lee and Mary about the fund-raising job was brief.

"Lee, you have to do it," said Mary.

So that February Iacocca, Cudlip, and some men from the National Park Service took a little government boat across New York harbor to the twenty-seven-acre island. It was one of those wind-tossed icebound days when the city's commuters can muster sympathy for Admiral Byrd fighting his way to the Pole. Iacocca, the hypochondriac who is never warm enough, seemed to wither under his fat overcoat with its upturned fur collar; his nose was wet as the group trooped down the long flight of steps into the decrepit Great Hall.

"You all right?" Cudlip asked Iacocca.

Iacocca made a hushing noise, and they kept going, eventually stomping around outside, among the stark, leafless trees and the rest of the shivering landmark waiting in ice to be reborn.

Watching his boss wilt under the wind, Cudlip again suggested that they cut the trip short, but Iacocca plowed through the remainder of the agenda without hesitation.

"Did you see it all?" he asked Cudlip* when they were warming up on the boat over a thermos of coffee. This was patriotism naked. "Couldn't you see and hear all our ancestors coming down

*It needs to be reported that Cudlip, who related this poignant story, is no Iacoccalyte. Not long after their trip to Ellis Island the two men stopped seeing eye to eye about Cudlip's job at Chrysler, and he left.

those steps?" asked Iacocca. *He* could see and hear it all. It *was* an island of tears, this place where the uniformed men almost didn't let his mother into the country—a moment of terror which his father must have remembered when he took five-year-old Lido up those interminable steps. Frozen as he was on his boat now, Chairman Iacocca was near tears himself.

And always his thoughts turned back to the Great Hall and how it had stirred him. "It's like a cathedral," he told an interviewer years later, "a churchlike setting, a place to pray. It brings tears to your eyes."

So tears are not alien to this man. They moisten his eyes when he speaks to friends of his father, and the more than 100 guests were touched to see tears in public at the party for his sixtieth birthday. It was a surprise affair at "21" in New York, arranged in secret by his daughters, Kathi, twenty-six, and Lia, twenty-one, and it really remained a surprise to the end. They told Iacocca they'd be joined only by his mother and sister, and they had a hard time luring him to the restaurant and cajoling him into wearing a dinner jacket. Lee was stubborn, as usual. "If there's a Tigers game, I'm not going," he threatened. Luckily there was no game, and when the Princeton Glee Club began to sing, the scene at "21" was straight from *This Is Your Life*.

Everyone was there, absolutely everyone who had mattered to Iacocca over the years (see Chapter 13, "The Company He Keeps and Keeps"), and as he rose to talk, slowly, lovingly, about friendship, his eyes were very wet. Friendship is loyalty. Loyalty is important, very important.

And Iacocca is sentimental about many other things. He is sentimental about the two old cars he keeps in his garage, a beloved 1931 Model A Ford convertible and a 1964 Mustang convertible. He is sentimental about April 17, the memorable day the Mustang was launched and therefore also the date he married his second wife. He appears, beaming, at the annual reunions of the Iacocca clan—full-throated, a couple of hundred strong—celebrating themselves in a public park at Emmaus, Pennsylvania, just outside Allentown. And when Iacocca Plaza was inaugurated at Lehigh University in honor of Papa Nick, Lee led so many Iacoccas that they filled two long rows out front.

Iacocca phones his mother in Allentown about every other day, and she is not too embarrassed to complain to reporters that she doesn't see enough of her distinguished son. The same openness prevails in his relationship with his daughters. The Iacoccalytes insist he is very close to the girls. They were given a private phone number where they can reach him in Detroit (if he happens to be there). After their mother died, Iacocca took the older girl to Europe, where the pair attended cooking classes, and when Kathi was single, working in Washington, her father often spent the night in the spare bedroom of her apartment.

For the young women, the closeness is not nearly close enough. "Sometimes I'd just like to rip the phone out of the wall," confesses Lia. She fantasizes about disguising her father with a big nose, false glasses, and mustache and wig and kidnapping him to a Caribbean island, presumably one without phones. Kathi, who runs the Juvenile Diabetes Foundation that her father established in New York in honor of her late mother (the foundation that gets the royalties from The Book), is more directly critical of the impatient, preoccupied dad with the backbreaking schedule of travel, board meetings, public appearances, on and on.

"He's all business," she has complained. "He doesn't like to hear run-of-the-mill details about your life, and he can freeze you out when he's no longer interested in what you are saying" (although he finds time to admonish her not to spend too much on furniture).

Kathi is talking about the shell that Iacocca draws around himself like an iron mantle, suddenly and often, the distancing from others that the Iacoccalytes also talk about. Perhaps most interesting about the gripes of the daughters is the fact that they were openly broadcast, and to a *Life* reporter at that. Young Lido would have dared no such mutinous indiscretions about Nick back in the Allentown days.

The women in Iacocca's life have never been meek or unintelligent or unattractive. He allows them to be seen as well as heard, and they are not entirely without influence. They are, however, never admitted to full partnership. Intellectually they have not been remotely his equal. In family matters the scope of their portfolios is conventional. In Iacocca's business concerns their voices count for little or nothing.

The mother is a full-time matriarch whose stardom centers on meatball soup. The sister is a small-town housewife. Both of the women Iacocca picked as his wives worked for a living, but their jobs were lowly. It is probably no coincidence that Mary, the plumber's daughter, never rose beyond the rank of receptionist at Ford, while the second Mrs. Iacocca, the sharecropper's daughter, had to keep smiling at airline passengers to maintain herself before she met Iacocca.

All of which makes it easier for Lee to remain in control as the star of his show.

Some stars anoint themselves with values that stretch society's rules beyond the conventional. Unlike Papa Nick, who fancied himself something of a star in Allentown, Lee Iacocca does not pull rank on school crossing guards and does not get arrested for drunken driving. But like Nick, he does sometimes fashion his own rules, and in rather draconian or devious ways, occasionally with unhappy consequences for himself and sizable numbers of fellow citizens (whose welfare does not, in the light of his immediate goal, seem to matter much to him when he is under the gun himself).

The Pinto absolutely *had* to be bullied into production, weighing 2,000 pounds and costing $2,000, and if the resulting climate of fear paralyzed the engineers and kept them from speaking up to Iacocca about the flammability of the fuel tank, whose human failure was this?

If the federal rule to make air bags mandatory *had* absolutely to be scuttled, that evidently made it all right for Iacocca to lobby secretly against this safety device before President Nixon personally and to deny even years later that he had brought up the subject at all in the White House.

If 5,000 Americans had to die each year because the sensationally selling new light trucks lack routine safety features required by law in passenger vehicles, why, that *had* to be acceptable because the lifesaving devices (such as that "one lousy little beam" Iacocca had grumbled about on the Connie Chung show) were not cost-effective.

What sanctified these rules for Iacocca? Blind ambition? Rigid belief that a course, once adopted, must not be modified for fear of appearing weak? Were these rules rooted in the dollar consciousness that sends Billy Fugazy into giggles when he tells how he and Papa Nick practically used to have to pull a stickup on Lee in a shoe store when they wanted to tease their rich companion into paying for a few pairs of shoes? Or do the Iacocca values express an extreme consciousness of rank, a surrender to the belief that if you are indeed *numero uno*, everybody else is indeed a lesser being and had better duck?

The Iacocca values were brought up by Harold Soper in my chat with this retired comptroller of the Parts and Services Division at Ford, the meticulous CPA who had been involved in the investigation of Iacocca's finances in the seventies. When Iacocca philosophized about budgets over a cigar after 5:00 P.M. Soper would grow uncomfortable.

"His idea of what was ethical and mine were different," he recalled.

No, there wasn't anything wrong with using the hunting lodges of suppliers or going to football games in trailers rented by Ford. Everybody did it, and everything was always documented. Soper just didn't care for it. He didn't like the way Iacocca acted *entitled* to perquisites.

"You're too much of a Pollyanna," Lee would tell Harold.

Soper did not think he was a Pollyanna at all. On the contrary. When Lee wanted to cut 100 people out of accounting so he could add 100 to sales—after all, he argued, the marketing department brought in the money—Soper fought the proposal successfully. He wanted tighter controls, not more loopholes so dealers could milk Ford more.

"The dealers will take advantage of you," Soper told Iacocca. Iacocca said Soper simply didn't understand how things had to be massaged so they'd get *done* in the real world of business.

The Iacocca-for-president boom was at its peak when I talked to Soper, yet no matter how ardently Soper admired Iacocca's brilliant mind, as he told me, he was one Republican who'd never vote for him.

"He's not president material," Soper said. "He's not the kind of man I'd like my kids to use as a role model."

Iacocca, the mushcake. Iacocca, the Pinto maker. There had to be at least two of him, maybe more. Maybe, actually, a president of the United States. There were Iacocca fans who between 1982 and 1987 were giving very serious thought to this role for him.

16.

IACOCCA FOR PRESIDENT

"THIS IS SOME-
THING I'VE GOT TO
DUCK," TERRY O'CONNELL REMEM-
BERS TELLING HIMSELF WHEN
DICK FITZPATRICK KEPT PHONING
HIM IN WASHINGTON TO LOBBY ON
BEHALF OF THE EMBRYONIC MOVE-
MENT.

It was 1984, and Fitzpatrick was cranking up the bandwagon by rallying his
friends. He was a Michigan state representative, a Democrat from
Battle Creek, home of breakfast cereals, and his infectious enthusiasm made up for what he lacked in political clout. Having
acquired a reputation for his earlier years of public relations
cheerleading on behalf of the Grand Ole Opry show, he thought
he'd finally hit on a great cause: drafting Iacocca to run for president.

O'Connell, forty-one, is a big, irrepressible rumpled bear, a jolly
promoter for causes of his choosing. He does lobbying in a well-
connected firm of consultants half a block from Capitol Hill. O'Con-

nell liked Fitzpatrick. They were fellow veterans of Vietnam, where O'Connell lost his left eye and arm to a grenade. (He convalesced for two years and eight months at Walter Reed Hospital and wears an eye patch and a steel hook.)

O'Connell held some useful political credentials. Mostly he had labored for principled losers such as Senators Henry ("Scoop") Jackson and George McGovern, but he had also served as political director of the Democratic National Committee. The trouble with Dick Fitzpatrick's siren song for Iacocca was that it sounded like a lot more work and aggravation than O'Connell needed. He had shifted to very lucrative lobbying for commercial causes. Iacocca meant no money. Worse, the draft movement was waddling like a baby turtle. Even that was putting it too strongly. The whole business was fluff, a joke.

Indeed, it had *started* as a joke of sorts. Iacocca traces its genesis to the Detroit Press Club bar and the generous alcohol consumption there. Specifically he put the finger on Jimmy Jones, the longtime *Newsweek* bureau chief. This, too, is a gag. Jones, an old friend of mine, remembers the bar talk. He says it was prevalent but vague, and he didn't start it.

The movement's first sign of semirespectability blossomed on the front page of Iacocca's busiest critic, the *Wall Street Journal*, on June 28, 1982, but not in the serious parts of the page. Slightly right of center the *Journal* daily spices up its gray fare with a light feature known to staffers as the "A-hed." It is coveted space for a bright writer to execute a frivolous pizzicato, and the Iacocca story was composed by a talented young Detroit correspondent, Amanda Bennett. Lately she had appeared in the same spot with her eyewitnesser on Michigan's last whorehouse.

The "A-hed" is not an out-and-out humor column, however. It's froth but not fantasy. Ms. Bennett had been hearing the Iacocca-for-president rumors around town. A popular sportscaster had mentioned it on his program. He had referred to the famous Iacocca TV commercials and asked more or less rhetorically whether the fellow wouldn't make one terrific president.

Then Ms. Bennett heard that Iacocca's crony George Steinbrenner, the owner of the Yankees, would launch a real Iacocca-for-president boom while introducing Lee as "Man of the Year" at a fundraiser for a local hospital. She attended the affair, and Steinbrenner did work around to the subject in stately terms, remarking: "I can't think of anyone I'd rather follow either as president of Chrysler or president of the United States."

Nothing happened, no applause, no yells of "We want Lee." People just looked at each other. Nevertheless, adequate ammunition had by then accumulated for Ms. Bennett's puckish wit to make an "A-hed" on the front page of the *Journal*.

"Lee Iacocca, it is whispered around Detroit, has a hankering for public office," she wrote. "Not just any public office, but one grand enough to satisfy a man with an ego as big as all outdoors. Lee Iacocca, it is said, the chairman of Chrysler Corporation, yearns to be the president of all the people. If a Hollywood star can, why not a Detroit car salesman?"

Most of the column was taken up by hoots from naysayers ("He'd be crazy to try" . . . "Good luck to him. He'll need it" . . . "I'd leave the country . . ."). Except for Steinbrenner and a couple of car dealers, nobody seemed to take the presidential possibility seriously except, just possibly, Iacocca himself.

"I'm running for any kind of office," he told Ms. Bennett. "I don't think I could handle politics." From this starting point he sailed into a stream of volunteered comments suggesting a frame of mind that seemed to lean in the opposite direction. He sounded pleased by the attention he was receiving on subjects far removed from automobiles.

"I could handle the economy in six months," he bragged without having been asked.

"Running Chrysler these last few years has been bigger than running the country," he claimed.

He followed up by offering Ms. Bennett a string of recommendations covering interest rates, the federal budget, energy policy, Social Security, school lunches, and more. And while he denied that the presidency was his thing, he conceded that he'd enjoy some public office, "maybe economic czar."

What was really on his mind about the presidency? "Some people think they know," wrote Ms. Bennett. "The suspicious see a grand design in Mr. Iacocca's recent activities, such as his TV commercials. 'He's not selling cars, he's selling Iacocca,' one says."

A grand design. A lot of kibitzers professed to detect in Iacocca's behavior a coy and careful game of hear-no-evil, see-no-evil pending the coming of the Call, preferably at the last dramatic moment in 1988. The Great Call, that is. Little calls had been filling his ears for years. They cascaded daily into the Chrysler offices in stacks of fan letters to which he paid rapt attention. He took them home and read them one by one.

The fan mail meant a great deal to Iacocca, and it filled several functions. It was, first off, applause—spontaneous approbation of the unreserved sort that Papa Nick had not dispensed when Lido was small in Allentown. It was unqualified approval and it still filled a need for Nick's son-the-folk-hero. The mail further represented a voice from the marketplace, from customers of Chrysler products. For a chief executive isolated from shopping malls and dealer show-rooms, the letters were a lifeline to reality. More, the letters set up individual relationships with their authors—brief and distant, yet highly personal.

Often the writers identified with the fate of the Chrysler Chair-man; at least this was true of the fans whose mail was leaked (with names omitted) to reporters by the company's public relations people.

The *Washington Post* was given access to this note from a man in Albuquerque: "The reason I am writing this letter is to let you know that I share the same trials and tribulations that you went through . . . at Ford. I was fired from a job which I felt like I had a bright future. . . ."

Iacocca was moved by such confidences and pored over his mail regularly and for many hours. "I try to read a hundred a night," he said. "You hear so much. They pour out their feelings. With some of them, I feel like a psychiatrist, and they're on a couch with me." He paused. "It's almost like—I wanna say—the priest in confes-sion."

For Iacocca, a Catholic who goes to mass on Sundays, this is a powerful statement, and it probably explains what the letter writers get out of the act of communicating with their hero. Iacocca, in his turn, gets more out of the mail than generalized applause and frag-mentary market research. The letters help to define him to himself. They assure him that he truly is a hero, revered by multitudes in search of a father figure, a confessor, a leader, and, back in 1982, a president of the United States.

"I've had a lot of letters in the last month saying I should run for President," he volunteered to Amanda Bennett of the *Wall Street Journal*. And to the *Washington Post* he leaked this letter from a young woman in New York City: "It is essential that you serve in this country's most powerful and influential position. . . . I am willing to do any work for you, and support you by any means possible."

Here, then, were voices from places beloved by marketers and politicians, the places ominously lumped together as the "grass roots" or "beyond the Beltway" or the "real world," and when letters start to arrive in piles, handwritten, pecked out on many different-lettered typewriters, mostly applause but not the canned applause turned on by professionally organized campaigns, then a tuned-in listener like Iacocca is impressed.

Dick Fitzpatrick was still phoning Terry O'Connell from Battle Creek, trying to get Terry interested in the Iacocca boomlet. O'Connell was still resistant, in part because of his own career objectives, also because the movement had few visible means of support except in places like *Time*. Speculating about dark-horse presidential possibilities, the magazine again mentioned the long-ago discovery of founder Henry Luce: Iacocca's "expressive face."

The new mention of this asset came in 1984, the year of the Iacocca autobiography. In The Book the author seemed to lay all his cards on the table. "While I might enjoy being President, it's strictly a fantasy because I couldn't imagine running for public office," the reluctant lion wrote. It would be "drudgery." He'd shaken too many hands, clutched too many cocktail glasses, inspected too many factories. He was exhausted, grown old, lacked the temperament for politics. "I'm candid to a fault, not a diplomat," he continued. He couldn't see himself hanging about for eight years to get some bill passed. He was far too impatient. And so on and on.

Yet this litany was followed—just as the earlier denials to Ms. Bennett of the *Wall Street Journal* had been followed—by further ruminations from Lee Iacocca, the poker player. He'd been talking to a "guy" in the advertising business, the autobiographer related. This guy had said that the country—that is, the people as in *the* "*pee-pul*"—wanted him to be a candidate because they didn't believe anybody anymore, especially not politicians. They did believe Iacocca.

"You don't bullshit them," the guy had said.

Iacocca could relate to that. He could see, he wrote, that "people" perceived him as a terrific manager, a leader who could manage a big institution, control a budget, restore a sense of purpose (come on, wasn't Chrysler really much like the country?). He could build confidence. His *mail* told him so. All that mail, all those guys writing, as he recalled their pleadings, "Why don't you turn this country around? Why are you wasting your time selling cars?" There is "a real vacuum out there," he wrote. "People are hungry to be led."

So, were his protestations perhaps a poker bluff, part of a grand design, a tactic to amble into the presidency without irksome factory inspecting, handshaking, baby nuzzling, to become the nation's *numero uno* by popular demand, by a draft from all those guys who sent him all that up-and-at-'em mail?

By 1985 some eager (and high-ranking) politicians hoped to smoke him out. In March former President Jimmy Carter joined the "I like Lee" fan club when he was questioned on *Sixty Minutes*. In April Senator Carl Levin of Michigan thought he had come upon the perfect occasion for an Iacocca response: the annual Freedom Fund Dinner of the NAACP's Detroit branch. Some 7,200 people, mostly blacks, were assembled in Cobo Hall.

Introducing Iacocca, the principal speaker, Levin simply stepped to the microphone and nominated him for the presidency. Just like that. This was followed by seconding remarks from a solid phalanx of Michigan's most potent Democrats: Governor Blanchard, Senator Riegle, Mayor Young. And before he got the entertainment program on the way, Sammy Davis, Jr., turned to Iacocca and chimed in: "If you'll run, I'll do everything I can to help you."

Cheers kept ringing through Cobo Hall.

Iacocca beamed. It was a breath-stopping moment. He dealt with it by not acknowledging the question, at least not directly. Instead, he launched into a slam-bang bombardment of President Reagan's fiscal policies and the president personally.

"The President is talking about the reindustrialization of America, the President thinks we're almost there," he began. The president was wrong, he said. "We're an America that's losing its ability to compete. . . . We've seen a budget deficit go abruptly and totally out of control. . . . It's going to crush us."

Iacocca suggested new taxes on energy and across-the-board budget cuts and kept swinging at the popular Mr. Reagan as an incarnation of Hollywood hype: "You mention 'tax' to the President now, and he goes into his Clint Eastwood routine. . . . I think we're headed for really big trouble. . . ."

Later Iacocca told Senator Levin that he had no presidential ambitions. Levin is a politician known for rare thoughtfulness and not given to airing whimsy. Iacocca had been cochairman of his campaign for the Senate.

"I wanted to show him how much support there was," the senator told me. "I think he'd be a good president and he'd win." The senator looked relaxed about Iacocca's apparent lack of interest. He shrugged. It was still early in the game, too early.

By September 1985 the editors of the remarkably well-oriented *Metropolitan Detroit* magazine were all but swept away when they dissected the results of a full national poll they had commissioned from the Market Resource Division of Urban Science Applications, Inc. The editors discovered that the "guys" who were swamping Iacocca with all that reverential fan mail were not unrepresentative aberrants. Not at all. They *were* the people. Market Resource had documented this fact of American life, much to the amazement of Kirk Cheyfitz, the magazine's editor and an experienced Iacocca watcher.

Cheyfitz wasn't pleased. He wrote that he found the figures "a bit terrifying." And: "On behalf of the Republic, I'm a little appalled." The headline above his commentary did not flatter Iacocca. It demanded incredulously, WHO FOR PRESIDENT?

The answer was undeniable. Cheyfitz concluded: "The numbers show, startlingly enough, that Lee Iacocca, a man who's never been elected dogcatcher, may just be the Democrats' best hope in '88."

First off, Iacocca carried phenomenal "name recognition." Of the respondents in the poll, almost everybody—92.7 percent—knew who he was. Whoever thinks that this is an affirmation of the obvious is decidedly wrong. Some people who get questioned in national polls are shaky about identifying Henry Kissinger. Even for nationally prominent figures, a recognition factor of 70 percent is whoppingly high.

Next, people simply *like* Iacocca. A "favorable" or "somewhat favorable" impression of him was registered by 78 percent of the interviewees; 52 percent couldn't think of anything they disliked about him. Further, they like Iacocca *a lot*. When he was rated against five other Big Names,* only President Reagan beat him by a

*Reagan, Bush, Ted Kennedy, Mario Cuomo, and Jack Kemp.

tiny margin, 66 against 61 degrees, on a "feeling thermometer" that asked respondents to register the emotional intensity of their leanings on a chart with gradings from 1 to 100.

Name recognition and personal liking proved convertible into political potency in this poll. In a presidential race held in August 1985, Iacocca would have beaten Vice President George Bush by 47 to 41 percent, according to this inquiry. Astoundingly, Iacocca was drawing almost as much support from registered Republicans as Democrats, and he achieved his strongest showing where Democrats have been running the weakest, among white middle-class voters.

In these figures Editor Cheyfitz spotted a crucial element of Iacocca's appeal to voters, the same nuclear power that dazzled Dick Fitzpatrick in Battle Creek and has been preoccupying his Draft Iacocca spear-carriers ever since. What Cheyfitz saw was "a potential Democratic Reagan in the making—a man with broad appeal to the white middle-class *regardless of their party affiliation.*"

Metropolitan Detroit dug up supporting evidence from—among others—Congressman Stewart B. McKinney, the moderate Republican from a predominantly white middle-class district of Connecticut, who had cheered Iacocca on during the Chrysler loan guarantee fight.

"I *adore* the guy," said the congressman, his choice of verb placing him on the upper end of the "feeling thermometer" scale. "If he went for President, I'd be for him, but I can't tell you whether he'd be a Democrat or Republican."

This lack of political labeling delighted not only the congressman, a millionaire tire dealer, but his friends back home in Fairfield, Connecticut, where Iacocca showed up for an "off the cuff" reception. "We had fifty people out on the porch," McKinney recalled with delight, "and Lee just tore into both parties, saying they were both full of crap."

When the Michigan pollsters asked their national sample, "What do you like about Lee Iacocca?" they were given a wide variety of responses, none directly related to politics, at least not overtly. The largest answer (39 percent) was that people "like the way he handled the Chrysler situation and saved the company." They thought he was a "good businessman." They liked his "persistence." They thought him honest, candid, dynamic, aggressive.

All this added up to what "appalled" Editor Cheyfitz.

"I don't want to take anything away from Lee Iacocca," he wrote. "I, too, admire the man. He *did* save Chrysler. He *is* one helluva businessman. He is, indeed, persistent. And I like him, too. But what on God's green earth does that have to do with being President?"

According to Cheyfitz, nothing. "From the viewpoint of the United States, the best answers to our poll would have been this: 'Vote for him for President? I don't even know what he stands for. You gotta be kidding!'"

According to Dick Fitzpatrick from Battle Creek and the tiny band of Iacocca-for-president drafters gathering around him by the spring of 1986, Cheyfitz had missed the point in a most spectacular way. Like it or not, the personality-directed replies to the Detroit pollsters had *everything* to do with Iacocca's qualifications for the presidency, at least as these attributes are weighed by voters in the 1980s. Never mind what President Iacocca would do about school lunches. The poll was attesting to Iacocca's *character*, defined by Webster as "moral excellence and firmness."

"Character in presidential politics is just about everything." So I was informed (long before Gary Hart's departure from the 1988 campaign) by Greg Schneiders, and Schneiders is the Washington thinker/strategist who endowed Iacocca's minimovement with the legs it badly needed. He created its character, and it was *his* character and expertise that finally convinced lobbyist Terry O'Connell to stop ducking Dick Fitzpatrick's entreaties and join the Iacocca cause.

Lean, agile, ferret-faced, Schneiders is partner in a suburban Washington polling and consulting firm and, at thirty-eight, another weathered soldier for principled losers.* He was deputy assistant for communications in the one-term Jimmy Carter White House and manager of Senator John Glenn's abortive run for the presidency in 1984—two all-American squares. Casting about to back a sexy winner for a change, Schneiders had been eyeing Iacocca when *Regardie's* magazine ("The Business of Washington") asked him to write the flag-carrying piece for a package of articles in the April 1986 issue.†

* The Draft Iacocca Committee's counsel and expert on party and state rules for primaries, David Ifshin, served as general counsel to former Vice President Walter Mondale in *his* unsuccessful 1984 race.
† The diligence and influence of local and regional magazines are a remarkable phenomenon. *Metropolitan Detroit* and *Regardie's* are far from alone. Magazines such as *New York*, *Washingtonian*, *Boston*, *Philadelphia*, and numerous others, also run ahead of national magazines in spotting some countrywide trends.

The cover displayed Iacocca, his right hand raised, his mouth ajar, towering above a rostrum bearing the seal of the president of the United States. The caption underneath fantasized, "President Iacocca takes the oath of office at noon yesterday." Across the center the red, white, and blue lettering offered a provocative choice: "Is this man running for President? Yes, the people want him. No, the politicians don't. The case for and against Lee Iacocca."

As the spokesman for the affirmative Schneiders stitched together such a peppy tract of advocacy that, as he tells it, he first off convinced himself. He decided that Iacocca ("Rocky Balboa in the Boardroom" he called him) would be the latest object of his own political affection—to have and to hold and to scheme for. Schneiders thought a draft could be brought off, and the heart of his case was the very theme that had shaken the boys at *Metropolitan Detroit* the previous year: a Democratic Reagan might be in the making.

The Detroiters had recoiled—another actor, another show— whereas Schneiders whooped. After experiencing Reagan, what would voters do for an encore? Move on to Iacocca, that's who, and Schneiders thought he knew why such a succession would succeed like apple pie after steak.

"America has been spoiled by Reagan's strengths and weaknesses in ways that will make life for his successor very difficult," he analyzed seven months before the Iran/Contra scandals broke. "We have been spoiled by his brand of strong leadership; we won't happily settle for anything less in our next president. We have also been spoiled by Reagan's happy-talk, morning-in-America glibness; the next President will have to demand that we make sacrifices, and that's an unpleasantness we won't easily accept.

"There's good reason to believe that Iacocca could handle this double-edged assignment," Schneiders ventured on, and right here he performed the great leap and enunciated what had been dawning on me and has surely not been lost on readers of these pages, to wit: "He has much in common with Reagan. He's mature and comfortable with himself. He's tough, knows his own mind, and knows how to lead. And he communicates with people in ways they understand. But Iacocca . . . is no Pollyanna. . . ."

Instead, so Schneiders enumerated, Iacocca is pragmatic ("neither too liberal nor too conservative—just like the voters"); without strong partisan commitments ("just like most Americans"); and "tough enough to stand up to Gorbachev."

Iacocca's ostensible drawbacks, as Schneiders analyzed them,

APRIL 1986: THE BOOM FOR PRESIDENT WAS GOING STRONG

were actually assets. Sure, his man lacked political experience; but so did General Dwight D. Eisenhower, and after Ike's landslide victory in 1952 a columnist voiced a thought that Schneiders now repeated: "[He] was above politics. That was part of his appeal. . . . In so many respects he was uncommitted, a clean slate on which each citizen could write his own hopes and aspirations." Voters could do the same with Iacocca. They could also rest secure in the knowledge that any survivor of Detroit's car wars must of necessity be a Houdini at political intrigue.

In Schneiders's upbeat script Iacocca's temper also became a plus factor: "He says what's on his mind and doesn't mince words. That trait worked for Harry Truman, and it could be even more appealing in this age of blow-dried, overcoached, smooth-talking candidates."

Even the Iacocca attribute most repulsive to the idealistic magazine journalists in Detroit warmed the heart of Schneiders, the political pro. So Iacocca's positions on some controversial issues were murky? Terrific!

"Candidates who have achieved fame outside of politics can beat the system," Schneiders wrote. "They have the advantage of being well known to voters without the disadvantage of having alienated a significant number of them."

Writing the "no" side of the Iacocca debate in *Regardie's*, John Margolis, the national correspondent of the *Chicago Tribune*, returned Schneiders's fire with dum-dum bullets. Historically, business people tend to make lousy politicians, Margolis argued. Iacocca is a thin-skinned despot who doesn't compromise or accept counsel. Politicians don't like him, and politicians know how to run the country. Iacocca is very vulnerable on pollution and car safety issues, especially on the Pinto. He has powerful and possibly talkative enemies, notably Henry Ford II, who keeps autobiographical tapes stored at the University of Michigan and could release them at any time ("like maybe if Iacocca runs for President"). Furthermore, Iacocca is not a gentleman, and he's not the coalescing force the country deserves to see at the top of the top.

"What it needs as its leader isn't someone who can run numbers and crack heads but someone who can understand its contradictions and enhance its sense of community," argued Margolis. "Sure, the government should be well managed, which is why the President should hire good managers. Let *them* be efficient; the President should be inspiring in times of weariness, comforting in times of trouble, calming in times of stress. There is absolutely no reason to think that Iacocca could be such a person. . . ."

In this "no" scenario Iacocca was transformed into a loser in an election. Margolis cited a national poll run in September 1985 for the Republican National Committee. Here, when matched against George Bush, Iacocca lost by approximately the same margin as Gary Hart and Ted Kennedy, even though he got more Republican votes. Iacocca alienated more Democrats than he won Republicans! How come? Those Democrats, said pollster Robert Teeter of Market Opinion Research in Detroit, "are strongly Democratic, lower status, and largely female. They just don't like Lee Iacocca."

Schneiders, O'Connell & Company scoffed. Democratic voters would "come home" and vote Democratic. The women would require heavy courting but would in time succumb to Iacocca's male charms. Nader and his "air bag nuts" were hobbyists tilting at a cause unpopular with drivers. Besides, what glitzy personage didn't have critics?

"You can't be a public figure without someone being against you," said O'Connell, shrugging.

Character: That was the buzzword Schneiders and O'Connell kept wanting to drill into me. "It's visceral," said Schneiders.

"He has tremendous character," chorused O'Connell. "And he's got warmth and empathy. You can see it in his family relationships, his friends, not the important people, the people he worked with. Why would they leave Ford and risk their pensions and jump on a sinking ship like Chrysler? But he feels compelled to hide his feelings. His nut-cutter image had to cover up what others might consider weakness."

"He's an adult," said Schneiders. "He knows his own mind. You know how Iacocca would approach a problem."

Their problem, Schneiders and O'Connell cheerfully confessed, was how to steer their noncandidate toward the nomination. Schneiders approached this conundrum in a nineteen-page document entitled "Drafting Lee Iacocca—A Preliminary Strategy." Addressing himself to his problem-within-the-problem, which he defined as "how to run without running," Schneiders puffed up clouds of creative smoke. "To draft a prominent and popular national figure," he wrote, "the process becomes the message."

And that message to the voters is: " 'We have to draft Iacocca *because* he is not a politician. Do you see him . . . kissing babies and asses? No.' "

According to Schneiders, this message reveals much happy meaning to voters about that ubiquitous all-American Iacocca character: "The process—the fact that Iacocca has to be drafted—provides critical information to the voters about Iacocca's *character*—that he is not a politician consumed by ambition. . . . His ideology, qualifications and position on specific issues will become important in time but are secondary to character. . . ."

The worst handicap for a presidential hopeful, Schneiders documented, is to be what Iacocca is not: a politician with a Washington orientation. Candidate Reagan ran against Washington. Candidate Jimmy Carter ran against Washington. Gary Hart almost beat a better-financed Mondale by tagging him as an old-school pol. Carter's momentum slowed as his exposure increased and he became "more political." The same stance hurt Hart. John Glenn peaked in 1984 with his patriotic, nonpolitical announcement speech, then sank in hand-to-hand combat with competing candidates.

By midsummer of 1986 Iacocca's old tormentor the *Wall Street Journal* had heard enough. It was time to squelch Schneiders, O'Connell, and their fellow drafters. An article taking up almost half a page and dipped in sarcasm blasted them and their "un-candidate" for exploiting the flag and Lady Liberty in the quixotic cause of a "wildly improbable enterprise."

Ignoring the fervor of the Anvil Chorus of the Michigan power brokers, the *Journal* exposed "this so-called grass-roots movement" as being hatched "in Washington office suites and at al fresco lunches at fancy French restaurants with a clear view of the Capitol."

Iacocca was profiting from an unfair free ride, according to a Democratic political consultant questioned by the newspaper: "He does the citizen-for-President number, and he has the advantage of having all that recognition without having to pay for it with funds regulated by the Federal Elections Commission." The power of personality would wilt quickly, the *Journal* predicted, and "the Iacocca effort offers little more than that." This would be the end because "the political Iacocca presents a slender profile."

The July 16 press conference at which Schneiders, O'Connell & Company made their public debut—the prayer meeting so rudely interrupted by Nader's Jim Musselman—received mixed reviews. Few took Iacocca's newly formalized disavowal seriously (BUT IF ELECTED I MIGHT SERVE, joked the *Newsweek* headline). Iacocca's copious pronouncements on public issues (see Appendix) were reviewed with reservations.

"People haven't focused on what he's really talking about," said one pol, "which is a hell of a lot of government."

Having started life as a joke, the noncandidate, supposedly running without running, was made-to-order raw material for the satirists.

Columnist Russell Baker in the *New York Times* deplored the ruination of a hero. "Does it make sense to remove a man from a job he does surpassingly well and place him in a job like the presidency, which has no relationship whatever to the automobile industry?" he asked. "Here is a classic case of promoting a successful performer to the level of his incompetence."

Baker went into mourning at the prospect of President Iacocca. "Whatever their lines of work, heroes are too scarce these days to risk sacrificing one by transfer to a job whose occupants are usually converted into bums until extreme old age turns them, when it no longer matters, into beloved elder statesmen."

In the *San Francisco Chronicle* columnist Arthur Hoppe offered a complete scenario of history-to-come. Hoppe pictured Iacocca being nominated while vacationing in Alaska. The candidate refuses to debate anyone and preempts no TV shows for paid political speeches. Press photos show him fishing and eating pizza with his wife. When he once appears on TV, it is to plead with the electorate not to vote for him.

"I simply lack the patience to get along with those idiots in Congress and the State Department," he says.

Following his landslide victory, Iacocca makes the briefest inaugural address in history. He turns to the microphone, beams, and says, "It worked."

While Art Hoppe gamed out the grand design of the noncandidate's noncampaign to its paradoxical conclusion, Schneiders, O'Connell & Company were casting about for signs of their hero's interest in their cause. They longed for signals, hints, whispers, emanations, anything, anything at all, to reassure them, at least to cheer them with some indication that they were chasing something less wispy than the political rainbow of the decade. Toward the end of 1986 they thought they had identified a friendly force: astrology.

The new Mrs. Iacocca, so Terry O'Connell learned, is a believer in astrology (I checked it out; it's true). This was the first intriguing bit of fresh intelligence the Iacocca drafters had picked up in months. O'Connell consulted an astrologer, not some dubious gypsy in a dark store but a concert violinist who did horoscopes as a hobby and enjoyed a reputation as a Washington source of data on the future.

It was true, said the astrologer. Iacocca was made of the right stuff for the presidency, and his chance at the job was real, according to the stars. The astrologer further saw plenty of delicate work ahead for the draft movement.

"He has to be very careful," O'Connell reported ominously. "She saw nasty, adamant opposition, lots of dangerous stuff ahead."

Would Mrs. Iacocca be given a similar analysis if she put the matter up to an astrologer of her choice? Absolutely. At least so O'Connell's astrologer assured him. But this good news brought further frustration. O'Connell and his friends had no way of discovering whether Mrs. Iacocca had perhaps elicited such intelligence from her stargazer or what her husband's reaction might have been, if any, printable or unprintable, because none of the drafters had ever met their candidate or even seen him except on television.

I asked O'Connell whether he was the least bit serious about any of this astrology business.

"We have to cover all bases," he said, which brings up the possible relevance of historical precedents that the Iacocca boosters were studying.

17.

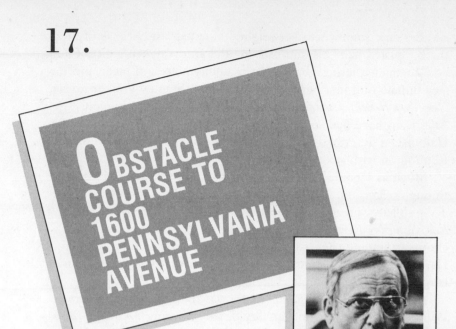

OBSTACLE COURSE TO 1600 PENNSYLVANIA AVENUE

IT HAD HAPPENED BE-FORE. In 1940 the Republicans nominated another businessman, Wendell Willkie, a utilities lawyer and Wall Street deal maker, in an abrupt switch abandoning several entrenched conventional candidates—all of them household names at the time. The political experts were left holding their prognostications in embarrassment. I've been reviewing the history of Willkie's rocketlike rise and find its parallels with Iacocca's early exposure to politics intriguing.*

The Willkie phenomenon was largely a product of his radiant charisma, magnified by media cheerleading. Henry Luce of *Time,* the candidate maker who spotted Iacocca's "expressive face" in the 1960s, called Willkie "a force of nature." The 1940 candidate was

---

*I am indebted for the details to the biography of Willkie by the *Chicago Tribune* political writer Steve Neal, *Dark Horse* (New York: Doubleday, 1984). The story gives off such rich bubbles of emotion that the drama overcomes an anticlimactic outcome not relevant to whatever could develop by 1988: Willkie had to run against the champ of champions, Franklin D. Roosevelt, and never stood a chance in the general election.

six feet one, somewhat overweight and stood out because of his thick, tousled hair, his enthusiasm, and an overflowing gift of gab.

"In any gathering he is about as anonymous and inconspicuous as a buffalo bull in a herd of cattle," wrote Stanley Walker in the *New York Herald Tribune*. Historian Bernard De Voto judged, "Few Americans have had so powerful a magnetism." Years later David Halberstam described him as "the rarest of things in those days, a Republican with sex appeal."

Much as Iacocca became part of the American consciousness through television, Willkie gained national status through the pre-TV publicity spreaders of the 1940s, mostly in magazines like *Time, Life, Saturday Evening Post,* and *Collier's*. All joined Henry Luce's chorus in singing cheers for the Republican whom Interior Secretary Harold Ickes, in a Democratic *mauvais mot* that became famous, lampooned as the "simple, barefoot boy from Wall Street."

And then there was radio. Radio was the lightning that struck Willkie on the evening of January 6, 1938, during *America's Town Meeting of the Air,* a weekly public affairs program carrying more political clout than *Sixty Minutes* does today. The format was a debate, popular then as it is in presidential competitions of the 1980s. The subject was the economy, still inching back out of the Depression. Willkie's opponent was Robert H. Jackson, a brilliant assistant U.S. attorney general who would ultimately be appointed a Supreme Court justice. In 1938 FDR was booming him for his own old job, governor of New York. For 1940 Jackson was considered presidential material if Roosevelt was to choose not to run.

The debate against Willkie incinerated Jackson forever for elective politics. As a popular columnist put it, Willkie made "a perfect monkey" of the Democratic aspirant in the give-and-take following the opening statements. A presidential boomlet was promptly born for his adversary.

Like Iacocca, Willkie laughed it off. In one letter to a fan he wrote: "Really, from my standpoint, it cannot constitute more than a joke. I do not think that the American people would even consider the election of a utilities executive . . . for constable, let alone President." In another letter he insisted, "Believe me, I do not have the slightest political ambitions."

In April 1940 a twenty-eight-year-old Wall Street lawyer, Oren Root, began forming Willkie clubs and circulating Willkie petitions that were enthusiastically received. "I have no illusions about your being nominated in Philadelphia," Root wrote Willkie. "I do know that if nominated you will win." Willkie mobilized influential friends in an abortive effort to stop Root. He was determined to stick to the shaggy, amateurish ways reminiscent of Jimmy Stewart in *Mr. Smith Goes to Washington*. He was interested in politics, he admitted. But he would never reach out for the nomination. Of course, he'd eventually have to accept if it fell to him.

"I couldn't go out and seek delegates and make two-sided statements," he protested. "I value my independence."

And yet, like Iacocca appearing on *Miami Vice*, Willkie showed up on the radio quiz program *Information Please* even though his friends told him it was undignified. Arriving at the Philadelphia convention, he told reporters that his headquarters were under his hat. With a wad of newspapers stuffed under his arm he laughed and said, "Ask me any damn thing in the world and I'll answer it. Nothing is off the record so shoot, ask anything you want."

Defending his history in business, again like Iacocca, he challenged California delegates: "If you can find any successful accusation against me, I want you to be against me!"

Hardly anybody took his chances seriously. Two callers from the *New York Times* were appalled when they discovered that he had no floor manager; he didn't know what that was. Governor Thomas E. Dewey, Senator Robert A. Taft, and former President Herbert Hoover, the principal candidates, were professionally organized. And they were opposed to aid for Britain or other American involvement in the European war. Willkie was an unabashed internationalist. A deadlock favoring Willkie was conceivable but considered extremely unlikely until Charles Halleck, the congressman from the underdog candidate's native Indiana, placed the name in nomination and the galleries went wild with a thunder of "We want Willkie! We want Willkie! We want Willkie!"

Halleck seized the emotion of the moment. "Is the Republican party a closed corporation?" he shouted. "Do you have to be born in it?"

"No! No! No!" the galleries roared back, and more than a million telegrams, letters, and cards to the convention delegates echoed the populist demonstration.

On the first ballot Dewey led with 360 votes. Taft had 189. Willkie trailed with 105.

"We want Willkie! We want Willkie!" yelled the chorus from the galleries, and kept it up for nearly eight hours through six ballots, frenetic behind-the-scenes intrigues and deals by the pros until, trying to establish order after midnight, the chairman of the chaos, Representative Joseph Martin, replied to the infectious chant with a phrase of concession that would be widely quoted: "Well, if you'll be quiet long enough, maybe you'll get him."

And they did. So it *can* happen.

It happened again in 1952, again involving an outsider alien to party politics, General Eisenhower, and again the similarities to Iacocca's situation are interesting* to trace.

While Willkie needed two years to be nudged into the candidacy that he relished once he got the taste of it, it took Ike's millionaire cronies eight years to drag the general, kicking and screaming,† into the smoky dens of slippery politicians whom he at heart disdained, actually despised.

The recalcitrant dragon's tortuous trek began with newspaper murmurs in 1943, when Ike commanded Allied wartime forces in Africa. He did not dignify the rumors with public comment, but privately he was disgusted. To his brother Arthur he wrote, "I will not tolerate the use of my name in connection with any political activity of any kind." And to a former superior officer: "I can scarcely imagine anyone in the United States less qualified than I for any type of political work."

Like Iacocca, he detested Washington and complained to his closest military associates about the city's primary product, deviousness. He wasn't "temperamentally fitted" to deal with politicians, Ike said. He could never make peace with them. "Politicians persist against all logic," he fumed. When he returned from the war, he told his wife, "My hatred of Washington is even greater than it used to be." He went there only with reluctance when President Truman assigned him to be chief of staff. He could hardly refuse a presidential order.

In 1946 a reporter pursued Ike into a Pentagon corridor after a press conference and persisted, "Now, General, isn't there some circumstance, some very remote circumstance, that might induce you to get into politics?"

---

*Details are drawn from Professor Stephen E. Ambrose's justly admired definitive biography, *Eisenhower* (New York: Simon & Schuster, 1983), Vol. I.
†I use this phrase with apologies to Ike's Democratic opponent, Adlai E. Stevenson, who depicted the general as "dragging" the Republican party "kicking and screaming into the 20th century." Reluctance, while a commonplace in politics, is usually overcome when the reward is right.

Ike spread his feet, plunged hands into pants pockets, and declared with emphasis: "Look, son, I cannot conceive of any circumstance that could drag out of me permission to consider me for any political post from dogcatcher to Grand High Supreme King of the Universe!" But to his diary he complained that even his friends did not believe him.

By 1947, as speculation would not stop, Ike confessed to his friend Walter Bedell ("Beetle") Smith that nomination and election by acclamation would constitute a "duty" he could not as a patriot refuse. He knew, however, that had happened to only one man, George Washington, so the possibility struck him as academic.

When a New Hampshire newspaper publisher entered a slate of Eisenhower delegates in that state's 1948 primaries, Ike responded: "My decision to remove myself completely from the political scene is definite and positive." Privately, too, he believed that he had finally managed to close the subject for good.

So why wouldn't he, as General William Tecumseh Sherman told the Republican National Convention of 1884, announce flatly, "I will not accept if nominated and will not serve if elected"? Ike was angry when he was taxed with reluctance to issue a Sherman statement. He offered a precision-tooled answer. He had taken the trouble to look up Sherman's dilemma and found it much different from his own.

"For twenty years many people hounded Sherman to take a part in politics and he steadfastly refused," the general lectured in a letter to an ex-classmate. "Finally in 1884 a political convention was actually in session. It deadlocked. The bosses communicated with him and asked him to step in as the one person around whom all might unite."

Only if such an offer were to hit him under the same circumstances, Ike wrote, would good taste allow him to follow Sherman's example, and he promised to do so "emphatically." Yet in June 1948 a lesser occasion roused him into a Shermanesque shudder when Florida Senator Claude Pepper threatened to nominate Eisenhower for president with or without his consent.

Ike replied: "No matter under what terms, conditions or premises a proposal might be couched, I would refuse to accept the nomination."

It didn't really count. Pepper had talked about the *Democratic* nomination. Ike had always been a closet Republican. Like Iacocca, the general had never disclosed his taste in parties. Iacocca unmasked himself in 1985 when a *Time* reporter wormed an answer out of him.

"You *are* a Democrat, aren't you?" the reporter asked.

"Yeah, I guess I am, when you put it that way," admitted Iacocca.

Ike was cagier and didn't take the bait until the Republican Convention of 1952 was less than a year away. He didn't really bite even then. He merely permitted his brother Milton to put out the word that the Eisenhower family had always been Republicans.

Meanwhile, Ike denied, denied, denied. He denied presidential ambitions in his diary, to his family, to Tom Dewey, who came to lobby him ("I do not believe that anything can ever convince me that I have a duty to seek political office," he told the former governor).

His denials even extended into private chats with intimate friends, the members of the "gang." These were his millionaire businessman golf buddies who eventually engineered his nomination, notably Bill Robinson, vice president of the *New York Herald Tribune*, the onetime Willkie house organ; Cliff Roberts, a New York investment banker; and former General (and comrade-in-Germany) Lucius D. Clay, now chairman of the Continental Can Company.

"And yet, his actions could not have been better calculated to put him in the White House," observes the biographer Stephen Ambrose. "No professional politician could have plotted a campaign for the general as successful as the one he directed himself."

All through the preconvention years both Eisenhower and Iacocca managed to run for office without running for office. Just as Iacocca kept busy selling automobiles, Eisenhower officiated in his first civilian job, the presidency of Columbia University. Just as Iacocca found time to travel about the country offering solutions to the problems of the federal deficit and farm subsidies at press conference after press conference, so Eisenhower kept touring and speaking out on behalf of a strong defense and against "paternalistic and collectivistic" domestic policies.

Were both men, consciously or not, plotting to capture the presidency all the time? Iacocca denied, denied, denied, and I know nobody to whom he has confided such a secret plan. The encyclopedic Professor Ambrose hints that Ike had his mind on the presidency for years, but his suspicions are unsubstantiated. Ambrose clearly doesn't know.

If there was such a secret, then, it probably was tucked away encapsulated in the ambivalent brains of both men, and for all the world both seemed to keep fighting off the presidential bug like a virus. As late as October 1951 Eisenhower was grouching (exactly like Iacocca): "I don't know why people are always nagging me to run for President. I think I've gotten too old." (Ike was then sixty-one; Iacocca would be sixty-four in 1988, when Reagan would be seventy-seven).

By then Ike had become the first commander of NATO in Paris. Emissaries with politics on their minds pursued him there, and the general began to waver just a little, strictly on ideological grounds. When the banker Winthrop Aldrich warned that the Republican party would vanish after the next election if he didn't run, Eisenhower said that would be a "disastrous possibility."

Other developments eroded his resistance more directly. His principal potential adversary, the starchy Senator Taft, Willkie's old rival and known as "Mr. Republican," signed a statement that "American troops should be brought home" from Europe which infuriated Ike, the soldier and internationalist. Truman submitted a budget with a $14 billion deficit which shocked Ike's fiscal sensibilities.

The mission was unmistakable. But politics? Did *he* belong in politics? "Politics . . . excites all that is selfish and ambitious in a man," he moralized to his oil baron crony Sid Richardson. "Wouldn't it be nice if we could just forget all this kind of thing?" he wrote to General Clay, by now retreating into wistfulness over what was destined not to be.

Finally, when Cliff Roberts and Bill Robinson came to smoke him out in Paris in December 1951, Eisenhower let drop that he was not only with them but ahead of them—and craftier at strategy and tactics.

"The seeker is never as popular as the sought," he told his callers. "People want what they think they can't get." He would not resign his NATO post, as they wanted him to. Not yet. He still wanted to be wanted. He still needed a sign, a signal from the people, a mandate, and on February 11, 1952, five months before the Republican Convention in Chicago, he considered that the Call had come.

It arrived in Paris in the form of a two-hour film of a midnight rally in Madison Square Garden and was delivered by Jacqueline Cochran, the aviatrix and spouse of another wealthy Ike supporter, Floyd Odlum, the financier. The movie showed a throng of about 15,000 Eisenhower loyalists waving "I Like Ike" placards and banners and shouting (shades of "We want Willkie!"), "We want Ike! We want Ike! We want Ike!"

The event had been set up and manicured by the Eisenhower cronies and an outfit called Citizens for Eisenhower; but Ike felt that the grass roots had spoken, and Cochran acted quickly to close the sale. When she and the general and his wife, Mamie, were holding drinks, Cochran toasted, "To the President!"

Historian Ambrose recorded the emotional aftermath of this gesture as reported by Cochran in a later eyewitness account: "I was the first person ever to say this to him and he burst into tears. . . . Tears were just running out of his eyes, he was so overwhelmed." He started to talk about his family, mostly his adored mother (shades of Iacocca's instant memory of his father at moments of triumph), and after about an hour Ike instructed Cochran: "You can go tell Bill Robinson that I'm going to run."

The general's view of politicians—as scathing as Iacocca's—did not change. "Everything is calculated," he wrote his friend General Alfred Gruenther. "The natural and the spontaneous are frowned upon." Yet when Ike resigned from the army and returned home, he overwhelmed visiting convention delegates with his charm, his famous grin, his grasp of issues, his larger-than-life presence, and his capacity to control a temper which (like Iacocca's) was notorious for a low boiling point and undeleted expletives.

"We're worried about your wife," a Nebraska delegate said.

"Yes?" said Ike quietly.

"We hear she's a drunk."

"Well, I know that story has gone around," said the general, "but the truth of the matter is that I don't think Mamie's had a drink for something like eighteen months."

As the convention opened, Taft's lead had shrunk to 530 delegates over Eisenhower's 427 and the "We want Ike!" tidal wave was rolling. The general's managers did his work while he reminisced with his brothers in his Blackstone Hotel suite about their youth in Abilene, Kansas. He won without ever dirtying his hands. His instincts about the Call had been correct. Prompted or not, the grass roots did like Ike, a sentiment which was handy but did not take solid shape until the convention was held.

Seen through the imperatives of the 1980s, this emergence was too late, for in 1960 the balance of nominating power shifted from the convention delegates to the voters in state primaries and party caucuses. The two-year campaign marathon was born—more democratic, more visible, more wearisome, infinitely more expensive, and seemingly rigged against a candidate who was running by not running.

Willkie? Eisenhower? Poof! They made psychologically riveting illustrations of the tug-of-internal-war through which a technically nonpolitical candidate wrenches himself (or is wrestled by tacticians) into running condition, but that was about all. Since the time of Willkie and Eisenhower there had come another turn of history that Schneiders, O'Connell, and the other Iacocca drafters did not minimize.

"While these are interesting precedents to use with the media and at the cocktail parties, they are of little strategic value to us," warned Schneiders in his "Drafting Lee Iacocca" strategy paper. And David Ifshin, the movement's counsel, admitted: "We're starting with a major handicap. The rules are all written for traditional candidates."

Yes, but the rules could be overcome, thought Schneiders, because another change had come since Willkie and Eisenhower. The democratic way of nominating candidates was no longer largely determined by politics and organization. "It is a message/communication process," wrote Schneiders. "Gary Hart won primaries and even caucuses in states where he had *no* organization against massive Mondale organization."

Words and images were reaching voters and delegates over the heads of bosses and organizations, so that a potential candidate could indeed run without running, could even gain in stature, but never as late as convention time, not anymore. His timing would have to be exquisite. Like that of a poker player.

"Iacocca has to become a candidate before the convention," wrote Schneiders. There is no way that he can be drafted at the convention. Most of the delegates will be pledged to specific candidates who ran in the primaries and caucuses. There has not been a second ballot at a Democratic convention in thirty-six years. The only way that Iacocca can be the nominee is to go to the convention with a majority of the delegates committed to him or at least more than any other candidate.

This would entail a considerable uphill struggle for the draft committee. The drafters would have to get Iacocca's name on the ballots of most (and preferably all) primary states. They would need to meet the requirements for access to the ballot just about everywhere. And yet Iacocca would still need to do nothing himself until . . . until . . . well, until sometime after the first primary in New Hampshire in February 1988.

In New Hampshire, Schneiders figured, "some significant show of voter support" was essential. History was implacable without that; nobody had ever won a general election without winning in New Hampshire. New Hampshire, however, could be conquered quite easily by write-in votes, and in the summer of 1987 I was reliably told that Iacocca secretly welcomed having his name written onto the ballots there, perhaps to test the waters, perhaps only to flex his muscles. Lyndon Johnson had managed nicely with write-ins in that state. And New Hampshire had been hospitable to such relatively unconventional candidates as Eugene McCarthy, George McGovern, and Gary Hart.

"New Hampshire's always been partial to outsiders and I suspect voters would respond quite well to Iacocca," said Richard Winters of Dartmouth College, a political scientist and Democratic state committeeman. "It isn't a wildly inappropriate candidacy for this state."

Iacocca's ultimate deadline would face him shortly after "Super Tuesday," Tuesday, March 8, 1988, when major primaries were scheduled in 13 southern and border states. Wrote Schneiders: "He could probably get past Super-Tuesday by announcing after New Hampshire that he will make a decision following the next round of primaries. Staying out any longer would become awkward."

Awkward? That would be rather too quiet a word if by then the voters, delegates, politicians, and media would still be plucking petals off their favorite flowers: "He loves us, he loves us not, he loves us. . . ."

18.

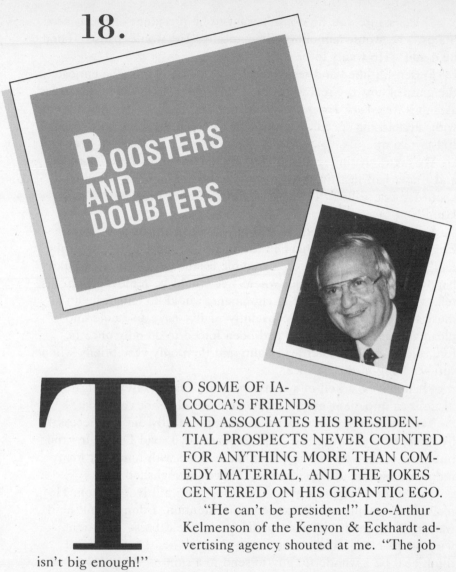

BOOSTERS AND DOUBTERS

To some of Iacocca's friends and associates his presidential prospects never counted for anything more than comedy material, and the jokes centered on his gigantic ego.

"He can't be president!" Leo-Arthur Kelmenson of the Kenyon & Eckhardt advertising agency shouted at me. "The job isn't big enough!"

And one of Kelmenson's executive vice presidents, noticing that Lee was not on the K & E boat en route to Ellis Island for the great Statue of Liberty anniversary spectacular, remarked, "He walked."

While making speeches around the country, Doug Fraser, the retired United Auto Workers leader, grew so accustomed to being questioned about Iacocca's intentions that he tried to dispose of the suspenseful topic as soon as he rose to face an audience, any audience, anywhere.

"I can assure you he doesn't want to be president of the United States," he would announce dramatically. He would pause. Then he'd add: "He wants to be king."*

Fraser still liked and respected Iacocca—the brains, the curiosity, the grasp of how the real world functions. Once he'd watched Iacocca assault a *New York Times* crossword puzzle. The puzzle surrendered with breathtaking speed. "Compared to Reagan, he's a literary critic," Fraser told me.

We were sharing a plane ride from Detroit to New York, and Fraser had just finished reading a *Detroit Free Press* editorial about Iacocca, called "If You Can Find a Better President, Elect Him!"

Fraser, a silver-haired, hearty giant, broke up in uproarious laughter. It could really happen, he mused, if the Democrats in the end were unable to agree on a credible candidate. But what would happen in the White House, where Lee would be removed from his relatively rarefied corporate environment, would no longer be an almost absolute boss, would constantly, daily, have to cajole and plead and compromise as he had been forced to do only once before, during the Chrysler loan fight, and then only very briefly when survival hung in the balance?

"It would be a hell of a transformation," said Fraser doubtfully. "Lee is an impatient man. His tolerance level is not very high."

Yet even people who dislike Iacocca personally did not necessarily disapprove of him as presidential material. David Davis, Jr., the publisher of *Automobile* magazine, had tangled with him over many industrial issues and doesn't enjoy Iacocca's roughshod ways.

"He's not a leader of men," he says; "he's a driver of men. He really beats people up just to get their attention. I don't think he'd want to go through behavior modification. He'd be so impatient with the process." There was a long pause. Then Davis said, "I think he'd be a wonderful guy to send to a summit."

Ah, yes, the summit and the Soviets. I spent a hilarious luncheon with one of Iacocca's former ghostwriters, an elfin soul who held the job for three years, probably an all-time record in a slot where heads tend to roll as they did in the French Revolution. Talk about Iacocca's need for control! This fellow had seen his speech drafts thrown to the floor and actually stomped upon by Iacocca.

*Iacocca's ambitions had long inspired near-identical hyperbole among acquaintances on his Detroit home ground. In 1983 publisher Keith Crain of *Automotive News* told a *Time* reporter: "Hell, Lee doesn't want to be President; he wants to be appointed Pope."

Yet he'd survived his chief's editorial evaluations, such as "Fuck that!" or "Don't give me that crap!"

"He's not into grays," the ghostwriter says dryly.

He recalled how his immediate superior had been "terrified" when Iacocca issued a summons to appear in his presence and how this boss rummaged in his desk drawer for pills that he seemed to swallow by the fistful before facing Iacocca. Fortunately the confrontations were often brief. Iacocca terminated them in the military manner by asking for questions and not waiting to hear any.

" 'Any questions?' means 'You're dismissed,' " remembers the ghost, chuckling.

A little disconcerted by this authentic peek into Iacocca's office ambiance, I asked my source how he would feel if Iacocca were to become the man with the finger on the nuclear button.

"I'd trust him more than Reagan," said the ghostwriter. "He's sane." Sane, probably, in the same way that the Russians are sane at the summit.

My inside source on the Pinto's troubles, Harley Copp, the persistent safety engineer, did not believe that Iacocca would become involved in presidential politics. Copp thought that his former nemesis would heed his own expressed view that he wasn't temperamentally suited.

"He doesn't know the art of compromise," Copp said. "With him, it's 'My way or the highway.' "

But suppose, I said, that Iacocca does somehow wind up in the White House?

"He'll make a great president," said Copp instantly and to my stark amazement, and he proceeded without hesitation to reel off his reasoning.

"He's the world's greatest salesman," said Copp, "and he has a deep sense of responsibility *if his ambition is not in the way*. He's tough; he's a real leader, someone that people will fall and die for. That jungle fight with Knudsen [for the Ford presidency], that was Lee at his worst. He was an animal. Now he's fifteen years older; he's reconstructed a defunct company; he follows a different morality. I think he'd have a deep sense of responsibility."

As Copp warmed to the topic, his earlier reservation about Iacocca's nonpractice of the art of compromise was forgotten. (I have encountered other voters who have come to think that compromise is a too much practiced art in politics.)

Would Copp *vote* for Iacocca despite his frustrating experience with him?

"Yes, I would," said the engineer whom Iacocca once exiled as a nonperson. "I sure would."

Most of my registered Iacoccalytes, as I'd expected, couldn't wait for their Rocky to put on the gloves and strut into the ring. "I think he would get things done," said Peter Facchiano, the retired Bethlehem Steel executive who went to Lehigh with Iacocca.

"Maybe he could get a few things *done*," echoed Hank Carlini, the sidekick from Ford and Chrysler.

Carlini had been telling me about watching his boss on his new farm in Italy, and those scenes were sinking in with him once more. "The man has got a heart," Carlini said. "He has feelings. He has what it takes to keep a family together. That type of man would make a good president."

Ben Bidwell, the Chrysler vice chairman, harked back to the fan mail that means so much to Iacocca. Bidwell thought that Lee's way of communicating stirred powerful vibrations in the hearts of voters. "There's a connection between Iacocca's mouth and the American psyche," he assured me. "The mail is emotional. Here's a letter from an army chaplain." Bidwell waved a letter and read from it: " 'If you don't like the way the government is run, change it! Don't screw around!' "

Bidwell looked up and beamed. "You wouldn't write a letter like that to George Bush," he said.

Iacocca's love affair with power also came up as a qualification for the presidency. It is an intimate relationship, and in the White House the direction in the *flow* of power might prove unconventional. "I'm not going to say that he'd be a good or a bad president," said Jay Dugan, the advertising man, sculptor, and Iacocca's close friend since Chester, Pennsylvania. "But he'd be an anomaly. Others get power from the office. He'd *bring* power to the office."

Could the office make constructive use of so much power? Even a devoutly loyal Iacoccalyte like Ron DeLuca, the Kenyon & Eckhardt president and behind-the-scenes hero of the Iacocca TV commercials, wasn't absolutely sure. He recalled how "very frightened" some of Iacocca's people are of him, how they find him an "intimidating guy" when he "exudes power."

How would this posture work out in the White House? It

seemed to me that DeLuca's response all but invoked the Fifth Amendment against self-incrimination. "I don't know enough about politics to know whether you can run a country that way," he said.

The outright naysayers also included certain witnesses whom I would classify as Iacoccalytes.

Lars Larsen, who had gotten to know his boss so well when Lars was chief Washington strategist during the Chrysler loan fight, agreed with the Iacocca watchers who spotted a limited but very real likeness to President Reagan.

"Some of the things Lee has tapped into are the same as Reagan," Larsen told *Time* in 1985. "The nation has been looking for a leader who is sure of himself, who calls a spade a spade—even if it isn't. He oversimplifies issues, and people like that. But Reagan is shallow. Lee is not. He's a hell of a lot smarter than Ronald Reagan and a hell of a lot deeper."

And yet when I asked Larsen directly about the presidency, his tune shifted abruptly into a minor key.

"He'd be a terrible president," Larsen said. "He's very thin-skinned. Any hint of criticism he can't stand." Though Larsen retained much affection and admiration for his former boss, the thought of Iacocca's bossing the country made Larsen, I could see, turn cold.

Steve Sharf, a brash ex-Berliner who owed Iacocca his elevation to high executive rank at Chrysler, thought he was doing his benefactor a huge favor by disqualifying him for a political career.

"I think politics would kill him," Sharf snapped the instant I'd popped the question. "He'd have to kiss everybody's rear end. He's too much of a boss's boss, I don't think he can do that. He wouldn't be happy. I hope for his sake he doesn't run."

Among the long-ago grammar and high school classmates in Allentown I found, in addition to overwhelming general acclaim, some intriguing reservations. Gene Giancarlo, the retired executive director of the American Society of Newspaper Editors, thought that the politicians in Washington were too devious for Iacocca. He wouldn't be able to handle them without violating his principles.

"I think he could do a hell of a job," Giancarlo said, "but he couldn't recycle his conscience; I don't think he could do that. I think he's too honest a person."

Bill Diehl, a retired steel executive, thought Iacocca would be too "rigid" to cope successfully with Congress. Diehl also thought that his old school friend was not sufficiently "rounded" to be the nation's *numero uno*. "If he runs, I hope there's a good alternative," Diehl told me, not quite foreclosing a vote for Allentown's favorite son.

Jim Leiby, the University of California history professor whom Iacocca remembers as his best friend in high school, was ambivalent about Iacocca's past *and* future.

"My main sense is the wonderful achievement," said Leiby. "He played the game and won. He won big. And that's wonderful."

How about the presidency? Leiby showed signs of discomfort.

"I think he'd like to give something back and doesn't know how to go about it."

Leiby was another Iacocca watcher who wondered how well rounded the man is; he feared his old schoolmate is too removed from the worlds of science, art, religion, the world of intellect, Leiby's own worlds.

How about integrity?

"Oh, I'm quite sure he'd be honest, and yes, he's tough and prioritized. He was always well organized, and he has a type A personality."

I classified Leiby in my mind as an intellectual's vote: "Yes, but . . ."

Don Frey, the Bell & Howell chairman who obtained a not-so-amicable divorce from Iacocca when he left Ford, was a believer—predictably—in the "grand design" theory, the devious notion that Iacocca was running hard by not running. Frey felt certain that Iacocca was "scheming to be nominated for president by acclamation." Surprisingly Frey was not dead set against an Iacocca presidency. Just very, very cautious. "Before I vote for him, I'd want to know who the opponent is," he said.

Having once been bitten by Iacocca's ambitions, Frey was in no doubt that his collaborator on the Mustang, the partner who took the credit, had the taste of the presidency coursing through his mouth. It would be like the hankering of a great mountaineer who needed to climb Everest mostly because it was there.

"President of the United States," said Frey slowly. "That's the only thing that's left."

I was given a near replay of this line, but with an upbeat twist, by Larry Domagall, one of the Ford cronies in whose eyes Iacocca has never done wrong, never could, and never will.

"It's the one great thing that's left," said Domagall. "Where do I sign up?"

* * *

The uninhibited Steve Miller, Iacocca's top financial man at Chrysler, considered it unlikely early in 1987 that voters would find many opportunities to sign up for his boss as president in 1988, even if the Democrats were to face unusual difficulties in agreeing upon a candidate.

Unless . . . unless, that is, a serious downturn were to hit the economy.

"If people are grasping for some dramatic savior—I'm spelling out a parallel to Chrysler in 1978—I think he could be elected," mused Miller. "People really believe him. Our market research on his commercials goes off the charts."

The same look-first-to-economics scenario also spooked the crystal ball of one of the canniest Democratic pollster/consultants, David Garth of New York. "If the economy has deteriorated by 1988," he has said, " people may well be fed up with politicians in general. That's when they'll say, 'Give us a guy who knows how to do something.' Iacocca's proven he can take a company back from bankruptcy and make it profitable again. That may be all the qualification the voters need."

Some liberal commentators were detecting Iacocca attributes they didn't like. In the *New Republic*, the prestigious columnist who signs himself "TRB" rejected the thought that Iacocca stood above politics, like Eisenhower. TRB sized up the savior from Chrysler as carrying around "a clear political agenda" in his knapsack, and he diagnosed in the Iacocca personality the sternness of a strong father (another Nick Iacocca?) rather than the kindly-caretaker qualities of a benign Eisenhower uncle. And the columnist spotted worse, much worse in the Iacocca charisma.

"There used to be a name for the political philosophy of a strong charismatic leader, a Darwinian struggle among nations, and a privately owned but centrally planned economy, with a heavy emphasis on heroic images and pageantry," wrote TRB. "That name was fascism."

Good heavens! Iacocca is a fascist?

No, not exactly, hedged the columnist, "but the flavor is definitely there," and here was why: "Iacocca's vision of an economy managed by tripartite boards of government, business, and labor leaders is the classic corporate state of fascist ideology. It is capitalism without free enterprise, socialism without social justice, a deeply conservative and disastrous arrangement that would freeze the economy in place for the benefit of current property owners."

So much for flights into ideology. Politicians, meanwhile, kept harrumphing about qualifications they missed in Iacocca altogether.

"He doesn't tolerate differences of views," I was lectured by a powerful Michigan Democrat, Congressman John ("Big John") Dingell of Detroit, chairman of the House Committee on Commerce and Energy. Mark Siegel, an uncommitted Democratic party official, found Iacocca wrong in age and image ("We have to look to the people who are thirty-five and under"). And some shrewd analysts suspect that Americans do want a politician for president, that their alleged detestation of the breed is barely skin-deep.

"It's hard to spend more than an hour in a saloon without hearing someone mutter that politicians are 'a bunch of crooks,' " wrote Jon Margolis of the *Chicago Tribune*. "As it turns out, though, most people hate politicians only in the abstract. That very saloon patron would be honored to meet his state legislator and no doubt greatly admires his congressman, whom he regularly returns to office."

Among the national pollsters, at least one was convinced that Iacocca would fall flat on his big nose in presidential politics. Louis Harris of the Harris Poll was reminded of George Romney, that other Michigander and automaker, whose presidential ambition was harpooned by a single verbal misstep. Harris guessed that Iacocca's verbosity would lead him into a similar trap.

"He's inherited the syndrome of the auto industry," said Harris. "When they go into politics they develop foot-in-mouth disease."

George Will, the conservative commentator, was not as dismissive. He appreciated Iacocca's appeal to voters.

"People like Iacocca because nothing is muffled as he approaches anything," he wrote. "People like his off-the-cuff pugnacity . . . his cantankerousness, so he could make it his tactic, even his platform. He could say: No way I am going to Iowa in winter. Or New Hampshire. My campaign will be part McKinley, part McLuhan. I will come out on my porch every day or so and snap at Sam Donaldson."

But no. "A chairman of a corporation is in a command position. A president is in a persuasion position. . . . So, Iacocca for President? The answer probably is: Good man, wrong job." The columnist followed this dictum with the hedging that Iacocca brings out in flesh appraisers: "But then, that is what Sam Rayburn said about another political newcomer—Dwight D. Eisenhower."

When I talked about Iacocca's potential with Harry Treleavan, the arch-Republican strategist/star of Joe McGinniss's anti-Nixon book *The Selling of the President*, his reaction was surprisingly benign.

"I don't know whether he has the patience to be president," Treleavan started out. Then he stopped to switch direction: "It'd be an interesting thing to try. He might be better than most people think. I have a great deal of respect for him."

Respect soars to adulation in the case of Joseph A. Califano, Jr., an "Italian boy" who made good in politics and, according to prevailing Washington opinion, still harbors an ego and political ambition as zesty as Iacocca's. Chrysler is a Califano law client, Joe Califano serves on the Chrysler board, and he ranks as an Iacoccalyte of such stellar standing that he is allowed to make fun of his pal Lee right in front of the Man himself.

"Does Lee Iacocca have what it takes to be president of the United States?" Califano asked while introducing Iacocca at a Washington fund-raising dinner.

Said he: "I've studied the presidency, I've written about it, I've worked in the White House, I've served two presidents at close hand, and I can tell you that Lee does have what it takes. When he reads cue cards, you cannot see his eye moving."

Califano can also be very serious about an Iacocca candidacy. "He says privately what he says in public—that he doesn't want it," Califano told *Time*. "But once he made the commitment Lee would be phenomenal as a candidate. He knows how to lead. He knows how to communicate."

About his own feelings toward his availability and competence for the presidency Iacocca communicated and communicated and communicated and then communicated some more. (See Appendix, page 355.) Despite his reputation as a master communicator, however, the message never quite came across without some ingredient of ambiguity, at least not from 1982 until perhaps late in 1986.

"I talked to my two kids about running," he told the *New York Times Magazine* in the summer of that year, "and I talked to my mother. And I thought no, no, no, I'd probably end screwing it up."

This would appear to cover Iacocca's process of earnest pondering, plus his apprehension and that of his mother and his daughters about doing a *good* job in the White House, but he didn't say he'd pass up an opportunity to do it if the chance were to present itself.

The door was not ajar by much, but it didn't look closed to me.

The year before, *Time* caught him in a state of excruciating ambivalence. "I've thought about it," he said then. "Sometimes I say, 'Maybe I should give it a shot. It's only four years. It'd be fun and an honor.' " Then he thought of his mail, God, all that mail, but there had just come a letter that wasn't all in the *avanti* mold. This lady had written and said that he owed it to the country to run but that he'd probably get killed in office.

Killed? Killed! That was just what his security-conscious nerves needed! He had already been through one horrifying demonstration of a president's helplessness in the face of possible danger. Driving in the presidential limousine with President Reagan in St. Louis, Iacocca had discovered, on arriving at their destination, that the car lacked interior door handles. The president was a prisoner of his Secret Service protectors, for crying out loud! It was scary as all hell!

So now Iacocca exploded at the hapless *Time* reporter who had flatteringly asked about the presidency. If he didn't get shot, he said, the frustrations of the goddamn job would get him for sure!

"It would destroy me," he said. "I couldn't survive. I would shoot myself first."

Why suicide? Now the prankster came out in the noncandidate.

"I couldn't take four years of [ABC White House correspondent] Sam Donaldson."

Then he resorted to the fatigue theme.

"I just don't have the desire. I don't want to climb another mountain."

When a man from *Life* came around to sound him out a bit later, he seemed a lot less tired. He said he knew that folks at the grass roots were stomping their feet on his behalf ("I don't bullshit them"), and he did not doubt that he had the right stuff. Again there came the disavowals, but then "I believe that if I wanted to be President, I could be President," he announced.

Also, he'd manifestly given thought to the nuts and bolts of a campaign, and he was cheerful about financing such a venture: "If it takes money to run a good TV campaign I guess I could accumulate $100 million for openers. I know all the Madison Avenue guys. I can read a TelePrompter as well as Reagan can now. I've been doing this crap all my life, so I imagine I could get elected."

Once Iacocca started to stew about "this crap"—that is, politics and the show biz glitzing that goes with it—his adrenaline level climbed. It's the Rocky Balboa lemme-at-'em syndrome, and early during Reagan's second term Iacocca often seemed sorry he wasn't already running against the currect administration.

"They're such asses," he told Bob Spitz, the man from *Life*. He jeered that they were practicing "acne economics," telling taxpayers not to worry about the trade balance and the deficits and the rest of the financial malaise because "we're gonna grow out of it." Ha!

Automobile industry economics—now, that was for real, and it was convertible into White House economics by no magic at all, according to Iacocca.

"If an automobile man does not talk exchange rates, interest rates, or fuel, he must be asleep because there ain't nothing else," he said. "The impact of those is the very lifeblood of our business. Most people never make the connection."

And Reagan! Reagan was an ignoramus. Iacocca went to see him in the White House to explain some problems about warrants Chrysler had issued as part of the government loan guarantee, and he might as well have been talking to the oval walls as to the president.

"He didn't know what the hell I was talking about," Iacocca told a friend.

With Bob Spitz, the free-lance writer who had interviewed him for *Life*, Iacocca opened up further. Surplus wordage from the interview wound up in *Newlook* magazine, and there his sniping at Reagan grew sharper—and this was months before the Iran scandals broke.

What were Reagan's real beliefs anyway?

"He's got cue cards," Iacocca sneered at Spitz. "They tell him what to say. I want a president with some convictions. I don't know what the hell Reagan's convictions are. I know he hates Communists, and I know he hates taxes. Other than that, I don't know a fucking thing about him." Why, Reagan wasn't the president at all! The real president was "that fucking Don Regan," incredible! Iacocca railed, "I never voted for the guy. I would never have voted for the guy. . . ."

In the more polite climate of *Vogue* magazine Iacocca was back at juggling his tantalizing worries: Could he? Should he? Would he?

"I could come close, and that's what worries me," he said. Then a most quixotic and hard-to-believe cop-out: "It would be nice to run and not make it." Then the usual climb down from that mountain that keeps obscuring his field of vision. "I have five hundred letters a day telling me what the people are looking for out there, but I have no desire for office. That's starting over again. How many mountains do you want to climb?"

The *Vogue* interviewer, a New York radio personality named Sherrye Henry, wasn't buying this routine. "For all his denials, Iacocca *sounds* like a potential candidate," she concluded after being exposed to the usual litany about the nation's economic crisis and his cures.

"By presenting a different set of policies, Iacocca is selling Iacocca," this interviewer, too, had to notice. "And he possesses the natural qualities of a political leader: he is alternately a cheerleader, pulling along the less inspired to his vision of victory; a preacher, delivering the folks fundamental down-home values; and a teacher, insisting that his students do their homework *now* and get the answers *right*."

By the autumn of 1986, talking to *Cosmopolitan*, Iacocca was peering down from the mountain and sounding more full of doubts than ever. "I'm at a peak now," he said, "and to come down into the ugly valley of politics now to get back up again, who needs it?" Ugly? What was really so ugly about politics? Well, having to keep your mouth shut: "If you believe something in your heart and can't say it, that goes from diplomacy to hypocrisy, and I couldn't hack that. I'd go nuts. People say, 'You could be President,' and I say 'Yeah, you've got to be political head of the party first, and I couldn't go out there and look for all those delegates and make promises."

So what *did* he want? "I will help elect the next President, I hope," he said. "I'd literally like to meet all the candidates and question them and then grade their papers and say, 'That's our man.' "

And was that all he wanted? Just to be inspector in charge of quality control? Well, a fat appointive job might still be fun. "If you could help your country in some job without going through the political process, and the right President asked you to serve in a way that you thought you could really do so good, I would probably do that," he allowed. "An economic job I could do, I think. . . ."

Iacocca functioning as a cog in a chain of presumed equals? Taking orders from another *numero uno*? Looking wistfully at the mountain from below? Did he need *that*? Yet if he still wanted to serve his country, what alternatives might suit him?

"Lee'd be a tremendous benevolent dictator," mused Billy Fugazy, whose judgment on this specialized point deserves respect. And if his job description dovetails with Iacocca's occasional ruminations about wanting to be the nation's "economic czar," it's a shame that the American system does not accommodate even informally crowned czars, except temporarily in wartime. As for a normal-sized cabinet post, it is difficult to visualize the Iacocca ego operating in harness with a team of cabinet members of roughly equal rank. Didn't Iacocca say years ago that he had been number two for too long?

A Bernard Baruch-style park bench advisership doesn't seem to fit him either. When one looks closely at a possible economic role for him in the light of the Washington realities, the proposed czardom is a naive notion anyway. No less an authority than Joe Califano, the former cabinet member and Iacocca loyalist, says so. The proposal suggests wishful thinking on Iacocca's part or else his innocence about the way government operates at the cabinet level. The concept is a pipe dream.

"There is no such job and there can't be," pronounced Califano. The czar's turf would first have to be snatched away from the secretary of the treasury, the secretary of commerce, and the chief executive. That would be an improbable raid, even in the unlikely event that a president would, in effect, volunteer to demote himself.

So if I'm reasonably close to judging the Iacocca potential correctly, the top post would seem to be better tailored for him than any other, and scrutiny of his life and record would be very intense.

Which reminds me of 1956, when my friend Sam Shaffer and I were working in the Washington bureau of *Newsweek* and were assigned to collaborate on the first cover story on John F. Kennedy, then the junior senator from Massachusetts and as yet unwilling to admit on the record what most reporters were pretty sure about: that he was eager to become president.

To Sam and myself the ambition seemed not outrageous but fairly farfetched. Sam in particular was full of doubts, and once Sam adopted a fixed view on an open political question, it was difficult to move him from his rock. Since he had covered Capitol Hill longer than any correspondent, he was a fixture with unusual privileges, such as asking impudent questions of senators as long as he pleased, without risk of being laughed off or evicted.

I recall the scene well. We'd been grilling Jack Kennedy several times, each time for an hour or two (and, yes, all reporters called him Jack then). Kennedy was leaning back on his rocking chair, one leg over an armrest, puffing on a cigar, responding to Sam's increasingly inventive provocations, each question minimizing Kennedy's qualifications to become president and painting the likelihood of his election in more and more ludicrous terms.

The game seemed to go on for a long time, and finally Kennedy just smiled and said, "Look, Sam, all these jobs have to be done by human beings."

19.

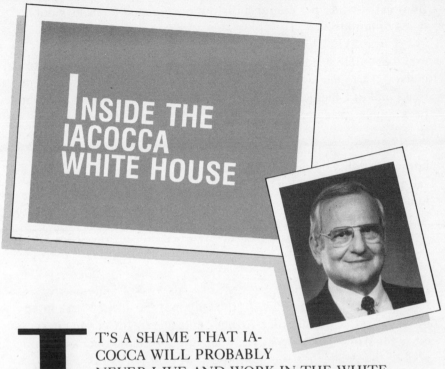

INSIDE THE IACOCCA WHITE HOUSE

IT'S A SHAME THAT IA-
COCCA WILL PROBABLY
NEVER LIVE AND WORK IN THE WHITE
HOUSE BECAUSE HE'D SURELY SAVOR THE
ELABORATE POMP. He'd take all of it quite for
granted because he has upheld the trappings of the Im-
perial Presidency since he became the mere president
of Ford.

A former executive of the company still chuckles at
the memory of the scene when Iacocca arrived to in-
spect the largest Ford dealership in California. A convoy of long
limousines drove up. Many men in dark suits jumped out. Iacocca
taking the lead, the retinue marched into a conference room to be
piped aboard. Nobody sat down until President Iacocca was seated.
Nobody spoke out loud until he spoke. No band strummed "Hail
to the Chief," yet the sanctity of the occasion was lost on nobody.

The privileges of office are important to Iacocca on pragmatic as
well as psychological grounds. Perquisites save time, eliminate such
inconveniences as standing in line, and help validate his self-image.
It's unlikely that other "Italian" kids from Allentown have drawn

wash water from a gold faucet aboard a private 727 jet, or slept in the double bed of such a flying palace, or lounged in solitude in the front cabin while the entourage is not encouraged (and does not dare) to intrude.

"It was like Air Force One," a former Ford speech writer remembers. "He can be unapproachable, like God, and he wants to convey that. One evening we boarded the plane in Detroit and got to a hotel in Chicago at ten P.M. He decided he wanted to go right back home, so fifteen people packed up and we returned to Detroit."

Such independence does not come easily without personal airborne capability, which explains why Iacocca became so incensed at the government nitpickers who decided that taxpayers should not finance private planes while Chrysler was operating under public loan guarantees. To Iacocca, being deprived of his plane was not like losing a luxury. It was like having his toothbrush confiscated.

Excessive significance can be read into this love of folderol, the tinfoil of the *numero uno* status. In the Imperial Presidency as defined by its inventor, the historian Arthur Schlesinger, Jr., comic opera dress for White House guards and heaters for the outdoor swimming pool of the president's summer home, all paid for by tax dollars, were not terribly important of themselves. They were, says Schlesinger, "the expression of a regal state of mind," of "Caesarism."

Presidents Johnson and Nixon both displayed such "monarchical yearnings." They lost touch with reality and grasped for powers that led to disgrace for Johnson and destruction for Nixon. Johnson could not conceive that he lacked the means to subdue a rabble of gooks, the North Vietnamese. Nixon thought that the illegalities of his "plumbers," his conspiracies against his domestic "enemies" by wiretapping and mail reading, were logical extensions of his imperial duties. Both men lost contact with the voters; both suffered from overprotective sheltering provided by subservient advisers. Both were, at bottom, brought down by gross flaws within themselves.

Does Iacocca wallow in a regal state of mind? Is he a Caesar afflicted by monarchical yearnings?

I have talked with some of his former colleagues who have imagined how he would set to work with new associates in the White House, and the old-timers break out in hives at the vision.

"I can see the dressing down he'll give the cabinet every morning," said a retired Ford public relations executive.

Iacocca loves to encourage this rugged reputation. "If someone stepped out of line in my administration, on a power trip, I'd stop it in a hurry," he told an interviewer in 1986. "After the second warning there'd be no tomorrow. They'd be gone." Moreover, he has always enjoyed operating that way. When a *Time* cover story in the 1960s described him as a "cold-assed operator," his PR people feared they would be held responsible for a case of lèse-majesté.

"We're dead," groaned the PR chief. He was wrong. Iacocca wasn't insulted; he chuckled.

"Yeah, that's me," he said.

So in an Iacocca administration the air would probably turn blue with four-letter language ("Who knows?" said the UAW's Doug Fraser. "Americans might like it"). The brief half-life of presidential speech writers might come down by several additional notches. Slogans resembling TV commercials might blossom to dramatize some rather too complex national issues, and the identity of the *numero uno* in the White House would never be in doubt.

At Chrysler headquarters just about every room is graced by an Iacocca photo with a quotation from Chairman Iacocca: "We have one and only one ambition. To be the best. What else is there?" The signature below is Iacocca's, and the meaning is the message: The world would be best off if run by Chairman Lee, assisted by formations of Iacocca-inspired deputies.

I detect a touch of Big Brotherism in all this but hardly a regal state of mind, surely no Caesar with monarchical yearnings, although the posteriors of some exposed personalities might feel President Iacocca's footsteps. Another thing: Caesar never had much fun running his country. Iacocca probably would, just as he talked about fun to the *Time* reporter who badgered him about the White House life back in 1985. It's just not much fun for those around him.

"Ass kicking, that's his environment," said a retired *Wall Street Journal* Detroit correspondent who for years ran elaborate feuds with Iacocca. But then, as Iacocca's critics persistently do, the critic from the *Journal* switched gears. "I admire the guy," he went on. "You gotta admire him for getting things done. I just can't always like *the way* he gets things done."

The former *Journal* man gave me a front-page article from the January 9, 1975, issue of the paper. It was headlined BRAKING THE

RULES. Underneath, it said, "Auto men use slump in seeking slow-down on safety, pollution." President Iacocca of Ford was placed in the front rank of carmakers demanding the relaxation of rules on auto safety and pollution. Iacocca quoted "statistics that he says show that Americans would enjoy 'one less day of coughing and chest discomfort every 33 years if smog were eliminated.'"

On February 10 the *Journal* published an indignant response from Iacocca, complaining about the quote on coughing and chest discomfort: "As your reporters know, the statistics are not mine. They come directly from a report by the National Academy of Science."

My retired *Journal* man was still furious about Iacocca's mirror trick. "The wonderful coughing quote is a masterpiece of verbal legerdemain," he told me. "Compare his letter. It correctly identifies an NAS report as his source of statistics, but it doesn't quite say that the conclusion and quote that were in the *Journal* were from the report, does it? That's because those were, in fact, entirely his incredible, sensational words, just as we said."

The *Journal* man thereupon simmered down. We were hardly talking plumbers and wiretaps.

"You gotta admire that he's not afraid to stand up and go for something he wants, and you can't help but *enjoy his company*," the retired correspondent said. "He's clever. He'll yell at you for ten or fifteen minutes, but he's such a great raconteur and you'll have another story for tomorrow's paper. He'll say, 'You know what happened *today* . . . ?'" And he'd be having *fun*.

. What about the awful anger, the rage that so many Iacocca-phobes talk and write about? Would it truly descend upon the cabinet every morning and turn the secretaries of state and defense into stone? Executives who have been populating the inner Iacocca sanctum at Chrysler think not.

"A lot of it is baloney," said Paul Bergmoser, the recently retired Chrysler president.

"If lightning struck and Lee became president of the United States, he'd surround himself with people who speak up," said Steve Miller, the vice chairman for finance. "He throws out nonperformers."

So what about the rage, Steve, the rage?

"Intimidation is an important fact of life with Lee," said Miller. "But it's always pointed, articulate, it's aimed at a business problem, it's not personal, and it's not incoherent expletives. It's focused on a particular problem: 'This is too much cost for the market; how did we get into this box?' "

The cutting edge of Miller's hand hit the table, imitating an Iacocca gesture of high fury.

Miller smiled. "It's not fun to be on the receiving end," he said, leaving the obvious unstated: Nobody has yet claimed that running a company (or a country) can be all fun all the time.

So what about Iacocca's way of listening?

Miller smiled once more and reported a profound discovery.

"He doesn't listen, but he hears," said Miller. "You find out later that things sink in. It does take fortitude to argue your point."

And, oh, yes, Iacocca listens to the mail and the TV, and he reads the papers and books, and he listens to gossipy friends like Billy Fugazy and the rest of his gang, and he does do his homework reading at night and constantly comes up with clippings for follow-up. He never, never seems to lose touch with the market, with what the customers want, with reality, and he sure as hell never stops asking questions.

His maligned *landsmann* Niccolò Machiavelli prescribed that a ruler "ought to be a great asker, and a patient hearer of the truth about those things of which he has inquired" and each adviser should "see that the more freely he speaks, the more he will be acceptable." Iacocca knew.

If Iacocca had not yet reached Machiavelli's standards for the second part of the ask/listen equation, he had stockpiled by early 1987 a respectable inventory of views on policy questions, especially in the field of economics.

"Lee has a passionate interest in economic affairs," Steve Miller said. "He's undeclared on abortion, school prayer, and other issues, but at the lunch table he rattles off his economic solutions like a tape—passionate and colorfully stated."

Since I didn't feel I should place an electronic bug into the executive dining room at Chrysler, I combed through the monthly syndicated newspaper column Iacocca has been writing and found that his political persona presents—the *Wall Street Journal* to the contrary—a far from "slender profile." (The *Journal* does credit him with ideas that add up to considerable government intervention in the economy: a Marshall Plan to rebuild American industry; a new agency to restructure industrial debt; trade barriers, including a special tax on Japanese automobile imports; interest rates to be set by law; and new taxes to battle the federal deficit, including a gasoline tax of up to twenty-five cents a gallon at the pump.)

Iacocca's newspaper columns address a much wider spectrum of concerns in fairly lively style and offer imaginative approaches for selling his philosophy to the voters. Take the federal deficit. "The truth is we are going broke," he wrote, "and not very slowly." The mortgage on our children would be out of reach soon. He argued that people are oblivious of the figures because they're impersonal; $2 trillion doesn't mean anything to an ordinary person. He would begin, he said, by learning from the truth-in-lending laws. He'd send out a debt statement with every income tax form. For the average-income family of four, this notice would say:

DEAR MR. AND MRS. TAXPAYER:
Your share of the national debt is now $34,737.32. In the past 12 months your share has increased by $4,233.56. Your share of the interest bill this year is $2,174.73. Have a nice day.

Wrote Iacocca: "If Americans saw the debt personalized like that it might start a revolution."

In 1983 he suggested getting a start on balancing the national books by cutting the deficit, then $120 billion, in half. He proposed his "four fifteens." (I wondered: Would they have worked as magically as his "56 in 56" formula sold Fords in 1956 or his "2,000 and 2,000" kept down the weight and price of the Pinto?) He would have sliced $15 billion (5 percent) from the defense budget and another $15 from domestic programs. He would have raised $15 billion from increased gasoline taxes and another $15 billion from a $5-per-barrel tax on imported oil. Presto, $60 million (half the deficit) would have vanished. Today all the figures would have to be more than doubled, Iacocca warns, but the formula would still work.

Yes, yes, he knew how Walter Mondale had lost his career through incineration when he merely hinted at necessary tax increases. Salesman Iacocca wrote that in Reagan's time he would have sold tax increases by showmanship, like this: "Ronald Reagan and Tip O'Neill would walk on camera (smiling), with their arms around each other, and announce that they had worked out a sensible compromise to keep our country from going down the tubes. Then, looking straight into the camera, they would ask all Americans to rally around them and share some of the sacrifice."

Sacrifice, yes, sacrifice. It's a large word in the Iacocca dictionary of leadership. "Blood, sweat, and tears," Churchill had promised. "Ask not what your country can do for you," John Kennedy had admonished. Iacocca knew that our times are less idealistic, more pragmatic, numbers-oriented. "The people in Washington live by polls," he wrote. "They don't lead public opinion. They follow it. Democracy works from the bottom up. So the answer is to change the polls."

Which gets him back to the crucial necessity for informing the people of the facts so convincingly that they will appreciate how the deficit affects them and their children. "I'm convinced that if Americans really understood how deep in the hole they are, and just what they are doing to their kids' future, they would not only accept sacrifice, they'd *demand* it."

To my surprise, Iacocca also lectured in his writings about the "honorable old art of compromise," the very art that his critics claim is alien to him. It seems that he does appreciate its value and is quite put out with people who don't.

"We've been on an ideological kick in Washington lately," he wrote. "Compromise is out! It's Rambo time on the Potomac. Pick your side and fight to the last ditch, and anybody caught in the middle is a wimp." He says we're "like the little kid who won't play football unless he's quarterback," so polarized that our forefathers' system of checks and balances, which Iacocca lauds, is breaking down.

To hear Iacocca discuss the art of compromise, he seems to understand it well, including the need to place reins on the negotiators' egos.

"It's not a sign of weakness to bargain as hard and as fairly as you know how, and then compromise in the interest of both sides," he wrote. "I've never made a deal in my life that had any lasting value unless the other guy felt he had won a little, too."

In the real world of Iacocca's business dealings, he does (more often than not) practice compromise (more or less) according to this pious preaching. He just doesn't go about it quite so peacefully, not even when negotiating with close friends.

Well aware that Iacocca was scouting for new ways to tuck his rapidly increasing wealth into solid investments, Billy Fugazy in 1986 suggested that Lee become a partner in a real estate venture of their mutual pal Donald Trump, the famous forty-year-old billionaire.

In a spare moment between other deals, Trump had acquired the tallest building in the exclusive West Palm Beach, Florida, resort area, a brand-new thirty-two-story condominium. It was Trump's kind of place: The walls of the lobby were three stories high and covered with leather; its armchairs were done in elephant skin. Exercising his usual modesty, the new owner named the project Trump Plaza.

I was not invited when Trump, Iacocca, and Fugazy sat down to negotiate Iacocca's partnership—a $1 million penthouse was thrown into the deal for Lee—but Fugazy talked to me guardedly about the proceedings shortly after (to Billy's great relief and somewhat to his surprise) the deal had been locked up. I felt I was listening to Sancho Panza's tale of his headaches in brokering a compromise between two lance-carriers, both named Don Quixote.

"Lee is used to getting things done his own way," Fugazy began. Trump is used to driving iron-hard bargains. Lee thought Donald was being too tough with his figures and got mad, especially at Billy. "He screamed at me," Fugazy related, "but at nine o'clock that night he called. It had all been forgotten, and he had an entirely new approach that worked."

Fugazy grinned. "He doesn't *like* to compromise," he said. "He doesn't want to be detoured. But that doesn't mean he won't *accept* the detour."

Iacocca had learned the need for compromise at Ford, to be sure. Otherwise he could never have survived there as long as he had. And he had given thought to the process of giving and taking.

"I live in a world of accommodation and compromise," he told the writer Gail Sheehy shortly before the great Ford firing. "They always talk about the rugged individualist who just says, 'I'm the boss, I'm going to order it.' Well, whoever that is, in government or in business, usually ends up getting his head knocked off. The higher up you go in an organization, the more you compromise."

That year he didn't compromise enough and his head did get knocked off. It was the last time. Live and learn.

Since I'd heard from quite a few Iacocca boosters and doubters that unpleasant things might happen to the country if Iacocca had to transfer his talents from the private to the public sector, it was interesting to read in one of his newspaper columns how nicely he seems to understand the crucial difference between the two systems. Again, he used the deficit problem as his example:

"In business, the process is fairly simple. You call all your key people into a room and say, 'okay, sales are down and costs are up, so we have to take 10 per cent out of the budget, starting right now. Come back tomorrow and tell me what you're going to give up . . .' But America isn't the typical company; it's a democracy. It's accountable to the people. . . ."

One helpful technique, he said, would be his old hobbyhorse: list making. He proposed that we all make lists of the most important services that government supplies us ("Protection from the Russians? A social security check?"). Then each of us should ask, "How much more tax am I willing to pay to keep the ones I don't want to touch?" We should send our lists to our congressmen and senators because "the budget won't get cut until we tell the politicians to do it and send them a list of sacrifices we are willing to make."

Simplistic? Certainly. Precampaign campaign oratory? Possibly. But not unworkable, not unimaginative, not lacking in insight into the behavior of people, and not lacking in the attractive human quality that none of my informants had brought up in any connection with Iacocca: humility. Could it be that humility accounts for some measure of the shyness his friends do talk so much about?

One category of strangers with whom Iacocca is not shy at all—indeed, he sometimes leaves himself breathtakingly self-revealed—is interviewers, uncelebrated journalists whom he invites so they can listen to him pontificate. They provide audiences he craves, listeners outside the inner circle of his converts in the executive lunchroom. On a lucky day, when these listeners tap vulnerable nerves with the right mix of anesthetic and surgical probing, they walk away with interesting ruminations about his noncandidacy, as we have seen earlier, and sometimes about substantive matters as well.

In September 1986 one fortunate visitor to Detroit was Fritz Wirth, Washington correspondent for *Die Welt*, a leading national newspaper in West Germany. Wirth had asked the usual questions about the presidency. Iacocca had issued the usual denials, again and again, no, no, no, no way.

"Good," said Wirth. "You don't want to be president. But what would happen if you were president of the United States here and now? What would be your first action and your first decision?"

Iacocca could not resist.

"My first action would be very difficult," he said. "I would take on the dual scandal of our time, the budget and trade deficits. I would declare them to be bipartisan national problems and it would be like in World War II: We must bury our differences. And since I come from industry, I'd submit a five year plan and I'd say: we'll start with it tomorrow."

One more issue would require even more urgent attention, he said, and he was all set with a tactic for handling it, too.

"I believe in the benefits of continuing dialogue," he said. "Maybe it wouldn't be possible, but *it would be my style to hold at least four summit meetings per year* [emphasis added] because the discussion of the nuclear threat to the world must have absolute priority. One can't solve these problems by saying, 'We won't talk to these people, they're bad.' "

At least four summits a year? So much chummying up to the "guys" in the Kremlin might smack of weak-kneed courtship to conservative American cold warriors. To pragmatic, solutions-oriented voters it would probably seem a refreshing new notion for loosening up ancient suspicions and injecting movement into fossilized East-West stalemates. At the very least, this is not the kind of ready response an interviewer would get from someone who hasn't thought about the gut question in the conduct of the nation's foreign affairs.

Several of the Iacoccalytes had been contemplating Lee-at-the-summit on their own long before I met up with them, and they liked the view that appeared in their crystal balls. "He'd be terrific with Gorbachev," said Fugazy, and so thought others, especially the buddies who had seen him win at poker.

Predicting presidential performance. At least one leading historian has won the acceptance of his peers for his method of turning this art into something closer to the precision of a science (see Chapter 21, "The Iacocca Character," page 329). But it still demands strong lenses to foresee Harry Truman's ascent from the cronyism of his Kansas City courthouse to the majesty of his Marshall Plan or Jimmy Carter's comedown from his élan in running the state government in folksy Georgia to his disintegration in the fragmentation of micromanagement when the voters promoted him to be *numero uno* in cutthroat Washington.

While nobody can gauge in advance what heat and direction a new president's "internal fires" would produce, Iacocca's past performance offers clues. His would surely have been a strong, decisive, pushy presidency and a wordy one given to much showmanship, hoopla, many press conferences, innumerable speeches and briefings and photo opportunities, considerable sparring with the *Wall Street Journal*, Sam Donaldson, and other skeptics.

He would have kept a tight, informed rein on his staff, and its members would have toed the Iacocca line with devotion. He'd have taken endless office hours for granted. His homework would have gotten done thoroughly and in good time. His concern for his personal security would have been welcomed by his Secret Service detail. The TV people would have enjoyed his mastery of their medium. His hypochondria would have kept the White House physician intrigued. Instead of Reagan's rich Californians and Carter's homespun Georgians, Iacocca's kitchen cabinet would have contained a contingent of tight-lipped "car guys" from Detroit.*

He probably would have had some labor people around, but he would not have worked on close terms with any woman whom he might, for political reasons, perhaps have felt forced to appoint to a ranking administration post.

The record shows that Iacocca prefers to seek no counsel from women at all. In his youth and his days at Ford, mature females stayed at home, took care to be good listeners, gave quiet, tactful advice on anything but business matters, and sent their men off to work on decent breakfasts. As in Papa Nick's day, the women were either hallowed as homemakers on their kitchen pedestals or collectively regarded as sexually available, and they were so discussed by Lee and his intimates. A young male visitor to Iacocca's office once asked him why he and his colleagues called their female secretaries by their first names but didn't let the women address the men with equal informality. Iacocca was taken aback. "If a man's secretary here called him by his first name everybody would think he's laying her," said The Chairman.

To Lee's generation of males, old-fashioned midwesterners,

---

*Friends from the BBDO advertising agency presented Chrysler Vice Chairman Ben Bidwell with a mock version of a Dewar's whiskey "profile" ad. According to this gag, the last two books read by Bidwell had been *Iacocca* and *The Making of the President* and Bidwell's "secret ambition" was to become presidential press secretary.

women were still tidily boxed in two categories. They were either wives or, actually or potentially, "pussy." It is an appallingly degrading word dating back to a time that seems long ago but is not. Its continued usage is a reality and conveys true, deep disrespect. In the Iacocca school, women are for home or play, and a blurring of their status was slow to come. Important work was still men's work.

Iacocca was enough of a marketing man to realize that unliberated attitudes, if detected, might keep women buyers out of car dealer showrooms, and in 1986 his personnel people had been given orders to put a top-level female executive in place at Chrysler by the end of the year. Notwithstanding The Chairman's zest for meeting objectives, the assignment remained unaccomplished. (As of spring 1987, Ford had one female officer, General Motors had three.)

Bill Winn points out that Iacocca picked up his basic business attitudes from Charlie Beacham. "In that school there were no women," says Winn. "They didn't exist. Women executives were never part of Lee's life." Doug Fraser of the UAW recalls that Iacocca once expressed his admiration for one of the union chief's executives, but Lee automatically assumed she was a secretary.

In personal encounters Iacocca tends to impress even the most liberated women very favorably. Gloria Steinem, arguably America's most influential contemporary female, told me she sat next to him at large dinners on at least two occasions.

"I was impressed with him, and I liked him," she recalled. Their mutual admiration arose in part from their shared dislike of President Reagan. Iacocca regaled Steinem with irreverent stories of his visits to the White House. "He was open and funny," she said.

I mentioned Iacocca's reputation as an unreconstructed male chauvinist, but Steinem insisted that she could detect no antifeminist symptoms in his table talk. "I felt he didn't have personal hangups about women's issues," she remembered.

Was Iacocca changing his attitude toward women? That was possible, of course; his capacity for personal growth had shown itself repeatedly during my inquiries. And yet I think his ability to deal with Steinem on terms of full equality probably had more to do with her brains and personality. I first worked with Steinem on magazines some twenty years ago. She is exceptionally smart, well informed, personable, and good-looking—and not just on television. And there is nothing strident about this soft-voiced person with the gentle, almost shy smile and the big dark eyes. There may never have been a lower-keyed crusader. It was easy to picture Iacocca or any chauvinist melting in her presence as a dinner partner.

It also was not difficult to visualize Peggy Iacocca's performance as a first lady. While she lacked experience, age, and sophistication for becoming a senior adviser like Nancy Reagan or Rosalynn Carter, the former Peggy Jane Johnson was ambitious, a mover, a talker, and, like her husband, Lee, a living advertisement for an all-American specialty: self-improvement.

A cheerful charmer from a southern country crossroads, she had a sexy figure, soft blue eyes, but no trace of accent, and was, at thirty-five, twenty-six years younger than Iacocca. She was loaded with any number of enthusiasms and extraordinarily self-possessed. Although her last claim to prominence had come to her as runner-up to Miss Kinston in Kinston, North Carolina, her hometown, the possibility of taking up residence in the White House had not unsettled her one bit.

"If I had to manage it," she bubbled to a writer from *Metropolitan Detroit* magazine, "I'm sure I could, and quite well."

Too bad that fate—and Iacocca—dealt her a problematic hand.

20.

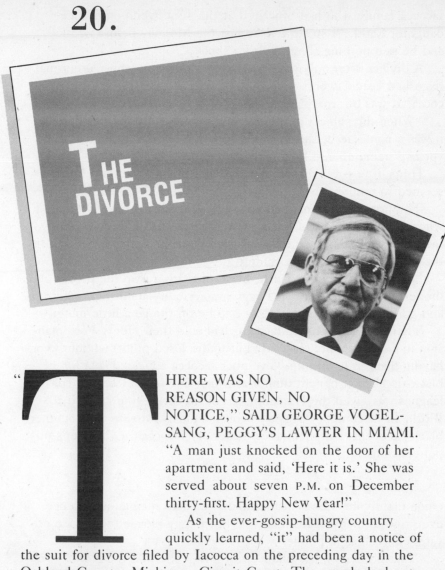

THE DIVORCE

"**T**HERE WAS NO REASON GIVEN, NO NOTICE," SAID GEORGE VOGELSANG, PEGGY'S LAWYER IN MIAMI. "A man just knocked on the door of her apartment and said, 'Here it is.' She was served about seven P.M. on December thirty-first. Happy New Year!"

As the ever-gossip-hungry country quickly learned, "it" had been a notice of the suit for divorce filed by Iacocca on the preceding day in the Oakland County, Michigan, Circuit Court. The couple had not lived together since October 15, 1986, the petition disclosed, less than seven months after the Iacoccas were married. There was a "breakdown in the marriage relationship to the extent there remains no reasonable likelihood that the marriage can be preserved." The court was asked for an "equitable distribution" of "certain property acquired during the term of the marriage."

The news created a sensation because the surprise was total. "It really floored me," said Father John Mericante, a close friend of the

Iacocca family who had officiated at the June wedding of Lee's daughter Kathi. "I spoke to Lee just the Monday before he filed, and he said nothing about it. It's a shock."

A divorce after only *seven months* for a husband whose other marriage had lasted twenty-seven years? And for a Catholic like Iacocca? It was bizarre.

"When the subject of divorce was discussed at the prenuptials, it was a nonissue because Mr. Iacocca just doesn't believe in divorces," remembered Vogelsang, the attorney.

Hints of possible discord had, in fact, emerged earlier, but they seemed so tenuous that they were ignored except in hindsight.

The first storm signal had gone up right after the April wedding when Peggy's matron of honor, Karen Clark, had offered a comment to *People* magazine that was prescient but was drowned out in the swirl of congratulatory confetti.

"Lee is on the go so much, he would rather skip the parties and dinners," said Mrs. Clark. "Peggy has a vitality about her, a get-up-and-go. Sometimes she would like to be on the go a little more."

Then, in October, the Iacoccas had sold their Henry Ford mansion in Grosse Pointe (at a tidy but undisclosed profit) without ever having lived in it. In mid-November Iacocca appeared solo for a black-tie Detroit benefit dinner at which one of his Chrysler colleagues was given the Humanitarian of the Year Award by B'nai B'rith. In December Peggy was conspicuously missing from another black-tie event, a dinner/dance hosted by Iacocca for Chrysler's upper echelons.

Once the divorce news hit the media, Iacocca maintained silence, even toward many of his relatives, but Peggy pleaded with Lee privately as well as in public.

"I have been on the phone with him," she told the *Detroit Free Press*. "How much of a reconciliation there can be, I don't know." Manifestly she was strongly hoping that her moody husband would kiss and make up. To her the divorce suit was only another of their routine fights.

"If this were anyone else, this would be just a marital spat that no one would pay any attention to," she claimed at first. And attorney Vogelsang told the press what was apparent from the start of the sad episode: His client wanted to be taken back; she was still "deeply in love" with her husband.

The Detroit newspapers labored hard to activate the tear ducts of their readers. "A heartsick Peggy Iacocca, in seclusion in her East Side Manhattan apartment and comforted by her Yorkshire terrier Sassy, said she spent most of her Tuesday morning on the phone trying to reconcile with her husband Lee," began a front-page article in the *Detroit News*.

Even the *New York Times*, usually above any marital fray, caught a momentary attack of gossip fever. DETROIT ABUZZ ABOUT IACOCCA DIVORCE PLANS, said its four-column headline across an article rounding up all the excitement with an un-*Times*ian smack of the lips. So intense was the general preoccupation with the unanticipated social news, reported the *Times*, that Iacocca—"in Detroit his status approaches that of royalty"—felt compelled to stay away from the great annual Auto Show.

Nor was the titillation limited to Iacocca's hometown, the *Times* found. It told about the visiting executive of a California-based automobile company who interrupted a Detroit business meeting to blurt out: "I don't care about any of that. I want to know what the inside story is: are Peggy and Lee getting back together?"

The *Times* could be forgiven for its peek into Iacocca's marital closet. After all, Lee and Peggy *were* something like royal personages. Furthermore, both had courted publicity diligently, thus casting themselves as public figures with little excuse for insisting on privacy. But now they went into hiding, and the gossipmongers, mostly unnamed, took over the many attempts to explain what had gone wrong.

The big trouble, mused several of the anonymous friends, was that Peggy had gone on strike about moving to stodgy, business-oriented Detroit, where Lee had to spend much of his time with Chrysler. She pretty much refused to be there with him, preferring the more entertaining New York environment and her apartment there. Lee felt deserted.

"Just ask yourself how many meals you like to eat alone," said one Iacocca crony.

According to another friend, it was only after he had married Peggy that it dawned on Lee that his new wife, unlike the late Mary, had no wish to spend most evenings out of public view, quietly at home, with Lee engrossed in his papers and his crossword puzzles, away from partying strangers in search of small talk.

The contrast between Mary and Peggy hit Lee like a sledge-hammer after the excitement of the dating and the wedding had died down. "When Peggy declined to move to Detroit, it became apparent to Lee that he was dealing with a different breed of woman," said one source.

Another informant, an anonymous Chrysler executive, blamed much of the couple's travail on his boss. "Lee's problem is that he tried to treat her like an employee on the production line, not a partner," reported this observer. "It's unfortunate because they probably still love each other. But they were just from different generations."

Different generations and clashing temperaments. Both partners were people of iron determination. More succinctly, both were stubborn as hell. Each had a strongly ingrained personal life-style. Each wanted control of their joint life. Each thought it would be possible to convert the other after the wedding. Both miscalculated.

No doubt, additional private factors played a role, but the irreconcilable clash of two powerful personalities is one key pattern among divorcing couples, although it isn't commonly recognized when the male partner is older, accustomed to command, and presumably wiser, while the younger female partner is outwardly ingratiating and compliant. In actuality, a liberated woman can be just as rocklike as such a man.

One of Peggy's former boyfriends, John F. Burton, Jr., who dated her for several years in the mid-1970s, said: "She's not going to be run over by anyone. It may have been more than he could take if she stood up to him a lot."

Standing up. It is a posture that had been Peggy Jane Johnson Iacocca's style since the high school drama coach back in Kinston, North Carolina, took her aside, informed her that she had the perfect personality for the stage, and asked her to join his class.

"From that day on, I wished I was Sarah Bernhardt," she recalled many years afterward.

Someone like the Divine Sarah could hardly flourish in the confinement of Kinston, the home of Peggy's daddy, Clarence, a share-cropper who advanced no farther than work in a tobacco warehouse. And when the Grainger High School newspaper asked the class of '68 for its life goals, Peggy announced that hers was to leave Kinston, just to get out.

A little community college failed to hold her interest, so she joined the world by enlisting in National Airlines as a flight attendant in Miami. She began flying to London and Paris and learned French from Berlitz. In 1975, strangely, she returned to Kinston and talked a longtime admirer into marrying her, much as she seems to have persuaded Iacocca to commit himself to her eleven years later—and with similar precipitous results.

The first husband was an upstanding salesman for Allstate Insurance, Brooks Rasor. The marriage lasted just fourteen weeks.

"That was my fault," she acknowledged subsequently. "I pushed him to get married."

Back to National Airlines she went on the rebound; but the company was gobbled up by Pan American, and she found herself bored flying the African routes, wanting to stand up to Pan Am. She did, joining the Statue of Liberty fund-raising efforts and then BBDO advertising, which did the Dodge ads for Iacocca.

Peggy and Lee were becoming an item—they appeared together in public for the first time in November 1983—but circumstances and timing of the early romance are unclear. The timing, in particular, remained classified news, presumably in deference to the memory of Mary Iacocca's death in the spring of 1983.

According to the official version, the couple was brought together at the Palm Bay Club in Miami by an unnamed mutual friend in an unknown year. It was a blind date officially. Unofficially they'd met previously at some time in some way. In any event, Peggy was in no mood to stand up to Lee then or, evidently, at other times during the courtship years.

She admired him in the style to which he was long accustomed. "He's the greatest education I've ever had," she said. "I learn something each day from him." He, in turn, was having the sort of fun time that he'd not experienced in a long while, and it felt marvelous.

"We make each other laugh," said Peggy. "I'm a very up person, and he needs that."

Lee agreed: Peggy's great and good cheer was a priceless asset to his chronically harassed existence. "She makes me feel happy," he said. "I like people who wake up every morning and are glad they're alive and are whistling and happy as hell."

But marriage? Iacocca seemed unenthusiastic. According to a rumor heard by the staff of the *Free Press*, he was supposed to have presented Peggy with an engagement ring. The editors, fearing rebuff, persuaded Jimmy Jones, the retired *Newsweek* man who was in good odor with Lee, to call up the great man and ask about the ring. Iacocca confirmed the report, but he sounded damned grumpy, anything but an eager groom. And two weeks before the wedding he was heard to remark: "You bet I'm nervous. It's a huge change in life."

His girls had been upset at the idea of acquiring such a young stepmother so soon after their mother's death. Kathi, the elder daughter, had remained behind in the car when she was drafted to chaperone the couple on one of their dates—and she had cried. By the time of Kathi's wedding—Peggy appeared radiantly in the same tucked and pleated pale blue Bill Blass dress she had worn for her own marriage eight weeks earlier—both daughters had become reconciled to their father's new marital status. At least somewhat. Lia's principal public compliment of her stepmother could be interpreted as sounding ambivalent toward her and downbeat toward him.

"The best thing is that she doesn't take any of his crap," she told a writer from *Life*.

The daughters had found an ally in Peggy, someone else to stand up to their forbidding father, to soften his workaholic ways, maybe, to get him to set aside more unscheduled time for some personal life for a change. Once Lee and Peggy did sneak off to go bowling at 11:00 P.M. Most of the time he was frozen into his old closed-off style.

"Getting his attention is very, very difficult," said the new Mrs. Iacocca within a few weeks of the wedding. "We just have to stand in line and wait our turn."

She was beginning to sound like another frustrated mutineer, like the daughters, because she, too, was registering her complaint to the man from *Life*. He, for one, was listening to her raptly. When Peggy did manage to collar the man she called Lido, the results were less satisfactory, especially when she attempted to sell him on some modest behavior modification.

"I tell him, 'Lido, why don't you back off a little?' " to which his response was revealing and beyond appeal. "I can't," he told Peggy, "I'm the star."

Peggy did her best to accommodate her husband's stardom— i.e., his need for dominance—at least before the wedding. She learned to cook his favorite Italian dishes. She converted from Methodism to Catholicism. She hit it off with his buddies, particularly with Billy Fugazy, whom she often phoned several times daily.

After scouting more than two dozen homes in Connecticut, even persuading Lee to look at two of them, she agreed to move into the Grosse Pointe mansion, if only to escape from the family home in Bloomfield Hills that threatened to become an intolerable shrine to Mary.

But by the time they gave up on the mansion—Lee roared in dismay at the fortune Peggy was planning to spend on redecorating—they no longer felt, as *Good Housekeeping* magazine had enshrined them, like one of America's "most beautiful" couples. And Peggy was definitely no longer taking "any of his crap."

"Peggy was basically a nice person, but she was too stubborn. She was always trying to change him. She thought she could change that old asshole, and she just wouldn't back down."

This was the judgment of Carroll Shelby when I asked him for the inside story of what had gone wrong. The old racing driver, born in Texas and still proud of the drawl that proved it, had often been a traveling companion to Lee and Peggy over the years, and he possessed a shrewd eye for relationships.

He'd been buddies with Lee since he came to Ford in 1961 for the financing of his great coup, the manufacture of the classic A.C. Cobra sports car. Currently he was buying Dodge cars from Lee and souping them up in his Los Angeles factory as sports models selling for up to $16,000. He qualified as a charter Iacoccalyte but was more outspoken than most.

"Peggy is quite a social climber," Shelby judged. "She wanted to be on the go all the time. After they were married, she didn't want to cater to his old-fashioned ways. She was impressed that she was Mrs. Lee Iacocca. And she wanted to spend a hell of a lot more money than he did. It hurts him to turn loose of big chunks of money."

Shelby watched Peggy change from a "good old country girl" into a jet-setter who adapted to the role of Mrs. Iacocca with a flair befitting her idol, Sarah Bernhardt. He knew that Lee liked the rewards and comforts of jet-setters but not their clubbiness. So Shelby was not surprised when the marriage seemed to collapse with apparent suddenness. He also knew that Peggy was flabbergasted by her husband's New Year's Eve decision to break up.

"She never dreamed in her wildest dreams that he'd walk out on her," he said. Lee and Peggy were simply two strong personalities, each looking for a partner to control, neither one finding enough "give" in the other to make a seven-day-a-week relationship function without intolerable stress. Carroll Shelby pronounced a sendoff: "They weren't meant to be."

And Peggy seemed to agree as the shock of the split had worn off and hope for reconciliation appeared to be fading. "We should always just have dated and never married," she told Eleanor Breitmeyer, the mother confessor and doyenne of Detroit women writers.

As a mere date Peggy would again have faced hectic competition from other women, not all of them with marriage on their minds. For Iacocca's sex appeal is one of the nation's most open secrets.

"I'd rather kiss you than shake your hand," murmured a woman lined up in the front row of an adoring mob at a New Orleans car dealers' convention.

"He has an earthiness that is pure sex—it's those eyes," said a friend of the late Mary Iacocca when *People* magazine questioned her for an article elevating Lee to "Sex Symbol for a Corporate Age." Numerous other women testified to this thesis on a variety of grounds. The wife of a rival auto executive called him "a modern-day caveman. . . . You'd never be afraid of anything with Lee Iacocca around." A "glamorous 51-year old Detroit career woman" observed: "I think his need to succeed would make him want to satisfy a woman in bed."

Karen Clark, Peggy's matron of honor, addressed herself to the less erotic elements of Iacocca's appeal to women. "He's extremely courtly, opening doors, standing up when women leave the table," she said. "And Lee is an immaculate dresser with exquisite taste: suits always pressed, stunning cuff links. He takes care of himself." And then Mrs. Clark put her finger on Iacocca's ultimate source of sex appeal: power.

"You know he is a man on the move," she said. "A lot of women are attracted to movers and shakers."

Iacocca, in turn, was relishing his regained freedom. "We've had more good conversation than we've had in ten years," said Carroll Shelby, presumably speaking for the male Iacoccalytes.

Shelby further said that Iacocca was delighted to be "back in the automobile business." Sure enough, a few days later the business news reverberated with word of Chrysler's tentative agreement to take over American Motors with its desirable line of four-wheel-drive Jeeps. Vice Chairman Ben Bidwell had run the complicated international negotiations together with Steve Miller, the top financial man, yet whenever fatigue or doubts arose, it was The Chairman who pushed and shoved them along like a drill sergeant.

Said Bidwell: "Iacocca kept banging us over the head, saying, 'This is for the long haul. This is a once-in-a-lifetime opportunity to broaden the distribution network, get a brand and a new plant and go forward. You take the pimples and the warts along with the beauty marks.' "

So Lee was pushing on again, warning his men that if they didn't go forward, they would be going backward. And in the department of female companionship he was also pushing on. One of my Detroit sources reported that Lee was dating a local cop. Yes, a cop. "She's a part-time model, in her thirties, and gorgeous," said the informant.

But wait! Hold everything! The judge in the divorce case was getting impatient with the apparent stalling of the parties. If there was no divorce agreement or reconciliation by June 30, 1987, he announced, he would appoint a mediator to settle the case.

That was in April. By May Iacocca's friends were watching the relationship like a tennis match. Would they or wouldn't they? Peggy still wasn't being seen in Detroit, but here she was arm in arm with Lee, both of them wearing happy smiles, posing at the Kentucky Derby for *People* magazine. What kind of a divorce was that?

Well, quite likely no divorce at all because in June the couple was back from a trip to Lee's farm in Italy. Listen again tomorrow. . . .

21.

THE IACOCCA
CHARACTER:
MEASURING UP
IN THE GAME OF
LEADERSHIP

MY INTER-
VIEWING AND
EFFORTS AT ANALYSIS LEFT
ME DISSATISFIED AT SEVERAL
LEVELS. Given the crosscurrents of
Iacocca's years—one thinks of his life
as a journey aboard a storm-tossed
whaling boat—what is the bottom
line for him? What is he truly like?
What key character qualities had I
failed to sort out of the facts? Or overemphasized? Or undervalued?
What might be his ultimate potential as a *numero uno*, perhaps in
some kind of public service? And if he is not to be a candidate for
president, why did so many voters believe that he ought to be?

His apparent elimination from the field of dark horses in the
spring of 1987 had nothing whatever to do with his qualifications or
lack thereof. I discussed his vanishing act with Greg Schneiders,
the chief strategist of the Draft Iacocca Committee. The group was
quietly disbanding. Like a revolutionary general whose junta has
taken to the hills, Schneiders was casting about for a new hero de-

serving of his allegiance for 1988. He was regretful about Iacocca, but one had to be practical and think of the fellow's marital difficulties; his increasingly resolute resistance against the call to duty; and, especially, the conviction in Washington, based on Reagan's troubles with Iran and the associated scandals, that the election of a Democratic president in 1988 seemed pretty much assured. The market for an Iacocca appeared to have evaporated.

"There is no longer the need for an outsider to come as a savior," said Schneiders. Iacocca's perennial scold, the *Wall Street Journal*, scolded him again, this time calling him a "draft dodger." Schneiders remained cheerfully professional.

"We're saving the bumper stickers for 1992," he said.

The election of 1992 was also on Iacocca's mind. At a ruminative year-end press conference in December 1986 he announced that he planned to stay at Chrysler through late 1990. "I'm so sure of that, I'd bet money on it if I were you people," he told reporters.

Warning for the umpteenth time that economic problems were about to overwhelm the nation, he now added a defeatist note. He said he was running out of suggestions for cures. What could anyone still do about the budget and trade deficits?

"I'll be damned if I know," he added. Then came a new rationale for his old disavowal: *"That's* why I don't want to be President" (emphasis added).

Not in 1988 anyway. He would probably confine himself to nominating another candidate and trying to act as that man's power broker. But 1992 would present a more interesting opportunity. A depression might be raging. It could be time for the "Roosevelt-type administration" that he might just possibly be willing to lead.

Physically the great marketer from Detroit has aged dramatically under the stresses of recent years. He has studied current photos of himself and compared them to pictures taken before he went to Chrysler in 1978; the contrast, once laid out before him, startled and worried him because the changes in his face are dramatic (not that he looked like a youngster by the time he left the frustrations at Ford).

"Iacocca's face is that of a man not often or easily made happy," wrote Gail Sheehy in the watershed year of 1978. "It is the face of a swordsman; no small anxiety lines, no tension wrinkles, no laugh lines, none at all. What there are, though, are three vertical slashes—deep mark-of-the-sword slashes from hairline to brow." By 1987 there were many more lines of wear and still no laugh lines.

Still, Iacocca's intimates report no slackening of their man's drive, his gluttony for work. So perhaps he would not be too aged in 1992 to be drafted at sixty-eight as a national savior, especially in the event of a calamitous national emergency.

His Depression-triggered anxiety about his material well-being has surely subsided with the years. Friends estimate that his wealth amounts to at least $50 million, perhaps quite a bit more, and still much, much more money was contractually guaranteed to fall into his lap soon. His salary, bonus, and stock options, rose to a whopping $23.6 million for 1986, making him by far the most highly paid person in the land.* His cash income for that year was a relatively piffling $1.7 million, including a bonus of $975,000. But he also received 337,500 shares of Chrysler stock which didn't add up to much when he went to work for Chrysler but were worth $11.8 million when they reached him in the fall of 1986. (The rest of his income that year was accounted for by dividends from that stock and interest on the dividends.)

All this is just a downpayment for Iacocca's services. In the fall of 1987 he could collect another 112,500 shares of stock and in November 1990 he would receive an outright grant of 127,500 shares of Chrysler common stock, worth $6.4 million (as of February 1987). If he stayed on the job a further year, he would get a gift of another 42,500 shares. He could also buy still another 480,000 shares at favorite-son prices.† The options for the 480,000 future shares would be exercisable as follows: 360,000 shares in December 1990 at the February 5, 1987, market price and another 120,000 shares if he stays on the job until December 1991. No other poker players ever ran up so small a stake into such a gigantic pot.

And even as Chrysler had begun to look great financially, it had also become, at least in some significant respects, a model corporate citizen under Iacocca. Not only that it was the first major American carmaker to concentrate on fuel-efficient vehicles. It set up the industry's first employee stock ownership plan and, later, a relatively generous profit-sharing program for everybody on the payroll. And it disposed of its military and South African interests.

---

*Iacocca's public reaction to the windfall: "That's the American way. If little kids don't aspire to make money the way I did, what the hell good is this country?"
†In a publicly held company like Chrysler such largess must be based on performance, and Iacocca has unquestionably delivered appropriate value. As recently as 1980 Chrysler lost $1.7 *billion*. In 1984 it earned $2.3 billion; in 1985, $1.6 billion; in 1986, $1.4 billion. Between 1982 and 1987 the company's aggregate market value increased twenty-five times.

* * *

Meanwhile, a question kept troubling me: If the end of Iacocca's noncandidacy in 1988 was unrelated to his potential capacity as president, did its rise have nothing to do with his qualifications either? An issue far bigger than Iacocca was buried here, and his brief career in politics made me want to deal with it.

Like the Detroit magazine editors who were flabbergasted in 1985 when their national poll showed that Iacocca—the man "who's never been elected dogcatcher"—could actually be the Democrats' best hope in 1988, I wondered what this utter amateur's sudden political standing tells us about the way we elect presidents. Is the selection process mostly a crapshoot? If not, what accounts for our record of bipartisan failures of the last fifteen years: Lyndon Johnson, Nixon, Carter, Reagan, two Republicans and two Democrats?* Are we playing Russian roulette with our future and the destiny of our children? Is there no way to peel away the hoopla of the plotting for high office, to look behind the scenery of the wire pulling, the debates, the posturing on TV, to X-ray the inner (along with the outer) lives of the contenders? Must we wait for an anonymous tip to the *Miami Herald* (and its dubious sleuthing) to unmask a frontrunner like Gary Hart as an arrogantly heedless gambler with his own cause? Are there no tests to detect the rot in presidential timber and in other potential top-level leaders?

There are.

Until recent years the hunt for failures and masters among our chief executives had been, in the word of the behavioral scientists, "retrodictive"—that is, confined to analyses of past performance, to largely unproductive detective work probing the condition of the proverbial barn after the departure of the horse. It was a chase for souvenirs.

Teams of distinguished historians lined up all of the presidents since George Washington under their microscopes and rated their records for "greatness." In 1948 fifty-five professor/experts launched such an exercise. In 1962 a tribunal of seventy-five undertook a reprise under the chairmanship of Harvard's Arthur M. Schlesinger, Sr., and came away with substantially the same results.†

The findings brought little surprise, nor did they yield indicators

---

*I omit the forgotten caretaker years of Gerald Ford as an undistinguished neutral experience.
†Five presidents were "great"; an additional six were "near great." The "great" presidents were, in the order of the votes they received, Lincoln, Washington, Franklin Roo-

sufficiently specific to be helpful to future voters. The professors equated greatness with activism, found that great presidents held the stage at critical moments in American times, that they "acted masterfully and farsightedly in foreign affairs" and suffered lots of abuse (Jefferson was called "Mad Tom"; Lincoln was the "baboon in the White House"). And that was about all.

In 1972 the hunt for much more specific human qualities suggesting greatness or failure in our leaders suddenly turned less amorphous and frustrating. Two scholars published respected books that year announcing new detective tools. Both of these academics applied more rigorous, scientific methods than the historians had mustered in the past. One author supplied a firmer underpinning to "retrodictive" interpretations of our leaders' past lives; the other had managed to design something of a scientific crystal ball, a systematic examination of past careers with the frank objective of adding the "predictive" element. He wanted to pinpoint measurable qualities in the lives of candidates that would constitute tips to voters about the *future* behavior of the hopefuls once they are elevated to high office.

The retrodictive effort, which happened to focus on the then-incumbent President Nixon, was the first important exercise in "psychohistory." Its author was Bruce Mazlish, a renowned historian at MIT who has since, by remarkable coincidence, become my brother-in-law. The book was well received, but the label of "psychohistory" remains controversial. Many scholars now use the technique, but its name is none too popular, even reviled by some, probably because some of its practitioners rely heavily on traditional Freudian theories that have become unfashionable.

(The controversy is much like the furor between qualified cancer specialists about the relative merits of radiation and surgery in the treatment of breast malignancies. No one any longer doubts that rigorous digging into the past behavior of leaders can, in professional hands, be a richly rewarding treasure hunt. Unsettled is only the method of choice and what to call it.)

The Mazlish work, *In Search of Nixon*, explicitly disclaimed any ambition to predict the future, and yet it did. Within months of its publication the Watergate scandals had broken open, triggering a

---

sevelt, Wilson, and Jefferson. To the historians of a generation later, the nomination of Wilson would be surprising. His insistence on maneuvering an unwilling electorate into the League of Nations is now considered so obsessive that the rating of his overall performance has dropped. The "near great" were Jackson, Teddy Roosevelt, Polk, Truman, John Adams, and Cleveland. Presidents starting with Kennedy were necessarily not rated in this 1962 poll.

fallout that lasted almost two years. Having concluded in his book that Nixon was an untrustworthy, dangerous neurotic, Mazlish looked all but prescient. I thought he was nicely qualified to comment on the objectives of this chapter: to look closely and objectively at (1) Lee Iacocca's qualifications for leadership and (2) what can be done to eliminate candidates who shouldn't be entrusted with high office.

So I sent Mazlish the preceding chapters. I also enlisted, for the same purpose, the author of the second groundbreaking study of 1972: James David Barber, professor of political science at Duke University and author of *The Presidential Character*, which bears the provocative subtitle, *Predicting Performance in the White House*. The book has gone through three editions, the last having come out in 1985. Each reappearance updated the White House triumphs and follies since the proliferating work's previous incarnation.

Writing nearly two years before the Iran scandals, Barber dismissed President Reagan as an entertainment celebrity, an intellectual drifter, a lazybones who once confessed that his favorite moment of the week was "climbing into that helicopter to go to Camp David."

Barber quotes accounts of White House reporters who found the president "eerily detached, oblivious," and a former White House staffer who lamented his erstwhile colleagues' lack of curiosity. "They have no questions," this defector said. "It's an administration without questions."

Relying on "Reagan dramatics," wrote Barber, the president was often "unplugged" from reality and dangerously vulnerable to staff people who misperformed or misbehaved. He could only "lurch" from crisis to crisis. Barber's conclusion: "At the center of it all was a President continually in search of directors to tell him what to do."

I thought that Barber's 1985 analysis of Reagan's "character," as it fell into shape prior to his presidency, came astonishingly close to foreshadowing the political collapse of this amiable man whom Barber called "as hard to dislike as a laughing baby." So I was delighted that Barber, too, agreed to act as my consultant.

My third and last authority is a professor with a workaday slant on leadership—an ability to stand the heat in the political kitchen—that Messrs. Mazlish and Barber cannot list among their credentials. He is Richard E. Neustadt of Harvard, who took leaves of absence from his classroom to serve the Kennedy, Johnson, and Carter White Houses and therefore brings to our scene here what the hard-nosed *Wall Street Journal* calls "a rare combination of intimacy and detachment."

Neustadt's classic course, *The American Presidency,* and its companion book, *Presidential Power,* have brought him more than recognition. He has influence. His work has helped to shape the thinking of the intellectual and political elite for a quarter of a century.

And so, after allowing them some weeks to acquaint themselves with the foregoing pages, I set out to visit my advisers.

Character. To Professor Barber, this is the name of the leadership game. Having spent the better part of a lifetime dissecting the lives of all presidents, paying closest attention to the presidents of this century, and having expended enormous persistence to comb through every shred of respectable evidence concerning the records of these men, he points to character as the ultimate criterion for assessing leadership and predicting a leader's future course.

Eschewing psychological constructions and jargon, Barber applies his standard where the stakes are exorbitant—to the man with the finger on the nuclear button, the president of the United States. I believe that this guidepost also applies to performance at any other leader's desk where the buck stops, to all places of ultimate managerial responsibility, to life at the top, where the leader is surrounded by innumerable eager courtiers yet is emotionally alone.

Barber's definition of character is explicit and commonsensical: "Character is the way the president orients himself toward life—not for the moment, but enduringly. Character is the person's stance as he confronts experience."

Character, as Barber views it, is mainly (though not wholly) developed in childhood. From it flow a person's *worldview,* shaped in adolescence, and then, finally, his *style,* the product of early adulthood. Worldview is the sum total of a leader's primary beliefs. Style is his habitual way with rhetoric, personal relations, and homework. Says Barber: "Style is his way of acting; worldview is his way of seeing."

What Barber politely refrains from saying outright is that the Freudian view of character development is too limited. Mother, father, childhood, id and ego aren't everything. *Adaptation* to the turbulence of one's life experience is relevant as well, and the leader's way of coping with life doesn't settle into a mold until long after the time when Freud says a personality is shaped.

I found this a marvelously serviceable scheme for systematizing a welter of discouragingly slippery concepts, a logical way of creating a structure to work from.

According to Barber's detective work, all presidents beginning with Theodore Roosevelt cluster into four types. The initial baseline for his evaluation is *activity versus passivity*. The extreme cases are illustrative: Does the president operate like a whirlwind, as Lyndon Johnson did, or like Coolidge, who often slept eleven hours a night and also took a midday nap?

The next basic dimension is *positive versus negative*. Does the president suffer and complain about his job like Eisenhower, or does he have a wonderful time wielding power, the way Franklin Roosevelt did?

Barber summarizes: "Active-positive presidents want most to achieve results. Active-negatives aim to get and keep power. Passive-positives are after love. Passive-negatives emphasize their civic virtues." Obviously, "active-positive" is meant to suggest soundness, perhaps greatness. The leaders in all other categories tend to be troubled by serious flaws.*

His scheme gives Barber four categories that work out like this:

Active-Positive	Active-Negative	Passive-Positive	Passive-Negative
Theodore Roosevelt	Wilson	Taft	Coolidge
Franklin Roosevelt	Hoover	Harding	Eisenhower
Truman	Johnson	Reagan	
Kennedy	Nixon		
Ford †			
Carter †			

Barber's categories transcend the limited and often empty definitions that offer little guidance to a leader's performance. Is he a Republican or a Democrat, a conservative or a liberal? These labels seem to make relatively little difference. A glance at the above tabulation is evidence that such specifications are without much meaning in gauging a leader for quality of performance, for *effectiveness*. Even the more sophisticated category of "self-esteem" is useless.

---

* Remarkable exceptions exist; George Washington was one. Barber admires him but rates him "passive-negative."
† I was surprised to see relative mediocrities like Gerald Ford and Jimmy Carter lumped together with the two Roosevelts, Truman, and Kennedy, but "active-positive" is meant to suggest only sound character.

True, without it a leader is nothing. Yet with it he can be either a Harding or an FDR.

More meaningful is what Barber calls the "climate of expectations," the national mood, the times into which a leader is thrust. Has recent experience left his constituency receptive to surcease, consolidation, and reassurance, for example? Or to moral renewal? Or restless for fresh initiatives? Effectiveness may depend on whether a leader's character can meet current demand.

My task was to apply the Barber system so as to extract answers to the main questions in my mind: (1) What are the most revealing qualities of promise to look for in Iacocca or any other leader? (2) What are the meaningful qualities to avoid?

The accuracy of the answers would naturally depend on the reliability of the data on a leader's character, worldview, and style, and for sheer plenitude of research materials Barber enjoyed a huge advantage. No group of humans is more aggressively dissected than the American presidents. Even the most reticent among them give press conferences and interviews and leave entire libraries crammed with papers. Many of them are prolific writers. Their friends and enemies, relatives, teachers, doctors, bodyguards, groundkeepers reminisce, analyze, lament, applaud. The outpouring is practically limitless, and the historians can select from a smorgasbord feast. So even though his aim was to "predict performance in the White House," Barber could mine a treasure of richly documented *past* careers.

Assessing the future prospects of an Iacocca—or any other *prospective* leader—entails greater risks. The Iacocca autobiography, as we have seen, is less than a fully reliable data base. Other sources I have used, especially my interviewees, also have limitations. For example, they shed only the sketchiest insight into one key to personality development, a factor that even researchers less avid for intimate detail than the Freudians would want to know more about: the relationship of the parents as it impacted on the raising of the son.

It would have been helpful for me to talk to Iacocca, but he resisted numerous approaches over nearly a year. I appealed to him directly by several letters, through associates, through friends, through my publisher, through his publisher. He passed word that he wanted to maintain "neutrality" toward my project. As a practical matter this meant that he refrained from ordering Fugazy, Bidwell, Sperlich, et al. not to talk to me. When I pressed for an explanation of his untypical coyness, word trickled down via his public affairs people that he didn't wish to talk for a biography because he was thinking of writing another book.

As I first interpreted this message, he was saying, "Why should I give away stuff about myself if I can sell it?" But since he is hardly in need of additional income, perhaps he was saying, "Why should I disclose personal information to a stranger if I can put it out the way I prefer to see things myself?" (You'll recall that he doesn't care much for strangers anyway.)

Fortunately Professors Barber, Neustadt, and Mazlish concluded independently that the preceding chapters offered up enough raw material for fresh judgments that I found intriguing indeed, especially since the professors spotted revelatory points in Iacocca's history whose importance I hadn't weighed. Listening to their comments as I interviewed these scholars was a sobering experience, like being taken down a familiar road and being shown embarrassingly large landmarks that I'd not noticed on my first trip.

Thus, after visiting Professor Barber, I reread my Chapter 5, zeroing in on the ways Iacocca employed to arrive at the design and the market positioning for the Mustang. On my first pass at these events I had already concluded that the continuing intramural debate in the auto industry about the paternity of this radically new vehicle was meaningless; no matter how severely Iacocca offended various sensibilities by crowing that the car was his, his, his, the car was in fact his. It would have gone no place if Iacocca hadn't added two seats in the rear and turned it into a family car, a mass-production item.

What I had not realized was a much broader implication of the Mustang experience, especially the significance of Iacocca calling in the buffs, his racing driver friends, to judge the early too-small Mustang design and then very deliberately turning directly against their enthusiastic approval of what they'd seen.

Being a late bloomer who emerged relatively tardy from the dominance of Papa Nick and his second father, the redoubtable Charlie Beacham, Iacocca was forty when he sired the Mustang. Nevertheless, Barber pointed to the experience as the most reliable tipoff to Iacocca's future behavior pattern as a leader. For Iacocca, the Mustang was what Barber has for decades called the "first independent political experience," the time of emergence as a youngish man who has found himself.

As Barber explains this watershed event, the value of the concept as a road signal is overriding in the life of any leader:

> It was then he moved beyond the detailed guidance of his family; then his self-esteem was dramatically boosted; then he came forth as a person to be reckoned with by other people. The *way* he did that is profoundly important to him. Typically he grasps that style and hangs on to it. Much later, coming into the Presidency, something in him remembers this earlier victory and he re-emphasizes the style that made it happen.

How can Barber be so certain that a leader's first independent political (or, as in the case of the Mustang, quasi-political) success is such an overwhelmingly revelatory beacon? Because his study of all the presidents told him so. He found the clarity of this pattern consistently repeated. It was "stark," unmistakable.

As we'll see, Professors Neustadt and Mazlish do not agree with all of Barber's ideas. However, they do endorse the crucial role he assigns to a future leader's first independent political success experience, and they further agree with the high ranking Barber assigns to a second blockbuster factor, a deceptively low-key question that I had overlooked entirely: Does the leader have a sense of humor about himself; can he mock himself, especially in public? If he can, he is demonstrating confidence. If he invariably takes himself seriously, he most likely lacks this vital quality.

When I applied the Barber system to specific items in my findings on Iacocca, it turned out that Barber (as well as the other two consultants) shrugged off as neutral or unimportant six factors that I had considered vaguely negative about the Chrysler Chairman. The scholars detected few potentially troublesome notes in Iacocca's hypochondria, his anxieties, his temper, his shyness with strangers, or the dramatic discrepancies between his public and his private selves.

The sixth and last of these discounted items might actually rate as a factor in Iacocca's favor. Barber had reacted quizzically to my hero's distaste for crowds, to his being required to smile at strangers or shake hands with them. On reflection, the professor deferred to Bruce Mazlish's opinion on this point, and Mazlish was not bothered by Iacocca's standoffishness. On the contrary.

"Some need the reaffirmation of a crowd," he said. "Iacocca is more his own man."

Iacocca's success with the Mustang, as I have mentioned, impressed Barber strongly. The professor sees it as a pattern-setting event, a curtain raiser. "He is saying, 'I am not Beacham; I am Iacocca, and here's what I do as Iacocca,' " Barber explained. "A young man goes out like that and is on his own, he's cut the cord with his daddy and with substitute daddies and professors, how is he going to act? He's somewhat at sea, but he acts in a certain way, and by gosh, it succeeds. That puts a stamp in the guy's mind that is lasting and is returned to."

Moreover, Barber can document that a triumph experienced at an early crossroads can foreshadow success in all kinds of career situations. The admissions authorities at his university, Duke, used to ask applicants to compose essays about their aspirations. Now students are asked: "What is the most significant challenge you have encountered in the past and how did you deal with it?" Duke believes that the responses are useful as predictions of the students' skill for coping with advanced education and life beyond.

A leader's ability to poke fun at himself, the telltale character guide that I had ignored, is harder to trace, and the evidence isn't always unambiguous. When Barber questioned me about Iacocca's talent for self-mockery, I cited Iacocca's wife's asking him to moderate his pace and his reply, "I can't, I'm the star." Barber wasn't sure this was a case in point. It would depend on Iacocca's tone. If he said it merrily, the remark qualified as self-mockery. If he said it seriously, perhaps even imperiously, it was bragging.

But I had found other examples of Iacocca's lampooning himself, and these were conclusive, especially since they showed Iacocca kidding himself in public, which a rigid personality (like Nixon or LBJ) could not be expected to bring off.

"I've got to stop getting fired like this," said Iacocca after his dismissal from one of the Ellis Island commissions. "People are going to start thinking I'm a drifter."

"I wish you'd stop it, because you're making my campaign staff nervous as hell," he told reporters in a ploy to deflect speculation about his presidential ambitions.

"I would tell everybody what to do, and she would tell them how." So said Iacocca to the American Society of Newspaper Editors in nominating Dr. Ruth Westheimer, the sex expert, who was present, as a possible vice presidential running mate.

I had my loudest laugh over a wisecrack Iacocca tossed at automotive reporters who asked him why he went ahead with the (eventually so successful) K-cars when he first came to Chrysler. "I really had nothing to do with it," lied The Chairman jokingly; "it was too late to change it." The remark reminded me of JFK's great line when he was asked how he became a hero: "It was involuntary. They sank my boat."

Insecure, poorly adjusted people don't put out such cocky gags about themselves.

I was surprised at the wealth of additional predictive signals Professor Barber managed to glean from my research into Iacocca's actions over the years. Here, adapted from his comments, is my rundown of characteristics that foreshadow a *favorable* outcome for Iacocca's handling of future leadership challenges. (Unfavorable and uncertain elements will be discussed later in this chapter.)

First, just as Iacocca's creative handling of the Mustang's design had foretold, his subsequent history of decision making offers additional evidence of his *ability to break away from rigid, stereotypical thinking.* Thus, when congressmen charged him with violating the principles of free enterprise in his plea for Chrysler's federal loan guarantee, Iacocca didn't turn defensive or argumentative; he said he hated to ask for the money, but there was no practical alternative. For him, what counted was not ideology but results: saving jobs.

Barber diagnosed that Iacocca also breaks out of a common stereotype when he flaunts his pride in his Italian origin. Usually members of an immigrant generation decide that they cannot fully adjust to American ways, and so they live at least partly through their children and for their hopes. Iacocca's parents adhered to this pattern, but the stereotypical behavior stopped with Lido.

"The second generation of kids tend to become super-Americans and say very little about their foreign connections," Barber explained. Refreshingly Iacocca doesn't subject himself to such a limitation. He loves calling himself "Italian."

While compulsive types usually don't enjoy their work—Nixon could barely even abide his successes—Iacocca revels in his chores. And he gets a kick out of playing the game; he has fun scheming to reach his goal, and he articulates his joy. He talks about having "fun" with his victories. He crowed when he became president of Ford and when the revolutionary design for the Chrysler minivan lived up to his expectations. These are healthy signs, likely harbingers of *upbeat, energetic approaches to solving future problems.*

Realism and courage were implicit in Iacocca's vigorous proposals to fix Washington's budget and trade deficit problems, for example, by applying stern measures that probably would not be popular. For years he appeared to be turned on, intellectually excited, by the possibility that he might make a contribution toward mastering such challenges. Some of his prophetic warnings and his "Wake up, America!" exhortations reminded Barber of JFK ("Ask not what your country can do for you . . ."). Iacocca does not minimize unpleasant realities, and he did not hesitate to attack Reagan long before the president's popularity began to slip.

Iacocca's *devotion to "homework"*—his mastery of detail without bogging down in minutiae as Jimmy Carter did—is another considerable asset (and a dramatic contrast with Reagan's intuitive manner). "We're seeing a degeneration of political discourse in which the empirical test is going out of style, and it needs to be revived," Barber said.

"Homework," of course, is a shorthand term here. Iacocca is a crammer, reader, analyzer, systematizer, a digger who doesn't shrink away from skimming a hundred letters at one sitting. His style bespeaks the diligence needed to deal with highly complex issues. He pays attention. Not everyone does these days.

His *aggressive curiosity*, the relentless question asking to determine what policy to choose, and his probing for weaknesses in the solutions being offered for his approval—these characteristics are formidable assets as well, and they are uncommon. "Not many people are genuinely curious about the reality of what's beyond them," Barber pointed out. Such curiosity indicates openness, inner security, a special supercool that Barber likes to call "extraordinary sanity."

Iacocca's successful grappling with the difficulties of the Chrysler turnaround and the tedious making of his famous TV commercials suggest to Barber an *uncommon capacity to grow after the age of forty-five*. The loan guarantee fight required Iacocca to come to terms with national politics and its practitioners. To make the commercials, he had to override strong personal inhibitions. Despite his distaste for both roles, he succeeded at them brilliantly although he was well past the age of fifty, another healthy sign.

Finally Barber was impressed by my information about the *strong personalities who surround Iacocca*, the top executives I had met at Chrysler: Bidwell, Sperlich, and the others who are anything but yes-men. Barber wanted to know whether I thought Iacocca pays attention to these advisers. I said I thought so, and I reminded Barber of the Chrysler man who had joked that Iacocca "doesn't listen, but he hears." No question, The Chairman's thinking is influenced by his intake from people he trusts. He likes tough, independent-minded advisers.

On the negative side of the Iacocca leadership ledger, the primary item concerns his stubborn responses to safety issues: the Pinto crisis, the long controversy delaying the use of air bags, and his scathing attitudes about safety in general, as reflected in his TV appearance with Connie Chung (where he defended unsafe small trucks). Barber, as well as my two other consultants, confirmed my own conclusion that Iacocca's stance on these issues blemishes his profile considerably.

His coping techniques included stonewalling, lying, and the sort of duplicitousness that feeds public resentment. His methods are especially damaging in the light of the long-term disillusionment with leaders, lately further stirred by the political and business scandals of the Reagan years. Iacocca showed no flexibility here. Rigidity blots this portion of his record. His attitude is uncomfortably reminiscent of the see-no-evil, hear-no-evil single-mindedness, undeviatingly pursued over periods of years, that spelled dishonor for presidents: Wilson (in his abortive insistence that America join the League of Nations; Hoover (in forswearing "handouts" to ease the Depression); Nixon (in treating Watergate as a mere burglary); and Johnson (who wouldn't let go of the lost Vietnam War).

Barber's other potentially negative entries on Iacocca's ledger all deal with the likely outcome in the event of a career switch to public service.

If Iacocca were to seek the presidency, his foremost problem— and my other two consultants again agreed—would deal with what I call "convertibility." I had imagined that the rugged experience of dealing with the likes of Henry Ford and the politicians who tried to block the Chrysler loan guarantee constituted excellent training, readily transferable to the public arena. My consultants were firm in thinking otherwise.

"He'd be saying, 'I know I haven't played football before, but I played a lot of basketball, and so now please put me on the New York Giants as quarterback and watch me carry the ball,'" was the way Barber put it. He called such a switch "not totally implausible" but "one terrific leap," and he believed that many voters would dismiss the idea as excessively risky adventurism.

Moreover, business usually works along hierarchical lines, as Barber pointed out, while public service is pluralistic and operates largely by consensus, negotiation, compromise. The aims in the public and the private arena are often very different. To sell a car is a clear-cut objective; to manage a policy toward South Africa involves the orchestration of a great many (often dramatically diverging) elements. The principal policy coordinator may have to tread carefully and speak ambiguously, perhaps resorting to inspiring but airy epigrams ("The only thing we have to fear is fear itself"). Iacocca was not taught such a loftily diplomatic style by Papa Nick, Charlie Beacham, or his experience at Ford and Chrysler.

It therefore troubled Barber that Iacocca had never run for office and had never served in an appointive public job; that friends considered him thin-skinned, impatient, and sometimes unpredictable; that he seemed intolerant of critics, females, and competitors; and that he was apparently wary of people better educated or smarter than himself.

The Chrysler loan guarantee campaign did not strike Barber as a useful indicator of how a President Iacocca would get along with Congress. His professed dislike of politics might sour him on a public job, although his objections might be tactical, Carter and Reagan having found it useful to run for Washington office on an anti-Washington platform.

All these caveats seemed to add up to a formidable but not necessarily incapacitating handicap for achieving greatness as a top-level leader.

I was left with a few imponderables that allowed no predictions or even guesses.

Barber said he couldn't be certain that Iacocca falls into the category of "active-positive" leader types. The "active-negative" label might fit the Chrysler Chairman better. I couldn't persuade Barber to make the call.

Despite the evidence of Iacocca's flexible thinking, the "overwhelming risk" is what the professor regards as a potential for "rigidification," which is not the same as calling someone a "rigid" person.

Thus Nixon and Johnson, while notorious (and visible) as tricky maneuverers, froze in their greatest crises. Barber is pointing to the *potential* danger of a leader who turns rigid when he feels cornered and faces defeat or enormous frustration. The chief executive may then hover, as if paralyzed, in a fixed policy position and remain immobile, no matter how ineffective his stance becomes, while a Watergate scandal or a Vietnam War or (as in Hoover's case) a Great Depression slowly overwhelms him.

The meaning of Iacocca's insistence on measuring up as a *numero uno* star is also unclear to Barber. If this preoccupation represents an ambition to achieve results, then Iacocca is simply being true to the go-and-get-'em tradition of great athletic coaches. If the *numero uno* ideal is a goal in itself, then it could be obsessive behavior and worrisome. Barber explained: "It would be necessary to go beyond the literalness of what he has said and get at the emotional meaning such things have for him."

Barber was not as unreservedly impressed as I had been with Iacocca's lifelong talent for snapping back from adversities, personal and professional. Again, he wanted to dig deeper than my research (and Iacocca's reluctance to answer questions) would permit. Comebacks, Barber explained, can be mechanical, compulsive, neurotic behavior, almost like the need of a punch-drunk fighter to rise and face the punishment of more blows. "After all," said Barber, "Nixon kept coming back and back and back." On the other hand, comebacks can signify healthy resilience, wholesome strength.

In order to interpret Iacocca's recoveries from disasters, it would be necessary to know details about his early relationship with both parents, not only with the father. No symbolic Freudian nuances are involved. If a child's road to rescue from misery is cut off by the forbidding attitude of one parent (such as Nick Iacocca), not much harm is likely if the child feels he has "an alternative to the sense of failure" and finds a haven with the other parent. If the child feels trapped and cannot get help from the other parent for some reason, then the emotional fallout in adulthood may result in destructive, compulsive behavior, possibly frenzy or severe depression.

Clearly this could become a major Achilles' heel, and so I began to worry about an unusual vignette I had run across from Iacocca's boyhood.* Lido was about eight years old when he was fighting with a pal and the other lad accidentally pushed him through a basement window, which broke and cut Lido's hand. He had been instructed by Papa Nick always to come to *him* when he got into trouble or got hurt, and so Lido did not go home to his mother, as most youngsters would have done. He ran to his father's restaurant.

* See *Iacocca* by David Abodaher (New York: Zebra, 1985), p. 35.

Nick was surprised. Lido had to remind him that he was following orders.

I talked this incident over with Bill Fugazy, who confirmed that Iacocca had indeed been closer to his father than to his mother while he was growing up. I did not get the impression that the relationship with Mama Antoinette was poor, that Lido would have been unable to get help from her if he had asked for it. Still, the effect of Nick's apparent monopoly on the boy's affections is unclear.

Iacocca's feelings for humanity—for the well-being of people in general—is likewise open to conflicting interpretations. When he pursued the Chrysler loan guarantees, his humane desire to rescue the endangered employment of his people came across powerfully. But his handling of the controversies concerning the Pinto, the air bags, and truck safety suggests callousness. The mixed signals allow no conclusion.

For a simplified overview of the Barber system as I believe it applies to Iacocca, I constructed this table:

IACOCCA LEADERSHIP PROFILE

Qualities Suggesting Positive Outcome for Future Challenges	Qualities Suggesting Negative Outcome	Outcome Unpredictable
The pattern set by Iacocca's first independent career success presages active, imaginative future leadership.	Pinto and air bags controversies suggest stonewalling, duplicitousness.	Might he turn dangerously rigid if frustrated in his aims?
Ability to mock himself suggests confidence.	Business successes aren't readily convertible to jobs in public sector.	Is his drive to be *numero uno* a means to achievement or a dangerously obsessive end in itself?
His past business decisions indicate creative, nonstereotypical thinking.	Lack of experience with political operating patterns could pose great risk in public post.	Were his parents' dynamics in healthy balance or potentially destructive in their effects on the son?

Qualities Suggesting Positive Outcome for Future Challenges	Qualities Suggesting Negative Outcome	Outcome Unpredictable
His enjoyment of his successes suggests upbeat, energetic appraisal of problem tasks.	Impatience and professed dislike of politics may suggest unfitness for public service.	If Iacocca entered public service, would citizens benefit the way they did when Chrysler jobs were saved by U.S. loan guarantees, or would public interest be overridden as in the Pinto, air bags, and truck safety controversies?
His concrete, forward-looking proposals for future action indicate realism and courage.		
His diligence with "homework" is a major plus for mastering a complex top leader position.		
"Aggressive curiosity" suggests inner security.		
Chrysler turnaround and TV commercials indicate capacity to grow after age forty-five.		
His current team of strong Chrysler executives indicates capacity to work with independent-minded advisers.		

Finally, as a tactical observation Barber offered one more note of uncertainty. It concerns the climate of expectations likely to influence the 1988 presidential elections and turns on a striking coincidence: the outward resemblance between Reagan and Iacocca.

The paradox has come up in these pages before. Both Reagan and Iacocca come on strong, in control, down-to-earth, unequivocal, confident. Their rhetoric on TV is fluent, dramatic, persuasive.

Both are regarded as show biz celebrities. Both are fatherly, elderly. So their public image is much the same. Their emotional and ideological selves and their work habits, on the other hand, could hardly be more at variance. In 1987 no one could foresee how this picture of sameness/contrast would affect voters in 1988 in the unlikely event they had to respond to it.

"I think we're looking at a reprise of 1976, a time in which the people are going to be morally indignant and looking for someone who will restore values to the sleazeball political system," said Barber. "The reestablishment of the Puritan ethic by way of an Italian prophet would be interesting."

If we forget for a moment that Iacocca almost certainly wouldn't get a turn at bat in 1988, a most intriguing question arises: Would the voters perceive him as he really is? Or would they continue to confuse celebrity with qualifications? Says Barber: "People have no idea what a carmaker does. They just heard he's a good guy."

The main point is: It requires more than the variables of "character" to gauge the effectiveness of leadership and a leader's impact on constituents, whether they be stockholders and directors in business or voters in politics. Timing counts, and Iacocca's sharp-eyed appraisal of the public's likely political appetite in 1992 shows that he knows it.

From Richard Neustadt I had hoped to get an unadorned appraisal of what would happen to a spectacularly successful businessman like Iacocca if he entered presidential politics. The professor lived up to his reputation for outspokenness.

Right off, he was appalled, truly shaken, by Iacocca's notions of "running" the government. (You'll recall that The Chairman wrote he could run the country with twenty-five loyalists and that the job of president was no harder than operating Chrysler during its turnaround.)

"Running the country?" Neustadt demanded. "That's not what the president does! He articulates, he makes choices, he finagles—or he doesn't. He may *think* he runs the country, but that's dangerous. He'll get frustrated. It reminds me a lot of Lyndon Johnson."

It also reminded him of Richard Nixon's deepest difficulty: not a lust for power but the sense of powerlessness that makes such purportedly strong types almost go bonkers.

"What is hardest for a president to bear," Neustadt said, "is the sheer frustration of not being able to get the things done that he wants to get done." To lead under these constrained conditions, a president requires almost limitless internal security. Johnson and Nixon lacked it, and Neustadt's reading of Iacocca was not reassuring.

"Here's another one," the professor said. "He's anxious, a hypochondriac, antifeminist." Neustadt shook his head. "I'm scared about drivenness, and he sure as hell is driven, like Johnson and Nixon. They were asking themselves constantly whether they were up to standards they couldn't meet. These two people never came to terms with themselves."

Whom would Iacocca blame for not getting things done?

Neustadt said: "He'd ask: 'Is it life or is it me?' A president must be internally pretty satisfied with himself."

Iacocca's trouble would mount soon after his initial rhetoric sank in, Neustadt predicted. "He'd build up expectations that he'd have great trouble living up to." As voters turned frustrated, the president would get less done, which would frustrate him more.

And he'd not have an easy time recruiting help that would be congenial as well as experienced. Who would be his twenty-five comrades true? What would they know to make up for their chief's innocence about the inside workings of the government? I had visions of blustery Charles Wilson, old "Engine Charlie" from Detroit, Eisenhower's secretary of defense, the chairman of GM, who couldn't understand why folks got so upset when he said that what was good for General Motors was good for the country. Iacocca's only known friend with political skills is Joe Califano, a towering and tempestuous ego, too volatile even for the saintly Jimmy Carter, who fired him as secretary of health, education, and welfare.

I asked Neustadt about Iacocca's likely potential for what the Chrysler Chairman often described as his dream job in public life, to be appointed "czar" over the nation's economy.

Neustadt glared.

I said it might not be such a terrible idea to have another Bernard Baruch on the job and take him off the park bench where the old-time financial adviser used to hold court.

"I'd keep him on a park bench, preferably in another town," Neustadt cracked. "I've almost never seen a president willing to be upstaged." And my own research had never shown Iacocca working within a team without pushing, shoving, scheming to become *numero uno*.

* * *

From Bruce Mazlish I had expected to hear strenuous reservations about any number of obvious flaws in the Iacocca psyche. Mazlish is expert in applying psychoanalytic methods of personality analysis. These techniques tend to expose dark pools of deficiencies in almost anyone, anything from emotional warts to deadly trauma, veritable catalogs of symptoms usually set out in forbidding-sounding jargon. To a layman, such a psychological portrait can appear devastating even if in fact it is not. There is something in the psychoanalytic drill of scrutinizing people that makes anybody look rotten.

To my surprise, that's not how Iacocca emerged in the Mazlish appraisal.

"I think I'd like and admire the guy if I met him," he said. "He's got a lot of limitations, but he's done a lot to overcome them."

Mazlish felt that Iacocca had grown considerably since leaving Ford. But the man's shyness with strangers bothered this consultant of mine ("it does suggest some kind of basic insecurity"). The insistence on lording it over other people from the perch of *numero uno* troubled him because it suggests that everybody else, the losers who haven't made it to the top, do not merit treatment as equals.

Mazlish worried about the limitations of Iacocca's business experience and the possibly excessive competitive streak that it left behind ("there's still too much of the car salesman in him"). And how much maturing and mellowing had really occurred in Iacocca since he came to Chrysler? To Mazlish, the question remained unresolved.

"Is he a leader or a driver?" he demanded. "I think he falls in between the two."

If Iacocca were ever to appear on a presidential ballot, would Mazlish vote for him?

"I wouldn't be thrilled" was the cautious but affirmative response.

My other consultants had reacted differently. To Richard Neustadt the question was downright painful. To David Barber the decision was wide open. He said he'd want to know a lot more about Iacocca and about any future opponent.

Neither Neustadt nor Mazlish was enamored of the emphasis on the term "character" in Barber's system of ferreting out deficiencies in leadership timber and classifying contenders for high office accordingly. Neustadt rejected the labeling as too limiting. Instead of "character," his preferred leadership criteria are: first, temperament;

next, experience; third, sense of purpose and sense of self. Mazlish preferred "good judgment" over all other qualities.

Infinitely more important to the public welfare, so all four of us agreed, is the extraordinary fact that fairly sophisticated new tools now exist to screen candidates for high places and that the tools are not being used. Revelatory questions are not being asked of the contenders. When was a live presidential candidate ever examined about his first independent political or protopolitical success? When was a candidate's record for self-mockery researched?

"It's just awful," Richard Neustadt said when I asked for his views on the American record for selecting presidential candidates.

"Why don't the right questions get asked?" I wanted to know.

"The answers would be boring," Neustadt suggested. "You can't get sex into them, and it can't be done in two minutes."

And so television wound up as the scapegoat, which didn't satisfy me because not all question-and-answer sessions on TV are limited to two minutes, and if Dan Rather can't or won't ask the right questions and listen to replies of reasonable length, then certainly the *New York Times* and the *Washington Post* possess the skills and the space to do justice to a better vetting process.

Questions with penetration value need to be asked, and that's the bread-and-butter job of the media. Why they so often remain unasked is a mystery.

So what's the bottom line on Iacocca? For most readers, the sum of the preceding chapters should offer the basis for individual judgment. Personally, I liked much of what I found in my research, although I am suspicious of public figures who crave attention but clutch a fig leaf to their private parts when they get it.

What *are* they hiding, if anything? There is no way to know, and with a control-hungry leader, living a fishbowl existence, this is potentially troublesome. Who can tell? Conceivably Henry Ford or his henchman do still hold material on Iacocca that could damage or embarrass him.

Overall, I believe my three scholar/experts were too rough on him. I don't think they sufficiently appreciated that he is still evolving. "He never did anything he didn't learn something from," I remember having been told by his crony Bill Winn. Such persisting curiosity, such an appetite for new and better problem solving, is exceptional in anyone who has reached his mid-sixties. It suggests a greater capacity to adapt to new crises—possibly even crises of White House proportions—than my experts gave Iacocca credit for.

Temperamentally, too, he seems to me to be still in the process of changing. His nerves (the "Italian tenor syndrome" Ben Bidwell calls it) are calming. His "internal fires" have been considerably banked by his successes. He is a less anxious person than he used to be. Like Harley Copp, the safety engineer who crusaded against Iacocca's decision to make an unsafe Pinto, I doubt that Iacocca today would still pressure his engineers to push ahead with such a car, consequences be damned, or to manage by force of fear as he did at Ford then.

Iacocca's frenzy to rule undisputedly as *numero uno* strikes me, on reflection, not as worrisome as I'd viewed it when I first learned of this red thread running through his life. In today's ultracompetitive climate, who can reach the top without wanting—wanting desperately—to get there? Iacocca's fantasy of displacing Henry Ford still strikes me as quixotic, but the warning of my psychologist expert that people afflicted with the *numero uno* syndrome are artificial beings incapable of authenticity in relationships, actors who are always "on," does not seem to fit Iacocca. His carefree links with Billy Fugazy and other Iacoccalytes are pretty good evidence that he is open and real.

So who *is* the real Iacocca? The public or the private man? Both, of course. Why not? The one set of traits is not inconsistent with the other, and Iacocca is clearly comfortable with both of his images. It seemed to me that I had investigated and substantially resolved the contradictions that my interviewees had presented. Iacocca is considerably more *and* less than advertised. It happens.

Nor am I upset over the observation of Don Frey, the Bell & Howell chairman, who said he'd never met "a bigger prick" than Iacocca. Granted, the Chrysler Chairman can be ruthless and did not behave well toward Frey. But isn't it meaningful that Frey might nevertheless vote for this former boss if Lee were ever to run for president? And isn't it relevant to recall how consistently Frey (and many others whose toes were squashed by Iacocca) talk of having learned so much from Lee, how he expanded their capabilities as only a real leader can?

I admire resilient people who can weather life's knockouts over and over, can learn from them, can grow stronger with the punches, can come back again and again, more mature each time, better equipped to cope with still more adversity. Such comebacks can breed megalomania, I suppose, but I see nothing manic in Iacocca.

I agree with the ghostwriter who did speeches for him at Ford and watched his rages and told me nevertheless: "He's sane." Indeed, Iacocca is blessed with what Professor David Barber calls "extraordinary sanity."

By my estimate, Iacocca is without doubt an "active-positive" character (to apply Professor Barber's classification). In the event that he ever runs for president, I might well vote for this man. It's a gamble. All advancements are predictions and gambles, and predictions are dangerous by definition. Arrogance, hypochondria, and all other warts considered, Iacocca looks like a reasonable leadership risk to me. He may even be tough enough and shrewd enough and human enough to make a great president.

His standing in the history of business is certainly assured. When the *Wall Street Journal* conducted an informal survey of management professors, business historians, financial journalists, and management consultants in 1987, asking these authorities to name contemporary business heroes who would still be studied by M.B.A. classes in the year 2037, Iacocca led the list.

He was mentioned fifty times, an especially remarkable showing because the runners-up were such long-accredited supermen. Thomas Watson, Sr., of IBM came in second with thirty-nine votes; Henry Ford (the original model, not number II) scored thirty-four; Alfred Sloan, Iacocca's hero figure from General Motors, got thirty-one votes.

Iacocca also set off more quibbling than the other nominees. The responding experts split on how much his stature was a function of style and how much was attributable to substance. The *Journal* mostly cited commentators who tended to downgrade Iacocca. In the category of "substance," they seemed to think more highly of Iacocca's ability to manipulate the government into coming up with the Chrysler loan guarantee than his ability to turn around the company's fortunes so quickly and completely. The category of "style" was dismissed as outright fluff in this survey.

In my view these experts, too, judged Iacocca too severely.

In the Chrysler turnaround the manipulation of the government was, after all, only the first phase of an enormously complex and successful operation. Without Iacocca's follow-up with hot new product and without his creation of a strong new management team, along with his personal skills and drive, the federal money might not have been repaid, much less repaid seven years ahead of deadline.

And "style," in my scheme of ratings, weighs more than hot air.

To cite one illustration, it was no doubt the pizzazz of the Chrysler TV commercials that helped to whip up enough curiosity about the Iacocca persona to generate the basic demand for his autobiography. But TV noise would not have sufficed to ignite the word-of-mouth demand that in turn led to the sale of more than 5 million copies in this country alone. The book is not exactly rollicking entertainment.

No, Iacocca's book customers derived value from the autobiography because of its prescriptions for business success, its demonstration of belief in the self, its role modeling for every reader's own wrestling match with adversity. That adds up to authentic inspiration, psychological support, and that's not fluff.

To arrive at a true bottom line for Lido Anthony Iacocca, one would, of course, need to know still more about him.

Deep down, how does he feel about his parents, his childhood, his adolescence? What, at bottom, made him think he could snatch the Ford Motor Company away from a jealous proprietor? How deeply has he really changed in recent years? Why couldn't (or wouldn't) he recognize beforehand that his second marriage was subject to near-instant risk of self-destruction?

And about the presidency. Why and how did he talk himself out of the ultimate quest to reign as *numero uno* to the whole country, his rumored candidacy for 1988? Fatigue? A sense of his own limitations? Fear of being embarrassed or defeated? Or could it be contentment at last, peace with his lot in his beloved automobile game?

"You gotta live with yourself," he said when he was being boomed for 1988. "You have to know what you're good at, and you also got to know who you are. I think I know my limits."

Sure. But Iacocca is, first and last, a gamesman. So is the old poker player really still hoping to play his hand in 1992? And finally, why would he sit for interviews with *Cosmopolitan* and *Die Welt* but avoid answering questions for this biography?

Perhaps he'll explain all this and more in a sequel of his autobiography. Rocky Balboa and other folk heroes have established a tradition of successful sequels. Another round of Iacocca confessions should again make spirited reading. And as his friends might say, some of them will even be true.

Appendix

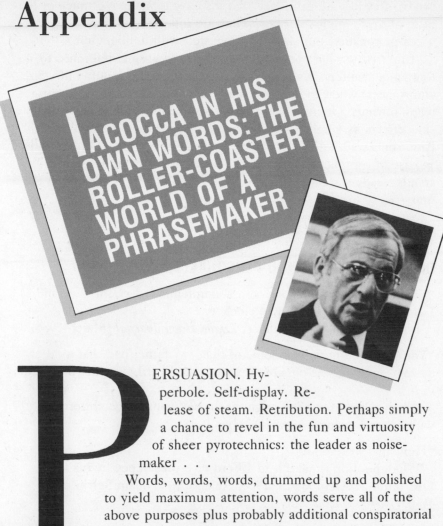

IACOCCA IN HIS OWN WORDS: THE ROLLER-COASTER WORLD OF A PHRASEMAKER

PERSUASION. Hyperbole. Self-display. Release of steam. Retribution. Perhaps simply a chance to revel in the fun and virtuosity of sheer pyrotechnics: the leader as noise-maker . . .

Words, words, words, drummed up and polished to yield maximum attention, words serve all of the above purposes plus probably additional conspiratorial designs for Lee Iacocca. How that man does love phrases! No wonder he makes so many of them. He fires them off like a commander of artillery. They're his personal *Bartlett's*, his own familiar quotations. They're his fireworks, and every day is the Fourth of July—different sounds and colors to fit his roller-coaster moods, purposes, stages of his life.

What follows is an informal album of such Iacoccaiana, sorted according to area of designed impact. Most of these sayings are spontaneous, though some are known to have been ghosted. All are gleaned from the public record (an audience being an essential ingredient for the launching of a bon mot, especially if you're Iacocca). Readers are cautioned that it's easy to make too much or too little of these miniexplosions. They are indeed revealing of the Iacocca personality, but should be ingested with deliberation.

DIRECTIONS: Do not consume without occasional reference to foregoing chapters. Note year (and Iacocca's corresponding life circumstances) when each phrase was launched. Discount pure noise when obvious. Grain of salt may not suffice to guard against such side effects as laughter or skepticism. Remember Ralph Waldo Emerson's warning that consistency is the hobgoblin of little minds. In case of complications, such as doubts about where Iacocca really stands, readers are urged to take bed rest and try calling him in the morning.

ON HIS CHARACTER AND PERSONAL STYLE

"I'm a ruthless commander . . . a simpleminded tyrant . . . and as I grow older I get even more crochety."
—Interview with Cindy Adams, *Ladies Home Journal* (March 1986).

"You might be born with some of that; my father had that kind of drive—anything was possible if you worked hard and put your mind to it."
—When asked about the origin of his self-confidence. Interview with Sherrye Henry, *Vogue* (October 1985).

"Hell, that's the end!"
—When he didn't make it to a Ford vice presidency by his thirty-fifth birthday, October 15, 1959. Related to William Serrin, *New York Times Magazine* (July 18, 1971).

"I think you have to have a little anger to get anything done in the world, as long as the anger is under control. If you're really an angry man, it'll wear you out. . . . It's a fine line."
—Interview with LeAnne Schreiber, *Cosmopolitan* (October 1986).

"If you're not enthusiastic, you don't sell anything. You don't have any fun, either. . . . I look for friends who are fun to be with."
—Interview with Cindy Adams, *Ladies Home Journal* (March 1986).

"I cook on weekends mostly. Mary says it's OK as long as I have three guys follow along behind me to clean up."
—Interview for cover story in *Time* (March 21, 1983).

"I don't want to have any more toys."
—When Cindy Adams (*Ladies Home Journal* [March 1986]) asked Iacocca why he lacked boats, horses, and other such acquisitions.

"Why should I tell everyone what I eat for breakfast Sunday mornings?"
—When Cindy Adams (*Ladies Home Journal* [March 1986]) asked

about his desire for privacy.

"I've had plenty of power. I don't need any more to satisfy my soul. I don't need any more notoriety, I need more privacy."
—Interview with LeAnne Schreiber, *Cosmopolitan* (October 1986).

"I can't, I'm the star."
—Said to his second wife, Peggy, when she asked him to slow down. Quoted in *Life* cover story (June 1986).

"I used to read a book a week. Then a book a month. Now I'm lucky if it's a damn book a year. That's symptomatic of the *disease* of success."
—Interview with Cindy Adams, *Ladies Home Journal* (March 1986).

"I'd really like to sleep late some morning."
—Ibid.

"It's adversity. They want to talk to someone who suffered a little. . . . People like grit and perseverance."
—When asked why readers of his autobiography send him so much fan mail; quoted in the *Washington Post* interview (September 8, 1985).

"At Chrysler they gave me 'before' and 'after' photographs [of myself] five years apart. It scared the hell out of me."
—When explaining that he'd like to slow down. Quoted in *New York Times Magazine* (May 18, 1986).

ON HIS MANAGEMENT STYLE

"I told a few people, 'Get with it. You're being observed. Guys who don't get with it don't play on the club after a while.' It worked because all of a sudden a guy is face to face with the reality of his mortgage payments."
—Explaining how he got moving after his 1960 promotion to head

the Ford Division at Ford Motor Company. Quoted in *Time* cover
story (April 17, 1964, date of the Mustang launching).

"You have to make up your mind. You can't go home and ask your
wife."
—Explaining how he kept raising production figures for the Mustang before it was launched. Quoted in *Newsweek* cover story (April
20, 1964).

"I never think of the car laying an egg. If I did, I think I'd go nuts."
—Describing his frame of mind before the Mustang launch. Quoted
in *Newsweek* cover story (April 20, 1964).

"A guy never gets canned for not doing enough. He gets canned for
working on the wrong thing."
—Ibid.

"Write down what your goal is."
—Ibid.

"You either get black in this business or you get out."
—Ibid. He was urging Ford dealers to work harder.

"Mustang will go 417,175!"
—On being told by reporters at a press conference in 1963 that
417,174 copies had been sold of the Falcon, Ford's last hit before
the Mustang.

"[Robert] McNamara was always operating with grocery sheets. He
wanted twelve alternatives even on a simple problem. Hell, that
takes time and a lot of paper. All I ask for is A, B and C and . . .
how to interpret these facts."
—Related to William Serrin, *New York Times Magazine* (July 18,
1971).

"They said I lacked grace and polish. That really hurts me."
—Comment on Ford family spokesman's explanation of Iacocca's
firing from Ford (July 1978). Quoted in news accounts.

"That f——— p——! You know what I just told him? That he was
a g——— f——— p——!"
—Iacocca relating his feelings about a Ford executive he had just
dressed down; quoted in *The Fords* by Peter Collier and David Horowitz (New York: Summit, 1987).

"I want a Rolls Royce grill on the front of the T-Bird!"
—Order to Ford chief designer Eugene Bordinat, key to the enormous success of the 1968 Mark III. Quoted in news accounts.

"If you get two years ahead of your market, you'll go bankrupt, but if you fall two years behind, you'll also go bankrupt."
—Explaining marketing strategy to Gail Sheehy in *Esquire* interview (August 15, 1978, time of Iacocca's firing from Ford).

"What is this shit? What the hell do we need outsiders coming in to tell us who we are?"
—Explaining his feelings (1976) about management consultants such as McKinsey & Company. Quoted in *Iacocca: An Autobiography*.

"You either have hardware or you don't."
—Sendoff for his first Chrysler K-cars, 1980. Quoted from off-the-cuff remarks to Detroit auto writers in *Car and Driver* magazine (September 1980).

"They can come in here and have their picture taken with me for a hundred thousand [dollars]."
—Explaining a money-raising technique for Statue of Liberty restoration. Quoted in *New York Times Magazine* (May 18, 1986).

"That borders on being un-American!"
—Iacocca's view of his getting fired from Statue of Liberty Advisory Commission. Quoted in February 1986 news accounts.

"I built it."
—Iacocca's appraisal of his role in Statue of Liberty restoration. Quoted in the *Nation* (March 8, 1986).

"We're all like the little kid who won't play football unless he's quarterback."
—Quoted from "The Fine Art of Compromise" by Lee Iacocca, *Newsweek* (December 23, 1985).

"I say, screw the *Wall Street Journal*!"
—Statement to Tom Brokaw in 1984 NBC television special on Iacocca's career, Iacocca was commenting on the *Wall Street Journal*'s criticism of him.

ON AUTOMOBILES

"Change, change, change. That's what makes this a fascinating business."
—Statement to Clay Felker in interview, *Esquire* (November 1962).

"All the buffs said, 'What a car!' [the Mustang] 'It'll be the greatest car ever built.' But when I looked at the guys saying it—the offbeat crowd, the real buffs—I said, 'That's for sure not the car we want to build because it can't be a volume car, it's too far out.'"
—Explaining the crucial decision that changed the Mustang from a limited-circulation sports car into a phenomenally successful family vehicle. Quoted in *Time* magazine cover story (April 17, 1964).

"They say people would rather spend their money for leisure. Will you tell me how the hell you get to a leisure spot in the world without a car? Did you ever see a guy get into an airplane without getting out of a car first?"
—Quoted by William Serrin in *New York Times Magazine,* July 18, 1971.

"Race'm on Sunday and sell 'em on Monday."
—Explaining why he put Ford back into car racing after the company had dropped out of that field to promote safety. Quoted in *The Reckoning* by David Halberstam (New York: William Morrow, 1986).

"I say give 'em leather. They can smell it."
—Explaining his marketing techniques at Ford. Ibid.

"We'll give you a dealer who will repair what we produce."
—Explaining his 1970 substitute for making quality cars. Ibid.

"Why should we be like Russia? . . . What the hell, I have lots of clothes, I like different foods. . . ."
—Defending frequency of automobile model changes. Quoted in *New York Times Magazine* (July 18, 1971).

"A bum rap."
—Comment on public belief that foreign cars were made better than American cars in the early 1970s. Ibid.

"We must have done something wrong. We must have been stupid or arrogant. I guess that for many years I said, 'Let them eat cake,'

because things were good. . . . I did the best I knew how."
—Explaining the sad record of the declining automobile industry.
Quoted in interview by Lally Weymouth, *Parade* (September 12, 1982).

ON HIS VALUES

"God, was I greedy! My generation wasn't looking for 'quality of life'; we were money-grubbers. I really wanted to make money fast."
—Explaining his philosophy during his high school and college days. Quoted in Gail Sheehy interview, *Esquire* (August 15, 1978).

"In those days, boy, you could really be an entrepreneur in a big company. You could gamble, you could do things that wouldn't be allowed today. I had my own little [design] playpen . . . with the clay and all the designers."
—Explaining the exciting work atmosphere at Ford in the 1960s.
Ibid.

"Our young people don't want to stand for anything. They want it now, and they want a lot. But everybody in his life has got to ask the question: 'I'm taking a lot out—what am I putting back in the pot?' "
—Commenting on today's yuppies. Quoted in interview by Bob Spitz, *Newlook* magazine (September 1986).

" 'Think for yourselves.' Let me repeat it: 'Think for yourselves.' This isn't the first time you've heard it, but it's the best advice you'll ever get from me or anybody else. . . . Remember, everything worthwhile carries the risk of failure. I have to take risks every day. I'd rather not, but the world doesn't give you or me that option."
—Commencement Address, Duke University (May 4, 1986).

"I'm convinced that if Americans really understood how deep in the hole they are and just what they are doing to their kids' future, they would not only accept sacrifice, they'd demand it."
—Syndicated newspaper column by Iacocca, 1985.

"What matters most is not the fame. It's people saying, 'I've got respect for you.' "
—Interview in *Cosmopolitan* (October 1986).

ON HENRY FORD II

"He picked me out of the mob."
—Commenting on his 1960 promotion to head the Ford Division and his gratitude to Henry Ford. Quoted in *New York Times Magazine* (July 18, 1971).

"I really think he took a hell of a gamble with a young guy. I could have failed and embarrassed the hell out of him."
—Commenting on Henry Ford's support of the Mustang. Quoted in *Newsweek* cover story (April 20, 1964).

"Henry Ford wants you to be blunt, and I happen to be blunt. We don't try to Alphonse and Gaston each other. . . ."
—*Time* magazine cover story (April 17, 1964).

"We just sat there, Mister Ford with his cigarette and me with my cigar, and blew smoke at each other."
—Describing his promotion to the presidency of Ford. Quoted in *New York Times Magazine* (July 18, 1971).

"Mister Ford is No. 1 in my mind. Always was and always will be. He hired me, he brought me along, he gave me my opportunities."
—Ibid.

"You don't get close to the king."
—Describing his relationship with Henry Ford. Quoted in *Never Complain, Never Explain* by Victor Lasky (New York: Marek, 1981).

"Because of my pension, he still pays me a lot of money to go to work every morning to see if I can knock his block off. It must drive him crazy."
—*Iacocca: An Autobiography*.

"I won't forgive the bastard."
—Interview with Tom Brokaw on NBC-TV special, 1984.

ON THE JAPANESE

". . . we're going to kick their asses back into the Pacific Ocean."
—Statement to Carroll Shelby, a personal friend, in 1971. Quoted in *The Reckoning* by David Halberstam.

"An incredible 86% of Japan's total trade surplus comes from what it sells in just one single market, America. . . . Japan has gotten hooked on the willingness of Americans to buy so many of its products. That over-dependence ought to really scare the Japanese."
—Syndicated newspaper column by Iacocca, 1985.

"We send Japan low-value soy beans, wheat, coal, and cotton. They send us high-value autos, motorcycles, TV sets and oil well casings. It's 1776 and we're a colony again, this time of Japan."
—1985 interview, *U.S. News & World Report*.

"They even pick on ravioli. Can you believe it? We can send them all the ravioli we want as long as they are filled with cheese. But if they are filled with meat, there is a quota. That's because they restrict U.S. beef. I guess they're scared we'll get around it by hiding tons of bootleg beef in all those little raviolis. Those guys don't take any chances."
—Syndicated newspaper column by Iacocca, 1986.

"I guess if we don't watch our step with Japan they'll pull their Seventh Fleet out of guarding San Francisco."
—Quoted in *Parade* (September 12, 1982).

"It was a little like asking General Custer to come to speak to the Sioux Nation."
—Commenting on his invitation to speak before the Japan Society in New York in syndicated Iacocca newspaper column, 1985.

"You've got thirty days. Sayonara!"
—Explaining his proposed ultimatum to the Japanese for cutting the U.S. trade deficit. Comment made to U.S. congressional Democrats, White Sulphur Springs, West Virginia, March 1985. Quoted in *Time* magazine cover story (April 1, 1985).

ON FINANCIAL MANAGERS ("BEAN COUNTERS")

"I don't think any of these goddam people know any real people."
—Quoted in *The Reckoning* by David Halberstam.

"Can you imagine that son of a bitch trying to hawk a car?"
—Ibid.

ON CRISIS MANAGEMENT AT CHRYSLER

"It was fun, in a way, but you finally wear out. . . ."
—Quoted by Lally Weymouth in *Parade* (September 12, 1982).

"Every Friday at four o'clock I looked for $260 million to meet my payments. . . . That tested everyone. . . ."
—Ibid.

"I got scared—it was just overwhelming, almost like events are out-running your ability to cope with them, and you suddenly say, 'Oh my God, I'm going to drown!' "
—Quoted by Sherrye Henry, interview in *Vogue* (October 1985).

"I contemplated it myself [suicide], I'm not kidding you, a couple of times, when we didn't have any money in the bank."
—Quoted by the Associated Press from Dallas press conference remarks concerning financial plight of farmers (March 16, 1986).

ON AUTO SAFETY AND THE ENVIRONMENT

"Safety has really killed all of our business."
—Statement to President Nixon at secret White House meeting on April 27, 1971. Quoted in the Nixon White House tapes.

"We get letters . . . on customer service. . . . We don't get any-thing on safety."
—Ibid.

"The shoulder harnesses, the headrests, are complete wastes of money."
—Ibid.

"I could never see putting a hundred dollars into making an engine cleaner, there were no data, no standards [in the 1960s]. . . . If GM wasn't putting a hundred dollars into clean air and we were, we'd go bust."
—Quoted by Gail Sheehy in *Esquire* interview (August 15, 1978).

"The air won't get dirty. More people won't get killed because sidebeams or bumpers aren't meeting the new requirements."
—Off-the-cuff talk to Detroit auto writers proposing a freeze on fed-

eral safety and environment control regulations. Quoted in *Car and Driver* magazine (September 1980).

ON NATIONAL AND INTERNATIONAL ISSUES

"Where do you stand? For your District first and your Country second or the other way around? Millions of jobs are pouring out of your country. Right now a lot of you are fighting each other instead of fighting the President. . . ."
—Remarks to Democratic party leaders, 1985. Quoted in *The Iacocca Management Technique* by Maynard M. Gordon (New York: Dodd, Mead, 1985).

"I'm no Communist, folks, but it's not Russia that's laying waste to my business and to most of the rest of business in this country—it's Japan. Our friend. While we stack up missiles in the front yard, all aimed at our enemy, our friend is taking over the backyard."
—Ibid.

"Right now, America is getting whipped. . . . So get mad. Get mad at those people in Washington. . . ."
—Graduation Address, Massachusetts Institute of Technology, 1984.

"I know cheap gas for what it is and it's a drug habit. . . . I've gotten some angry letters from people who say I'm all wet on raising energy taxes. But it makes sense, popular or not, and we ought to do it."
—Syndicated newspaper column by Iacocca, 1986.

"We're fiddling with the tax code when we ought to be carrying water to the fire."
—Address to Financial Analysts Federation, Washington, D.C. (June 10, 1985).

"We're turning ourselves into a colony again. And it all starts with the deficit."
—Remarks to Poor Richard Club, Philadelphia (January 17, 1985).

"We've got all kinds of economic incentives for American companies to pack up and move overseas. We need some incentives to keep them and their jobs in America."
—Address to Financial Analysts Federation, Washington, D.C. (June 10, 1985).

"Equality of sacrifice: I've watched it in my company. It can work for the country, too."
—Interview on *Good Morning America* (June 10, 1986).

"For a society as rich as ours, not to be taking care of our sick people is crazy."
—Quoted in *Life* cover story (June 1986).

"I go to some restaurants—$100 to eat, one person, rich food. . . . Then you go outside in New York and see all these homeless people. It makes me mad as hell."
—Ibid.

"I'd be damned if I know."
—Response at December 1986 press conference when asked whether he still had solutions for the nation's economic problems. Quoted in news accounts.

ON WASHINGTON AND POLITICIANS

"I hated it. I'm surprised I survived."
—Commenting on his personal experience in dealing with politicians in the capital, on *Good Morning America* (June 10, 1986).

"Washingtonians . . . live in a phony world of gossip and worry. By nature, they're schizos, I'm telling you!"
—Quoted in *New York Times Magazine* (May 18, 1986).

"The people in Washington live by the polls. They don't lead public opinion. They follow it."
—Syndicated newspaper column by Iacocca, 1986.

"When they do something right, they call in the cameras, but when they screw up, they hide all the mail."
—Syndicated newspaper column by Iacocca, 1985, regarding popular reaction to his firing from the Statue of Liberty Advisory Commission.

"The worst kept secret in Washington is that taxes are going up. It's only a question of when. Politicians are whispering about new taxes like little boys telling dirty jokes. They all know the facts of life, but they don't want to talk about them out loud. . . ."
—Syndicated newspaper column by Iacocca, 1985.

"We've been on an ideological kick in Washington lately. Compromise is out! It's Rambo time on the Potomac. Pick your side and

fight to the last ditch, and anybody caught in the middle is a wimp."
—Quoted from "The Fine Art of Compromise" by Lee Iacocca,
Newsweek (December 23, 1985).

"I don't think this administration gives a shit about that."
—Commenting on environmental problems. Quoted in *Newlook*
magazine (September 1986).

"I want a President with some convictions. I don't know what the
hell Reagan's convictions are. I know he hates Communists and I
know he hates taxes. Other than that, I don't know a fucking thing
about him."
—Ibid.

"They're such asses."
—Commenting on the Reagan administration in *Life* cover story
(June 1986, four months prior to the first disclosures of the Iran/
Contra scandals).

"And there's Congress, which our forefathers said *had* to be adversarial. But *500 guys?*"
—Quoted in *New York Times Magazine* (May 18, 1986).

ON THE PRESIDENCY

"I believe that if I wanted to be President, I could be President."
—*Life* cover story (June 1986).

"Big names want to give me $20 million at a clip."
—Ibid.

"I'd enjoy it. I sure as hell could do it."
—Quoted by Cindy Adams in *Ladies Home Journal* interview (March
1986).

"It's not my bag."
—Quoted in *New York Times Magazine* (May 18, 1986).

"No, no, no."
—Comment to reporters in his hometown, Allentown, Pennsylvania, in October 1986, when they asked whether he would *ever* run
for president.

"I stand by Sherman's quote."
—Reply to Detroit press conference question (July 1985), quoted
by Ven Marshall, Channel 7 TV, Detroit.

"I am not a candidate, do not plan to become a candidate and see no circumstances that would change my mind."*
—Public statement, July 17, 1986.

"[I] must request in the most unambiguous terms that you cease all efforts in my behalf. . . ."
—Letter of July 17, 1986, to Draft Iacocca Committee.

"I never want to be in that racket [politics]. To be right, you gotta be a goddamn conniving liar at times."
—Quoted in *Newlook* magazine interview (September 1986).

"Probably the worst of all is the bureaucracy is so big, you can't fire these asses who are in civil service . . . and don't do a goddamn thing."
—Ibid.

"Our national leadership consists of too many lawyers and not enough people from business."
—*Iacocca: An Autobiography*.

"The one thing I could do as President—but I never think about it—is surround myself like I did at Chrysler . . . just get yourself twenty good people and watch the fur fly . . . if somebody stepped out of line in my administration, on a power trip, I'd stop it in a hurry. After the second warning, there'd be no tomorrow."
—Quoted in *Newlook* magazine interview (September 1986).

"I won't submit to a draft."
—*Detroit Free Press* (September 4, 1983).

"They drink a lot."
—Ibid., commenting on reporters who, Iacocca claimed, invented his presidential boom in the Detroit Press Club bar.

"It would be my style to have at least four summit conferences a year."
—Explaining how he would handle Gorbachev if he were to become president. Quoted in interview with *Die Welt* (West Germany, October 6, 1986).

"I could handle the economy in six months."
—Quoted in the *Wall Street Journal* (June 28, 1982).

---

*Douglas Fraser, former head of the United Auto Workers and veteran Iacocca watcher, observed: "He says he doesn't 'see' circumstances. Doesn't that mean there might 'be' circumstances?"

"Running Chrysler these last few years has been bigger than running the country."
—Ibid.

"I don't think I could handle politics."
—Ibid.

"It's been quenched."
—Comment on whether he had presidential "fire in the belly." Interview in 1984 with Tom Brokaw on NBC-TV special.

"People are hard up. They're looking for somebody, *anybody*, to listen to, and, in the end, the thing that distinguishes me from all the others is that I don't bullshit them."
—Comment on why he continued to be courted for the presidency. Quoted in *Life* cover story (June 10, 1986).

"I'm getting old and you have to know your limits. I'd probably be mediocre anyway. And I promised my family I wouldn't."
—Address to American Society of Newspaper Editors (May 1986).

"The next president is going to feel just like Herbert Hoover. . . ."
—Explaining at December 1986 press conference why 1988 was not a presidential year for Iacocca.

THE IACOCCA WIT

"Our customers want economy, and apparently they don't care what it costs to get it."
—Explaining the market for economy cars loaded with optional equipment. Quoted by Clay Felker in *Esquire* interview (November 1962).

"Don't worry, I'll spend it very carefully."
—When asked about his pay cut to $1 per year at Chrysler. Quoted in the *Saturday Evening Post* (March 1982).

"When you're already losing your ass, what's another billion among friends?"
—Explaining why he went ahead with the new K-cars and minivans at Chrysler in 1978.

"I really had nothing to do with it. It was too late to change it."
—Off-the-cuff 1980 talk to Detroit auto writers overtly disclaiming (while actually claiming) credit for going ahead with the K-cars, al-

ready scheduled for production before Iacocca came to Chrysler. Quoted in *Car and Driver* magazine (September 1980).

"Then the shah left town."
—Explaining the onset of the oil crisis and its impact on the car industry. Quoted in news accounts (January 1979).

"I'm a catcher now, not a pitcher, and all I'm doing is catching hell."
—On cleaning house at Chrysler. Quoted in the *Saturday Evening Post* (March 1982).

"He has to say that. I'm the client."
—Responding to an advertising man's extravagant assessment of the Iacocca mind. Quoted in *Vogue* interview (October 1985).

"They wanted Walter Cronkite, but he wouldn't do it, so they asked me."
—Explaining why he made the Chrysler TV commercials. Quoted in *The Reckoning* by David Halberstam.

"We have a Treasury Secretary who developed what I call acne economics. He says, 'Don't worry, we're gonna grow out of it.' "
—Quoted in *Life* cover story (June 1986).

"I've got to stop getting fired like this. People are going to start thinking I'm a drifter."
—Quoted in news accounts after Iacocca was fired from the Statue of Liberty Advisory Commission.

"Five and eight dollars a head, and they didn't even get a drink."
—Marveling that 3,000 came to hear him at a lecture for businessmen. Quoted in *Time* magazine cover story (April 1, 1985).

"Cronkite and I were sitting around the house trying to figure out how much of a phony Reagan is. He said, 'Why don't the two of us be running mates? We both know television.' I said, 'Sure, what spot do you want?' "
—Ibid.

"Many people now think I'm an actor. But that's ridiculous. Everybody knows that being an actor doesn't qualify you to be President!"
—*Iacocca: An Autobiography*.

"I would tell everybody what to do, and she would tell them how."
—Address to American Society of Newspaper Editors, May 1986,

describing TV sex expert Dr. Ruth Westheimer's potential role as his vice presidential running mate. (Dr. Westheimer was a fellow speaker at the same convention.)

"I wish you'd all stop it, because you're making my campaign staff nervous as hell."
—Quoted in *U.S. News & World Report* (July 14, 1986), about his being pressured to admit presidential ambitions.

"I'm not running for anything but my life."
—Press conference comment (February 1986).

"I've got one big problem: what if I win?"
—Quoted in *Parade* interview with Lally Weymouth (September 12, 1982).

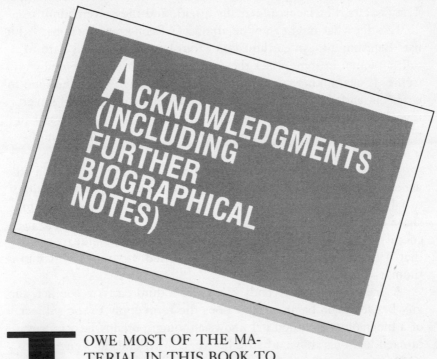

ACKNOWLEDGMENTS (INCLUDING FURTHER BIOGRAPHICAL NOTES)

I OWE MOST OF THE MATERIAL IN THIS BOOK TO THE MORE THAN 130 BRAVE SOULS WHO ALLOWED THEMSELVES TO BE INTERVIEWED. Arithmetically minded readers will note that only 109 names appear at the end of this section. The discrepancy offers a further sidelight of the Iacocca story.

In my forty-odd years of reporting I've found that just about any American loves to talk to a writer about almost anything. I think it's part of our general openness, a nice American trait, wanting to be counted, to be heard, to be understood.

Sometimes people waste their time and mine by telling a lot of lies, but not often, and the accessibility of eyewitnesses spreads a cheery light into an author's dreary existence. I discovered long ago that the same openness holds true for hired killers on Death Row and for CIA operatives who contributed mightily to the botching of historic events, along with others who have little to gain from putting even their very best foot forward.

Exceptions exist, of course, but rarely have I encountered so resistant a group of silent loyalists as Iacocca commands. Several dozen of them refused to talk to me at all, and some were barely civil about it. Others talked but didn't want their names mentioned. They're afraid of Iacocca, actually afraid, and they often admit it.

Exactly what might they be afraid of? Economic sanctions? A hit list? Banishment? An earthquake of four-letter words? It's hard to tell, although in some cases the free-floating anxieties seemed extreme. (I'm thinking of the former Ford executive who asked me to write out and sign, at lunch, a statement promising that I'd never reveal to another human being that we'd eaten lunch; nor was I to repeat anything this fellow said. Since this was, effectively, nothing, my conscience passed the test.)

Some of the interviewees named below consulted Iacocca in advance. They needed to know whether he considered it permissible to talk to me. A few took this precaution and then decided not to share their memories after all. I assume that Iacocca told these Iacoccalytes that he was "neutral" toward me and my endeavor and that they decided that mere neutrality carried the fumes of risk to themselves.

A "neutral," as everybody knows, is a third party to conflict, the guy between combatants. How does the term apply to the subject of a biography? Damned if I know, although perhaps Iacocca saw himself looming above a battle between his friends and enemies.

At any rate, "neutral" is how he described himself toward me in conversation with Jim Tolley. The genial James L. Tolley holds a job I wouldn't perform for $1 million a year plus bonuses and free convertibles. I don't know what Tolley earns, but it's not enough. He is vice president for public affairs at Chrysler, and I know something about the voluminous aspects of Iacocca's nonpublic affairs with me, all rounds having been conducted via the saintly Jim Tolley.

I won't stop to summarize the letters I wrote to Iacocca, alternately warm and demanding, or the sample interview questions I submitted. He replied to nothing, not even with a form letter. At the time I was reading Iacocca's interviews with *Ladies Home Journal, Vogue, Cosmopolitan,* and other publishers of history and felt neglected. But then Bill Novak, the fine collaborator on the Iacocca autobiography, confided that Iacocca doesn't answer his letters either. So I thanked my good fortune; at least Iacocca didn't threaten to meet me where his friend Frank Sinatra wanted to see Kitty Kelley, *his* biographer: in court.

What is one to make of so devoted a sense of privacy in such an aggressively public man? I speculate about Iacocca's motivations in the preceding text. Here I need to assure readers that every effort was made on their behalf to break the regal silence in Detroit, and I was not the only one who tried.

My thanks for kamikaze missions on my behalf go to Jim Tolley; Bill Fugazy (who also proved most accommodating in many other ways); Ben Bidwell, vice chairman at Chrysler; and Tom Clark, president of BBDO advertising. All their efforts to move me into the Iacocca presence were abortive. Even that master negotiator of publishing, my old comrade-in-arms Larry Hughes of William Morrow and Hearst, struck out in his effort to enlist the aid of Iacocca's publisher, Alberto Vitale of Bantam Books.

In the end the book probably benefited from Iacocca's stonewalling. It forced me to locate more sources, look under more rocks, ask more questions. It saved me from exposure to the spell cast by Iacocca's famous powers of persuasion, his self-salesmanship. Between the Iacoccalytes, the critics, and the small hard core of more or less objective witnesses, I probably arrived at a more balanced portrait than if Iacocca had dipped his heavy oar into the research.

In his absence, his magisterial autobiography was helpful. It is naturally the party line—Iacocca according to Iacocca, not always Iacocca according to the blunt facts.

The Iacocca biography by David Abodaher is embarrassingly servile—Iacocca for Little Folks—but it contains some useful material derived from its hero's family.

The literature on Henry Ford II and his vast clan is library-sized. I found the most recent available work, *Ford: The Men and the Machine* by Robert Lacey, painstakingly researched, and I relied on it. The long-awaited Ford opus by Peter Collier and David Horowitz, producers of blockbusters, had not yet appeared as this is written, except for brief newspaper excerpts. The biography of Henry II by Victor Lasky, *Never Complain, Never Explain*, contains unique material on Mr. Ford's bizarre investigation of Iacocca in the mid-seventies.

For the Chrysler story I relied largely on *Going for Broke* by Michael Moritz and Barrett Seaman and *New Deals* by Robert B. Reich and John Donahue.

David Halberstam is a throaty minnesinger of the automobile industry's lemming instinct. *The Reckoning* contains a closetful of vintage Iacocca anecdotes and quotes, as well as striking original sketches of two long-neglected powerhouses of the Ford Motor Company and automobile history: Charlie Beacham, Iacocca's role model, and Ed Lundy, the financial éminence grise.

Halberstam gave me some shrewd advice. Neal Shine and Keith Crain opened doors in Detroit. The Bryant Library in Roslyn, New York, as always had answers to innumerable questions, and the friendly assistance of the libraries at the *Detroit Free Press* and the Detroit *News* were indispensable.

The huge magazine literature on Iacocca includes some gems that I found enormously helpful and should be singled out:

William Herrin wrote the first shrewd basic biography in the *New York Times Magazine* as early as 1971.

The work of Kirk Cheyfitz in *Monthly Detroit* of 1979 is investigative journalism of a very high order; his political assessment in *Metropolitan Detroit* of 1985 (along with the work of Hillel Levin) is by far the most complete and imaginative.

Richard Geist clearly happened upon Iacocca in a manic and revealing stage of his life—Lee had just been remarried and was about to celebrate the rebirth of his very own Statue of Liberty—and Geist made the most of the occasion in the *New York Times Magazine* in 1986.

Bob Spitz pumped a larger and more authentic load of personal material out of Iacocca and his entourage than I found elsewhere. His timing was as good as Geist's. The results appear in the 1986 *Life* magazine cover story, and the unpublished material spilled over later into the remarkably frank verbatim question-and-answer material Spitz published in *Newlook* magazine.

The coverage of Iacocca over the decades in *Time* magazine and in the *Wall Street Journal* is, as usual, immensely hardworking, enterprising, and endless. The contrast is every bit as striking. I concluded that *Time* must love Iacocca as fervently as the *Wall Street Journal* detests him. Nothing dramatizes the Jekyll/Hyde split of the Iacocca personality as vividly as the black-versus-white colorings offered by these two media giants.

Lee can do it. He is, as the saying goes, a man of many parts. I tried to do justice to them all, and it couldn't have been attempted without the interviewees who did speak up, especially the hometown old-timers of Allentown, Pennsylvania, a refreshingly levelheaded and hospitable group* who deserve an extra bow.

P. W.
Ridgefield, Connecticut
June 1987

---

*Although several hometown folks also refused to be interviewed.

THE
INTERVIEWEES

Applebaum, Stuart (Bantam Books publicity director)

Barber, James David (historian, Duke University)

Bates, Baron (Chrysler public relations executive)

Beisel, Wilford ("Bob") (school friend)

Bennett, Amanda (*Wall Street Journal* correspondent)

Bergmoser, Paul (retired Chrysler president)

Bidwell, Ben (Chrysler vice chairman)

Boggs, Thomas Hale ("Tommy"), Jr. (Washington lawyer and lobbyist)

Boothby, Willard S. (college friend)

Bordinat, Eugene ("Gene") (retired Ford chief designer)

Bourke, William ("Bill") (Reynolds Metals president, former number three at Ford)

Breitmeyer, Eleanor (*Detroit News* editor and writer)

Califano, Joseph A. ("Joe"), Jr. (Washington lawyer, Chrysler board member)

Carlini, Hank (friend and Chrysler executive)

Charles, Edward (boyhood friend, Allentown, Pennsylvania)

Chung, Connie (NBC-TV interviewer)

Clark, Tom (friend and BBDO advertising president)

Claybrook, Joan (Washington safety activist)

Cody, Fred (Detroit friend, retired advertising executive)

Cole, David (University of Michigan, Auto in Michigan Project)

Conrad, Ruth (school friend)

Copp, Harley (retired Ford safety engineer)

Craig, Richard A. (college friend)

Crain, Keith (Detroit, president, Crain Communications)

Cudlip, Charles ("Chick") (Washington, former Chrysler lobbyist)

Curran, Bill (Detroit, friend and retired advertising executive)

Davis, David, Jr. (Ann Arbor, automobile magazine publisher)

DeLuca, Ron (Kenyon & Eckhardt advertising agency president)

Diehl, Bill (school friend)

Dinan, Alfred J. (college friend)

Dingell, John (Detroit congressman)

Domagall, Larry (friend, retired Ford executive)

Dugan, Jay (close personal friend)

Dunlap, Rosemary (Motor Voters lobbyist)

Duskin, Ken (Kenyon & Eckhardt executive vice president)

Facchiano, Peter (college friend)

Fleming, Al (*Automotive News* writer)

Flohr, Marjorie (school friend)

Franz, Paul J., Jr. (Lehigh University, vice president for development)

Fraser, Douglas (retired president, United Auto Workers)

Frey, Donald N. ("Don") (Bell & Howell chairman, former Ford executive)

Fugazy, William Denis ("Bill") (close personal friend, travel company president)

Giancarlo, Angelo ("Gene") (school friend)

Giorgio, Anthony ("Tony") (Detroit wine importer)

Gross, H. Edward (college friend)

Hafner, Charles G. (college friend)

Harbour, Jim (Detroit automobile industry consultant)

Harris, Louis (pollster)

Hefty, Robert ("Bob") (retired Ford public relations executive)

Hernandez, Gio (barber)

Iacocca, Julius (Allentown, Pennsylvania, cousin)

Jaroff, Leon (*Time* magazine, former Detroit bureau chief)

Jenkins, Dr. Al (school friend)

Jones, Jim (*Newsweek*, retired Detroit bureau chief)

Jouppi, Arvid (Detroit automobile securities analyst)

Kelmenson, Leo-Arthur (Kenyon & Eckhardt vice chairman)

Kern, Harry B. (college friend)

Klotz, Frank ("Buzz") (close personal friend)

Larsen, Wendell ("Lars") (IC Industries executive vice president, formerly Chrysler)

Laux, Elgar ("Gar") (close friend, former Ford and Chrysler executive)

Leiby, Jim (school friend)

Levin, Carl (U.S. senator, Michigan)

Lienert, Bob (automotive editor)

Lienert, Paul (automotive columnist)

Lundy, J. Edward ("Ed") (retired Ford financial executive)

MacAdams, Richard (college friend)

McLaughlin, Matthew ("Matt") (retired Ford executive)

Mazlish, Bruce (historian, Massachusetts Institute of Technology)

Miller, Robert S. ("Steve"), Jr. (Chrysler vice chairman)

Montgomery, John (retired Chrysler executive)

Morrissey, John J. (friend, Detroit advertising consultant)

Moschini, Floyd N. (school friend)

Murphy, Dr. Franklin D. (Ford director; retired chairman, Los Angeles Times-Mirror Company)

Murphy, Walter (Detroit public relations consultant, formerly Ford)

Musselman, Jim (Washington lawyer and consumer activist)

Neustadt, Richard E. (historian, Harvard University)

Novak, William ("Bill") (author, Iacocca collaborator)

O'Connell, Terry (Draft Iacocca politician)

Passino, Jacque (former Ford executive)

Potamkin, Victor (Cadillac and Chrysler dealer)

Purdy, Samuel M. (college friend)

Quinn, Charles (school friend)

Raber, Marion (grade-school teacher)

Reiff, John T. (school friend)

Reingold, Edwin (*Time* magazine, former Detroit bureau chief)

Romanos, Jack (former Bantam Books executive)

Romig, Bob (school friend)

Rutt, Dr. George (school friend)

Schneiders, Greg (Draft Iacocca politician)

Sharf, Steve (retired Chrysler executive vice president)

Shelby, Carroll (close personal friend)

Shine, Neal (*Detroit Free Press* editor)

Silfven, Sandra (*Detroit News* writer)

Small, Wes (friend, Chrysler and former Ford executive)

Smith, David C. (editor, *Ward's AutoWorld* magazine)

Snelling, Richard A. (school friend, former governor of Vermont)

Soltys, Henry (junior high school music teacher)

Soper, Harold (retired Ford accounting executive)

Sperlich, Harold ("Hal") (Chrysler president, former Ford executive)

Steinem, Gloria (feminist leader)

Sussman, Ben Ami (school friend)

Treleaven, Harry (New York advertising consultant)

Walker, George (Detroit, former Iacocca speech writer at Ford)

Warshaw, Dorothy (school friend)

Whispell, Rita (school friend)

Winn, Bill (close personal friend)

Witteman, Paul (*Time* magazine, former Detroit bureau chief)

Wolfe, Louis (former Bantam Books chairman)

Wright, J. Pat (Detroit automotive author)

NOTES ON SOURCES

CHAPTER 1. IN SEARCH OF THE REAL IACOCCA, PAGE 11

INTERVIEWS
Bourke, Bill; Frey, Don; Larsen, Wendell; Shine, Neal; Sperlich, Hal.

BOOKS
Iacocca, Lee, *Iacocca: An Autobiography* (New York: Bantam, 1984).
Lacey, Robert, *Ford: The Man and the Machine* (Boston: Little, Brown, 1986).

ARTICLES
Cheyfitz, Kirk, "Who for President?," *Metropolitan Detroit*, September 1985.
"Detroit's Comeback Kid," *Time*, March 21, 1983. Cover story.
"Ford's Young One," *Time*, April 17, 1964. Cover story.
Levin, Hillel, "Lee in '88," *Metropolitan Detroit*, September 1985.
"The Mustang: A New Breed out of Detroit," *Newsweek*, April 20, 1964. Cover story.
Sheehy, Gail, "Conversations with Iacocca upon Facing the Axe," *Esquire*, August 15, 1978.
"A Spunky Tycoon Turned Superstar," *Time*, April 1, 1985. Cover story.

CHAPTER 2. THE MAKING OF AN IACOCCA, PAGE 25

INTERVIEWS
Charles, Ed; DeLuca, Ron; Dugan, Jay; Fugazy, Bill; Iacocca, Julius; Klotz, Buzz.

BOOKS
Abodaher, David, *Iacocca* (New York: Macmillan, 1982).
Iacocca, op. cit.
Lacey, op. cit.

ARTICLES
"Nicola Iacocca, Father of Ford Co. President," *Allentown Morning Call*,
   February 7, 1973. Obituary.
"Builder Nicola Iacocca Dead at 83; Example for Son's Rise as Ford Head,"
   Allentown Morning Call, February 8, 1973.
"Challenging Life," *Allentown Morning Call*, February 7, 1973. Editorial on
   Nicola Iacocca
Cheyfitz, Kirk, and J. Patrick Wright, "The Rise and Fall and Rise of Lee
   Iacocca," *Monthly Detroit*, February 1979. Cover story.
Iacocca, Antoinette, "Antoinette Iacocca's Italian Meat Ball Soup," *Detroit
   News*, June 25, 1986.
Kita, Joe, "That's Our Lee! Family Views TV Show on Iacocca," *Allentown
   Morning Call*, January 30, 1984.
Rayner, Polly, "Mama Iacocca Has Best Idea When It Comes to Cooking,"
   Allentown Morning Call, September 26, 1975.

CHAPTER 3. THE MAKING OF AN ANXIOUS MAN, PAGE 33

INTERVIEWS
Beisel, Bob; Bidwell, Ben; Boothby, Willard S.; Charles, Ed; Conrad,
   Ruth; Craig, Richard A.; DeLuca, Ron; Diehl, Bill; Dinan, Alfred J.;
   Facchiano, Peter; Franz, Paul J., Jr.; Fugazy, Bill; Giancarlo, Gene;
   Gross, H. Edward; Hafner, Charles G.; Jenkins, Dr. Al; Kern, Harry
   B.; Larsen, Wendell; Leiby, Jim; MacAdams, Richard; Moschini,
   Floyd; Purdy, Samuel M.; Quinn, Charles; Raber, Marion; Reiff, John
   T.; Romig, Bob; Rutt, Dr. George; Smith, David; Snelling, Richard
   A.; Sperlich, Hal; Sussman, Ben Ami; Warshaw, Dorothy; Whispell,
   Rita; Winn, Bill; Zimbardo, Dr. Philip G.

BOOKS
Abodaher, op. cit.
Comus (Allentown High School Yearbook), 1942.
Epitome (Lehigh University Yearbook), 1945.
Iacocca, op. cit.
Zimbardo, Philip G., *Shyness* (Reading, Mass.: Addison-Wesley, 1977).

ARTICLES
Associated Press, "Iacocca on Suicide," *Newsday*, March 16, 1986.
Devlin, Ron, "The Dream Come True—Her Son Has Become an "Ameri-
   can Folk Hero," *Allentown Morning Call*, June 29, 1986.
Diedrich, Gary, "Lee's Other Lady—The New Mrs. Iacocca," *Metropolitan
   Detroit*, July 1986.

CHAPTER 4. LEARNING THE ROPES FROM THE MENTOR/TORMENTOR, PAGE 55

INTERVIEWS
Domagall, Larry; Dugan, Jay; Klotz, Buzz; Laux, Gar; McLaughlin, Matt; Potamkin, Victor; Winn, Bill.

BOOKS
Abodaher, op. cit.
Halberstam, David, *The Reckoning* (New York: William Morrow, 1986).
Iacocca, op. cit.

ARTICLE
Cheyfitz and Wright, op. cit.

CHAPTER 5. IF YOU KNEW HENRY . . . , PAGE 71

INTERVIEWS
Bordinat, Gene; Bourke, Bill; Davis, David; Domagall, Larry; Frey, Don; Hefty, Bob; Jaroff, Leon; Jones, Jim; Klotz, Buzz; McLaughlin, Matt; Morrissey, Jim; Murphy, Walter; Passino, Jacque; Reingold, Edwin; Walker, George; Winn, Bill.

BOOKS
Halberstam, op. cit.
Iacocca, op. cit.
Lacey, op. cit.
Lasky, Victor, *Never Complain, Never Explain* (New York: Richard Marek, 1981).

ARTICLES
Cheyfitz and Wright, op. cit.
Collier, Peter, and David Horowitz, "Watershed: Knudsen's Out and Iacocca's In," *Detroit Free Press*, June 18, 1986.
Eisenstein, Paul A., "Ford Pleads Mea Culpa," *Metropolitan Detroit*, December 1986.
Felker, Clay, "Iacocca: Whiz Kid, Senior Grade," *Esquire*, November 1962.
"The Mustang: A New Breed Out of Detroit," *Newsweek*, April 20, 1964. Cover story.
"Ford's Young One," *Time*, April 17, 1964. Cover story.
"Iacocca, Lee A.," *Current Biography*, 1971, pp 206–208.
Nikolaieff, George A., "Ford's Maverick: Lee Iacocca, Aggressive and Smart . . . ," *Wall Street Journal*, May 14, 1970.
Serrin, William, "Ford's Iacocca—Apotheosis of a Used-Car Salesman," *New York Times Magazine*, July 18, 1971.

CHAPTER 6. THE INVESTIGATION: HUNTING FOR SKELETONS IN IACOCCA'S CLOSET, PAGE 93

INTERVIEWS

Bergmoser, Paul; Bidwell, Ben; Bourke, Bill; Crain, Keith; Fleming, Al; Fugazy, Bill; Lienert, Bob; Lienert, Paul; Lundy, Ed; Murphy, Franklin D.; Soper, Harold.

BOOKS

Halberstam, op. cit.
Iacocca, op. cit.
Lacey, op. cit.
Lasky, op. cit.

ARTICLES

"Ford's Secret Probe of Iacocca," *Time*, August 7, 1978.
O'Toole, Patricia, "Power Steering," *Manhattan, Inc.*, September 1985. Profile of William Denis Fugazy.
Sullivan, Colleen, "William Fugazy and Friends," *New York Times*, November 4, 1979.
Yates, Brock, "Don't Do It, Lee," *Car and Driver*, August 1985.

CHAPTER 7. THE LOUDEST FIRING SINCE MACARTHUR, PAGE 103

INTERVIEWS

Bergmoser, Paul; Bordinat, Gene; Bourke, William; Crain, Keith; Dugan, Jay; Fugazy, Bill; Kelmenson, Leo-Arthur; McLaughlin, Matthew; Murphy, Franklin; Murphy, Walter; Sperlich, Hal; Winn, Bill.

BOOKS

Halberstam, op. cit.
Hailey, Arthur, *Wheels* (New York: Bantam, 1971).
Iacocca, op. cit.
Lacey, op. cit.
Lasky, op. cit.
Robbins, Harold, *The Betsy* (New York: Trident, 1971).

ARTICLES

Auletta, Ken, "Don't Mess with Roy Cohn," *Esquire*, December 5, 1978.
Breitmeyer, Eleanor, "Mary Iacocca: Spunk, Style and Honesty," *Detroit News*, May 19, 1983. Obituary.
Cheyfitz and Wright, op. cit.
McCluggage, Denise, "Never on Tuesday—II," *Auto Week*, October 20, 1986. Profile of Alejandro de Tomaso.
Nikolaieff, op. cit.
Rayner, Polly, "Wife Mary: I Do My Own Cooking . . . Lee Is a Fussy Eater" *Allentown Morning Call*, November 12, 1966.

Serrin, op. cit.
Sheehy, op. cit.

CHAPTER 8. THE JOB HUNT: "IF I'D HAD THE SLIGHTEST IDEA . . . ," PAGE 125

INTERVIEWS
Carlini, Hank; Harbour, Jim; Larsen, Wendell; Montgomery, John; Rutt,
    Dr. George.

BOOKS
Gordon, Maynard M., *The Iacocca Management Technique* (New York: Dodd,
    Mead, 1985).
Halberstam, op. cit.
Iacocca, op. cit.
Moritz, Michael, and Barrett Seaman, *Going for Broke: The Chrysler Story*
    (New York: Doubleday, 1981).
Reich, Robert B., and John B. Donahue, *New Deals* (New York: Times
    Books, 1985).

CHAPTER 9. THE MAKING OF THE BORN-AGAIN CHRYSLER CORPORATION, PAGE 135

INTERVIEWS
Bergmoser, Paul; Bidwell, Ben; Carlini, Hank; DeLuca, Ron; Fraser,
    Doug; Frey, Don; Kelmenson, Leo-Arthur; Laux, Gar; Miller, Steve;
    Potamkin, Victor; Small, Wes; Sperlich, Hal.

BOOKS
Gordon, op. cit.
Halberstam, op. cit.
Iacocca, op. cit.
Moritz and Seaman, op. cit.
Reich and Donahue, op. cit.
Stuart, Reginald, *Bailout* (South Bend, Ind.: And Books, 1980).

ARTICLE
Weymouth, Lally, "Has Chrysler Been Saved?," *Parade*, September 12,
    1982.

CHAPTER 10. MR. IACOCCA GOES TO WASHINGTON, PAGE 149

INTERVIEWS
Boggs, Tommy; DeLuca, Ron; Larsen, Wendell; Miller, Steve.

BOOKS
Califano, Joseph A., Jr., *America's Health Care Revolution* (New York: Random House, 1986). See chapter, "The Chrysler Story."

Gordon, op. cit.
Halberstam, op. cit.
Iacocca, op. cit.
Moritz and Seaman, op. cit.
Reich and Donahue, op. cit.
Stuart, op. cit.

ARTICLES
Bartley, Robert L., "Laetrile for Chrysler," *Wall Street Journal*, December 19, 1979. Editorial.
Weymouth, op. cit.

UNPUBLISHED MANUSCRIPT
Miller, Robert S. ("Steve"), Jr., "Personal Notes: The Chrysler Corporation Loan Guarantee Act of 1979."

CHAPTER 11. THE MAKING OF A "TV MONSTER," PAGE 169

INTERVIEWS
Bordinat, Gene; Bourke, Bill; Charles, Ed; DeLuca, Ron; Duskin, Ken; Frey, Don; Kelmenson, Leo-Arthur; Larsen, Wendell; Morrissey, John; Small, Wes; Treleaven, Harry; Winn, Bill.

BOOK
Iacocca, op. cit.

ARTICLE
Baker, Russell, "To Save a Hero," *New York Times*, April 25, 1984.

CHAPTER 12. THE MAKING OF THE AUTOBIOGRAPHY, PAGE 181

INTERVIEWS
Applebaum, Stuart; Hernandez, Gio; Novak, Bill; Rapoport, Nessa; Romanos, Jack; Wolfe, Louis.

ARTICLES
Apcar, Leonard M., "Motor Mouth Speaks Out," *Wall Street Journal*, November 8, 1984. Book review.
Davis, Joann, "A Talk with Nessa Rapoport," *Publishers Weekly*, March 1, 1985.
Dickstein, Risa, "William Novak," *Interview*, March 1987.
Friedman, Jack, "Power Barber Gio Hernandez Has a Tip for Lee Iacocca's Publisher: Give Me a Cut," *People*, March 18, 1985.
McDowell, Edwin, "Publishing: 'Iacocca' Reaches Millionth Copy," *New York Times*, December 14, 1984.
Menn, D. Joseph, "Iacocca Book Nets Big Gain for Harvard Diabetes Work," *Harvard Crimson*, January 1, 1985.
Minsky, Terri, "The House of Hits," *New York*, May 5, 1986.
Romano, Lois, "The Hired Pens," *Washington Post*, June 12, 1985.

————, "Is Lee Iacocca Driven? You Betcha," *Washington Post*, September 8, 1985.

Serrin, William, "The Importance of Being Iacocca," *New York Times*, December 23, 1984.

DOCUMENT

Gio Hernandez, Plaintiff, versus Bantam Books, Inc., Defendant, Supreme Court of the State of New York, Index No. 14505/1985, June 19, 1985, and July 24, 1985.

CHAPTER 13. THE COMPANY HE KEEPS AND KEEPS, PAGE 221

INTERVIEWS

Bidwell, Ben; Carlini, Hank; Charles, Ed; Clark, Tom; Dugan, Jay; Fugazy, Bill; Frey, Don; Kelmenson, Leo-Arthur; Klotz, Buzz; Shelby, Carroll; Small, Wes; Soltys, Henry; Winn, Bill.

ARTICLE

Breitmeyer, Eleanor, "Kathi Iacocca Has Gala Wedding," *Detroit News*, June 22, 1986.

CHAPTER 14. SAFETY: IACOCCA'S ACHILLES' HEEL, PAGE 235

INTERVIEWS

Bates, Baron; Bidwell, Ben; Chung, Connie; Claybrook, Joan; Copp, Harley; Dunlap, Rosemary; Musselman, Jim.

BOOKS

Halberstam, op. cit.

Iacocca, op. cit.

Lacey, op. cit.

Nader, Ralph, *Unsafe at Any Speed* (New York: Grossman, 1965).

ARTICLES

Dowie, Mark, "Pinto Madness," *Mother Jones*, September/October 1977, reprinted in *The Big Business Reader*, ed. Mark Green et al. (New York: Pilgrim Press, 1983).

Emshwiller, John, and Albert Karr, "Braking the Rules: Auto Men Use Slump in Seeking Slowdown on Safety, Pollution," *Wall Street Journal*, January 9, 1975.

Fleming, Anne, ed., "Myths and Facts About Air Cushions" (Washington: Insurance Institute for Highway Safety, 1984).

————, "About Air Bags" (Washington: Insurance Institute for Highway Safety, 1985).

McGinley, Laurie, "Auto Makers Offer to Put in Air Bags if Deadline Extends," *Wall Street Journal*, December 12, 1986.

Mitchell, Greg, "Iacocca's Untold Story—Puncturing the Air-Bag Rule," *Nation*, February 16, 1985.

Motor Voters, "Lee Iacocca and Airbags," April 14, 1986. Press release.
———, "Victims Protest 15th Year of Iacocca's War Against Airbags,"
April 24, 1986. Press release.
Parachini, Allan, "Ford, Iacocca at Secret '71 Meeting: Tape Reveals
Nixon Move to Suppress Air-Bag Rules," *Los Angeles Times*, November
29, 1982.
Ryan, Richard A., "Protesters Assail Iacocca on Auto Safety," *Detroit News*,
July 17, 1986.

DOCUMENT
National Archives and Records Administration, Nixon Presidential Mate-
rials Project, Part of a Conversation Among President Nixon, Lide (*sic*)
Anthony Iacocca, Henry Ford II, and John D. Ehrlichman.
In the Oval Office, April 27, 1971, between 11:08 and 11:43 A.M.

CHAPTER 15. THE IACOCCA VALUES, PAGE 251

INTERVIEWS
Bidwell, Ben; Carlini, Hank; Cody, Fred; Cudlip, Chick; Curran, Bill;
Fugazy, Bill; Giorgio, Tony; Jouppi, Arvid; Silfven, Sandra; Soper,
Harold.

ARTICLES
Bennett, Amanda, "Who Made Iacocca Not Quite So Shy? It Was Dale
Carnegie," *Wall Street Journal*, June 16, 1986.
Bohy, Ric, "Iacocca May Hanker Henry's Old Home," *Detroit News*, June
14, 1986.
Breitmeyer, Eleanor, "Iacoccas Plan to Move into Ford Home in the Fall,"
Detroit News, June 17, 1986.
Gamarekian, Barbara, "Iacoccas Raise Cudgels Against Diabetes," *New
York Times*, May 1, 1985.
Geist, William E., "The Iacocca Touch," *New York Times Magazine*, May
18, 1986. Profile.
———, "About New York: 800 Car Dealers Salute Liberty and Iacocca,"
New York Times, July 5, 1986.
Gottlieb, Martin, "Restoring Ellis Island: Bitter Dispute over the Future
of a National Shrine," *New York Times*, Feburary 23, 1986.
———, "An 80's Folk Hero: Lee A. Iacocca" *New York Times*, July 3,
1986. Profile.
———, "For Iacocca, a Day of Accolades Around the City," *New York
Times*, July 5, 1986.
Gratz, Roberta Brandes, and Eric Fettmann, "Mr. Iacocca Meets the
Press," *Nation*, March 8, 1986.
———, "Whitewashing the Statue of Liberty," *Nation*, June 7, 1986.
Hoelterhoff, Manuela, "Bickering and Dickering: The Storm over Ellis Is-
land," *Wall Street Journal*, April 17, 1986.
Iacocca, Kathi (as told to Anne Cassidy), "Our Work Would Make Our
Mother Happy," *McCall's*, May 1986.

Iacocca, Lee, "Day of the Recall Is Recalled by Iacocca," *New York Daily News*, March 30, 1986.
———, "In Pursuit of Liberty," *Parade*, June 1, 1986.
———, "What Liberty Means to Me," *Newsweek*, July 7, 1986.
Pear, Robert, "Iacocca and Secretary of Interior Clash over Statue Panel Ouster," *New York Times*, February 14, 1986.
Penn, Stanley, "Taking Liberties: Iacocca Controversy Is Latest in Series of Tiffs over Statue's Renewal," *Wall Street Journal*, February 14, 1986.
"The Politics of Liberty," *Newsweek*, February 24, 1986.
Rayner, Polly, "Lee Iacocca, Automaker—and Family Man, Too," *Allentown Morning Call*, November 12, 1966.
Rice, William, "Iacocca: "Wine and Olive Oil Next," *Danbury* (Conn.) *News Times*, October 10, 1986.
Ritenour, Jennifer, "Iacocca Gift Honors Parents," *Allentown Morning Call*, October 27, 1986.
Silfven, Sandra, "Iacocca Vintage Hailed," *Detroit News*, April 2, 1986.
———, "Wine, Etc.: Restaurateurs Enjoy Iacocca Vino," *Detroit News*, April 16, 1986.
"Sing Me No Torch Songs," *Time*, February 24, 1986.
Spitz, Bob, "Mr. America," *Life*, June 1986. Cover story.

CHAPTER 16. IACOCCA FOR PRESIDENT, PAGE 265

INTERVIEWS
Bennett, Amanda; Dingell, John; Jones, Jim; Levin, Carl; O'Connell, Terry; Schneiders, Greg.

BOOK
Iacocca, op. cit.

ARTICLES
Baker, op. cit.
Bennett, Amanda, "President Iacocca? No, but in Detroit It Sounds Plausible," *Wall Street Journal*, June 28, 1982.
Cheyfitz, op. cit.
Hoppe, Arthur, "President Iacocca," *San Francisco Chronicle*, July 21, 1986.
Levin, op. cit.
Margolis, Jon. "Is This Man Running for President? No," *Regardie's*, April 1986.
Marshall, Steve, "Fan Test-Drives Lee Bandwagon," *USA Today*, July 17, 1986.
May, Jeanne, "NAACP Crowd Says Yes to an Iacocca Bid," *Detroit Free Press*, April 29, 1986.
Schneiders, Greg, "Is This Man Running for President? Yes," *Regardie's*, April 1986.
Shribman, David, "Draft Iacocca Committee Expects Lady Liberty Will Brighten His Road for a Presidential Drive," *Wall Street Journal*, July 3, 1986.

Tyson, Remer, "Draft Iacocca Group Maps Strategy," *Detroit Free Press*, April 27, 1986.

UNPUBLISHED MANUSCRIPT

Schneiders, Greg, "Drafting Lee Iacocca—A Preliminary Strategy," prepared for the Draft Iacocca Committee, Washington, April 4, 1986.

CHAPTER 17. OBSTACLE COURSE TO 1600 PENNSYLVANIA AVENUE, PAGE 281

BOOKS

Ambrose, Stephen E., *Eisenhower* (New York: Simon & Schuster, 1983), Vol. I.

Neal, Steve, *Dark Horse* (New York: Doubleday, 1984).

CHAPTER 18. BOOSTERS AND DOUBTERS, PAGE 291

INTERVIEWS

Bidwell, Ben; Carlini, Hank; Copp, Harley; Davis, David, Jr.; DeLuca, Ron; Diehl, Bill; Dingell, John; Domagall, Larry; Dugan, Jay; Facchiano, Peter; Fraser, Doug; Frey, Don; Giancarlo, Gene; Kelmenson, Leo-Arthur; Larsen, Wendell; Leiby, Jim; Miller, Steve; Treleaven, Harry.

BOOKS

McGinniss, Joe, *The Selling of the President* (New York: Trident, 1969).

ARTICLES

Geist, "The Iacocca Touch," loc. cit.

Henry, Sherrye, "Iacocca: The Great White House Hope?," *Vogue*, October 1985.

Schreiber, LeAnne, "Lee Iacocca: America's Most Famous Businessman," *Cosmopolitan*, October 1986.

Spitz, "Mr. America," loc. cit.

———, "Lee Iacocca: The Man Who Would Be President," *Newlook*, September 1986.

"A Spunky Tycoon Turned Superstar," *Time*, April 1, 1985. Cover story.

TRB, "Strongmen," *New Republic*, December 2, 1985.

CHAPTER 19. INSIDE THE IACOCCA WHITE HOUSE, PAGE 305

INTERVIEWS

Fraser, Doug; Fugazy, Bill; Hefty, Bob; Miller, Steve; Steinem, Gloria; Walker, George.

BOOK

Schlesinger, Arthur M., Jr., *The Imperial Presidency* (New York: Popular Library, 1974).

ARTICLES

Diedrichs, Gary, "Lee's Other Lady—The New Mrs. Iacocca," *Metropolitan Detroit*, July 1986.

Emshwiller, John, and Albert Karr, "Braking the Rules: Auto Men Use Slump in Seeking Slowdown on Safety, Pollution," *Wall Street Journal*, January 9, 1975.

Iacocca, Lee, "Psst—The U.S. Is Going Broke," *New York Daily News*, November 24, 1985.

———, "The Fine Art of Compromise," *Newsweek*, December 23, 1985.

———, Commencement Address, Duke University, Durham, North Carolina, May 4, 1986.

Sheehy, op. cit.

Spitz, "Lee Iacocca: The Man Who Would Be President," loc. cit.

"A Spunky Tycoon Turned Superstar," *Time*, April 1, 1985. Cover story.

Wirth, Fritz, "Ich bin ein verdammt schlechter Verlierer," *Die Welt*, October 6, 1986. Iacocca interview.

CHAPTER 20. THE DIVORCE, PAGE 319

INTERVIEWS

Jones, Jim; Shelby, Carroll.

ARTICLES

Bernstein, Fred, "Power Romance," *People*, February 2, 1987.

Blosser, John, Charles Montgomery, and Ed Sussman, "Why Lee Iacocca Slapped New Wife with Divorce Suit—The Untold Story," *National Enquirer*, January 20, 1987.

Breitmeyer, Eleanor, "Peggy Sounds Resigned," *Detroit News*, February 5, 1987.

Diedrichs, op. cit.

Golz, Earl, "Why Lee Iacocca's Marriage Careened Off Course," *Star*, January 20, 1987.

Holusha, John. "Detroit Abuzz About Iacocca Divorce Plans," *New York Times*, January 16, 1987.

Neill, Michael, "Lee Iacocca Forsakes Liberty as he Weds a Statuesque Ex-Stewardess, Peggy Johnson," *People*, May 5, 1986.

CHAPTER 21. THE IACOCCA CHARACTER: MEASURING UP IN THE GAME OF LEADERSHIP, PAGE 329

INTERVIEWS

Barber, James David; Mazlish, Bruce; Neustadt, Richard E.; Schneiders, Greg.

BOOKS

Barber, James David, *The Presidential Character: Predicting Performance in the White House*, 3d ed. (Englewood Cliffs, N.J.: Prentice-Hall, 1985).

Mazlish, Bruce, *In Search of Nixon* (New York: Basic Books, 1972).

ARTICLES

Bussey, John., "Iacocca Agrees to Keep Chrysler Posts, Settling for Now the Issue of Succession," *Wall Street Journal*, February 6, 1987.

"But If Elected I Might Serve," *Newsweek*, July 28, 1986.

Iacocca, Lee, "Quotations from Chairman Lee," *Car and Driver*, September 1980.

Mazlish, Bruce, "The Presidential Character," *New York Times Book Review*, October 8, 1972. Book review.

Schlesinger, Arthur M., Sr., "Our Presidents: A Rating by 75 Historians," *New York Times Magazine*, July 29, 1962.

"Thanks but No Thanks," *Time*, July 28, 1986.

REPORTS

Chrysler Corporation, "Report to Shareholders 1985."

Chrysler Corporation, "Report to Shareholders 1986."

BIBLIOGRAPHY

Abodaher, David. *Iacocca*. New York: Macmillan, 1982. New York: Zebra, 1985.

Adams, Cindy. "Lee Iacocca in High Gear!" *Ladies Home Journal* (March 1986).

Allentown High School. *Comus*, 1942. Yearbook.

Ambrose, Stephen E. *Eisenhower*. New York: Simon & Schuster, 1983, Vol. I.

Apcar, Leonard M. "Motor Mouth Speaks Out." *Wall Street Journal*, November 8, 1984. Book review.

Associated Press. "Iacocca on Suicide." *Newsday*, March 16, 1986.

Auletta, Ken. "Don't Mess with Roy Cohn." *Esquire*, December 5, 1978.

Baker, Russell. "To Save a Hero." *New York Times*, April 25, 1984.

Barber, James David. *The Presidential Character: Predicting Performance in the White House*, 3d ed. Englewood Cliffs, N.J.: Prentice-Hall, 1985.

Bartley, Robert L. "Laetrile for Chrysler." *Wall Street Journal*, December 19, 1979. Editorial.

Bennett, Amanda. "President Iacocca? No, but in Detroit It Sounds Plausible." *Wall Street Journal*, June 28, 1982.

———. "Who Made Iacocca Not Quite So Shy? It Was Dale Carnegie." *Wall Street Journal*, June 16, 1986.

———. "How to Make Business History." *Wall Street Journal*, March 20, 1987.

Bernstein, Fred. "Power Romance." *People*, February 2, 1987.

Blosser, John, Charles Montgomery, and Ed Susman. "Why Lee Iacocca Slapped New Wife with Divorce Suit—The Untold Story." *National Enquirer*, January 20, 1987.

Bohy, Ric. "Iacocca May Hanker Henry's Old Home." *Detroit News*, June 14, 1986.

Breitmeyer, Eleanor. "Mary Iacocca: Spunk, Style and Honesty." *Detroit News*, May 19, 1983.

———. "Iacoccas Plan to Move into Ford Home in the Fall." *Detroit News*, June 17, 1986.

———. "Kathi Iacocca Has Gala Wedding." *Detroit News*, June 22, 1986.

———. "Peggy Sounds Resigned." *Detroit News*, February 5, 1987.

"Builder Nicola Iacocca Dead at 83; Example for Son's Rise As Ford Head." *Allentown Morning Call*, February 8, 1973.

Bussey, John. "Iacocca Agrees to Keep Chrysler Posts, Settling for Now the Issue of Succession." *Wall Street Journal*, February 6, 1987.

"But If Elected I Might Serve." *Newsweek*, July 28, 1986.

Califano, Joseph A., Jr. *America's Health Care Revolution: Who Lives? Who Dies? Who Pays?* New York: Random House, 1986. See chaper entitled "The Chrysler Story."

"Challenging Life." *Allentown Morning Call*, February 7, 1973. Editorial on Nicola Iacocca.

Cheyfitz, Kirk. "Who for President?" *Metropolitan Detroit*, September 1985.

———, and J. Patrick Wright. "The Rise and Fall and Rise of Lee Iacocca." *Monthly Detroit*, February 1979. Cover story.

Chrysler Corporation. "Report to Shareholders 1985."

———. "Report to Shareholders 1986."

Collier, Peter, and David Horowitz. "Watershed: Knudsen's Out and Iacocca's In." *Detroit Free Press*, June 18, 1986. Excerpt from forthcoming book, *The Fords*.

Davis, Joann. "A Talk with Nessa Rapoport." *Publishers Weekly*, March 1, 1985.

"The Democrats' Reluctant Dragon." *U.S. News & World Report*, July 14, 1986.

"Detroit's Comeback Kid." *Time*, March 21, 1983. Cover story.

Devlin, Ron. "The Dream Come True—Her Son Has Become an American Folk Hero." *Allentown Morning Call*, June 29, 1986.

Dickstein, Risa. "William Novak." *Interview*, March 1987.

Diedrichs, Gary. "Lee's Other Lady—The New Mrs. Iacocca." *Metropolitan Detroit*, July 1986.

Dowie, Mark. "Pinto Madness." *Mother Jones*, September/October 1977, reprinted in *The Big Business Reader*, ed. Mark Green with Michael Waldman and Robert K. Massie, Jr. New York: Pilgrim Press, 1983.

Eisenstein, Paul A. "Ford Pleads Mea Culpa." *Metropolitan Detroit*, December 1986.

Emshwiller, John, and Albert Karr. "Braking the Rules: Auto Men Use Slump in Seeking Slowdown on Safety, Pollution." *Wall Street Journal*, January 9, 1975.

Feinberg, Andrew. "Might as Well Call It the Iacoccamobile." *New York Times*, October 11, 1986.

Felker, Clay. "Iacocca: Whiz Kid, Senior Grade. *Esquire*, November 1962.

Fleming, Anne, ed. "Myths and Facts About Air Cushions." Washington: Insurance Institute for Highway Safety, 1984.

———, ed. "About Air Bags." 3d ed. Washington: Insurance Institute for Highway Safety, 1985.

"Ford's Secret Probe of Iacocca." *Time*, August 7, 1978.

"Ford's Young One." *Time*, April 17, 1964. Cover story.

Friedman, Jack. "Power Barber Gio Hernandez Has a Tip for Lee Iacocca's Publisher: Give Me a Cut." *People*, March 18, 1985.

Furlong, William B. "Chrysler's Lee Iacocca." *Saturday Evening Post*, March 1982.

Gailey, Phil. "Push May Be Coming to Shove for Iacocca." *New York Times*, July 16, 1986.

———. "Iacocca Disavows Effort to Draft Him as a Presidential Candidate." *New York Times*, July 18, 1986.

Gamarekian, Barbara. "Iacoccas Raise Cudgel Against Diabetes." *New York Times*, May 1, 1985.

Geist, William E. "The Iacocca Touch." *New York Times Magazine*, May 18, 1986.

———. "About New York: 800 Car Dealers Salute Liberty and Iacocca." *New York Times*, July 5, 1986.

Gio Hernandez, Plaintiff, versus Bantam Books, Inc., Defendant, Supreme

Court of the State of New York, Index No. 14505/1985, June 19, 1985, and July 24, 1985.

Golz, Earl. "Why Lee Iacocca's Marriage Careened Off Course." *Star*, January 20, 1987.

Gordon, Maynard M. *The Iacocca Management Technique*. New Y rk: Dodd, Mead, 1985.

Gottlieb, Martin. "Restoring Ellis Island: Bitter Dispute over the Future of a National Shrine." *New York Times*, February 23, 1986.

———. "An 80's Folk Hero: Lee A. Iacocca." *New York Times*, July 3, 1986. Profile.

———. "For Iacocca, a Day of Accolades Around the City." *New York Times*, July 5, 1986.

———. "Iacocca's Bandwagon Rolls Without Him." *New York Times*, July 13 1986.

Gratz, Roberta Brandes, and Eric Fettmann. "Mr. Iacocca Meets the Press." *Nation*, March 8, 1986.

———. "Whitewashing the Statue of Liberty." *Nation*, June 7, 1986.

Hailey, Arthur. *Wheels*. New York: Bantam, 1971.

Halberstam, David. *The Reckoning*. New York: William Morrow, 1986.

Hampton, William J. "The Next Act at Chrysler." *Business Week*, November 3, 1986.

Henry, Sherrye. "Iacocca: The Great White House Hope?" *Vogue*, October 1985.

Hoelterhoff, Manuela. "Bickering and Dickering: The Storm over Ellis Island." *Wall Street Journal*, April 17, 1986.

Holusha, John. "Detroit Abuzz About Iacocca Divorce Plans." *New York Times*, January 16, 1987.

Hoppe, Arthur. "President Iacocca." *San Francisco Chronicle*, July 21, 1986.

Iacocca, Antoinette. "Antoinette Iacocca's Italian Meat Ball Soup." *Detroit News*, June 25, 1986.

Iacocca, Kathi (as told to Anne Cassidy). "Our Work Would Make Our Mother Happy." *McCall's*, May 1986.

"Iacocca, Lee A." *Current Biography*, 1971, pp. 206–208.

Iacocca, Lee. "Quotations from Chairman Lee." *Car and Driver*, September 1980.

———, with William Novak. *Iacocca: An Autobiography*. New York: Bantam, 1984 and 1986).

———. "Psst—The U.S. Is Going Broke." *New York Daily News*, November 24, 1985.

———. "The Fine Art of Compromise." *Newsweek*, December 23, 1985.

———. "Day of the Recall Is Recalled by Iacocca." *New York Daily News*, March 30, 1986.

———. Commencement Address, Duke University, Durham, North Carolina, May 4, 1986.

———. "In Pursuit of Liberty." *Parade*, June 1, 1986.

———. "What Liberty Means to Me." *Newsweek*, July 7, 1986.

"The Iacocca Conundrum." *Newsweek*, November 18, 1985.

Kita, Joe. "That's Our Lee! Family Views TV Show on Iacocca." *Allentown Morning Call*, January 30, 1984.

Lacey, Robert. *Ford: The Men and the Machine*. Boston: Little, Brown, 1986.

Lasky, Victor. *Never Complain, Never Explain*. New York: Richard Marek, 1981.

Lehigh University. *The 1945 Epitome*. Bethlehem, Pa.: Lehigh University. Yearbook.

———. *Alumni Directory 1983*. White Plains, N.Y.: Bernard C. Harris Publishing Co., 1983.

Levin, Doron P. "What Iacocca Didn't Mention in Latest Display." *Wall Street Journal*, February 20, 1986.

Levin, Hillel. "Lee in '88." *Metropolitan Detroit*, September 1985.

McCluggage, Denise. "Never on Tuesday—II." *Auto Week*, October 29, 1986.

McDowell, Edwin. "Publishing: 'Iacocca' Reaches Millionth Copy." *New York Times*, December 14, 1984.

McGinley, Laurie. "Auto Makers Offer to Put In Air Bags If Deadline Extends." *Wall Street Journal*, December 12, 1986.

McGinniss, Joe. *The Selling of the President*. New York: Trident, 1969.

Margolis, Jon. "Is This Man Running for President? No." *Regardie's*, April 1986.

Marshall, Steve. "Fan Test-Drives Lee Bandwagon." *USA Today*, July 17, 1986.

May, Jeanne. "NAACP Crowd Says Yes to an Iacocca Bid." *Detroit Free Press*, April 29, 1985.

Mazlish, Bruce. *In Search of Nixon*. New York: Basic Books, 1972.

————. "The Presidential Character." *New York Times Book Review*, October 8, 1972. Book review.

Menn, D. Joseph. "Iacocca Book Nets Big Gain for Harvard Diabetes Work." *Harvard Crimson*, January 1, 1985.

Miller, Robert S., Jr. "Personal Notes—The Chrysler Corporation Loan Guarantee Act of 1979." Unpublished manuscript.

Minsky, Terri. "The House of Hits." *New York*, May 5, 1986.

Mitchell, Greg. "Iacocca's Untold Story—Puncturing the Air-Bag Rule." *Nation*, February 16, 1985.

Moritz, Michael, and Barrett Seaman. *Going for Broke: The Chrysler Story*. New York: Doubleday, 1981.

Motor Voters. "Lee Iacocca and Airbags," April 14, 1986. Press release.

————. "Victims Protest 15th Year of Iacocca's War Against Airbags," April 24, 1986. Press release.

"The Mustang: A New Breed Out of Detroit." *Newsweek*, April 20, 1964. Cover story.

Nader, Ralph. *Unsafe at Any Speed*. New York: Grossman, 1965.

National Archives and Records Administration, Nixon Presidential Materials Project. Part of a Conversation Among President Nixon, Lide (*sic*) Anthony Iacocca, Henry Ford II, and John D. Ehrlichman. In the Oval Office, April 27, 1971, between 11:08 and 11:43 A.M.

Neal, Steve. *Dark Horse*. New York: Doubleday, 1984.

Neill, Michael. "Lee Iacocca Forsakes Liberty as he Weds a Statuesque Ex-Stewardess, Peggy Johnson." *People*, May 5, 1986.

"Nicola Iacocca, Father of Ford Co. President." *Allentown Morning Call*, February 7, 1973. Obituary.

Nikolaieff, George A. "Ford's Maverick: Lee Iacocca, Aggressive and Smart, Maneuvers Way into Top Auto Job." *Wall Street Journal*, May 14, 1970.

O'Toole, Patricia. "Power Steering." *Manhattan, Inc.*, September 1985. Profile of William Denis Fugazy.

Parachini, Allan. "Ford, Iacocca at Secret '71 Meeting: Tape Reveals Nixon Move to Suppress Air-Bag Rules." *Los Angeles Times*, November 19, 1982.

Pear, Robert. "Iacocca and Secretary of Interior Clash Over Statue Panel Ouster." *New York Times*, February 14, 1986.

Penn, Stanley. "Taking Liberties: Iacocca Controversy Is Latest in Series of Tiffs over Statue's Renewal." *Wall Street Journal*, February 14, 1986.

"The Politics of Liberty." *Newsweek*, February 24, 1986.

Rayner, Polly. "Lee Iacocca, Automaker—and Family Man, Too." *Allentown Morning Call*, November 12, 1966.

―――. "Wife Mary: I Do My Own Cooking . . . Lee Is a Fussy Eater." *Allentown Morning Call*, November 12, 1966.

―――. "Mama Iacocca Has Best Idea When It Comes to Cooking." *Allentown Morning Call*, September 26, 1975.

Reich, Robert B, and John B. Donahue. *New Deals*. New York: Times Books, 1985.

Rice, William. "Iacocca: Wine and Olive Oil Next." *Danbury* (Conn.) *News Times*, October 10, 1986.

Ritenour, Jennifer. "Iacocca Gift Honors Parents." *Allentown Morning Call*, October 27, 1986.

Robbins, Harold. *The Betsy*. New York: Trident, 1971.

Romano, Lois. "The Hired Pens." *Washington Post*, June 12, 1985.

―――. "Is Lee Iacocca Driven? You Betcha." *Washington Post*, September 8, 1985.

Ryan, Richard A. "Protesters Assail Iacocca on Auto Safety." *Detroit News*, July 17, 1986.

Schlesinger, Arthur M., Jr. "Our Presidents: A Rating by 75 Historians." *New York Times Magazine*, July 29, 1962.

―――. *The Imperial Presidency*. New York: Popular Library, 1964.

Schneiders, Greg. "Drafting Lee Iacocca—A Preliminary Strategy." Unpublished manuscript prepared for the Draft Iacocca Committee, Washington, April 4, 1986.

―――. "Is This Man Running for President? Yes." *Regardie's*, April 1986.

Schreiber, LeAnne. "Lee Iacocca: America's Most Famous Businessman." *Cosmopolitan*, October 1986.

Serrin, William. "Ford's Iacocca—Apotheosis of a Used-Car Salesman." *New York Times Magazine*, July 18, 1971.

―――. "The Importance of Being Iacocca." *New York Times*, December 23, 1984.

Sheehy, Gail. "Conversations with Iacocca upon Facing the Axe." *Esquire*, August 15, 1978.

Shribman, David. "Draft Iacocca Committee Expects Lady Liberty Will Brighten His Road for a Presidential Drive." *Wall Street Journal*, July 3, 1986.

―――. "Harvard Professor's Course Has Shaped Views of a Generation on the Power of the Presidency." *Wall Street Journal*, December 4, 1986. On Richard E. Neustadt.

Silfven, Sandra. "Iacocca Vintage Hailed." *Detroit News*, April 2, 1986.

———. "Wine, Etc.: Restaurateurs Enjoy Iacocca Vino." *Detroit News*, April 16, 1986.

"Sing Me No Torch Songs." *Time*, February 24, 1986.

Spitz, Bob. "Mr. America." *Life*, June 1986. Cover story.

———. "Lee Iacocca: The Man Who Would Be President." *Newlook* (September 1986).

"A Spunky Tycoon Turned Superstar." *Time*, April 1, 1985. Cover story.

Stuart, Reginald. *Bailout*. South Bend, Ind.: And Books, 1980.

Sullivan, Colleen. "William Fugazy and Friends." *New York Times*, November 4, 1979.

"Thanks but No Thanks." *Time*, July 28, 1986.

Trausch, Susan. "Wanted: Candidates Who Don't Look Like Politicians." *Boston Globe*, April 6, 1986.

TRB. "Strongmen." *New Republic*, December 2, 1985.

Tyson, Remer. "Draft Iacocca Group Maps Strategy." *Detroit Free Press*, April 27, 1986.

Weymouth, Lally. "Has Chrysler Been Saved?" *Parade*, September 12, 1982.

Wirth, Fritz. "Ich bin ein verdammt schlechter Verlierer." *Die Welt*, October 6, 1986. Iacocca interview.

Yates, Brock. "Don't Do It, Lee." *Car and Driver*, August 1985.

Zimbardo, Philip G. *Shyness*. Reading, Mass.: Addison-Wesley, 1977.

INDEX

Hagerty, Jim, 117
Hailey, Arthur, 72
Halberstam, David, 101*n*, 128, 143, 282
Halleck, Charles, 283
Hammer, Armand, 188
Harding, Warren, 336
Harris, Louis, 298
Hart, Gary, 21*n*, 22*n*, 277, 278, 289, 290
Heiskell, Marian (née Sulzberger), 117
Henry, Sherrye, 302
Hentz, Kathryn Lisa Iacocca (Kathi)
    (daughter), 109, 110, 260, 261,
    299
  marriage of, 221–226
  Peggy Iacocca and, 324
Hentz, Ned (son-in-law), 221
Herblock, 154
Herman, Woody, 52–53
Hernandez, Gio, 183–186, 195–197, 224
Hewlett, William, 132
Higdon, Lee, 130
Hilson, Jefferey, 83
Hilson, Luvinia, 83
"Hiring and Training Truck Salesmen"
    (Iacocca and Dugan), 63
Hitler, Adolf, 74
Hodel, Donald P., 258
Hodel & Co., 258
Honda (firm), 105
Hoover, Herbert, 22, 283, 336, 343, 345
Hope, Bob, 226, 230
Hoppe, Arthur, 279
Horizon, 150
"House of Hits, The" (Minsky), 182*n*
House of Representatives, U.S., 154,
    161, 162
  Banking Committee of, 156, 161
  Judiciary Committee of, 160
human engineering, 76–77, 79
Humphrey, Hubert, 175
hydraulic brakes, 126
hypochondria, 15, 45–46, 259, 315, 339,
    353

Iacocca (Iacocca autobiography; The
    Book), 14, 20–21, 30, 35, 45, 78,
    181–198, 337
  Beacham in, 55, 56
  Bidwell on, 143
  Cohn suit and, 113–114
  editing of, 193–194
  father in, 25, 29
  Henry Ford II in, 192, 193–194
  "herd effect" and, 194–195
  interviews for, 190–192
  as literary collaboration, 186
  lobbying mission in, 119
  motivation for, 182

Novak's earnings and, 194, 195
  organization of, 189–190
  presidency in, 269
  private papers and, 191–192
  reader identification and, 197–198
  rewriting of, 193
  safety in, 236
  sales of, 194
  success of, 194–195, 197–198
  TV commercials in, 170, 172, 179
  World War II years in, 48, 49
Iacocca, Antoinette (mother), 28–29, 34–
    35
  cooking of, 44, 110, 252
  on Ellis Island, 29, 229
  Smith and, 46–47
  son's relationship with, 166, 260–261,
    299, 346
Iacocca, Delma (sister), 34, 40, 44, 260,
    261
Iacocca, Julius (cousin), 25, 26, 46
Iacocca, Kathi, *see* Hentz, Kathryn Lisa
    Iacocca
Iacocca, Lee (Lido Anthony Iacocca):
  acceptance craved by, 254–256
  adversities overcome by, 197–198,
    255–256
  advice accepted by, 155, 309, 342
  aging of, 330
  ambitions of, 48, 111, 116, 241, 292,
    293, 296
  anxiety of, 33–53, 351–352
  appearance of, 15–18, 53, 88, 104, 326
  as athlete, 43–44, 45
  autobiography of, *see Iacocca*
  bigger-than-life appearance of, 18
  birthdays of, 91, 260
  as bull crazy, 110–111, 255
  Caesarism of, 306–307
  callousness of, 256
  in campus organizations, 53
  as Catholic, 268, 320
  character and personal style of, 100,
    273–278, 302, 329–354, 356–357
  children of, *see* Hentz, Kathryn Lisa
    Iacocca; Iacocca, Lia
  concentration powers of, 176, 178
  controlling behavior of, 22, 145, 155,
    171, 247, 249, 262, 326
  cooking of, 252, 261
  coping techniques of, 343
  curiosity of, 342
  dating of, 40, 49–50, 64, 323, 327
  death feared by, 46–47
  dreams of, 62
  drive of, 39–41, 51
  dual identity of, 14–15, 20, 43, 63,
    64*n*
  as "economic czar," 303

PHOTO CREDITS

All photos on opening pages of chapters courtesy Bozell, Jacobs, Kenyon & Eckhardt

Page 27: *Allentown Morning Call*

Page 57: No credit

Page 65: Courtesy Matthew McLaughlin

Page 73: Wide World

Page 80: J. Edward Bailey/*Time*

Page 183: Courtesy Bozell, Jacobs, Kenyon & Eckhardt

Page 199: J. Edward Bailey/*Time*

Pages 200–201: All courtesy Bozell, Jacobs, Kenyon & Eckhardt

Pages 202–203: Courtesy Chrysler Corporation

Pages 204–205: No credit

Page 205: Courtesy Chrysler Corporation

Pages 206–207: All courtesy John T. Reiff

Page 208: Courtesy Chrysler Corporation

Page 209: *Allentown Morning Call*

Page 210: No credit

Page 211: (Top) *Allentown Morning Call;* (middle) no credit; (bottom) Wide World

Page 212: *Allentown Morning Call*

Page 213: (Top) Courtesy Chrysler Corporation; (bottom) Wide World

Page 214: No credit

Page 215: Both courtesy Bozell, Jacobs, Kenyon & Eckhardt

Pages 216–217: All courtesy Chrysler Corporation

Page 218: (Bottom) Courtesy Chrysler Corporation

Pages 219–220: All courtesy Bozell, Jacobs, Kenyon & Eckhardt

Page 227: No credit

Page 275: No credit